The Religious Life of Man:

Guide to Basic Literature

compiled by

LESZEK M. KARPINSKI

The Scarecrow Press, Inc.
Metuchen, N.J. & London
1978

Library of Congress Cataloging in Publication Data

Karpinski, Leszek M
The religious life of man.

Includes indexes.
1. Religion--Bibliography. I. Title.
Z7751.K36 [BL41] 016.2 77-19338
ISBN 0-8108-1110-3

Manufactured in the United States of America

I wish to express my deep appreciation to Margaret Burke and Iza Laponce for reviewing the annotations and making suggestions on arrangements. I want also to thank my colleagues in the Humanities and Social Sciences Division for giving me helpful advice and generous practical assistance.

In conclusion, I am grateful to Michael Kasper and David Sheldon for consultations and supplying additions to the last two parts of the guide.

Leszek M. Karpinski
University of British Columbia Library

FOREWORD

Religion has been the subject of scholarly study from the beginnings of recorded time to the present and in almost every society. The number of publications thereby produced and eventually accumulated in libraries is almost terrifyingly large. Add in the fact that religious literature tends by its very nature to be abstruse and partisan and it becomes clear that the serious student of this subject, perhaps more than of any other, requires the assistance of a well-informed, objective, bibliographic guide in order to help him track down those publications which are reliable and truly appropriate to his needs.

The Religious Life of Man is designed to fill just that need and succeeds admirably. Leszek Karpinski is a scholar of religious studies who has explored his subject in half a dozen languages. Perhaps even more important in the present instance, he is a skilled reference librarian who has made his selection of listings on the basis of ample experience in assisting students. Like the outstanding cookbooks, which offer only "kitchen-tested recipes," The Religious Life of Man provides the indispensable ingredient of bibliographic guidance: proven usefulness. Mr. Karpinski's bibliography has helped hundreds of students at the University of British Columbia. In its present revised form, it should be of equal value to a wider audience.

Samuel Rothstein,
School of Librarianship,
University of British Columbia.

INTRODUCTION

This selected and annotated bibliography is designed to guide its users to important books, periodicals, and other reference materials in the field of religious studies. With few exceptions, only English language materials have been listed, since the work has been designed mainly for undergraduate students as well as the general public. The few foreign-language publications are in fact bibliographies, international in scope, which list English language materials as well as foreign sources.

The guide is an outgrowth of an extensive file of information notes compiled during the course of conducting reference services in the libraries of the University of British Columbia. It is limited to works most frequently appearing in the standard bibliographies and encyclopedic articles and is divided into six separate parts:

1. Religions of Mankind (General)
2. Religions of the Past
3. Judaism, Christianity, Islam
4. Asian Religions (Hinduism, Buddhism, Confucianism, Taoism, etc.)
5. The Beliefs of Native Peoples; Miscellaneous
6. The Occult

Each of these sections lists certain materials which provide a clearly written survey of a subject. The survey includes references to further pertinent literature, be they in the form of bibliographic footnotes or a bibliography. These bibliographic references in turn lead users to a fuller coverage of the particular subject under discussion as well as to the foreign language materials available but omitted from this guide.

LIST OF ABBREVIATIONS

Aus. P.A.I.S.	Australian Public Affairs Information Service
Bibliog. As. St.	Bibliography of Asian Studies
Bibliog. Hist. Sci.	Bibliography of the History of Science
Br. Hum. Index	British Humanities Index
Cath. Index	Catholic Index
ed., eds.	edition, editor, editors
Hist. Abstr.	Historical Abstracts
Int. Bibliog. Hist. Rel.	International Bibliography of the History of Religion
Int. Bibliog. Per. Lit.	International Bibliography of Periodical Literature
Int. Bibliog. Soc. Cult. Anthro.	International Bibliography of Social and Cultural Anthropology
Int. Bibliog. Sociology	International Bibliography of Sociology
P.A.I.S.	Public Affairs Information Service
Phil. Index	Philosopher's Index
Rel. Theol. Abstr.	Religious and Theological Abstracts
Rel. Per.	American Theological Library Association. Index to Religious Periodical Literature
SSCI	Social Sciences Citation Index
Soc. Abstr.	Sociology Abstracts
Soc. Sci. Hum. Index	Social Sciences and Humanities Index. Now published separately as (1) Humanities Index, (2) Social Sciences Index.

BRIEF TABLE OF CONTENTS
Showing Inclusive Entry Numbers

Part One. Religions of Mankind (General). 1-256

Part Two. Religions of the Past. 257-413

I. Prehistoric and Primitive Peoples (257-272)

II. Antiquity
General (273-278)
Near East (279-318)
Greek ... Roman (319-353)
Hellenistic; Manicheism (354-358)
Germanic (359-367)
Celts (368-373)
Slavs (374-376
Pre-Columbian America (377-388)
Journals (389-413)

Part Three. Judaism, Christianity, Islam. 414-1198

I. Judaism (414-518)

II. Christianity
Reference works (519-757)
Journals (758-783)

III. Gnosticism (784-787)

IV. Biblical Studies
English translations; Reference works (788-986)
Journals (987-994)

V. Islam (995-1198)

Part Four. Asian Religions. 1199-1688

I. General
Books (1199-1229)
Journals (1230-1251)

II. India and Hinduism (1252-1363)

III. Jainism, Sikhism, Tibetan (1364-1392)

IV. Buddhism (1393-1517)

V. Chinese (1518-1613)

VI. Japanese (1614-1678)

VII. Eastern Religions in the West (1679-1688)

Part Five. Native Peoples; Miscellaneous. 1689-1946

I. General (1689-1714)

II. Africa (1715-1793)

III. The Americas (1794-1827)

IV. Australia and New Zealand (1828-1859)

V. Oceania; Siberia (1860-1892)

VI. Church and State (1893-1915)

VII. Contemporary Trends in North America (1916-1946)

Part Six. The Occult, Magic, Parapsychology. 1947-2032

General Index (Authors, Titles, Subjects)

Periodicals Index

FULL TABLE OF CONTENTS

Foreword v
Introduction vii
List of Abbreviations viii
Brief Table of Contents ix

Part One: Religions of Mankind (General)

I Definition of Religion 1

II Methodology 1

III Reference Works [general; see also under subtopics IV-XIV]

Dictionaries and encyclopedias 2
Bibliographies and guides 4
Indexes and abstracts 6
Handbooks and surveys 7

IV Theses and Dissertations 10

V Journals [general; see also under subtopics VII-XIV] 12

VI Geography of Religion 14

VII Comparative Religion 15

VIII Mythology, Symbolism, Rites 17

IX Mysticism 22

X Philosophy of Religion 24

XI Anthropology of Religion 28

XII Psychology of Religion 31

XIII Sociology of Religion 34

XIV Religious Education 37

Part Two: Religions of the Past

I Prehistoric and Primitive Peoples 41

II Antiquity

General Works, Handbooks, Surveys 44

Near East 45

Ancient Egypt 47
Ancient Mesopotamia 49
Ancient Syria and Palestine 50
The Hittites 51
Ancient Iran 51

Ancient Greek, Etruscan, and Roman 52

Greek 55
Etruscan and Roman 56

Hellenistic 58

Manicheism 58

Germanic 59

The Celts 60

The Slavs 61

Pre-Columbian America 61

Ancient Mexico 62
Ancient Peru 63

Journals 63

Part Three: Judaism, Christianity, Islam

I JUDAISM

Reference Works

Dictionaries and encyclopedias 67
Bibliographies and guides 69
Index 70

Texts in Translation

Introductory surveys 70
Scriptures 71
Historical works 72
Anthologies 72
Jewish legends 73

Handbooks and Surveys

History--General 73
History of religion, theology, philosophy 75
Sects 80
Liturgy 81
Mysticism 82
Kabbalah 82
Calendar, festivals 82

Journals 83

II CHRISTIANITY

Reference Works

Dictionaries and encyclopedias 85
Bibliographies and guides 88
Indexes 88
Atlases 89

Handbooks and Surveys

History
General works 89
Early church 93
Medieval church 94
Crusades 95
Reformation, Counter-Reformation 96
Modern church since Reformation 98
Creeds and doctrines 99
Ecumenical movement 100
Heretics 101
Liturgy 101
Miracles 103
Missions 103
Monasticism and religious orders 104
Mysticism 105
Myth and symbolism 105
Papacy and popes 105
Saints 106
Vestments and ecclesiastical dress 107

Christian Churches and Sects 107

Eastern Orthodox Church 108
Roman Catholic Church 110
Protestantism--General 112
Anglican and Episcopal 113
Baptists 113
Christian Science 114
Congregational Church 114
Episcopal (see Anglican)
Jehovah's Witnesses 115
Lutheran Church 115
Mennonites 116
Methodism 117
Mormons 118
Pentecostalism 118
Presbyterianism 119
Quakers 119
Salvation Army 119
Shakers 119
Unitarian Church 120
Christianity in North America 120
Christianity in Canada 122
Christianity in the United States 124

Journals 125

III GNOSTICISM 129

IV BIBLICAL STUDIES

English Translations, Reference Works

Introductions 130
Principal versions in English translation 130
Dictionaries and encyclopedias 132
Bibliographies, guides, indexes 135
Commentaries 137
Companions 138
Concordances 139
Subject guides 139

Handbooks and Critical Works

Introductions 140
Chronology 140
Biblical geography 140
Biblical archeology/historical surveys 142
Textual and literary criticism 146
Old Testament studies 149
New Testament studies
Bibliographies 151
Dictionaries and guides 152
Companion 153
Abstracts 153
Handbooks and critical works 153
Jesus studies 157
Pauline studies 159
Studies in Apocrypha 160
Qumran [Dead Sea scrolls] studies 160

Journals 163

V ISLAM

Reference Works

Dictionaries and encyclopedias 165
Bibliographies and guides 166
Indexes and abstracts 169
Geographical works and atlases 169
Chronology 170

Qur'an [Koran]

Texts in English translation 170
Guide 171
Critical works 172
Muhammad 173
Tradition (Hadith) 174
Jesus in Islam 175

Anthologies of Texts in English Translation 175

Handbooks and Critical Works

General introductions 176

History
General 179
Early Islam 182
Medieval Islam 183
Modern Islam 183
Islamic art and architecture 184
Calendar 186
Ethics 186
Islamic institutions (social/political) 186
Islamic law (Fikh, Shari'a) 187
Literature of Islamic peoples 188
Arabic 189
Persian 189
Turkish 190
Mysticism (Sufism) 190
Philosophy (Falsafah) 191
Theology (Kalam) 192
Worship 193
Islam and the West 193
Islam in Africa 194
Islam in North America 195
Islam in Persia (Iran) 195
Islam in the Soviet Union 196
Islam in Spain 196
Islam in Turkey 197
Islam in Indian subcontinent 197
Islam in Indonesia 197

The Baha'i 198

Journals 198

Part Four: Asian Religions

I GENERAL INTRODUCTION

Reference Works

Bibliographies and guides 201
Dictionaries and encyclopedias 202
Scriptural collections 203
Anthologies 203

Critical Works 204

Journals 206

II INDIA AND HINDUISM

Indian Background of Asian Religions

Bibliographies 209
Dictionaries and encyclopedias 209
Critical works
Indian civilization 210
Religions of India--general 211
Festivals; pilgrimage 213

Indian art 213
Mythology 214

Hindu Religious Tradition

Bibliographies and guides 215
Dictionary 216

Scriptural Writings

Critical survey 216
Scriptural collections 216
Anthologies 216
The Vedas 217
The Upanishads 218
The Mahabharata 220
The Ramayana 221

Critical Studies

Philosophical systems--general 222
Vedanta 223
Yoga 224
General studies on Hinduism 224
Modern religious movements 227
Sects 227

Journals 228

III JAINISM, SIKHISM, TIBETAN RELIGIONS

Jainism

Bibliographies and guides 229
Scriptures in English translation 229
Critical studies 230

Sikhism

Bibliographies and guides 230
Scriptures in English translation 231
Critical studies 231
Journal 232

Tibetan Religions

Bibliography 233
Texts in English translation 233
Critical studies 233

IV BUDDHISM

Reference Works

Bibliographies and guides 235
Dictionaries and encyclopedias 236
Index 237

Scriptural Collections and Anthologies 237

Critical Studies

General 239
Life of Buddha 242
Mahayana Buddhism 243
Zen Buddhism
Reference works 244
Critical studies 245
Zen and Western culture 247
Theravada Buddhism 247
Buddhism in Tibet; Tantric tradition 248
Buddhism in China 249
Buddhism in India and Sri Lanka [Ceylon] 251
Buddhism in Japan
Bibliography 252
General studies 252
Sects 253
Buddhism in Southeast Asia 254

Journals 255

V CHINESE RELIGIONS

Reference Works 256

Critical Studies

History of Chinese civilization 257
Religious history 258
Modern religious life 260
Festivals 260
Mythology 260
Chinese philosophies 261

The "Five Classics" and the "Four Books"

Complete "Five Classics" 263
Shu Ching 263
Shih Ching 264
I Ching 264
Ch'un Chiu 265
Li Chi 265
The "Four Books" 265

Confucianism

Anthologies 265
Critical Works 266
Works of Confucius 267
Critical studies of Confucius 267
Works of Mencius 268
Critical study of Mencius 268
Neo-Confucianism 268

Other Works and Beliefs

Mohists and Legalists 269
Folk religions 270

Taoism

Bibliography 270
Classic texts 271
Chuang-Tzu 271
Lao-Tzu 271
Lieh-Tzu 272
T'ai I Chin Hua Tsung Chih 272
Critical studies 272

Journals 273

VI JAPANESE RELIGIONS

Reference Works

Ancient Documents (in English)

Anthologies 276
Fudoki 276
Kojiki 277
Nihongi 277
Norito 277

Critical Studies

History of Japanese civilization 277
Religious history 279
Mythology 281
Folk religion 281
Festivals 281
Ainu religion 282
Confucianism in Japan 282

Shintoism 283

Modern Religious Life

New religions 285
Religious life 286
Sociology of Japanese religion 286

Journals 286

VII EASTERN RELIGIONS IN THE WEST 288

Part Five: Native Peoples; Miscellaneous

I GENERAL

Dictionaries 291
Bibliographies, catalogs, abstracts 292
Critical studies 293
Journals 294

II AFRICA

Reference Works 296

Critical Studies

Historical background 297
Studies in religious beliefs 299
African cults in the Americas 306

Journals 307

III THE AMERICAS

North America

Reference works 309
Critical studies
Indian beliefs 310
Eskimo-Aleut (Inuit) beliefs 313

South America 314

The Caribbean 314

IV AUSTRALIA AND NEW ZEALAND

Australia

Reference works 316
Critical studies 317

New Zealand 319

V OCEANIA; SIBERIA

Pacific Islands

Reference works 322
Critical studies 322
Journals 325

Java 326

Okinawa 326

Siberian (Altaic) Peoples 326

VI CHURCH AND STATE

General 328

Eastern Europe and the Soviet Union 330

VII CONTEMPORARY TRENDS IN NORTH AMERICA 333

Part Six: The Occult, Magic, Parapsychology

Reference Works

Encyclopedias 339
Bibliographies 340

Critical Studies

General 341
Alchemy 346
Apparitions and ghosts 347
Astrology 347
Crystallomancy 348
Exorcism 348
Numerology 348
Prophecy and fortune-telling 349
Secret societies; Masonry 349
Witchcraft and demonology 350

* * *

General Index (Authors, Titles, Subjects) 353
Periodicals Index 396

Part One

RELIGIONS OF MANKIND (GENERAL)

I DEFINITION OF RELIGION

1 Eliade, Mircea. The Sacred and the Profane; the Nature of Religion. Transl. from the French by Willard R. Trask. New York, Harper, 1961 (1957). 256 p.
This very systematically written book includes a series of imaginative reconstructions based on critically selected materials which attempt to explain human religious life in all its manifestations. Bibliography, and an index are provided.

2 Kishimoto, Hideo. "An Operational Definition of Religion." Numen, v. 8:3 (1961), p. 236-40.
"Religion is an aspect of culture centered upon activities which are taken by those who participate in them to elucidate the ultimate meaning of life and to be related to the ultimate solution of its problems. Many religious systems contain the notion of deity and/or holiness in relation with such activities"--Text.

3 Saliba, John A. Homo religiosus in Mircea Eliade; An Anthropological Evaluation. Leiden, Brill, 1976 (Supplementa ad Numen, altera series: Dissertationes ad historiam religionum pertinentes, v. 5). 210 p.
This interesting collection is comprised of studies on various aspects of the study of religion. Of special interest is the last section: The Study of Religion; The Definition of Religion. A useful bibliography is appended.

II METHODOLOGY

4 Bianchi, Ugo. The History of Religions. Leiden, Brill, 1975. 228 p. (Transl. of Storia delle religioni, 6th ed., 1970.)
Provides a translation of an outstanding work by the Italian scholar which deals with the object and methodology of the history of religions; religion and the various religions; studies and problems in the history of religions; modern problems of methodology and interpretation. A selective classified bibliography is provided.

5 Helfer, J. S., ed. On Method in the History of Religions. Middletown, Conn., Wesleyan Univ. Press, 1968 (History and Theory. Beiheft 8, 1968).

6 Penner, Hans H. "The Fall and Rise of Methodology: A Retrospective Review." Religious Studies Review, v. 2: 2 (1976), p. 11-16.

Provides a brief but informative overlook of new approaches to the study of religion. A list of bibliographic references is provided.

7 Pummer, Reinhard. "Religionswissenschaft or Religiology." Numen, v. 19: 2-3 (1972), p. 91-127.

8 Waardenburg, Jean J. Classical Approaches to the Study of Religion. The Hague, Mouton, 1973-4 (Religion and Reason). 2 vols.

Provides an excellent source-book to the history and methodology of the study of religion. It contains excerpts from the works of scholars who laid the foundation for religious studies. Bibliographic citations are included. An index is divided into: personal names, scholarly concepts, and concrete subjects.

III REFERENCE WORKS [works pertinent to subtopics IV-XIV are entered thereunder]

DICTIONARIES AND ENCYCLOPEDIAS

9 Canney, Maurice A. An Encyclopedia of Religions. London, 1921; Detroit, Gale, 1970. 397 p.

A reprint of "a volume of moderate size information about most of the ancient and modern religions: ethnic and historical" with short bibliographies.

10 Dictionary of the History of Ideas: Studies of Selected Pivotal Ideas. P. P. Wiener, 1973. 4 vols. Index.

Contains a selection of topics which intend to exhibit the important relationship of ideas in a variety of disciplines. Consult the Analytical Table of Contents: v. 1, The history of religious and philosophical ideas; and the index volumes.

11 Encyclopedia of Religion and Ethics. Ed. by James Hastings with the assistance of J. Selbie and Louis H. Gray. Edinburgh, Clark; New York, Scribner's, 1908-27. 12 vols. Index.

Recognized as the most comprehensive source of information for this topic in English. Contains articles on all religions, religious beliefs and customs, ethical systems and movements, philosophical ideas, moral practices; and related subjects in anthropology, mythology, folklore, biology, psychology, economics, and sociology. Names of people and places known in the history of religion are also included. Bibliographies are outdated but still of great informative value. The index volume is divided into four parts, which include: general, foreign words, scripture passages, and authors of the articles indexed.

12 Ferm, Vergilius T. A. Encyclopedia of Religion. New York, Philosophical Library, 1945. 844 p.
Contains a wide range of articles by people of different religious and specialty background, with bibliographies.

13 Forlong, James G. R. Faith of Man; Encyclopedia of Religions. Introd. by M. Silver. London, 1906; New Hyde Park, N.Y., 1964. 3 vols.
Its informative articles, with frequent bibliographical citations, are recognized as a model of the 19th-century comparative method. Subject Index in the introductory section enables the user to notice at a glance headings which contain more information.

14 Glasenapp, Helmuth von. Non-Christian Religions, A-Z. New York, Grosset and Dunlap, c1963 (Universal Reference Library). 278 p.
Translation of the author's Die nichtchristlichen Religionen, the introductory volume in the Fischer Lexicon Series. Each article explains the name of the religion, symbols, sacred writings, cults, priesthood, and social life. At the end one finds: statistical comparison map, chronological tables, bibliographies in subject arrangements, and an index.

15 International Encyclopedia of Religion and Philosophy. New York, Worldwide Reference Books, 1976- .
Divided into regional volumes, e.g. Africa, Middle East, South Asia.... Each volume contains articles arranged in alphabetical order. Annotated bibliographies and an author-title index are added.

16 McCasland, S. Vernon; G. E. Cains; and David C. Yu. Religions of the World. New York, Random House, 1969. 760 p.
Presents major living religions of the world with historical, geographical, and cultural background. Has a well organized index, and accurately selected bibliography. This work is highly recommended as a superbly organized reference work.

17 Mathews, Shailer, and Gerard B. Smith, eds. Dictionary of Religion and Ethics. New York, Macmillan, 1921. 513 p.
Defines terms in religion and ethics, especially useful for primitive and ethnic religions. Includes biographies of deceased persons known in the field. Classified bibliography is provided at the end of the volume.

18 Parrinder, E. Geoffrey. Dictionary of Non-Christian Religions. Amersham, Bucks., England, Huton, 1971. 320 p.
Special attention given to Hinduism, Buddhism and Islam, but contains also information on the other Far Eastern religions, ancient Middle East, Greece and Rome, Celtic, Teutonic and Scandinavian religions, ancient American cultures of Mayas, Aztecs, and Incas, and those of Australasia and Africa. Selective bibliography is included.

19 ______. Religions of the World, from Primitive Beliefs to Modern Faiths. New York, Grosset and Dunlap, 1971. 440 p.
Provides articles on major religions with references to history, geography, social life, current affairs, and international relationship. Detailed alphabetical index refers user back to the great many small topics discussed within the work. Bibliography at the end of the book is arranged by subject, e.g. Prehistoric, Africa, etc.

20 The New Schaff-Herzog Encyclopedia of Religious Knowledge. Embracing Biblical, Historical, Doctrinal, and Practical Theology; and Biblical Theological, and Ecclesiastical Biography from the Earliest Times to the Present Day ... prepared ... under the supervision of S. M. Jackson. Grand Rapids, Mich., Baker, 1949-50. 13 vols. (Vol 13: Index by G. W. Gilmore.) Supplemented by: Twentieth Century Encyclopedia of Religious Knowledge; an Extension of the New Schaff-Herzog.... Grand Rapids, Mich., Baker, 1955. 2 vols.
An expanded translation of the Realencyclopädie für protestantische Theologie und Kirche, valuable for its bibliographies listed in the general bibliographical survey at the beginning of each volume, and appended to the articles.

21 Zaehner, Robert C., ed. Concise Encyclopedia of Living Faiths. London, Hutchinson, 1964, 1959. 431 p.
Describes only the living religions. No account is given of religious beliefs of extinct cultures. At the end of the book one finds a classified bibliography as well as an index.

BIBLIOGRAPHIES AND GUIDES

22 Adams, Charles J., ed. A Reader's Guide to the Great Religions. 2nd ed. New York, Free Press, 1977 (1965). 364 p.
A collection of eight essays, written by specialists, which survey bibliographical resources available in the subjects of: Primitive religion, The religions of China (except Buddhism), Hinduism, Buddhism, The religions of Japan, Judaism, Christianity, and Islam. Includes an index of authors, editors, translators and compilers, as well as a subject index. For advanced research it must be supplemented by newer works, e.g. McCasland, (no. 16) or Parrinder (no. 19).

23 Barrow, John G. A Bibliography of Bibliographies in Religion. Ann Arbor, Mich., Edwards, 1955. 489 p.

"Attempts to bring together all separately published bibliographies in the field of religion"--Preface. From the 15th century to the present, covers all languages, and provides brief annotations. Gives locations in American and European libraries.

24 Berkowitz, M. I., and J. E. Johnson. Social Scientific Studies of Religion; A Bibliography. Pittsburgh, Univ. of Pittsburgh Press, 1967. 258 p.

Presents a survey-bibliography of 6000 published, verified, and available English-language items classified into 132 subjects.

25 Diehl, K. S. Religions, Mythologies, Folklores; An Annotated Bibliography, 2nd ed. New York, Scarecrow Press, 1962. 573 p.

Its very broad coverage includes items of general and specific reference ranging from scriptures and commentaries to magic and crystal gazing. Concise annotations inform user if cited items carry a bibliography, footnotes or indexes. Contains an author-title index but the lack of a subject index is a serious omission.

26 France. Centre National de la Recherche Scientifique. Sciences Humaines. Section 527: Sciences religieuses.

Formerly part of Bulletin analitique: Philosophie (v. 1-9; 1947-55: ZB 1 F73) then continued in Section 19: Philosophie of Bulletin signalétique. Science Humaines, since v. 25 (1972) in Section 527: Sciences religieuses. International in coverage, includes about 4000 abstracts divided into three sections: Science of religion, History of religions, and Exegesis and Biblical Criticism.

27 International Bibliography of the History of the Religions. Leiden, Brill, 1954- .

An important current bibliography published with the support of the International Council for Philosophy and Humanistic Studies and the Association for the History of Religions. Contains books and articles on the history of religions in classified arrangement. An author index is included since 1960.

28 Kennedy, James R. Library Research Guide to Religion and Theology: Illustrated Search Strategy and Sources. Ann Arbor, Mich., Pierian Press, 1974. 53 p.

Introduces many useful reference sources for religion. A classified bibliography of titles is added.

29 Mitros, Joseph F. Religions; A Select, Classified Bibliography. Louvain, Nauwelaerts, 1973. (Philosophical Questions Series, 8.) 435 p.

"...Submits material which opens avenues to subsequent sources..."--Preface. Also provides a detailed table of contents, and an index.

INDEXES AND ABSTRACTS

30 American Theological Library Association. Index to Religious Periodical Literature; An Author and Subject Index to Periodical Literature, Including an Author Index to Book Reviews. Chicago, American Theological Library Association, 1949- .
Published twice a year in paperback edition, and cumulated in the second year, includes about 9000 articles from nearly 200 scholarly journals. Indexes journals in English, French, German, and Italian. Separate section contains book reviews listed by author's name.

31 British Humanities Index. London, Library Association, 1962- .
A general index of British periodicals, which covers numerous topics in religious studies. References to selected journal articles are listed under following headings: "Religion," "Buddhism," "Muhammad," etc. Indexes some 22 religious journals, e.g. Religious Studies, Recusant History, etc.

Humanities Index see entry 36.

32 International Bibliography of Periodical Literature, Covering all Fields of Knowledge. Osnabrück, Dietrich, 1965- .
Provides a world index of articles from over 7600 journals, many of them in English. Subject headings are in German but in many instances cross references are provided from French and English.

33 Regazzi, J. J., and T. C. Hines. Guide to Indexed Periodicals in Religion. Metuchen, N.J., Scarecrow Press, 1975. 314 p.
It is "a new type of reference aid for librarians, teachers, and library users generally," which covers some 2700 periodicals, indexed some 3545 times in 17 abstracting and indexing services.

34 Religious and Theological Abstracts. Youngstown, Ohio, Theological Pub., 1958- .
Provides brief English abstracts of papers in various languages which appeared in journals of Christian, Jewish, Muslim, or Buddhist orientation. Each volume has an author, subject, and scripture indexes.

35 Richardson, E. C. An Alphabetical Subject Index and Index Encyclopedia to Periodical Articles on Religion, 1890-1899. New York, Scribner's, 1907-11. 1168 p.

Contains a list of some 58,000 articles selected from 600 journals in English as well as other languages.

36 *Social Sciences and Humanities Index*. New York, Wilson, 1916-1974. Then followed by separately issued: *Social Sciences Index*; *Humanities Index*, 1975- .

A general index limited to English language journals. Selected journal articles are listed under the following subject headings: Religions, Christianity, Islam, Muhammad, etc. Indexes a number of well recognized journals, e.g. *Church History*, *The Ecumenical Review*, *The Journal of Religion*.

37 *Social Sciences Citation Index*. Philadelphia, Institute for Scientific Information, 1970- . Three times a year, the third being the annual cumulation.

Covers some 1000 of the world's most important social science journals. Consists of three related indexes: Citation Index, Source Index, and the Permuterm Subject Index. For subject searches use the Subject Index, looking under such headings as Religion, Religiosity, Buddhism, Christianity, Islam, Occult, etc.

HANDBOOKS AND SURVEYS

38 Bleeker, Claas J., and Geo von Widengren. *Historia Religionum; Handbook for the History of Religions*. Leiden, Brill, 1969-71. 2 vols.

A survey of all religions in the world. It presents them in such a way that any structural similarities can be easily found. Each article follows the same basic scheme, including: a short description of the religion, its historical development, worship, influences, a short survey of research, and a select bibliography.

39 Braden, Charles Samuel. *The World's Religions*, rev. ed. Nashville, Abingdon Press, 1954. 256 p.

A short account of the development of the world religions which gives a broad social, economic, and political background. The bibliography includes larger reference works in which more specific topics may be found and a list of books on each religion. In this book one can also find information on scriptures and available translations.

40 Capps, Walter H. *Ways of Understanding Religion*. New York, Macmillan, 1972. 399 p.

This is a textbook which selects representative materials from writings by outstanding scholars in the field of religious studies. Each selection is followed by a selective bibliography. An index is provided.

41 Clemen, C. C., ed. *Religions of the World, Their Nature*

and Their History. Freeport, N.Y., Books for Libraries Press, 1969 (c1931) (Essay Index Reprint Series). 482 p.

Translation of Die Religionen der Erde. Comprises well chosen collection of articles written by specialists. Includes valuable information on primitive and prehistoric religion, national religions, and great world religions. Contains a bibliography and an index.

42 Comstock, W. Richard. Religions and Man; an Introduction. New York, Harper and Row, 1971.

Presents an excellent study of the history of religion. Includes a well selected bibliography and indexes.

43 ______. The Study of Religion and Primitive Religions. New York, Harper and Row, 1972. 117 p.

An up-to-date survey that contains a useful bibliography and an index.

44 Eister, Allan W., ed. Changing Perspectives in the Scientific Study of Religion. New York, Wiley, 1974 (Contemporary Religious Movements). 370 p.

Includes a selection of papers reexamining the current approaches to the study of religious institutions. Selected bibliographic references are appended at the end of each paper. Index.

45 Finegan, Jack. The Archeology of World Religions, the Background of Primitivism, Zoroastrianism, Hinduism, Jainism, Buddhism, Confucianism, Taoism, Shinto, Islam, and Sikhism. Princeton, N.J., Princeton Univ. Press, 1952. 599 p.

Deals with the early history of religions. Bibliography and indexes are included.

46 Frazer, James G. Golden Bough; a Study in Magic and Religion, 3rd ed. London, Macmillan, 1963. (1st ed., 1911-15.) 12 vols. And his Aftermath; A Supplement to The Golden Bough. London, Macmillan, 1936. 494 p.

This is a famous classic in the field of religious studies. Contains information about almost all forms and phases of religious belief and practice, from the most primitive to the most advanced. One has to bear in mind that certain methods and theories are obsolete, and that newer works should be consulted to supplement this one.

47 The History of Religions; Essays on the Problem of Understanding, by Joachim Wach et al. Ed. by Joseph M. Kitagawa, with the collab. of Mircea Eliade and Charles H. Long. Chicago, Univ. of Chicago Press, 1967 (Essays in Divinity, vol. 1). 264 p.

A collection of essays which present major problems confronting a modern study of religion. Includes bibliographical references in the footnotes, and a subject index.

48 Jurji, Edward J., ed. The Great Religions of the Modern World: Confucianism, Taoism, Hinduism, Buddhism, Shintoism, Islam, Judaism, Eastern Orthodoxy, Roman Catholicism, Protestantism. Princeton, N.J., Princeton Univ. Press, 1946. 387 p.

A collection of ten essays on major contemporary religions. Includes a selected bibliography and an index. It has been criticized for somewhat outdated scholarship, however the information contained in this work is still of great value.

49 Landis, Benson Y. World Religions; A Brief Guide to the Principal Beliefs and Teachings of the Religions of the World, and to the Statistics of Organized Religion. New York, Dutton, 1957. 127 p.

A survey of religions which gives a summary of their organization, administration, and membership.

50 Moore, George F. History of Religions, rev. ed. with corrections and additions. New York, Scribner's, 1949 (1919-20) (International Theological Library).

Provides a scholarly introduction to the field which is still useful for factual material. Contains a selective bibliography which has been updated in this new revised edition, and a very detailed subject index.

51 Noss, John B. Man's Religions, 5th ed. New York, Macmillan, 1974 (1949). 624 p.

A well-balanced introduction to the history of major religions divided into four parts: primitive and bygone religions, the religions of India, the religions of the Far East, the religions of the Near East. At the end of each chapter, it provides a list of bibliographical references. A subject index is also included.

52 Potter, Charles F. The Faiths Men Live By. Englewood Cliffs, N.J., Prentice-Hall, 1954. 323 p.

Chronologically arranged discussion of world religions which describes their divisions and denominations. In the appendix one finds a number of significant sects and important religious organizations.

53 Ringgren, Helmer and Åke V. Strøm. Religions of Mankind Today and Yesterday. Ed. by J. C. G. Greig, trans. by Niels L. Jensen. Philadelphia, Fortress Press, 1967. 426 p.

Translation of Religionerna i historia och nutid. Included are excellent bibliographic references and a useful index.

54 Schoeps, Hans J. The Religions of Mankind. Translated from the German by Richard and Clara Winston. Garden City, N.Y., Doubleday, 1966. 320 p.

Translation of: Religionen: Wesen und Geschichte.

Provides a study of basic religious concepts and their development from ancient times to the present. Includes bibliography.

55 Smith, Huston. *The Religions of Man.* New York, Harper, 1958 (paperback repr., New York, Mentor Books, 1959). 328 p.
An intelligent, clearly-written study which attempts a comparative evaluation of Christianity, Judaism, Buddhism, Hinduism, Confucianism, and Taoism. Each section includes a selection of bibliographic references.

56 Smith, Wilfred Cantwell. *A Meaning and End of Religions; A New Approach to the Religious Traditions of Mankind.* New York, New American Library, 1964 (A Mentor Book). 340 p.
Contains a bibliography and an index.

57 Spiegelberg, Friedrich. *Living Religions of the World.* London, Thames and Hudson, 1957. 511 p.
Provides an informative survey of great religions with selective bibliography and an index.

58 Toynbee, Arnold. *An Historian's Approach to Religion.* London, Oxford University Press, 1956. 318 p.
The author of *A Study of History* in 10 vols. presents his views on the role of religion in the rise of modern civilization.

59 Vos, Howard F., ed. *Religions in a Changing World; A Presentation of World Religions in the Mid-Twentieth Century Facing the Onslaughts of Rising Nationalism.* Chicago, Moody Press, 1967 (1953). 443 p.
Each chapter carries a selective bibliography. Contains also a list of general books which deal with several religions.

60 Walhout, Donald. *Interpreting Religion.* Englewood Cliffs, N.J., Prentice-Hall, 1963. 481 p.
Examines major problems which arise in the scholarly study of religion. Includes bibliographic references in the footnotes and a subject index.

IV THESES AND DISSERTATIONS

61 *American Doctoral Dissertations.* Ann Arbor, Mich., Univ. Microfilms, 1934- (annual).
A list of dissertations for which doctoral degrees were granted in some universities in the U.S. Represents also a few Canadian universities and is more complete than

Dissertation Abstracts. Lists items by subject; see under the heading: "Religion." See also no. 65.

62 ASLIB. Index to Theses Accepted for Higher Degrees in the Universities of Great Britain and Ireland, and the Council for National Academic Awards. London, Aslib, 1950/51- (annual).
Lists M.A. and Ph.D. theses, in a subject arrangement. Also includes an author index. Section "Religion" and its sub-divisions should be checked.

63 Black, Dorothy M., comp. Guide to Lists of Master's Theses. Chicago, American Library Assoc., 1965. 144 p.
Contains published sources of masters' theses in the U.S., and Canada to 1964. "Religion" and "Religious Education" are listed under "Theses in Special Fields." (See also no. 68.)

64 Canada. National Library. Canadian Theses. Thèses canadiennes. Ottawa, 1962- (annual).
Lists M.A. and Ph.D. theses and dissertations. Arranged by subject; section: "Religion."

65 Dissertation Abstracts. Ann Arbor, Mich., University Microfilms, 1938- (monthly).
Contains abstracts of dissertations available for purchase on film or xerox. Arranged alphabetically by topics and then by university. Section: RELIGION should be checked.

66 Humanities Research Council of Canada. Canadian Graduate Theses in the Humanities and Social Sciences, 1921-46. Ottawa, Canadian Bibliographic Centre, 1951.
Lists mainly masters' theses. Arranged by subject, with an author index.

67 Little, Lawrence C. Research in Personality, Character, and Religious Education; Bibliography of American Doctoral Dissertations in Religious Education, 1885-1959. New York Columbia Univ. Press, 1962. 215 p.

68 Masters Abstracts. Ann Arbor, Mich., Univ. Microfilms, 1963- (quarterly).
Includes abstracts of selected masters' theses from American universities. Section: "Religion." (See also no. 63.)

69 Reynolds, Michael M. Guide to Theses and Dissertations; An International Annotated Bibliography of Bibliographies. Detroit, Gale, 1975. 599 p.
Consult the section U: "Theology and Religion," p. 499-511. An Index of Names and Titles and a Subject Index are provided.

V JOURNALS [journals pertinent to subtopics VII-XIV are entered thereunder]

70 American Academy of Religion. Journal. Philadelphia, 1933- .
Supersedes Journal of Bible and Religion, 1933-1966. Includes extensive book reviews and critical notices.

71 American Schools of Oriental Research. Bulletin. New York, 1919- .
Cumulated index every five years. Indexed: Soc. Sci. Hum. Index.

72 Archiv Orientalní. Prague, 1929- .
Papers are published in English, French and German. Indexed: Bibliog. As. St.; Int.. Bibliog. Hist. Rel.

73 Cithara; Essays in the Judeo-Christian Tradition. New York, 1961- .
Published by Saint Bonaventure University. Cumulated index every two years.

74 Daedalus. Cambridge, Mass., 1846- (quarterly).
Indexed: Psych. Abstracts; Soc. Sci. Hum. Index.

75 Diogenes; An International Review of Philosophy and Humanistic Studies. New York, 1953- (quarterly).
Published by the International Council for Philosophy and Humanistic Studies.

76 East and West. Quarterly published by the Istituto Italiano per il Medio ad Estremo Oriente under the Auspices and with the Grant of the Consiglio Nationale delle Ricerche. Rome, 1950- .
Indexed: Int. Bibliog. Hist. Rel.

77 Eranos; Acta Philolgica Suecana. Uppsala, 1896- .
Contains papers in several foreign languages as well as in English. Cumulative index is published every 50 years.

78 The Expository Times. Edinburgh, 1889- .
Indexed: Br. Hum. Index; Rel. Per.; Rel. Theol. Abstracts.

79 History of Religions; An International Journal for Comparative Historical Studies. Chicago, 1961- .
Published by University of Chicago. Indexed: Rel. Per.; Rel. Theol. Abstracts.

80 Journal for the Scientific Study of Religion. Notre Dame, Ind., 1961- .
Published by the Society for the Scientific Study of

Religion. Indexed: Rel. Per.; Soc. Abstr.

81 Journal of Asian and African Studies. Toronto, 1966- .
Published by York University, Canada. Indexed: Canadian Periodical Index; Int. Bibliog. Soc. Cult. Anthro.

Journal of Bible and Religion see entry 70.

82 Journal of Oriental Studies. Hong Kong, 1954- .
Published in Chinese and English on behalf of the Centre of Asian Studies at the University of Hong Kong. Index: v. 1-5; indexed: Hist. Abstracts.

83 Journal of Religion. Chicago, 1882- .
Indexed: Soc. Sci. Hum. Index.

84 Journal of Religion of Africa. Leiden, 1966- .
Papers in English and French.

85 The Journal of Religious History. Sydney, Australia, 1960- .
Indexed: Rel. Per.

86 London. University. School of Oriental and African Studies. Bulletin. 1917- .
Indexed: Br. Hum. Index.

87 Monumenta Serica; Journal of Oriental Studies. Tokyo, 1936- .
Published by the Monumenta Serica Institute at the University of California, Los Angeles. Indexed: Bibliog. As. St.

88 Numen: International Review for the History of Religions. Leiden, 1954- .
Published by the International Association for the History of Religions. Papers are published in English, French, German and Italian. Indexed: Rel. Per.; Int. Bibliog. Hist. Rel.

89 Orientalia. Rome, 1920-30; new series v. 1, 1932- .
Published by the Pontifical Biblical Institute. Papers in English, German, and Italian. Includes comprehensive subject bibliographies, e.g. Keilschriftbibliographie. Indexed: Int. Bibliog. Hist. Rel.

90 Religion in Communist Dominated Areas. New York, 1962- .
Published by the National Council of the Churches of Christ in the U.S.

91 Religious Humanism; Quarterly Journal of Religious and Ethical Humanism. Yellow Springs, Ohio, 1967- .
Published by the Fellowship of Religious Humanists. Indexed: Phil. Index; Rel. Theol. Abstracts.

92 Religious Studies. New York, 1962- .
Contains articles which discuss historical and comparative aspects of religions, psychology, and sociology of religion. Indexed: Rel. Per.; Rel. Theol. Abstracts.

93 Religious Studies Review; A Quarterly Review of Publications in the Field of Religion and Related Disciplines. Hanover, Pa., 1975- .
Contains review essays, bibliographic surveys, and brief notes on recent publications.

94 Review of Religious Research. New York, 1959- .
Index: v.1-10 (1959-69). Indexed: Rel. Per.; Rel. Theol. Abstracts; Soc. Abstracts.

95 Studies in Religion. Sciences Religieuses. Toronto, 1970- .
Published by the Corporation for the Publication of Academic Studies in Religion in Canada. Indexed: Rel. Per.; Rel. Theol. Abstracts.

96 Thought; A Review of Culture and Idea. New York, 1926- .
Published by Fordham University, Bronx, N.Y. Indexed: Soc. Sci. Hum. Index; P.A.I.S.

97 Zygon; Journal of Religion and Science. Chicago, 1966- .
Published by the Meadville/Lombard Theological School and the Institute on Religion in an Age of Science. Indexed: Rel. Per.

VI GEOGRAPHY OF RELIGION

98 al-Faruqi, Ismail R., and D. E. Sopher. Historical Atlas of the Religions of the World. Macmillan, 1974. 346 p.
Provides an excellent introduction to understanding historical patterns of the interaction of religions. It is a great help to the student of religion, history, and civilization. Also includes an appendix: chronologies, a subject index, and an index of proper names.

99 Sopher, David E. Geography of Religions. Englewood Cliffs, N.J., Prentice-Hall, 1967 (Foundations of Cultural Geography Series). 128 p.
The only English publication which gathers and organizes scattered publications on the subject. This pioneering study deals with four cultural geographic topics: (1) the significance of the environmental setting for the evolution of religious systems and particular religious institutions; (2) the way religious systems and institutions modify their environment; (3) the different ways whereby religious systems occupy and organize segments of earth space; (4) the

geographical distribution of religions and the way religious systems spread and interact with each other. Includes bibliographical footnotes and a subject index.

VII COMPARATIVE RELIGION

100 A Dictionary of Comparative Religion. S. G. F. Brandon, gen. ed., London, Weidenfeld and Nicolson, 1970. 704 p.
An alphabetically-arranged dictionary which provides an easy reference for all religious beliefs and practices of mankind. Frequently used cross-references show interrelationship of topics and facilitate comparative research. Each article contains a bibliography. Also includes two indexes, a synoptic list of all entries related to major topics, and a general index of names and subjects not given a special entry with an indication under what entry to look it up.

101 Bouquet, A. C. Comparative Religion; A Short Outline, 5th ed. Harmondsworth, Penguin Books, 1958 (1942).
Provides a comparative survey of all religio-philosophical schools; from religious origins, through polytheism, Indian, Chinese, Semitic origin religions, and ending with mysticism. Includes a selective bibliography divided by religion and country and an index.

102 Burtt, Edwin A. Man Seeks the Divine; A Study in the History and Comparison of Religions. 2nd ed. New York, Harper and Row, 1964 (1957). 514 p.
A comparative review of major world religions which attempts to explain what religion is in the varied cultural and social settings. Subject bibliography is limited to books in English. Includes also an index.

103 Eliade, Mircea. Patterns in Comparative Religion. Transl. by R. Sheed. London, Sheed and Ward, 1958. 484 p.
Translation of Traité d'histoire des religions. A remarkable book which applies a comparative method for such major religious subjects as the meaning of the sacred, sun and moon worship, water symbolism, sacred stones, fertility cults, and the myth of eternal renewal. Contains a detailed bibliography at the end of each chapter, and two separate indexes: names and subjects.

104 James, Edwin O. Comparative Religion: An Introductory and Historical Study, rev. ed. London, Methuen, 1962 (1938). 334 p.
A survey of major religions which compares rituals and concepts. Provides a selective bibliography divided by subject.

105 ________. The Concept of Deity; A Comparative and Historical Study. London, Hutchinson, 1950 (Wilde Lecture in the University of Oxford). 200 p.

Contains a collection of comparative discussions on the primitive conception of providence, the worship of nature, Oriental pantheism, etc. Bibliographic references are given in footnotes. Also includes an index.

106 Jordan, Louis H. Comparative Religion, Its Adjuncts and Allies. London, Oxford Univ. Press, 1915. 574 p.

Presents annotated bibliography which has established "avenues of approach to comparative religion"--Preface. The contents shows clearly that comparative religion has been always an interdisciplinary study depending heavily on social sciences and languages studies.

107 Lessa, William A., and E. Z. Vogt, eds. Reader in Comparative Religion; An Anthropological Approach, 2nd ed. New York, Harper and Row, 1965 (1958). 598 p.

A basic guide to literature which surveys anthropologists' attitudes toward religion in the last 100 years. Each chapter has an introductory paragraph which places the selected material in context and provides bibliographic references. Includes biographies of authors, a list of selected books on non-Western religious systems, general bibliography and an index of authors and titles.

108 Parrinder, Edward G. Comparative Religion. London, Allen and Unwin, 1962. 128 p.

This book explains what comparative religion is, what are its attitudes, implications and tasks. Contains bibliographical references in the footnotes, and a general index.

109 Smart, Ninian. The Religious Experience of Mankind. New York, Scribner's, 1969 (Fontana Library, Collins, 1971).

A comprehensive survey which applies historical and comparative techniques. Marxism, humanism, and some observations on the present state of religion are added. Also contains a supplementary bibliography for each chapter at the end, and a detailed subject index with numerous cross-references.

110 Wach, Joachim. The Comparative Study of Religions. Ed. with an introd. by Joseph M. Kitagawa, New York, Columbia Univ. Press, 1961 (1958) (Lectures on the History of Religions, sponsored by the American Council of Leanred Societies. New Ser. no. 1).

A collection of papers which discuss the development of meaning and methods in the comparative study of religions, the nature of experience, and the expression of religious experience in dogma, ritual, and communion. Includes bibliography and an index.

JOURNALS

111 Studies in Comparative Religion: Metaphysics, Cosmology, Tradition, Symbolism. Bedford, England, 1941- .
Originally published under the title: Tomorrow; Journal of Psychical Research. See also nos. 79, 80, 83, 88, 94, 95, 97.

VIII MYTHOLOGY, SYMBOLISM, RITES

METHODOLOGY

112 Mathiot, Madelaine. "Cognitive Analysis of a Myth; an Exercise in Method." Semiotica, v. 6:2 (1972), p. 101-42.
Provides the definition and analyzes methods used in research. "By myth is meant a folk narrative that is believed to be true. As with most folk narratives, a myth has as many versions as there are narrators."--text.

BIBLIOGRAPHY

113 Bibliographie zur Symbolik, Ikonographie und Mythologie (Bibliography of Symbolism, Iconography, and Mythology). Int. Referatorgan. Baden-Baden, Heitz, 1968- .
An annual international bibliography which consists of an annotated list of books and articles arranged alphabetically by author. Contains a very detailed subject index in German.

114 Goodland, Roger. A Bibliography of Sex Rites and Customs; An Annotated Record of Books, Articles and Illustrations in All Languages. London, Routledge, 1931. 752 p.
Lists 9000 items which are concerned with sexual ideas throughout the progress of civilization.

115 Lurker, Manfred. Bibliographie zur Symbolkunde. (Bibliography of Symbolism.) Baden-Baden, Heitz, 1968 (Bibliotheca bibliographica aureliana, 12).
An international bibliography of selected monographs and journal articles available in the field: bibliographies, journals, dictionaries, and works from the 16th to 18th centuries. Chapters are arranged by subjects, e.g. ethnology, folklore, literature, etc. Also contains an author, and a very detailed symbols index in German.

DICTIONARIES

116 Bonnerjea, Biren. A Dictionary of Superstitions and

Mythology. London, Folk Press, 1969 (1927). 314 p.
A reliable guide to mythology and folklore which includes a bibliography of works used in the compilation of this work.

117 Bulfinch, Thomas. Mythology: The Age of Fable, the Age of Chivalry, Legends of Charlemagne, new ed. New York, Crowell, 1970 (1867). 980 p.
This "work is ... for the reader of English literature ... who wishes to comprehend the allusions ... made by public speakers, lecturers, essayist, and poets"--Preface. Contains also a list of archaeological sites, and an index with page references to appropriate paragraphs in the dictionary.

118 Cirlot, Juan E. A Dictionary of Symbols. London, Routledge and Kegan, 1967 (c1962). 400 p.
Provides explanation of many symbols which are encountered in the arts and in the literature. Includes bibliography of principal sources, and a subject index with numerous cross-references.

119 Funk and Wagnalls Standard Dictionary of Folklore, Mythology and Legend. Ed.: Maria Leach. New York, Funk and Wagnalls, 1949-50. 2 vols.
Includes information on gods, heroes, tales, motifs, customs, beliefs, songs, dances, games, proverbs, etc. Provides also "survey articles" with bibliographies on regions, and on special subjects.

120 Goldsmith, Elizabeth. Ancient Pagan Symbols. New York, Putnam, 1929. 220 p.
Provides explanation of numerous symbols. Arranged by subject, e.g. lotus, swastika, birds. Also includes a subject index with cross-references.

121 Hangen, Eva C. Symbols--Our Universal Language. Wichita, Kan., 1962. 308 p.
Entries are arranged in alphabetical order with abundant cross-references. Provides a list of honored patrons, guardians and protectors of the various occupations and a selective bibliography to more explanatory reading.

122 Jobes, Gertrude. Dictionary of Mythology, Folklore and Symbols. New York, Scarecrow, 1961-62. 3 pts.
An alphabetically arranged list of myths, legends, and symbols. Bibliography is listed at the end of pt. 2. Pt. 3 contains an index divided into two parts (a) Table of deities, heroes, and personalities; and (b) Table of mythological affiliations.

123 Larousse Encyclopedia of Mythology; with an introd. by Robert Graves. London, Hamlyn, 1962 (1959). 500 p.

A "Who was who: of the better known gods, goddesses, heroes, monsters, demons, angels, and saints from all over the world"--Preface.

124 Macculloch, John A., ed. The Mythology of All Races. Boston, Archeological Institute of America, 1937 (1916-31). 13 vols.

"A comprehensive collection ... of myths from all quarters of the earth and all ages..."--Preface. Vol. 13 contains a very detailed index with numerous cross-references. Is still regarded as a most useful reference work in English.

125 Man, Myth, and Magic; An Illustrated Encyclopedia of the Supernatural. Richard Cavendish, ed. London, Purnell, 1970- .

A comprehensive survey of magic, mythology and religion. Pt. 1 contains introductory articles, explaining more clearly the alphabetically arranged dictionary section. Most of the entries are followed by selective bibliographies. A complete index, with cross-references to related subjects appears at the end.

126 Sykes, Egerton, ed. Everyman's Dictionary of Non-classical Mythology. London, Dent, 1968 (1961). 282 p.

Contains 2000 condensed articles which cover American, Chinese, Japanese, Teutonic and Norse, and Middle Eastern mythologies.

127 Vries, Ad de. Dictionary of Symbols and Imagery. Amsterdam, North Holland, 1976. 515 p.

Contains an alphabetical listing of symbols or images which are known in western civilization. Some critical sources are cited.

HANDBOOKS AND SURVEYS

128 Campbell, Joseph. The Masks of God. New York, Viking Press, 1968-69. 4 vols.

First comprehensive history of mythology which makes a full use of the new science of comparative mythology. Vols. 1-3 deal with the anonymous mythological past; vol. 4 discusses the individual creators of myth, like Dante, Joyce, Mann, and T. S. Eliot. Includes a detailed index and a selective bibliography.

129 ________. The Mythic Image. Princeton, N.J., University Press, 1974 (Bollingen Series). 552 p.

This is a popularly presented survey of the origins of myths from the oral non-literate traditions to monumental literate civilizations of Europe, the Near East, India, Far East, and South America. Some bibliographic citations in notes and an index are provided.

130 Dillistone, F. W. Traditional Symbols and the Contemporary World. London, Epworth, 1973 (Bampton Lectures, 1968). 179 p.

First, provides a historical survey, then deals with symbols in the modern world. Some bibliographic references are included in notes. Indexes of names and subjects are supplied.

131 Douglas, Marj. Natural Symbols; Explorations in Cosmology. London, Barrie & Rockliff, Cresset Press, 1970. 177 p.

The author explores the relationship between cultural symbols, and social experiences of particular human groups where such symbols are found. A selective bibliography is provided.

132 Eliade, Mircea. Images and Symbols; Studies in Religious Symbolism. Transl. by P. Mairet. New York, Sheed and Ward, 1969 (1962). (Search Book.) 189 p.

A collection of studies which analyzes the structure of religious symbolism. Each chapter presents a discussion of a symbol or a group of symbols. The final chapter gives a summary of all findings. Bibliographical references are given in the footnotes. Also contains a subject index.

133 ________. Myth and Reality. Transl. from the French by W. R. Trask. New York, Harper and Row, 1964 (1963). (World Perspectives, vol. 31.) 204 p.

The author discusses the significance of such related myths as those concerned with the origin, creation, renewal, and the end of the world. A selective bibliography is included.

134 Firth, Raymond. Symbols: Public and Private. Ithaca, N.Y., Cornell University Press, 1973 (Symbol, Myth, and Ritual). 469 p.

"The aim of this book is to help to give perspective to the anthropological study of symbolic forms and processes and the functions of symbolism"--Introd. Extensive bibliographic references to monographs and periodical articles and an index are added.

135 James, Edwin O. Origins of Sacrifice; A Study in Comparative Religion. London, Murray, 1933. 313 p.

A survey of numerous rites which are comprehended under the term sacrifice. It provides a definition and a preliminary classification comprising; blood offering, vegetation ritual, human sacrifice, cannibalism, etc. Also includes a bibliography divided by chapters and an index of names and subjects.

136 Leeming, David A. Mythology: The Voyage of the Hero. Philadelphia, Lippincott, 1973. 337 p.

"This book of myths is built upon a simplified form of the mono-myth which is divided into eight basic events ... in the life of the hero..."--Introd. Select bibliography of works of importance to the student of mythology. The index is appended.

137 Lévi-Strauss, C. The Raw and the Cooked. Transl. by J. D. Weightman. New York, Harper and Row, 1969 (Introduction to a Science of Mythology, 1). 387 p.

Translation of Le Crut et le cuit. A famous new interpretation of mythology which applies a method of structural analysis in anthropology. Includes a bibliography.

138 ________. The Savage Mind. London, Weidenfeld and Nicolson, 1966 (The Nature of Human Society Series). 290 p.

Translation of La Pensée sauvage. Applying his own structural method in anthropology, the author demonstrates how each culture has its own system of concepts such as space and time, myth and rituals, etc. Also included are a selective bibliography and an index.

139 Mythology. Ed. by Pierre Maranda. Hardmondsworth, Penguin, 1972 (Penguin Modern Sociology Readings). 320 p.

An introduction to the topic which surveys new developments in the modern anthropological theory of myth. Comprises a brief historical review, a discussion of fundamental aspects of the modern theory of myth, and "the glance at the codes our literate and technological societies couch their myths." Bibliography provides a reasonably good coverage of recent works on myth. Also includes author and title indexes.

140 Parrinder, Edward G. Worship in the World's Religion. London, Faber and Faber, 1961. 239 p.

This remarkable book attempts to explain what is the nature of believer's worship and what is his faith and prayer. A brief bibliography and a subject index with cross-references are included.

141 Whittick, Arnold. Symbols, Signs and Their Meaning. London, Hill, 1960. 408 p.

This study is confined to visual symbolism as used in the West. However, also included are the better known Oriental examples. Pt. 1. explains meaning and types of symbolism; Pt. 2. describes its applied forms; Pt. 3. provides an encyclopedic dictionary of traditional and familiar symbols, their origin, meaning and history; and Pt. 4. deals with individual and collective expression, note especially on p. 307: Religious symbolism. Also contains a subject index.

142 Whittlesey, E. S. Symbols and Legends in Western Art; A Museum Guide. New York, Scribner's, 1972. 367 p.
Explains symbols which appear in most popular myths and legends. The listing is arranged alphabetically with numerous cross-references to bring all related subjects together. A short selective bibliography comprises works used for compilation of this work.

JOURNALS

143 Folk Lore; A Quarterly Review of Myth, Tradition, Institution. London, 1878- .
Incorporates the Anthropological Review and the Folk Lore Journal. Contains bibliographies, book reviews. Cumulated index: 1878-1958. Indexed: Br. Hum. Index; Int. Biblio. of Soc. and Cult. Anthro.

See also no.: 71, 81, 82, 84, 85, 86.

IX MYSTICISM

BIBLIOGRAPHY

144 Sharma, U., and I. Arndt. Mysticism: A Select Bibliography. Waterloo Lutheran University, 1973. 109 p.
"... Brings together some 1500 of the best works that have appeared in English or in English translation since 1900. It is designed to serve scholars, students, and librarians"--Introd. Encompasses the religions of the East and West: Christianity, Judaism, Islam, Hinduism, Buddhism, Taoism, etc., and the literary, psychological, and philosophical aspects of the subject. An index of persons, religions, etc. is provided.

DICTIONARY

145 Gaynor, Frank, ed. Dictionary of Mysticism. New York, Philosophical Library, 1953 (Midcentury Reference Library). 208 p.
Entries are listed alphabetically with cross-references.

INTRODUCTORY

146 Smart, Ninian. "Mysticism, History of." Encyclopedia of Philosophy. Vol. 5, p. 419-429.
Provides a brief informative introduction to the subject, with well-selected bibliographical sources.

HANDBOOKS AND SURVEYS

147 Happold, F. C. Mysticism; A Study and Anthology. Harmondsworth, England, Penguin, 1963 (Pelican Originals). 364 p.
A study which is divided into two parts: first the historical and biographical survey then an anthology. Bibliographical references are included in footnotes. The index is limited to proper names and works cited in the text.

148 O'Brien, Elmer. Varieties of Mystic Experience; An Anthology and Interpretation. New York, Holt, Reinehart and Winston, 1964. 321 p.
Presents a survey of mysticism from the 3rd to the 7th century. Includes selections of the chief mystics and their discussions. Chapter bibliographies are provided for more extensive studies.

149 Scharfstein, Ben-Ami. Mystical Experience. Oxford, England, Blackwell's, 1973. 195 p.
Attempts a definition of the mystic state discussing such issues as everyday mysticism, creator's mysticism, mystical techniques, Freud's psychoanalysis, and Patanjali's yoga, and finally the eleven quintessences of the mystic state. Bibliographic notes and an index are provided.

150 Spencer, Sidney. Mysticism in World Religion. Pelican Books, Harmondsworth, England, Penguin, 1963.
Is recognized as the best comprehensive survey of the field. Includes bibliographic references and an index.

151 Staal, Frits. Exploring Mysticism: A Methodological Essay. Berkeley, University of California Press, 1975. 230 p.
Provides a review of methods by which mysticism is generally studied. Glossary, bibliography, and index are appended.

152 Stace, Walter T., ed. The Teachings of the Mystics, Being Selections from the Great Mystics and Mystical Writings of the World. Ed. with introd., interpretative commentaries and explanations. New York, New American Library, 1960 (A Mentor Book). 240 p.
Bibliographic references are included in footnotes.

153 Underhill, Evelyn. Mysticism; A Study in the Nature and Development of Man's Spiritual Consciousness. New York, Noonday Press, 1955 (1911) (Meridian Books, MG 1). 519 p.
A classic which by its new edition marks the revival of interest in theoretical and practical mysticism. Contains abundant biographical information and extremely exhaustive bibliography.

X PHILOSOPHY OF RELIGION

ENCYCLOPEDIA

154 Encyclopedia of Philosophy. Paul Edwards, Editor in Chief. New York, Macmillan, 1967. 8 vols.

This most comprehensive reference work in the field covers Eastern and Western philosophy from ancient to modern times. Contains about 1500 articles with selective bibliographies. Subject of religion is discussed in vol. 7, but for more complete information index in vol. 8 must be consulted.

BIBLIOGRAPHIES

155 Bibliography of Philosophy: A Quarterly Bulletin. Published by the International Institute of Philosophy with the aid of UNESCO, of the Conceil International de la Philosophie et des Sciences Humaines.... Paris, Librairie Philosophique, 1937- .

Contains an annotated bibliography of monographs. Annotations are given in English, French, German, Italian, and Spanish. Includes a section which lists reprints, new editions, paperbacks, and translations. Especially important is the section "Philosophy of Religion." Issued quarterly with an annual and a cumulative author and subject index.

156 Répertoire bibliographique de la philosophie. Publié sous les auspices de l'Institut International de Philosophie avec le patronage de l'UNESCO.... Louvain, Editions de la l'Institut Supérieur de Philosophie, 1937- (three issues a year).

Literature on the subject is listed in the section: Philosophie de la réligion. Includes author and title indexes.

HANDBOOKS AND SURVEYS

157 Abernethy, G. L., and T. K. Lanford, eds. Philosophy of Religion. New York, Macmillan, 1962. 542 p.

Provides a large selection of readings which includes discussions on the problem of evil, immortality, nature of revelation and faith, and problems of religious language. Bibliography for more extensive reading is provided.

158 Arnett, Willard E. A Modern Reader in the Philosophy of Religion. New York, Appleton-Century-Croft, 1966 (Century Philosophy Series). 563 p.

A selection from major writings in the philosophy of

religion which "is intended primarily as a text for use in college..."--Preface. Each part includes bibliographical references.

159 ________. Religion and Judgement. New York, Appleton-Century-Crofts, 1966 (Century Philosophy Series). 335 p.
This book attempts to explain scientifically certain chosen aspects of religion in terms of non-religious elements of culture. Bibliography is divided into two parts: books which were extensively cited in the text, and a selection of other more important readings.

160 Bertocci, Peter A. Introduction to the Philosophy of Religion. New York, Prentice-Hall, 1955 (1951). 565 p.
Provides a discussion of central philosophical aspects of religion. Recognized as a most useful text for students who have no previous philosophical training. Each chapter provides a set of questions for repetition and a bibliographical guide. An index of names and subjects is included.

161 Bronstein, D. J., and H. M. Schulweis, eds. Approaches to the Philosophy of Religion; A Book of Readings. New York, Prentice-Hall, 1954. 532 p.
A collection of papers which deals with basic issues in the philosophy of religion. Arranged systematically with an introduction to each selection. Each chapter is provided with a selection of bibliographic references. Contains author and subject index.

162 Ducasse, Curt J. A Philosophical Scrutiny of Religion. New York, Ronald Press, 1953. 441 p.
An objective inquiry into the nature of religion which provides a clear and comprehensive account of typical religious experiences like prayer, conversion, mystical illumination; and concepts like: supernatural, miraculous, magical, divinity, sin, sacredness, soul, spirit, etc. Bibliographical leads are included in footnotes. Contains an index.

163 Feaver, J. C., and W. Horosh, eds. Religion in Philosophical and Cultural Perspective; A New Approach to the Philosophy of Religion Through Cross-disciplinary Studies. Princeton, N.J., Van Nostrand, 1967. 504 p.
Pt. 1 reviews the philosophy of religion in the historical perspective; Pt. 2 analyzes various contemporary ideals in their interaction with religion. Each chapter includes a set of questions for repetition and a list of selected references. Separate name and topic indexes are provided.

164 Ferré, Frederick. Basic Modern Philosophy of Religion. New York, Scribner's, 1967. 465 p.
A survey which presents in a generalized form a historical development of philosophies of religion. Includes

annotated chapter bibliographies.

165 Freeman, David H. A Philosophical Study of Religion. Nutley, N.J., Craig, 1964. 270 p.
The author examines various opposing definitions of religion. Bibliographical references are presented in the footnotes.

166 Hick, John. Philosophy of Religion. Englewood Cliffs, N.J., Prentice-Hall, 1963 (Foundations of Philosophy Series). 111 p.
Provides an analysis of phenomena of religious experience and all the activities of worship.

167 ________, ed. Classical and Contemporary Readings in the Philosophy of Religion. Englewood Cliffs, N.J., Prentice-Hall, 1964. 494 p.
Material is presented in two separate tables of contents: the Readings; and the Topical Table of Contents. Contains an appendix providing introductory notes and bibliographies, and a subject index.

168 Hutchinson, John J. Faith, Reason, and Existence; An Introduction to Contemporary Philosophy of Religion. New York, Oxford University Press, 1956. 306 p.
Introduces basic ideas and issues of new religious thought. One will find bibliographic references to primary sources, chapter bibliographies, a list of general works on the topic, and an index.

169 Kristensen, William B. The Meaning of Religion; Lectures in the Phenomenology of Religion. With an Introd. by H. Kraemer; transl. by J. B. Corman. The Hague, Nijhoff, 1960. 532 p.
A series of classroom lectures which deal with various religious phenomena. The subject is subdivided into three groups: religious cosmology, religious anthropology and cults. Bibliographies are included in the notes. Also contains an index.

170 Leeuw, Garaldus van der. Religion in Essence and Manifestation. Transl. by J. E. Turner. New York, Harper and Row, 1963 (1933; English transl., 1938) (Harper Torchbooks. The Cloister Library).
Translation of Phänomenologie der Religion. A monumental work which surveys and provides a critical appraisal of all phenomenological studies of religion. Includes bibliographical references in footnotes, and an index.

171 Lewis, H. D. Philosophy of Religion. London, English Universities Press, 1965 (Teach Yourself Books).
An excellent survey of philosophical problems of religion

which explains how they are solved today. Each chapter has an annotated selection of references. Contains a name and subject indexes.

172 MacGregor, Geddes. Introduction to Religious Philosophy. Boston, Houghton Mifflin, 1959. 366 p.
Discusses basic conception of God, the traditional case for the destiny of man, the mystery of evil, and religious language.

173 Smart, Ninian, ed. Historical Selections in the Philosophy of Religion. London, SCM, 1965 (Library of Philosophy and Theology). 510 p.
Contains a selection of writings of prominent philosophers pertaining to religion. Each selection is accompanied by a biographical note, an evaluation of the achievements, and a brief bibliography. A full index with numerous cross references is provided.

174 Thompson, Samuel M. A Modern Philosophy of Religion. Chicago, Regnery, 1955. 601 p.
A highly valued handbook which provides clear and comprehensive answers to such complicated concepts as faith and knowledge; truth; the nature of man; the idea of god; the existence of god; our knowledge about god; god and the world, etc. One finds ample notes with questions and topics for more extensive study. A selective bibliography is provided.

175 Trueblood, David E. Philosophy of Religion. New York, Harper, 1957. 324 p.
Recent general text which deals with the logic of religion, theistic realism, dialectical materialism, freudianism, the problem of evil, and such concepts as good, freedom, etc. Includes a bibliography.

JOURNALS

176 International Journal for Philosophy of Religion. The Hague, 1970- (irregular).
Sponsored by the Society for Philosophy of Religion. The section: Philosophy of religion in the journals should be scanned.

177 Philosophy and Phenomenological Research. Buffalo, 1940- (quarterly).
Published by the University of Buffalo Foundation and the International Phenomenological Society. Indexed: Int. Biblio. of Period. Lit.

178 Research in Phenomenology. Pittsburgh, Pa., 1971- (annual).

Published by the Duquesne University.

179 Sophia; A Journal for Discussion in Philosophical Theology. Parkville, Australia, 1962- (three times a year).
Published by the University of Melbourne, Dept. of Philosophy.

XI ANTHROPOLOGY OF RELIGION

INTRODUCTORY

180 Bharati, Agehananda. "Anthropological Approaches to the Study of Religion; Ritual and Belief System." Biennial Review of Anthropology, 1971, p. 230-82.
A survey article which provides a historical outline of progress in this field. Also includes a selective bibliography.

DICTIONARIES AND ENCYCLOPEDIAS

181 Encyclopedia of the Social Sciences. New York, Macmillan, 1950. 15 vols.
Includes all the main concepts of the Social Sciences; anthropology, psychology, sociology, etc. Subject and author indexes are included at the end of the last volume. Chapter: Religion, v. 13, p. 229-239, should be consulted. Especially helpful are cross-references and bibliography which is appended at the end of the article. In the index check, "Religion," etc.

182 Geertz, Clifford. " Religion; I. Anthropological Study." International Encyclopedia of the Social Sciences, v. 13, p. 398-406. New York, Macmillan, 1968. 17 vols.
Contains articles on important topics in the social sciences; anthropology, psychology, and sociology, etc. Articles deal with concepts, theories, and methods of each discipline. Selected bibliographies are appended. Topics can be easily located either by means of numerous cross-references in the text of encyclopedia or in vol. 17: Index.

183 Winick, Charles. Dictionary of Anthropology. New York, Philosophical Library, 1956 (Midcentury Reference Library). 579 p.
A dictionary of anthropological terms which is very useful for definitions of more specialized terms not listed in general dictionaries. Includes some biographical information and many proper names. Must be used, with caution, however, because of numerous errors.

BIBLIOGRAPHIES

184 International Bibliography of Social and Cultural Anthropology. London, Tavistock, 1956- (annual).

Prepared by the International Committee for Social Science Documentation. Lists monographs and journal articles selected for their scholarly value. Excluded are works dealing in polemics and those of only informative nature. Religious topics are covered by Section F: Religion, Magic, and Witchcraft. Subject index should be checked for related topics, e.g., Rites, Religious minorities, etc.

185 International Folklore and Folklife Bibliography. Ouvrage publié par la Société Internationale d'Ethnologie et de Folklore sous les auspices du Conceil International de la Philosophie et des Sciences Humaines et avec le concours de l'UNESCO. Rédigé ... par R. Wildhaber. Bonn, Habett, 1939- .

An irregularly published bibliography which covers folklore of all countries. Especially important is the section, "Popular Beliefs." In the subject index check: "Mythus," "Religionsgeschichte," "Symbol," etc.

HANDBOOKS AND SURVEYS

186 Conference on New Approaches in Social Anthropology, Cambridge, 1963. Anthropological Approaches to the Study of Religion. London, Tavistock, 1966 (Association of Social Anthropologists. Monographs). 176 p.

A collection of papers which survey and evaluate the theories and methods used in the past and outline the new perspectives for research in the field. Bibliographical references are provided at the end of each chapter.

187 Wallace, Anthony F. C. Religion; An Anthropological View. New York, Random House, 1966. 300 p.

After outlining traditional anthropological theories of religion, the author analyzes the categories under which religion is described by statistical and cross-cultural methods. He also surveys present state of information on the function of religion. An extensive bibliographical references and an index are included.

JOURNALS

188 Anthropologica. Ottawa, 1955- (2 issues a year).

Published by the Canadian Research Centre for Anthropology. Features articles in the fields of cultural and social anthropology and related disciplines.

189 Anthropological Journal of Canada. Ottawa, 1963- (quarterly).
Published by the Anthropological Society of Canada. Indexed: SSCI.

190 Anthropological Quarterly. Washington, D. C., 1928- .
Published by the Catholic Anthropological Society. Indexed: Int. Bibliog. Soc. Cul. Anthro.; Cath. Ind.

191 Anthropological Society of Oxford. Journal. Oxford, 1970- (3 issues a year).
Published by the Institute of Social Anthropology. Indexed: Int. Bibliog. Soc. Cult. Anthro.

192 Anthropos; Revue international d'ethnologie et de linguistique. Salzburg, 1906- (3 issues per year).
Papers in English, French, and German. Cumulated index, v. 1-54 is provided. Indexed: Int. Bibliog. Soc. Cult. Anthro.

193 Annual Review of Anthropology. Palo Alto, Calif., 1972- .
Supersedes Biennial Review of Anthropology. Indexed: Int. Bibliog. Soc. Cult. Anthro.

194 Current Anthropology; World Journal of the Sciences of Man. Chicago, 1960- (5 issues per year).
Cumulated index, 1960-68 is provided. Indexed: Soc. Sci. Hum. Index; Int. Bibliog. Soc. Cult. Anthro.

195 Ethnology; An International Journal of Cultural and Social Anthropology. Pittsburgh, 1962- (quarterly).
Indexed: Soc. Sci. Hum. Index; SSCI.

196 Ethnos. Stockholm, 1936- (quarterly).
Papers in English and German. Cumulated index is issued every 10 years. Indexed: Int. Bibliog. Soc. Cult. Anthro.

197 Indiana. University, Folklore Institute. Journal. Bloomington, 1940- (3 issues a year).
Supersedes Midwest Folklore. Indexed: Int. Bibliog. Soc. Cult. Anthro.

198 Journal of Anthropological Research. Albuquerque, N. M., 1973- (quarterly).
Continues Southwestern Journal of Anthropology. Indexed: Soc. Sci. Hum. Index; SSCI.

199 Man. London, 1966- (quarterly).
Published by the Anthropological Institute of London. Continues its Journal. Indexed: Int. Biblio. of Soc. and Cult. Anthro.

200 Mankind. Sydney, 1931- (2 issues a year).
Published by the Anthropological Societies of Australia. Indexed: Aus. P.A.I.S., Soc. Sci. Hum. Index.

XII PSYCHOLOGY OF RELIGION

DICTIONARIES AND ENCYCLOPEDIAS

201 Ditties, James E. "Religion. III. Psychological Study." International Encyclopedia of the Social Sciences. V. 13, p. 414-21.
See no. 182. A survey of concepts, theories and methods in this field. List of related entries and selective bibliography are provided at the end.

202 Encyclopedia of Psychology. Eds.: H. J. Eysenck and W. Arnold. New York, Herder and Herder, 1972. 3 vols.
Includes two kinds of entries: short definitions, and lengthy articles of up to 4000 words, covering important concepts and terms and containing selected bibliographical references for further reading. Particularly useful is the article: Kretchmer, W. "Religion, Psychology of," Vol. 2, p. 136-46.

INDEX ABSTRACTS

203 Psychological Abstracts. Lancaster, Pa., 1927- (monthly, cumulated semi-annually).
Published monthly with an index for each six-month issues. Each issue contains: table of contents, complete list of journals regularly searched, cumulative author index, cumulative subject index. For reference the entry: Religion should be checked.

BIBLIOGRAPHIES AND GUIDES

204 Capps, Donald; L. Rambo; and P. Ransohoff. Psychology of Religion. Detroit, Gale, 1976 (Information Guide Series: Philosophy and Religion). 352 p.
The contents are organized according to six dimensions: mythological, ritual, experiential, dispositional, social, and directional. Author, title, and subject indexes are appended.

205 Lindzey, Gardner, and Elliot Aronson, eds. Handbook of Social Psychology, 2nd ed. Reading, Mass., Addison-Wesley, 1968 (1954). 5 vols.
A survey of literature in every field of social psychology.

Each volume covers a particular aspect: vol. 1: Historical Introduction; vol. 2: Research Methods; vol. 3: The Individual in the Social Context; vol. 4: Group Psychology and Phenomena of Interaction; and vol. 5: Applied Social Psychology. At the end of each chapter one finds extensive bibliographical references. Author and subject indexes are provided separately at the end of each volume.

206 Meissner, W. W. Annotated Bibliography in Religion and Psychology. New York, Academy of Religion and Mental Health, 1961. 235 p.
Includes about 3000 references which are organized into 47 well-defined and workable categories, e.g. psychology and conscience; psychoanalysis and religion, etc. It covers monographs and journal articles in all languages. An author index is provided.

HANDBOOKS AND SURVEYS

207 Allport, Gordon W. The Individual and His Religion; A Psychological Interpretation. New York, Macmillan, 1960 (1950) (Macmillan Paperback). 147 p.
Includes an index of authors and subjects.

208 Argyle, Michael. Religious Behaviour. London, Routledge and Paul, 1958 (International Library of Sociology and Social Reconstruction). 196 p.
Surveys studies in the field of psychology of religion, completed in Britain and North America since 1900. Shows how religious behavior and belief vary with personality factors, age and sex, environmental experiences, social belonging, etc. Provides a bibliography, and name and subject indexes.

209 Clark, Walter H. The Psychology of Religion. New York, Macmillan, 1958. 485 p.
An inquiry into psychological aspects of religion, its effects upon human behavior, and the relationship between religion and psychotherapy. Contains research questions, a selective bibliography and name and subject indexes.

210 A Dialog between Theology and Psychology. By L. Aden, and others. Ed. by Peter Homans. Chicago, Univ. of Chicago Press, 1968 (Essays in Divinity). 295 p.
An excellent collection of papers which deals with various topics in the field of religious psychology. Bibliographic references are provided in the footnotes; also contains an index.

211 Freud, Sigmund. The Future of an Illusion. Transl. by W. D. Robson-Scott. Rev. and newly ed. by James Strachey. Garden City, N.Y., Doubleday, 1964 (1928)

(Anchor Books, A 381). 105 p.
A classic essay on the future of religion.

212 Fromm, Erich. Psychoanalysis and Religion. New Haven, Conn., Yale Univ. Press, 1950 (The Terry Lectures). 126 p.
A scholarly discussion of Freud and Jung's attitudes towards religious problems. No index provided.

213 James, William. The Varieties of Religious Experience. New York, Longmans Green, 1929 (1902) (Gifford Lectures on Natural Religion. A Modern Library of the World's best books). 534 p.
A highly valued work which founded a basis for broad analysis of psychic experience in connection with religious practices.

214 Jung, Carl G. Psychology of Religion. New Haven, Conn., Yale Univ. Press, 1960 (1938). 131 p. Also in his: Collected Works. Pt. 1. London, Routledge and Paul, 1953- .
An monumental essay which deals with the autonomy of unconscious, dogma and natural symbols, history and psychology of natural symbol.

215 Rudin, Josef. Psychotherapy and Religion. Transl. by E. Reinecke and P. C. Bailey. Notre Dame, Ind., Univ. of Notre Dame Press, 1968. 241 p.
Presents new insights on dynamic activity of the psyche and the effects of its study on the understanding of man's spiritual life.

216 Scobie, Geoffrey E. W. Psychology of Religion. London: Batsford, 1975. 189 p.
First, attempts a definition of religion and then discusses variables of religious belief and behavior, and their definitions; psychological factors associates with religious behavior; attitude change in religious behavior, etc. Bibliography and Index.

217 Spinks, G. S. Psychology and Religion; An Introduction to Contemporary Views. London, Methuen, 1963 (Methuen's Manuals of Modern Psychology). 221 p.
Contains a critical survey of theories which treat religion as psychological activity based on analytical and psychoanalytical methods. Includes a very detailed bibliography, and name and subject index.

218 Zunini, Giorgio. Man and His Religion; Aspects of Religious Psychology. Transl. ... with a foreword by Sean O'Riordan. London, Chapman, 1969 (1963). 365 p.
Originally published as Homo religiosus; il saggiatore. Provides an excellent survey of all aspects of psychology of religion with selected bibliographical references.

JOURNALS

219 Journal of Religion and Health. New York, 1961- (quarterly).
Published by the Academy of Religion and Mental Health. Indexed: Rel. Per.

220 Journal of Social Psychology. Provincetown, Mass., 1929- (3 issues a year).
Indexed: Psychological Abstracts; Biological Abstracts.

XIII SOCIOLOGY OF RELIGION

ENCYCLOPEDIA

221 Bellah, R. N. "Religion. II: The Sociology of Religion." International Encyclopedia of the Social Sciences. V. 13, p. 406-13.
See no. 182. Discusses relations between religion and social structure. Also includes a selective bibliography.

BIBLIOGRAPHIES

222 International Bibliography of Sociology. London, Tavistock; Chicago, Aldine, 1952- (annual).
Published by the International Committee for Social Sciences Documentation. Monographs and journal articles on religion are listed in the section D13 but the subject index should be checked for related topics. Includes book reviews.

223 LeBras, Gabriel. "Sociology of Religion; A Trend Report and Bibliography." Current Sociology, V. 5:1 (1956), 87 p.
Evaluates items included in the bibliographic section. The bibliography is limited to living religions. Studies prior to 1940 are omitted.

ABSTRACTS

224 Sociological Abstracts. Brooklyn, N.Y., 1953- (6 issues per year).
A classified list of abstracts with annual cumulative subject and author indexes. Abstracts of works on religious topics are included in the class, 1500:35, "Sociology of Religion." Indexes: Daedalus, Encounter, Religious Research, etc.

HANDBOOKS AND SURVEYS

225 Berger, Peter. Sacred Canopy; Elements of a Sociological Theory of Religion. Garden City, N.J., Doubleday, 1967. 230 p.

British edition published under title, The Social Reality of Religion. This interesting book surveys a developing sociological theory of religion, drawing examples from both ancient and modern religions. Includes bibliography, and subject and names indexes.

226 Birnbaum, Norman, and Gertrud Lenzer, eds. Sociology and Religion; A Book of Readings. Englewood Cliffs, N.J., Prentice-Hall, 1969. 452 p.

Presents various schools of thought in the field of sociology of religion. Discusses the anthropological tradition, structural functionalism, and contemporary studies which employ quantitative techniques. One finds also an excellent bibliography which indicates the sources.

227 Demerath, N. J., and P. E. Hammond. Religion in Social Context: Tradition and Transition. New York, Random House, 1969. 246 p.

This work provides a perceptive analysis of the most important and challenging sociological works in the field.

228 Durkheim, Emile. The Elementary Forms of the Religious Life. Transl. from the French by J. W. Swain. New York, Free Press, 1965 (1912).

Translation of Les Formes élémentaires de la vie religieuse. Based partly on Spencer and Gillen's study of an Australian tribe, it is an outstanding pioneer work on the social aspects of religious beliefs and practices.

229 Fallding, Harold. The Sociology of Religion. Toronto, McGraw Ryerson, 1974. 240 p.

This is a textbook written for the student of sociology. Pt. I deals with unity found in religion. Pt. II, with diversity. In chapter 1 is found an interesting attempt to develop a sociological definition of religion. Bibliographic references are included in notes. Also indexes.

230 Nottingham, E. K. Religion; A Sociological View. New York, Random House, 1971. 332 p.

This excellent textbook discusses the varying roles that religion has played in societies of differing types. It provides an extensive bibliography, and an index.

231 O'Dea, Thomas F. Sociology and the Study of Religion, Theory, Research Interpretation. New York, Basic Books, 1970. 307 p.

An excellent collection of papers which form a consistent body of research, interpretation, and theoretical discussion in the field of sociology of religion. Contains bibliographical references in the footnotes, and an index.

232 Robertson, Roland. The Sociological Interpretation of Religion. New York, Schocken Books, 1970 (Introductions to Sociology). 256 p.

A survey of basic issues which is presented in a very condensed form. Constitutes an excellent annotated guide to the field.

233 Schneider, Louis. Religion, Culture, and Society; A Reader in the Sociology of Religion. New York, Wiley, 1964. 663 p.

A fine selection which brings together modern as well as classical sources providing a sound basis for understanding of various sociological problems in studies of religion. Includes bibliographical footnotes, and an author index.

234 _______. Sociological Approach to Religion. New York, Wiley, 1970. 188 p.

A comprehensive account of structural-functional analysis of religion which emphasizes the importance of historical and comparative materials. Includes bibliographical information in footnotes, and an index.

235 Stark, Werner. The Sociology of Religion; A Study of Christendom. London, Routledge and Paul, 1966-70 (International Library of Sociology and Social Reconstruction). 4 vols.

An extensive analysis of established and sectarian religions, the universal church, and types of religious man. Each volume is provided with its own index. Bibliographical references are included in the footnotes.

236 Wach, Joachim. Sociology of Religion. London, K. Paul, 1951 (1944) (International Library of Sociology and Social Reconstruction). 412 p.

Presents a summary of findings of theologians, and social scientists on the interaction of religion and society in different cultures and ages. The author provides a working typology of religious groups, their cult expressions, leadership, and symbols integration. Includes bibliographical references in footnotes.

237 Weber, Max. The Sociology of Religion. Transl. by E. Fischoff. Introd. by T. Parson. Boston, Beacon Press, 1963 (1922). 304 p.

Translation of his Religionssoziologie. A classic work which makes rewarding but difficult reading. First analyzes the nature of religion, then turns to the question of sources for religious beliefs, and finally discusses the consequences of religious belief and activity for other areas of human life.

238 Yinger, J. M. Religion, Society, and the Individual; An Introduction to the Sociology of Religion. New York, Macmillan, 1957. 655 p.
A comprehensive introduction which surveys the more significant literature on the topic. Includes a good selective bibliography.

239 ________. The Scientific Study of Religion. New York, Macmillan, 1970. 593 p.
An elaborate treatment of major theoretical issues which surround religion, society, and the individual.

JOURNALS

240 American Journal of Sociology. Chicago, 1895- (bi-monthly).
Indexed: Soc. Sci. Hum. Index; Int. Bibliog. Sociol.

241 Internationales Jahrbuch für Religionssoziologie. International Yearbook for the Sociology of Religion. Köln, Opladen, 1965- .
Papers are published in English and German. Each issue is devoted to a specific topic. Concentrates on studies of theoretical problems, lists summaries of descriptive studies, and includes essays on religious phenomena. Footnotes are provided but no bibliographies.

242 Religion and Society. Bangalore, India, 1954- (quarterly).
Published by the Christian Institute for the Study of Religion.

243 Social Compass; International Review of Socio-Religious Studies. The Hague, 1953- (quarterly).
Text in English and French. Indexed: Rel. Theol. Abstracts; Int. Bibliog. Sociology.

244 Sociological Analysis; A Journal in the Sociology of Religion. Chicago, 1940- (quarterly).
Published by the Association for the Sociology of Religion. Indexed: Soc. Abstr.; Cath. Index.

XIV RELIGIOUS EDUCATION

ENCYCLOPEDIA

245 The Encyclopedia of Education. Lee C. Deighton, Editor-in-Chief. New York, Macmillan and the Fortress Press,

1971. 10 vols.

Contains more than 1000 articles which deal with history, theory, research, and philosophy, as well as with structure of education. Most of the articles conclude with a bibliography for more extensive study. Vol. 7, p. 465-98 includes following articles: Religion in the public schools; Religious education in the church; Religious education, Urban; Religious service, education for professional career. For related topics the index in Vol. 10, p. 528-9 should be consulted.

BIBLIOGRAPHIES AND GUIDES

246 Clebsch, William A. "Religious Studies in American Colleges and Universities: A Preliminary Bibliography." Religious Studies Review, v. 1:1 (1975), p. 50-60.

This brief essay, with a classified bibliography, surveys the development of religion in higher education over the last half-century.

247 Guide to Religious Studies in Canada. Comp. and ed. by C. P. Anderson, under auspices of Canadian Society for the Study of Religion. Toronto, Corp. for the Publication of Academic Studies in Religion in Canada, 1969- (irregular).

This guide, sponsored by the Canadian Society of Biblical Studies, the Canadian Society of Church History, and the Canadian Theological Society, surveys the state of religious studies in Canada.

248 Politella, Joseph, ed. Religion in Education; An Annotated Bibliography. Oneonta, N.Y., American Assoc. of Colleges for Teacher Education, 1956. 90 p.

Contains an annotated bibliography of books representing the Jewish, Protestant, and Catholic points of view.

INDEX

249 Education Index. New York, Wilson, 1929- (monthly, then quarterly and annually cumulated).

A cumulative author and subject index to educational materials in the English language. For bibliographical references one should look under the subject: Religious education.

HANDBOOKS AND SURVEYS

250 Holbrook, C. A. Religion, A Humanistic Field. Englewood Cliffs, N.J., Prentice-Hall, 1963 (The Princeton Studies: Humanistic Scholarship in America). 299 p.

This book reviews and evaluates the entire field of religious instruction and scholarship, the materials and methods, the problem of indoctrination, curricular content, the relationship of undergraduate and graduate schools. The author indicates that a scholarly study of religion should be included in the humanistic curriculum.

251 Smart, N., and D. Horder, eds. New Movements in Religious Education. London, Temple Smith, 1975. 271 p.

This collection of papers brings together many ideas and experiences which have changed the concept of religious education in schools during the past decade. A select bibliography for further reading is provided. Lacks an index.

252 Strommen, M. P., ed. Research on Religious Development; A Comprehensive Handbook. A Project of the Religious Education Assoc. New York, Hawthorn Books, 1971. 904 p.

Includes abundant bibliographical references.

253 The Study of Religion in Colleges and Universities. Ed. by P. Ramsey and J. F. Wilson, with chapters by W. A. Clebsch and others. Princeton, N.J., Princeton Univ. Press, 1970. 353 p.

A collection of papers which provide an excellent evaluation of contemporary religious studies and probably future development. Includes a bibliographical essay at the end.

254 Taylor, M. J., ed. Religious Education; A Comprehensive Survey. New York, Nashville, Abingdon Press, 1960. 445 p.

Pt. 1 explores such areas as philosophy of education, psychology, and objectives; Pt. 2 discusses programs, materials, and methods; Pt. 3 deals with administration, building and equipment, etc.; Pt. 4 describes eight agencies for religious education. Each chapter has a useful bibliography of selected older and recent works. There is also a biographical index, and an author subject index.

JOURNALS

255 Journal of Christian Education. Sydney, 1957- (3 issues a year).

Published by the Australian Teachers' Christian Fellowship. Indexed: Rel. Per.

256 Religious Education. Chicago, 1906- (bi-monthly).

Published by the Religious Education Association. Indexed: Education Index.

Part Two

RELIGIONS OF THE PAST

I PREHISTORIC AND PRIMITIVE RELIGIONS

DICTIONARY

257 Wedeck, H. E., and W. Baskin. Dictionary of Pagan Religions. Secaucus, N.J., 1974 (1971). 363 p.
This popular work covers the cults of Egypt, the Middle East, the Mediterranean area, as well as the cults from other parts of the world. Lacks bibliographic references for further reading.

BIBLIOGRAPHIES AND GUIDES

258 Buchholz, Peter, comp. Bibliographie zur alteuropäischen Religionsgeschichte, 1954-64. (Bibliography of the History of Ancient European Religions.) Literatur zu den antiken Rand- und Nachfolgekulturen im aussermediterranen Europa unter besonderer Berücksichtigung der nichtchristlichen Religionen. Berlin, de Gruyter, 1967. (Arbeiten zur Frümittelalterforschung, Bd. 2.) 299 p.
An international bibliography which contains a listing of 5298 items arranged by country and subdivided by subject. Much English language material is included.

259 Long, C. H. "Primitive Religion." Adams, C. J. A Reader's Guide to Great Religions. 2nd ed. New York, Free Press, 1977 (1965), p. 1-38.
See no. 22. A bibliographical essay which reviews literature for the study of primitive religion. Contains a list of journals relevant to the subject, and bibliographies subdivided by geographical areas.

260 "Prehistoric and Primitive Religion." International Bibliography of the History of Religions. Leiden, Brill, 1954- .
See no. 27. This section includes 1. Prehistoric religion; 2. Primitive religion; 3. Early European religions. Contains monographs and journal articles.

261 "Religion of Primitive People." McCasland, S. V. Religions of the World. New York, Random House, 1969. p. 9-27.
See no. 16. An informative introduction which defines the subject and discusses fundamental terms, such as animism, mana and taboo, animitism, totemism, etc. Also provides a list of basic bibliographic references.

HANDBOOKS AND SURVEYS

262 Evans-Pritchard, E. E. Theories of Primitive Religion. Oxford, England, Clarendon Press, 1965 (Sir D. Owen Evans Lectures, 1962). 132 p.
A valuable textbook which emphasizes that religious phenomena must be understood in a situational context rather than against the background of their past. Includes a bibliography and an author subject index.

263 Frazer, J. G. Totemism and Exogamy; A Treatise on Certain Early Forms of Superstition and Society. London, Macmillan, 1910. 4 vols.
A classic which provides a systematic ethnological survey of totemism. Vol. 4 contains an extensive index of subjects with abundant cross-references.

264 Freud, Sigmund. Totem and Taboo; Some Points of Agreement Between the Mental Lifes of Savages and Neurotics. Transl. by J. Strachey. London, Routledge and Paul, 1950 (1913). 172 p.
This is a reprint of Freud's famous and disputed hypothesis about the origins of religion and culture. A bibliography and subject index are provided.

265 Goode, W. J. Religion Among the Primitives; with an introd. by Kingsley Davis. Glencoe, Ill., Free Press, 1951. 321 p.
Provides a detailed functional analysis of comparative materials drawn from cultural anthropology. Includes bibliography and a subject index.

266 Howell, William. The Heathens; Primitive Man and His Religions. Garden City, N.Y., Doubleday, 1948. 306 p.
Explores such topics as the nature of religion, mana, taboo, and magic in its various forms. Contains a very detailed subject index. Bibliography is included in footnotes.

267 James, Edwin O. Prehistoric Religions; A Study in Prehistoric Archaeology. London, Thames and Hudson, 1963 (1957).
An excellent comparative survey which attempts to bring together all available materials relating to the earliest

religious manifestations prior to recording of events in written documents. It deals with burial rituals; cremations, inhumation, and mummification; the cult of dead, the mystery of birth, the sky-religion, etc. Includes chapter bibliographies, chronological tables, and an author subject index.

268 Jensen, A. E. Myth and Cult among Primitives. Chicago, Univ. of Chicago Press, 1963 (1951). 349 p.

Translation of the author's Mythos und Kult bei Naturvölkern. A study which employs anthropological methods in discussion of such topics as: man and reality, deity, sacrifice, ethos, magic, souls, ancestors cults and spirits. A bibliography and an author subject index are provided.

269 Lowie, R. H. Primitive Religion. London, Owen, 1960 (1952). 382 p.

Pt. 1 draws sketches of the Crow, Ekoi, Bukana, and Polynesian religions; Pt. 2 reviews critique and theories; Pt. 3 "while not avoiding the historical problems of comparative religion calls attention to the neglected psychological facets to the subjects." Contains an extensive bibliography and an index.

270 Norbeck, Edward. Religion in Primitive Society. New York, Harper and Row, 1961. 318 p.

Contains a good summary of many ethnographic accounts of religion in pre-literate societies. Pt. 1 provides an overview of primitive religions; Pt. 2 discusses the role of religion. Index of name and subjects is included. Bibliographic references are provided in footnotes.

271 Radin, Paul. Primitive Religion; Its Nature and Origin. New York, Dover Publications, 1957 (1937). 322 p.

A scholarly treatise by a noted anthropologist which attempts to describe the religion and the religious experience of aboriginal peoples. The author emphasizes the importance of the social and economic factors and defines more specifically the psycho-physical make-up of individuals. The discussion comprises: the nature and substance of religion, the economic determinants, the approach to supernatural, monolatry and monotheism, etc. Bibliographical references are included in the notes at the end. Also contains an author subject index.

272 Swanson, G. E. The Birth of the Gods; The Origin of Primitive Beliefs. Ann Arbor, Univ. of Michigan Press, 1960. 260 p.

On the basis of statistical analysis of anthropological data gathered from fifty primitive societies, the author develops an interesting theory about the relationship of deistic beliefs and social structure. Includes a selective bibliography and an index.

Part Two--Religions of the Past (cont.)

II ANTIQUITY

GENERAL WORKS, HANDBOOKS, SURVEYS

BIBLIOGRAPHIES

273 Archäologische Bibliographie. (Archaeological Bibliography.) Berlin, Gruyter, 1913- .
Supplement to Jahrbuch des Deutschen Archäologischen Instituts. Information on religion is included in the section H: Religion, Mythos, Kult. Covers monographs and journal articles. Includes English language materials.

274 Bibliotheca orientalis. Leiden, 1943- (quarterly).
Journal published by the Nederlands Instituut het Nabije Oosten; lists book reviews which are arranged in classified order, e.g., Egyptology, Mesopotamia-Assyriology, Hethitica, Vetus Testamentum, Classics, Islam-Arabica, Iran-Asia Centralis-India, Historia Religionum.

See also no. 22.

HANDBOOKS AND SURVEYS

275 Brandon, Samuel G. F., ed. Religion in Ancient History; Studies in Ideas, Men, and Events. N.Y., Scribner's, 1969. 412 p.
A collection of essays which discuss religions in ancient Egypt, Mesopotamia, Israel, Greece, and Iran. The author analyzes such topics as creation, death, soul, and the judgment of the dead. One finds also studies on Osiris, Job, Zarathustra, and events in the first three centuries of the Christian era. Contains an annotated selective bibliography, and an index of names and subjects.

276 The Cambridge Ancient History. Cambridge, Cambridge Univ. Press, 1924-56. 12 vols.; new rev. ed. 1970- (in progress, vol. 1, pt. 1-2, and vol. 2, pt. 1-2 already published, some papers available in fascicules).
Provides the most authoritative and up-to-date treatment of all cultures and periods of the antiquities.

Bibliographies and indexes are provided.

277 Ferm, Vergilius T. A., ed. Forgotten Religions, Including Some Living Primitive Religions. New York, Philosophical Library, 1950. 392 p.

A collection of essays which review the most important aspects of the old religions. They discuss religious beliefs of Egypt, Mesopotamia, the Hittite Empire, Greece, and Rome. Analyzes basic ideas of Mithraism, Manicheism, and Mazdakism. Also includes a number of forgotten but still existing religions. Each chapter is provided with a selective bibliography.

278 Kramer, Samuel N. Mythologies of the Ancient World. Garden City, N.Y., Doubleday, 1961 (Anchor Books, A229). 480 p.

Provides excellent source material for studies of Egyptian, Sumerian, Akkadian, and Greco-Roman myths. Also deals with Far East Asian and pre-Columbian Mexican myths. A subject index and a bibliography are included.

NEAR EAST

BIBLIOGRAPHIES

279 "Keilschriftbibliographie" (Cuneiform Bibliography). Orientalia, N.S. 1932- (annually).

An exhaustive bibliography which is published in each March issue of Orientalia. Lists in classified arrangement monographs and journal articles. Class 5, 1-9: Religion, Mythologie, Weltanschauung is of special importance for religious research. English language materials are included.

280 Orlin, L. L. Ancient Near Eastern Literature; A Bibliography of One Thousand Items on the Cuneiform Literatures of the Ancient World, Partially Annotated, and with a Special Section on Literary Contacts and Interrelations between Greece and the Near East. Ann Arbor, Mich., Campus Publishers, 1969. 113 p.

Contains a number of references which are relevant to the study of religion, e.g., myths, psalms, hymns, etc.

HANDBOOKS AND SURVEYS

281 Bratton, F. G. Myths and Legends of the Ancient Near East. New York, Crowell, 1970. 188 p.

Explains the nature and meaning to the ancient Near Eastern mythology providing a critical analysis of Sumero-

Akkadian, Egyptian, Ugaritic-Canaanite, and Hittite myths. Bibliographical references contain monographs and journal articles. Also included are pantheon charts, glossary, and an index.

282 Drioton, Etienne; G. Contenau; and J. Duchesne-Guillemin. Religions of the Ancient East, transl. by M. B. Loraine. New York, Hawthorn, 1957 (Twentieth Century Encyclopedia of Catholicism, 141; Sect. 14: Non-Christian Beliefs). 164 p.

Provides a review of religious beliefs of ancient Egypt, Mesopotamia, and Iran presented by the outstanding authorities in the field.

283 Gaster, Theodor. The Oldest Stories in the World, Originally Translated and Retold with Comments. New York, Viking, 1952. 238 p.

Contains a selection of Babylonian, Hittite, and Canaanite myths; each myth is accompanied by a critical comment. Includes an index of motifs.

284 Gray, John. Near Eastern Mythology. Felthan, Hamlyn, 1969. 141 p.

Presents a survey of Mesopotamian, and Canaanite myths. A select bibliography is provided.

285 James, Edwin O. The Ancient Gods; The History and Diffusion of Religion in the Ancient Near East and Eastern Mediterranean. London, Weidenfeld and Nicolson, 1960 (Weidenfeld and Nicolson History of Religion).

Provides a comprehensive survey of principal religious forms which developed in Egypt, Assyria, Palestine, Syria, and Asia Minor. Gives accounts of seasonal festivals, burial customs, cosmology, prophesy, etc. Also contains a bibliography and an index.

286 ________. Myth and Ritual in the Ancient Near East; An Archaeological and Documentary Study. London, Thames and Hudson, 1958. 352 p.

Presents an excellent survey based on available textual and archaeological materials. Deals with seasonal cults, sacral kingships, mother-goddess, creation and immortality, etc. Bibliography and an index are provided.

287 Mendelsohn, Isaac, ed. Religions of the Ancient Near East; Sumero-Akkadian Religious Texts and Ugaritic Epics. New York, Liberal Arts Press, 1955 (Library of Religion, v. 4). 284 p.

Contains a collection of texts in English translation. Each selection is supplied with prefatory notes. A classified select bibliography, list of gods, and an index of Biblical references are provided.

288 Pritchard, J. B., ed. The Ancient Near East; An Anthology of Texts and Pictures. Translators and annotators: W. F. Albright et al. Princeton, N.J., Princeton Univ. Press, 1958.

A combined and condensed edition of the Ancient Near Eastern Texts... and The Ancient Near East in Pictures.... For details see below.

289 ______. The Ancient Near East in Pictures Relating to the Old Testament. Princeton, N.J., Princeton Univ. Press, 1954.

______. Ancient Near Eastern Texts Relating to the Old Testament. 2nd ed., corr. and enl. Translators and annotators, W. F. Albright et al. Princeton, N.J., Princeton Univ. Press, 1955. 3 v.

______. The Ancient Supplementary Texts Relating to the Old Testament, consisting of Supplementary materials for the Ancient Near East in Pictures and Ancient Near Eastern Texts. Princeton, N.J., Princeton Univ. Press, 1969.

Presents the most authoritative collection of English translations of significant texts as well as illustrations of monuments of the ancient Near East accompanied by a complete critical apparatus.

290 Ringgren, Helmer. Religions of the Ancient Near East. Transl. by J. Sturdy. Philadelphia, Westminster, 1973 (1967). 197 p.

Transl. of Främre Orientens Religioner i Gammal Tid. "It is intended to represent the religions of the Ancient Near East in their context, but at the same time to emphasize certain elements which are of special interest for the study of the Old Testament"--Preface. Deals with Sumerian, Babylonian, Assyrian, and West Semmitic Religions. A select bibliography, and an index are provided.

ANCIENT EGYPT

BIBLIOGRAPHY

291 Janssen, Jozef M. A., comp. Annual Egyptological Bibliography. Leiden, International Association of Egyptologists, 1947- .

Contains an exhaustive bibliography of monographs and journal articles, also includes reprints. Entries are arranged alphabetically by author; subject approach is not provided.

HANDBOOKS AND SURVEYS

292 Bleeker, C. J. "The Religion of Ancient Egypt." Bleeker, C. J. Historia religionum, v. 1, p. 40-114.
See no. 38. A survey article which deals with historical development of beliefs, conception of God, conception of man, worship, and subsequent influences. The final part provides a historical review of research in the field of Egyptian Religion. Includes a bibliography of more important monographs and journal articles.

293 Breasted, J. H. Development of Religion and Thought in Ancient Egypt; Lectures Delivered on the Morse Foundation at Union Theological Seminary, new ed. New York, Wilson, 1959 (1912). 379 p.
A classic, which is in many respects out-dated. It should be consulted, however, as an example of thorough scholarship. Includes revised bibliographical references in the footnotes.

294 Budge, E. A. T. W. From Fetish to God in Ancient Egypt. London, Oxford Univ. Press, 1934. 545 p.
Deals with the predynastic religious beliefs as well as the cults, theological systems and religions of the dynastic period. Pt. 1 analyzes the principal ideas and facts such as the conception of God, magic, cult of animals, etc. Pt. 2 contains a collection of English translations of hymns, myths, and legends of the gods. Also includes an index.

295 Cerny, Jaroslav. Ancient Egyptian Religion. London, Hutchinson, 1952 (Hutchinson's University Library. World Religions). 159 p.
Introduces a completely new approach to the study of the subject by presenting the Egyptian religion as a part of the political and social history of the country. Discusses character of the gods, relations between men and gods, the cult, and foreign influences. Includes a selective bibliography and an index.

296 Egyptian Mythology. Based on the text transl. by Delano Ames, from Mythologie générale Larousse. London, Hamlyn 1965. 152 p.
Includes discussions of early cults and their deities, creation myths, protective divinities of the Pharoah and the Kingdom, sacred animals, etc. Provides a list of sacred animals whose heads appear on Egyptian gods and an index; no bibliography included.

297 Frankfort, Henri. Ancient Egyptian Religion; An Interpretation. New York, Harper, 1961 (1948). (Harper Torchbooks, the Cloister Library). 172 p.
Provides a reliable discussion of Egyptian deities and

religious customs in everyday life based on the analysis of literary documents and objects of art. Bibliography and an index are provided.

298 Morenz, Siegfried. Egyptian Religion. Ithaca, N.Y., Cornell Univ. Press, 1973 (1960). 379 p.
"This book has been written ... from the heart"--Foreword. It deals with the sources and meaning of religion in Egyptian, the gods, worshipping, cult and piety, ethics and its relationship to religion, cosmogonies, death and the dead, sacred writings, and the Egyptian religion and the outside world. Also contains a glossary of the characteristics of the gods, chronological tables, bibliography and indexes.

ANCIENT MESOPOTAMIA

HANDBOOKS AND SURVEYS

299 Römer, W. H. P. "The Religion of Ancient Mesopotamia." Bleeker, C. J., ed. Historia religionum, v. 1, p. 115-194.
See no. 38. Reviews the essence of the Mesopotamian religious beliefs presenting their historical development, the pantheon, and the worship. A brief sketch of the history of research in the field is included. Also contains a select bibliography.

300 Hooke, S. H. Babylonian and Assyrian Religion. London, Hutchinson, 1953. 128 p.
A reliable account which presents religious beliefs and practices of the Mesopotamian peoples. An index and bibliographical references are included.

301 Jacobsen, Thorkild. The Treasure of Darkness; A History of Mesopotamian Religion. New Haven, Conn., Yale Univ. Press, 1976. 273 p.
Gives a comprehensive synthesis of sources pertaining to the ancient Mesopotamian religious world view. Provides an in-depth study of two great religious epics the Gilgamesh and Enuma Elish. Also includes bibliographical references and an index.

302 Kramer, S. N. Sumerian Mythology; A Study of Spiritual and Literary Achievements in the third Millenium B.C., rev. ed. New York, Harper, 1961 (1943) (Harper Torchbooks. Academy Library, TB 1055). 125 p.
Provides a detailed study of the Sumerian myths from cuneiform inscriptions now available with a brief outline of their concepts.

303 Oppenheim, Leo. Ancient Mesopotamia; Portrait of a Dead Civilization. Chicago, University of Chicago Press, 1964. 433 p.
Presents a detailed survey of Mesopotamian civilizations. Especially important is Chapter IV which discusses various religious problems. Provides extensive footnotes with annotated bibliographic references.

ANCIENT SYRIA AND PALESTINE

304 Driver, G. R. Canaanite Myths and Legends. Edinburgh, Clark, 1956 (Old Testament Studies, 3). 168 p.
Presents a collection of myths and legends from discoveries of cuneiform tablets at Ugarit (now Ras Shamra). Provides a transliteration and translation of the text into English with complete critical references to works consulted for decipherment of the cuneiforms. The glossary contains a number of alternative words, readings, and interpretations.

305 Gray, John. The Canaanites. London, Thames and Hudson, 1964 (Ancient People and Places, v. 38). 244 p.
Describes all aspects of the history of peoples who lived in this area in the second millenium B. C. Chapter V: Canaanite Religion, is of special interest. Contains a bibliography and an index.

306 Kaperlund, A. S. Baal in the Ras Shamra Texts. Copenhagen, Gad, 1952. 156 p.
An excellent analysis of Baal which is based on the Ugaritic texts. It deals with names of the god, his family, accompanying minor gods, and his character and task. Includes a subject index, index of authors, and a list of bibliographic references.

307 Obermann, Julian. Ugaritic Mythology; A Study of Its Leading Motifs. New Haven, Conn., Yale Univ. Press, 1948. 110 p.
A study of Ugaritic texts that provides a fair picture of Canaanite religion. Bibliographic references are included in the footnotes.

308 Oldenburg, Ulf. The Conflict between El and Baal in Canaanite Religion. Leiden, Brill, 1969. (Numen, altera series: dissertationes ad historiam religionum pertinentes, v. 3.) 216 p.
A study of Canaanite religion which reviews all the available sources for knowledge of the Canaanite religion and investigates its relationship with other religions especially the religion of the early Hebrews. Contains an excellent selection of bibliographic references, an index of authors, and a subject index.

309 Ringgren, H. "The Religion of Ancient Syria." Bleeker, C. J., ed. Historia religionum, v. 1, p. 195-222.

See no. 38. A survey article which deals with historical development of religious concepts of early Syria, the conception of the deity and worship; the final part provides a historical review of studies undertaken in the field. Select bibliography is included.

THE HITTITES

310 Gurney, O. R. The Hittites, 2nd ed. Harmondsworth, England, Penguin Books, 1954 (1952) (Pelican Books). 240 p.
Provides an outline of the Hittite history and culture. Chapter VII, Religion, presents all available materials on religion, from archaeological explorations and decipherment of texts. Includes a select classified bibliography.

311 Lloyd, Seton. Early Highland People of Anatolia. London, Thames and Hudson, 1967 (Library of the Early Civilizations). 144 p.
Presents a survey of early Anatolian civilizations in the Bronze and Metal Ages, especially Phrygians, Urartu, and Hittites. Includes a bibliography and an index which should be checked for religious topics.

312 Otten, H. "The Religion of the Hittites." Bleeker, C. J., ed. Historia religionum, v. 1, p. 318-22.
See no. 38. Provides an outline of our knowledge about religious life of the Hittites. Discusses conceptions of deity and man, of worship, etc. Also includes a brief select bibliography.

ANCIENT IRAN

BIBLIOGRAPHY

313 Pearson, James D., ed. A Bibliography of Pre-Islamic Persia. London, Mansell, 1975 (Persian Studies Series). 288 p.
An extensive classified bibliography covering languages and literatures, history, religion, art and archaeology. Consult Section C: Religion, p. 149-230. An author index.

HANDBOOKS AND SURVEYS

314 Cumont, F. V. M. The Mysteries of Mithra. Transl. from the 2nd rev. French ed. by T. J. McCormack. New York, Dover Publications, 1956. 238 p.
An excellent presentation of this important religious movement which became a rival of Christianity. Provides bibliographic references and an index.

315 Duchesne-Guillemin, J. "The Religion of Ancient Iran." Bleeker, C. J., ed. Historia religionum, v. 1, p. 323-76.

See no. 38. This informative review contains discussion on the essence of religious movements in Iran, their historical development, worship, myths, and the history of research. Also includes a select bibliography.

316 Oxtoby, Willard G. Ancient Iran and Zoroastrianism in Festschriften; An Index. Shiraz, Iran, the Asia Institute of Pahlavi University, 1973 (Bibliographic Studies in Religion, no. 1). 207 p.
Lists some 1808 articles in 18 languages from 421 collections published between 1875 and 1973. Of special interest is the section Religion, p. 112-73. Author index.

317 Vermaseren, M. J. Mithras, the Secret God. New York, Barnes and Noble, 1963 (1959). 200 p.
Translation of Mithras de geheimzinnige god. The author presents an excellent summary of the knowledge about the ancient worship of the great Iranian deity. Contains a selection of bibliographical references and an index.

318 Zaehner, R. C. The Dawn and Twilight of Zoroastrianism. New York, Putnam, 1961 (Putnam History of Religion). 371 p.
Presents a comprehensive survey of Zoroastrianism. Pt. 1 describes the message of the prophet Zoroaster; Pt. 2 is devoted to schisms and sects. Includes a bibliography and an index.

ANCIENT GREEK, ETRUSCAN AND ROMAN

DICTIONARIES AND ENCYCLOPEDIAS

319 Aken, Andreas R. A. The Encyclopedia of Classical Mythology. Transl. from the Dutch by D. R. Welsh. Englewood Cliffs, N.J., Prentice-Hall, 1955. 155 p.
Translation of Elseviers mythologische encyclopedie. Entries are arranged alphabetically under the Latin form with transliterated Greek forms added; cross-references are made to variant forms. References to ancient authors are cited in the text. Lists deities and heroes, principal religious festivals, significant places: temples and oracles.

320 The Encyclopedia of the Classical World. Comp. by J. H. Croon, transl. by J. Müller-van Santen, with emandation by C. Jones. Englewood Cliffs, N.J., Prentice-Hall, 1965. 239 p.
Translation of Elseviers encyclopedia de antieke wereld. Entries are arranged alphabetically under the Latin form. Comprises a great amount of information on ancient history, persons, places, etc. References to classical authors are included.

321 Evans, Bergen. Dictionary of Mythology, Mainly Classical. Lincoln, Neb., Centennial Press, 1970. 293 p.
Provides explanation of mythological figures from Absyrtus to Zeus. Lists parallel Greek and Roman gods and heroes. Abundant cross-references, select bibliography, and an index are provided.

322 Grant, M., and J. Hazel. Who's Who in Classical Mythology. London, Weidenfeld and Nicolson, 1973. 447 p.
Contains an alphabetical listing of names. Maps, genealogical trees, and a list of Greek and Latin authors are added.

323 The New Century Handbook of Greek Mythology and Legend. Ed. by C. B. Avery. New York, Appleton-Crofts, 1972. 565 p.
Contains information on places of historical, mythological and archaeological interest, biographies, etc. Presentation is based mainly on the ancient authors' descriptions. Includes a pronounciation guide.

324 The Oxford Classical Dictionary. Oxford, England, Clarendon Press, 1970.
This new edition contains the most up-to-date materials on almost every aspect of classical life. Entries vary in length from two lines to over six pages. Each article has a bibliography of the most significant works on the topic in English and foreign languages. One finds information on cults, religious practices, and on myths. Also includes a general bibliography in appendices.

325 Tripp, Edward. Crowell's Handbook of Classical Mythology. New York, Crowell, 1970. 631 p.
Presents a collection of articles alphabetically arranged with numerous cross-references. Includes a list of classical sources and a pronouncing index.

326 Zimmerman, J. E. Dictionary of Classical Mythology. New York, Harper and Row, 1964. 300 p.
Includes 2100 entries with their pronounciation. For characters with both Greek and Latin names or other variant spelling, all versions are listed. More important entries are provided with both ancient and modern bibliographic references.

BIBLIOGRAPHIES AND GUIDES

327 L'Année philologique; bibliographie critique et analytique de l'antiquité gréco-latine. (Philological Annual; Critical and Analytical Bibliography of the Greek and Roman Antiquities.) Paris, Société d'Edition "Les Belles Lettres,"

1924- .

For earlier publications consult no. 329. Contains a classified list of monographs, noting their reviews, and journal articles with brief annotations. One should pay special attention to Chapter V, Section D: Histoire religieuse et mythologie (History of religion and mythology). Includes English language materials.

328 McGuire, Martin R. P. Introduction to Classical Scholarship; A Syllabus and Bibliographical Guide, new rev. ed. Washington, D. C., Catholic Univ. of America Press, 1961. 257 p.

Contains detailed bibliographies on ancient history, literature, science, art, and archaeology. There is also a section--no. 15--on religion, mythology, and magic, p. 132-8.

329 Marouzeau, Jules. Dix Années de bibliographie classique, 1914-24. (Ten Years of Classical Bibliography). Paris, Société d'Edition "Les Belles Lettres," 1927-29. 2 vols.

Includes an exhaustive list of monographs and journal articles. Book reviews are indicated. Section: Histoire; D. Histoire religieuse et mythologie (History; D. History of Religion and mythology) should be checked. Continued by L'Année philologique, no. 327.

330 Peradotto, John. Classical Mythology: An Annotated Bibliographical Survey. Urbana, Ill., 1973. 76 p.

Provides a selective list of materials on comparative mythology, myth and art, myth and literature, myth and anthropology, some general studies and collections of essays, translations etc. Index of authors and titles, and an index of publishers are supplied.

HANDBOOKS AND SURVEYS

331 Grant, Michael. Myths of Greeks and Romans. Cleveland, World Publ. Co., 1962. 487 p.

Provides a selection of most important myths in their best modern translation. Each myth is followed by a critical discussion of the concepts of hero, glory and fighting, from Homer to Giraudoux. Includes genealogical tables, select bibliography and an index.

332 Kerényi, Karoly. The Religion of Greeks and Romans. Transl. by C. Holme. New York, Dutton, 1962. 303 p.

This book describes all the cult places of the Greek and Roman religion. Contains bibliographical notes at the end of the book and an index.

333 Loverdo, Costa de. Gods with Bronze Swords. Transl. by N. Amphoux. Garden City, N.Y., Doubleday, 1970 (1966). 273 p.

Translation of Les Dieux aux epées de bronze. The author attempts to review the development of such myths as Perseus, Jason, Heracles, Bellerophon, Amphitryon, etc. Includes comparative chronologies tables, a list of principal sites of the Heroic Age, a bibliography of classical and modern authors, and a subject index.

334 Reinhold, Meyer. Past and Present; The Continuity of Classical Myths. Toronto, Hakkert, 1972. 449 p.
This is a textbook written for the general student. Provides a selective classified bibliography an index of recurrent themes, and a general index.

335 Rose, Herbert J. Religion in Greece and Rome, with a new introd. New York, Harper, 1959 (Harper Torchbook, TB 55).
A combined revised edition of the author's Ancient Greek Religion (1946), and Ancient Roman Religion (1948). Traces the development of Greek and Roman beliefs from earliest time to the beginning of Christianity. Includes a select bibliography and an index.

GREEK RELIGION

336 Adkins, A. W. H. "Greek Religion." Bleeker, C. J., Historia religionum, v. 1, p. 377-441.
See no. 38. A review of Greek religious beliefs which discusses the conceptions of deity and man, worship, and provides a short history of research in this field. Also contains a select bibliography.

337 Barthell, Edward E. Gods and Goddesses of Ancient Greece. Coral Gables, Fla., Univ. of Miami Press, 1971. 146 p.
Comments individually on various gods and demi-gods who compose the Greek Pantheon, attempting to systematize them into a single family tree. Bibliography comprises of source material from the ancient writers and modern critical works. Also includes an index of mythological names.

338 Dietrich, B. C. The Origins of Greek Religion. Berlin, de Gruyter, 1974. 345 p.
An excellent scholarly study which traces the development of Greek religion from its beginnings in the East, through the Minoan, Mycenaean periods. Select bibliography, names and subject indexes are included.

339 Graves, Robert. The Greek Myths. London, Cassell, 1958 (1955). 774 p.
Collects scattered elements of a myth, and then analyzes various historical and anthropological issues. Contains full bibliographic materials for the ancient sources.

340 Guthrie, William K. C. The Greeks and Their Gods. London, Methuen, 1950. 388 p.
An informative survey which provides an account of the Greek religious conceptions from the earliest times to Plato and Aristotle. Includes bibliographic footnotes and an index.

341 ______. The Religion and Mythology of the Greeks. Cambridge, Cambridge University Press, 1961.
Provides an excellent survey of Greek religion with selective bibliography and an index.

342 Nilsson, Martin P. A History of Greek Religion, 2nd ed. Transl. from the Swedish by F. J. Fielden. Oxford, Clarendon Press, 1949 (1925).
A classic in the field. Deals with various problems of Greek religious life: such as the Minoan-Mycenean past, origins of myths, primitive belief and ritual, gods of nature and human life, the Homeric anthropomorphism, and rationalism, legalism and mysticism, civic religion, the religion of cultural classes and that of peasants, etc. Contains bibliographic notes and an index.

343 Pinsent, John. Greek Mythology. London, Hamlyn, 1969. 141 p.
Provides a condensed review of basic Greek myths with a classified selected bibliography.

344 Rose, Herbert J. A Handbook of Greek Mythology; Including Its Extention to Rome, 6th ed. London, Methuen, 1965 (1928). 363 p.
An accurate summary of Greek myths which takes into account all modern findings. Bibliography includes ancient writers and contemporary critical works. Index is divided into: A. Mythological names; Greek and Latin, including fabulous places; B. Names of historical persons and places, and subjects.

345 Zielinski, Tadeusz. The Religion of Ancient Greece; An Outline. Transl. by G. R. Noyes. Freeport, N.Y., Books for Libraries Press, 1970 (1926). 235 p.
Translation of the author's Religja Grecji Starożytnej, presents this valuable classic dealing with various aspects of religious life of the Greeks. Contains an index; no bibliography provided.

ETRUSCAN AND ROMAN

346 Dumézil, Georges. Archaic Roman Religion; With an Appendix on the Religion of the Estruscans. Transl. by P. Krapp. Chicago, Univ. of Chicago Press, 1971 (1966). 2 vols.

Transl. of La Réligion romaine archaique.... Presents the development of Roman beliefs from the Indo-European comparative perspective. Application of this new method allows to trace all the subsequent influences and relationships. Contains bibliographic references in the footnotes and an index.

347 Fergusson, John. The Religions of the Roman Empire. Ithaca, N.Y., Cornell Univ. Press, 1970 (Aspects of the Roman Life). 296 p.

Provides an informative survey of Roman religious life through the third century A.D. Contains discussion on grandmother, god of the heaven, god-sun, function gods, Tyche, and deified effigy of an emporer. Also included is an extensive bibliography and indexes.

348 Grant, Frederick C. Ancient Roman Religion. New York, Liberal Arts Press, 1959 (The Library of Religion, 8). 252 p.

Provides a thorough study of various cults and beliefs that developed in the course of Roman history. It discusses the old agricultural religion, religion under the republic, Augustan restoration, the Empire, and closes with the Christian victory. Some bibliographical references in the footnotes; no index provided.

349 Grant, Michael. Roman Myths. London, Weidenfeld and Nicolson, 1971. 293 p.

A detailed study of elements of Roman myths which explains how they were acquired and developed specifically Roman characteristics. Bibliography consists of two parts: mythical Rome, and mythology in general; it includes references to ancient writers and modern critical works. Also contains a subject index with numerous cross-references.

350 Ogilvie, Robert M. The Romans and Their Gods in the Age of Augustus; Ancient Culture and Society. London, Chatto and Windus, 1969. 135 p.

Contains an informative study of religious beliefs and practices with references to ancient sources listed directly in the text and a selective bibliography.

351 Palmer, Robert E. A. Roman Religion and Roman Empire: Five Essays. Philadelphia, University of Pennsylvania Press, 1974 (Haney Foundation Series). 291 p.

Deals with Juno in archaic Italy; Adherence to the Adventine Canon and the Lex Tiburtina; the Gods of the Grove Albunea; Saturn and the Saturnian verse; on Mutinus Titinus. Also contains a bibliography and an index.

352 Perowne, Stewart. Roman Mythology. London, Hamlyn, 1969, 141 p.

Includes discussion of gods, worship, state cults, newcomers beliefs, Epicureans and Stoics, immortal longings, foreign influences: Egyptian, Syrian, Hebrew, Persian; and early Christianity.

353 Schilling, R. "The Roman Religion." Bleeker, C. J., ed. _Historia religionum_, v. 1, p. 442-94.
See no. 38. Presents an informative review of problems which are encountered in research of the complex beliefs of the Romans. Contains a selective bibliography.

HELLENISTIC

354 Grant, Frederick C. _Hellenistic Religions: The Age of Syncretism._ New York, Bobbs-Merrill, 1953 (Press Library of Liberal Arts). 196 p.
Consists of the introductory part which discusses a number of religious systems in the Mediterranean and the Middle East after the fall of the Macedonian Empire; and a selection of ancient texts supplied with critical commentary and bibliography. No index is provided.

355 Vermaseren, M. J. "Hellenistic Religions." Bleeker, C. J., ed. _Historia religionum_, v. 1, p. 493-532.
See no. 38. Provides a brief survey of various Hellenistic cults and creeds with bibliography restricted to significant studies on each topic.

MANICHEISM

356 Asmussen, J. P. "Manicheism." Bleeker, C. J., ed. _Historia religionum_, v. 1, p. 580-610.
See no. 38. Provides a condensed survey with bibliography of sources and selected critical works. Consult also the author's _Manichean Literature._ Delmar, N.Y., Scholars' Facs., 1976.

357 Ort, L. J. R. _Mani; A Religio-Historical Description of His Personality._ Leiden, Brill, 1967 (Supplementa ad _Numen_, altera series. Dissertationes ad historiam religionum petinentes). 286 p.
"The first chapter contains a survey of studies about Mani and his religion. The second chapter enumerates the sources which we have at our disposal. The third chapter derives Mani's religious self conception from the texts"--Introd. Includes an excellent bibliography, indexes of names and subjects, modern authors, middle Iranian texts, and Coptic texts.

358 Widengren, George. _Mani and Manicheism._ Transl. by C. Kessler, rev. by the author. London, Weidenfeld and

Nicolson, 1965. 167 p.
Recognized as a best presentation of this oriental religious movement; includes bibliographic references and an index.

GERMANIC

359 Davidson, Hilda R. E. "Germanic Religion." Bleeker, C. J., ed. Historia religionum, v. 1, p. 610-28.
See no. 38. Contains a condensed review of the essence of religion; its historical development, and a brief history of research in the field. Includes a select bibliography.

360 _______. Gods and Myths of Northern Europe. Baltimore, Penguin Books, 1964 (Pelican Books, A670). 251 p.
A reliable survey of Germanic and Scandinavian religious beliefs and customs, with a selective bibliography and an index.

361 _______. Scandinavian Mythology. London, Hamlyn, 1969. 143 p.
Presents a review of Scandinavian myths from about 1600 to 450 B.C. The study is based on comparison of the ancient sources from various areas outside Scandinavia. A selective bibliography and an index are included.

362 Dumézil, Georges. Gods of the Ancient Northmen. Ed. by E. Haugen. Introd. by C. S. Littleton and U. Strutynski, Berkeley, Univ. of California Press, 1973 (UCLA Center for the Study of Comparative Folklore and Mythology. Publications, 3). 157 p.
This collection of translations offers the reader a sampling derived from writings by the famous French comparativist: Pt. 1, Gods, of the Ancient Northmen; Pt. 2, Minor Scandinavian Gods. Numerous bibliographic footnotes and an index are added.

363 Grimm, Jacob L. K. Teutonic Mythology. Transl. by T. S. Stalybrass. London, Bell, 1882-88. 4 vols.
Includes a collection of Teutonic myths in English translation with an appended scholarly treatise. Contains a detailed analysis of each myth with numerous critical notes about various versions and interpretations. A comprehensive index is provided.

364 Larson, Gerald J., ed. Myth in Indo-European Antiquity. Berkeley, Univ. of California Press, 1974 (UCSB Institute of Religious Studies). 197 p.
Contains a selection of 13 essays dealing with various issues in mythology and comparative mythology with special reference to Germanic myths and beliefs. Also includes a

bibliographical note and an index.

365 Munch, P. A. Norse Mythology; Legends of Gods and Heroes, in the revision of M. Olsen. Transl. from the Norwegian by S. B. Hustvedt. New York, American Scandinavian Foundation, 1954 (1940).

This new revised version of this classic work attempts an up-to-date treatment of the entire subject. The content is subdivided into: myths of the gods; the heroic legends; and worship of the gods. Provides extensive notes, bibliography, and an index.

366 Rydberg, Viktor. Teutonic Mythology; Gods and Goddesses of Northland.... Transl. from the Swedish by R. B. Anderson. London, Noroena Society, 1907. 3 vols.

Contains a comprehensive history of Teutonic myths and religious beliefs; especially well documented is the section dealing with Scandinavia. Includes a dictionary of principal proper names with character attributes, and an index.

367 Turville-Petre, Gabriel. Myth and Religion of the North; The Religion of Ancient Scandinavia. New York, Holt, Rinehart, 1964. 340 p.

Provides a survey of the early religions in Scandinavia. Discusses myths and theories of gods such as Odin, Thor, Baldr, Vanir as well as the divine heroes, sacrifice, beginning and the end of the world, etc. Contains a bibliography and an index.

THE CELTS

368 Chadwick, Nora. The Druids. London, Verry, 1967. 119 p.

Due to the scarcity of sources, the author tries to review all the information about the Druids handed down by the ancient writers. She comes to the conclusion that they were primitive philosophers and teachers. Includes an index but no bibliography.

369 Draak, Maatje. "The Religion of the Celts." Bleeker, C. J., ed. Historia religionum, v. 1, p. 629-47.

See no. 38. Evaluates the results of research in this field, where because of the lack of religious texts, special methods of investigation have been employed. A selective bibliography is included.

370 MacCana, Proinsias. Celtic Mythology. Feltham, Hamlyn, 1970. 143 p.

A review of Celtic myths with a selected bibliography and an index.

371 Piggott, Stuart. The Druids. New York, Praeger, 1968 (Ancient People and Places, v. 63). 236 p.

An attempt to reconstruct the truth about Druids as priests which is based on the author's enormous archaeological expertise, previous theories and even fiction--e.g. William Blake. Includes a selective bibliography and an index.

372 Rees, Alwyn, and Brinley Rees. Celtic Heritage; Ancient Tradition in Ireland and Wales. London, Thames and Hudson, 1961. 427 p.
Provides comprehensive survey of research of various aspects of Celtic civilization including religious beliefs. Bibliographic references in notes and an index are provided.

373 Sharkey, John. Celtic Mysteries; The Ancient Religion. London, Thames and Hudson, 1975 (Art and Imagination). 96 p.
A briefly presented essay with some selected readings.

THE SLAVS

374 Gimbutas, Marija. The Slavs. London, Thames and Hudson, New York, Praeger, 1971 (Ancient People and Places, v. 74). 240 p.
This is a basic textbook in English for pre-Christian Slavic history from the beginning to the early second millenium B.C. to the rise of the Slavonic states in the 9th and 10th centuries A.D. The subject of religion is discussed in Chapter 8, Religion. Short bibliography is provided on p. 194.

375 "Slavonic Mythology." Larousse Encyclopedia of Mythology. p. 293-310; Bibliography p. 493.
See no. 123. Surveys scarce data of the ancient Slavonic religious beliefs and customs.

376 Vyncke, F. "The Religion of the Slavs." Bleeker, C. J., ed. Historia Religionum, v. 1, p. 649-66.
See no. 38. A review article which presents a brief description of the essence of beliefs, their historical development, and the history of the studies. Includes a selected bibliography.

PRE-COLUMBIAN AMERICA

377 Burland, Cottie A.; I. Nicholson; and H. Osborne. Mythology of Americas. London, Hamlyn, 1970. 407 p.
Originally published as: North American Indian Mythology, 1965; Mexican and Central American Mythology, 1967;

South American Mythology, 1968. Presents a well selected collection of myths with informative comments on religious beliefs. Contains a selective bibliography and an index.

378 Pre-Columbian American Religions, by Walter Krickenberg and others, transl. from the German by S. Davis. London, Weidenfeld and Nicolson, 1968 (1961) (History of Religion). 365 p.
Translation of Die Religionen des alten Amerika. Contains material on Mexico, South America, North America, as well as West Indies. Provides a selective classified bibliography and an index.

379 Spence, Lewis. The Myths of Mexico and Peru. London, Harrap, 1917. 366 p.
Contains a collection of Mexican and Peruvian myths with a bibliography of sources, an index, and glossary.

ANCIENT MEXICO

380 Burland, Cottie A. The Gods of Mexico. New York, Putnam, 1967. 219 p.
Provides an unusually clear picture of pre-Columbian beliefs arrived at mainly through the thorough knowledge of the Aztecs and efficient comparisons of the relics of other cults. Includes a bibliography and an index.

381 Caso, Alfonso. The Aztecs; People of the Sun. Transl. by L. Dunham. Norman, Univ. of Oklahoma Press, 1958 (1953) (Civilization of the American Indians Series, 50). 125 p.
Translation of El pueblo del sol. Surveys religious life of the Aztecs. It deals with the magic, calendar, sacerdotal organization, etc.

382 Morley, Silvanus G. Ancient Maya, 3rd ed., rev. by G. B. Brainerd. Stanford, Calif., Stanford Univ. Press, 1956. 494 p.
An exhaustive survey of the Maya history from its origin, rise, renaissance, to its final decline. Religion and Deities chapter, p. 208-58, should be noted. Contains a classified bibliography and an index.

383 Séjourné, Laurette. "Ancient Mexican Religion." Bleeker, C. J., ed. Historia religionum, v. 1, p. 667-79.
See no. 38. Provides condensed information on the essence, worship, and history of research of Mexican religions. Select bibliography is provided.

384 Thompson, J. E. S. Maya History and Religion. Norman, Univ. of Oklahoma Press, 1970. 415 p.
Comprised of a collection of papers which derive various

data from confrontation of contemporary observation of modern Indians, colonial writings, and archaeological material. Contains an extensive bibliography of sources and modern critical works. One should also read the author's earlier publication, The Rise and Fall of Maya Civilization, especially chapter VI: Maya Religion, p. 259-98.

ANCIENT PERU

385 Kelm, Antje. "The Religion of Ancient Peru." Bleeker, C. J., ed. Historia religionum, v. 1, p. 680-91.
See no. 38. A condensed survey of the state religion of the Incas discussing its development, worship, and history of research. Includes a selected bibliography.

386 Mason, John A. The Ancient Civilization of Peru. Baltimore, Penguin Books, 1968 (1957) (Pelican Book, A 395). 331 p.
Presents a comprehensive survey of historical developments in Peru. Pt. 3, Sect. 13, discusses religious beliefs of the Incas. Classified bibliography and an index are provided.

387 Means, P. A. Ancient Civilizations of the Andes. New York, Gordian Press, 1964 (1931). 586 p.
Presents a comprehensive study of the Incas' history. Deals with their government, arts, and religion (Chapter IX: The life and official religion of the Incaic State; Chapter X; Some other religions of the ancient Andeans, and their intellectual life in general). Bibliography is appended at the end of each chapter.

388 Meltraux, Alfred. The History of the Incas. Transl. from the French by G. Ordish. New York, Pantheon Books, 1969. 205 p.
Translation of Les Incas. An account of the history of the Incas which describes its social and political structure, the daily life of the people, religion (p. 121-42), etc. Includes a bibliography and chronological tables.

JOURNALS

389 American Academy in Rome. Memoirs. Rome, 1917- (irregularly).
An official publication of the Academy. Each issue contains several articles discussing one subject.

390 American Anthropologist. Menasha, Wis., 1888-98; New ser. 1899- (6 issues a year).

Published by the American Anthropological Assoc. Index: 1888-1928, 1929-38, 1939-48. Indexed: Soc. Sci. Hum. Index.

391 American Antiquity; A Quarterly Review of American Archaeology. Menasha, Wis., 1935- .
Published by the Society for American Archaeology. Indexed: Hist. Abstr.; Soc. Sci. Hum. Index.

392 American Journal of Archaeology. New York, 1885- (quarterly).
Published by the Archaeological Institute of America. Contains excellent articles by American and European scholars about excavations in the Near East, Greece, Egypt, and the Mediterranean area. Indexed: Soc. Sci. Hum. Index; Chemical Abstracts.

393 American Journal of Philology. Baltimore, 1880- .
Covers the field of Greek and Roman antiquities. Contains analysis of literature, history and philosophy. Indexed: Soc. Sci. Hum. Index.

394 American Museum of Natural History. Anthropological Papers. New York, 1908- (irregularly).
Includes scholarly articles covering all aspects of North American culture. Indexed: Int. Bibliog. Soc. Cult. Anthro.

395 Anatolian Studies; Journal of the British Institute of Archaeology at Ankara. London, 1951- (irregularly).
Brings the most recent reports on archaeological research in Turkey; is especially important for Hittite studies. Indexed: Archäeologische Bibliographie.

396 Antiquity; A Quarterly Review of Archaeology. Gloucester, England, 1927- .
Reviews archaeology in Europe and the British Isles. Book reviews are in each volume. Index v. 1-25. Indexed: Art Index; Br. Hum. Index.

397 Archaeology; A Magazine Dealing with the Antiquity of the World. New York, 1948- (quarterly).
Published by the Archaeological Institute of America. Contains a "news" section important for recent information about new excavations. Index vol. 1-10.

398 Berytus; Archaeological Studies. Beirut, 1934- (1 or 2 issues a year).
Published by the American University in Beirut. This journal is primarily devoted to historical and archaeological studies of Syria and Lebanon from prehistoric to early Islamic times.

399 British School at Athens. Annual. London, 1894- .
Presents reports on the work of the school each year. Three indexes covering vols. 1-48 are provided. Indexed: Archäeologische Bibliographie.

400 British School at Rome. Papers. London, 1902-1937; New ser. 1938- (irregularly).
Covers all aspects of all periods of Roman and Italian history and arts. Indexed: Archäeologische Bibliographie.

401 Classical Philology, Devoted to Research in the Languages, Literatures, History, and Life of Classical Antiquity. Chicago, 1906- (quarterly).
Articles are usually devoted to critical analysis of texts and historical and comparative studies. Indexed: Soc. Sci. Hum. Index; L'Année philologique.

402 Classical Quarterly. London, 1906- .
Published by the Classical Association. Includes long articles on literature, history and archaeology. Indexed: Br. Hum. Index; L'Année philologique.

403 Classical Review. London, 1886-1950; New ser. 1950- (3 issues per year).
Published in cooperation with the Classical Association. Contains excellent signed book reviews. Index vols. 1-64. Indexed: Br. Hum. Index; Soc. Sci. Hum. Index.

404 Classical World. Newark, 1907- (monthly).
Its greatest value is in its extensive critical bibliographies, and brief informative articles.

405 Greece and Rome. London, 1931- (semiannually).
Published for the Classical Association. Indexed: Br. Hum. Index.

406 Hesperia. Cambridge, Mass., 1932- (quarterly).
The journal of the American School of Classical Studies at Athens. Cumulative index is published separately every ten years. Indexed: Art Index; L'Année philologique.

407 Iraq. London, 1934- (semiannually).
Published by the British School of Archaeology in Iraq. Indexed: L'Année philologique.

408 Journal of Hellenic Studies. London, 1880- (semiannually).
Provides a comprehensive examination of all aspects of antiquity together with the Journal of Roman Studies. It also includes book reviews. Indexed: L'Année philologique.

409 Journal of Cuneiform Studies. New Haven, 1947- (quarterly).
Published by the American Schools of Oriental Research.

Contains long articles and book reviews.

410 Journal of Roman Studies. London, 1911- (semiannually). Published by the Society for the Promotion of Roman Studies. Contains the proceedings of the Society, articles, book reviews. Indexed: Soc. Sci. Hum. Index.

411 Journal of Near Eastern Studies. Chicago, 1942- (quarterly). This journal is published by the Department of Near Eastern Languages and Civilizations at the University of Chicago. Contains informative articles on recent research in the field and book reviews. Indexed: Soc. Sci. Hum. Index.

412 World Archaeology. Henley-on-Thames, 1969- (3 issues per year). Contains informative articles and book reviews.

413 Yale Classical Studies. New Haven, 1928- . Published by Yale University Department of Classics. Usually contains a collection of articles on one subject. Indexed: L'Année philologique.

Part Three

JUDAISM, CHRISTIANITY, ISLAM

I JUDAISM

REFERENCE WORKS

DICTIONARIES AND ENCYCLOPEDIAS

414 Encyclopedia Judaica. Ed. by Cecil Roth et al. Jerusalem, Encyclopedia Judaica; New York, Macmillan, 1972. 16 vols.

The most up-to-date source of information on all aspects of Jewish life, literature, philosophy, religion, customs, and history. Includes hundreds of biographical articles, which are followed by short bibliographies. Vol. 1 contains supplementary materials such as Hundred Years Jewish Calendar, 1920-2020; a list of places in Israel; Hebrew Newspapers and Periodicals; and an extensive index with abundant cross-references.

415 Encyclopedia of Zionism and Israel. Ed. by Raphael Patai. New York, Herzl Press; McGraw-Hill, 1971. 2 vols.

Contains 3000 articles. Covers place names in Israel, Jewish and Israeli biographies, and various subjects such as history of Zionist movement and its organizations; social, economic, political, cultural and religious development. Its coverage is up to the Six-Day-War.

416 Encyclopedia Talmudica; A Digest of Halachic Literature and Jewish Law from Tannaitic Period to the Present Time Alphabetically Arranged. Founder and Ed. M. Berlin; Ed. S. J. Zevin. English transl., I. Epstein and H. Freedman. Jerusalem, Talmudic Encyclopedia Institute, 1969- .

"Provides a comprehensive presentation, arranged alphabetically, of the halakhic subjects dealt with in the Talmud and in post-Talmudic rabbinic literature, from the gaonic period to the present day"--Preface. Each volume contains a subject index and a glossary of Hebrew terms.

417 The Jewish Encyclopedia; A Descriptive Record of the History,

Religion, Literature and Customs of the Jewish People from the Earliest Times to the Present Day. I. Singer, ed. New York, Funk and Wagnalls, 1901-6. 12 vols.

This work is superseded by the new Encyclopedia Judaica (see no. 414). However it is still useful for its biographies and for its articles on such topics as the basic elements of the Jewish religion and the older Jewish literature.

418 The New Jewish Encyclopedia. Ed. by David Bridger. New York, Behrman House, 1962.

"The facts of Jewish religion, history, ethics, literature, and national life are included in a practical comprehensive digest"--Preface.

419 The New Standard Jewish Encyclopedia. Cecil Roth and Geoffrey Wigoder, Editors in Chief. Garden City, N.Y., Doubleday, 1970. 2028 cols.

A compilation of facts on various aspects of Jewish life. Special emphasis is placed on recent developments in Jewish history especially in the American community. Biographies include also living people.

420 Schulman, Albert M. Gateway to Judaism; Encyclopedia Home Reference. South Brunswick, N.J., T. Yoseloff, 1971. 2 vols.

Provides information on history and structure of Jewish religion and communities. Contains a comprehensive index.

421 The Universal Jewish Encyclopedia; An Authoritative and Popular Presentation of the Jews and Judaism since the Earliest Times. Ed. by Isaac Landman. New York, Universal Jewish Encyclopedia, 1939-44. 11 vols.

Contains 15,000 articles covering every facet of Judaism and Jewish life, history, religion, and culture from the earliest times to 1939. Also includes biographies and geographical information. Articles are signed and accompanied by bibliographies. Vol. 11 comprises a brief Reading Guide and Index.

422 Werblowsky, R. J. Z., and G. Wigoder, eds. The Encyclopedia of Jewish Religion. New York, Holt, Rinehart, Winston, 1966 (1965). 415 p.

Provides accurate and non-technical information on Jewish beliefs and practices, religious movements and doctrines, as well as information on prominent persons in Jewish religious history. There are numerous cross-references but no bibliographies.

BIBLIOGRAPHIES AND GUIDES

423 Berlin, Charles, comp. Index to Festschriften in Jewish Studies. Cambridge, Mass., Harvard College Library; New York, KTAV, 1971. 319 p.
Contains an index to 259 collections of Festschriften published after 1937.

424 Celnik, Max and Isaac Celnik. A Bibliography on Judaism and Jewish-Christian Relations; A Selected Annotated Listing of Works on Jewish Faith and Life, and the Jewish-Christian Encounter. New York, Anti-Defamation League of B'nai B'rith, 1965. 68 p.
Contains a guide to "currently obtainable 300 books ... representing various Jewish viewpoints, generally not including Christian scholars."

425 Goldin, Judah and S. Cain. "Early and Classical Judaism. Medieval and Modern Judaism." Adams, C. J. A Reader's Guide to Great Religions, 2nd ed. New York, Free Press, 1977 (1965), p. 283-341.
See no. 22. Provides an excellent survey of materials available for studies of Judaism. Reviews histories and other standard works, primary sources available in translation. Scriptures, and the sects are also included.

426 "[IV.] Judaism." International Bibliography of the History of Religions. Leiden, Brill, 1954- .
See no. 27. The contents of this bibliography, published annually, is divided into: 1. Scriptures; 2. Qumran (Dead Sea Scrolls); 3. Institutions; 4. Philosophy; 5. History.

427 Leiman, Sid Z. "Jewish Ethics 1970-1975: Retrospect and Prospect. Bibliography." Religious Studies Review, v. 2: 2(1976), p. 16-22.
Presents a list of recent discussion, and views it from a critical perspective. Includes monographs and periodical articles.

428 Shunami, Shlomo. Bibliography of Jewish Bibliographies, 2nd ed. enl. Jerusalem, Magnes, 1965. 992 p. Suppl. 1975. 464 p.
Lists some 7000 bibliographies on a variety of topics in Jewish studies. Of special interest are the sections: IX. Religion, Philosophy, Cabala; XI. Bibl.; XII. Talmudic and Midrashic Literature; XIII. Liturgies, Synagogue. Music. Homiletics; XIX. Sects. Index of names and subjects.

429 Stern, Malcolm H., comp. "American Reform Judaism: A Bibliography." American Jewish Quarterly, V. 63:2 (1973), p. 120-137.
Includes monographs and periodical articles in subject arrangement: history, biography, sociological studies,

principles and practices. Also contains a list of Jewish American periodicals arranged chronologically and then by state.

430 The Study of Judaism; Bibliographical Essays. Contrib. Richard Bavier (and others). New York, KTAV for Anti-Defamation League of B'nai B'rith, 1972. 229 p.
Concentrates on four major subjects: Judaism in the New Testament times; Jewish-Christian relations; contemporary Judaic theology; and modern Jewry.

431 Werblowsky, R. J. Z. "Judaism." Bleeker, C. J., ed. Historia religionum, v. 2, p. 1-48.
See no. 38. A survey article which presents the essence of Judaism; its history; the doctrine of God; ritual, liturgy, and ethics; contemporary development in Judaism; and a brief survey of research history. Provides a select bibliography of sources and critical materials.

INDEX

432 Index to Jewish Periodicals. Cleveland, Ohio. College of Jewish Studies Press, 1963- (biennially).
Provides an author and subject approach to selected American and Anglo-Jewish periodicals of general and scholarly character. Indexes: American Jewish Historical Quarterly; Israel Exploration Journal; Jewish Social Studies; and elsewhere.

TEXTS IN TRANSLATION

INTRODUCTORY SURVEYS

433 Casper, Bernard M. Introduction to Jewish Bible Commentary. New York, Yoseloff, 1960. 128 p.
Presents a survey of the development of Biblical exegesis. Discusses the Targums, fixing of the Canon, the Mishna, the Massora, etc. A selective bibliography and an index are included.

434 Gersh, Harry. The Sacred Books of the Jews. New York, Stein and Day, 1968. 256 p.
Contains a brief review of all the classic Jewish literature which includes the Bible and the Talmud with its medieval and modern tracts. A strong accent is placed on the role of the Bible as an incentive for recording of every change in religious practice. Provides bibliographic references in footnotes and an index.

435 Kolatch, Alfred J. Who's Who in the Talmud. New York, J. David, 1964. 315 p.

Consists of an introductory explanation about the origin of the Talmud and its history; facsimile reproductions of the basic text with additional tracts; glossary of popular terms and expressions; and biographical part of great personalities in the Talmud.

436 Neusner, Jacob, ed. The Formation of the Babylonian Talmud; Studies in the Achievements of Late Nineteenth and Twentieth Century Historical and Literary-critical Research. Leiden, Brill, 1970 (Studia Post-Biblica, v. 17). 187 p.

A collection of papers which offer an account of the research of some of the more important historians and literary critics. A bibliography and an index are provided.

437 Sandmel, Samuel. The Enjoyment of Scripture; The Law, the Prophets, and the Writings. New York, Oxford Univ. Press, 1972. 300 p.

Presents a purely literary appraisal of the Hebrew Bible. Contains a chart of history and literature, and a selective bibliography. No index is provided.

438 ________. The Hebrew Scriptures; An Introduction to Their Literature and Religious Ideas. New York, Knopf, 1963. 552 p.

A well written introduction which presents an informative explanation of complicated nature of the Old Testament prophecy, the characteristics of Hebrew poetry, etc.

439 Strack, Hermann L. Introduction to the Talmud and Midrash. New York, Meridian Books, 1959 (1931) (Jewish Publication Society Series, JP8). 372 p.

Provides an easy popular explanation of the complicated study of the Talmud and Midrash. Bibliographical references are included.

SCRIPTURES

440 Bible. O. T. Pentateuch. English. 1963. Jewish Publications Society. The Torah, the Five Books of Moses. Philadelphia, Jewish Publications Soc. of America, 1963. 393 p.

A revised translation into modern language which was drawn directly from ancient Hebrew texts. Takes into consideration the archaeological and philological discoveries made in recent years, especially the Qumran scrolls.

441 The Midrash rabbah. English. Midrash rabbah; transl. into English with Notes, and Indices, under the Editorship of H. Freedman and M. Siman, with a Foreword by I. Epstein. London, Soncino Press, 1939. 10 vols.

A collection of commentaries which contains the homiletical, ethical, and moral interpretations of the Scriptures as expanded by the rabbis in the synagogues and colleges.

442 Moses ben Maimon. The Code of Maimonides. New Haven, Conn., Yale Univ. Press, 1949- (in progress) (Yale Judaica Series). 15 vols. published.

Contains a collection of religious and legal treatises written by this celebrated philosopher and translated by various translators.

443 Talmud. English. The Babylonian Talmud; Transl. into English with Notes, Glossary, and Indices under the Editorship of I. Epstein. London, Soncino Press, 1961 (1935-52). 18 vols.

The first complete English translation of the Babylonian Talmud. It has been recognized as "a monument of modern scholarship." The index is comprehensive, it covers all cited passages and terms. Lists names of rabbis mentioned in the text.

444 ______. ______. The Talmud, with English Translation and Commentary. Ed.: A. Ehrman. Jerusalem, el-'Am, 1965- (in progress).

A new critical edition of the Talmud which has been undertaken by leading theologians, historians and linguists in Israel.

HISTORICAL WORKS

445 Josephus Flavius. Josephus, with an English Transl. by H. St. John Thackeray. London, Heinemann; New York, Putnam, 1926-65 (Loeb Classical Library. Greek Authors).

Presents a standard English translation of the works of the famous historian of Palestine who lived in the first century A.D. Contains Jewish Antiquities and Jewish War.

ANTHOLOGIES

446 Baron, Salo W., and J. Blau, eds. Judaism: Post-biblical and Talmudic Period. New York, Liberal Arts Press, 1954 (History of Religion, v. 3). 245 p.

Comprises a selection from the Judaic traditional texts on theology, religious life, legal problems, philosophy, folklore, etc.

447 Glatzer, Nahum N. The Judaic Tradition; Texts ed. and introduced by N. N. Glatzer. Rev. ed. with New Introd. Boston, Beacon Press, 1969 (Beacon Paperback, no. 316). 838 p.

Presents a selection from post-Biblical Jewish literature

on theology, philosophy, folklore, etc. Contains a selective bibliography. This is a consolidated edition of the author's previous anthologies: Hillel the Elder; The Emergence of Classical Judaism, 1966; Faith and Knowledge; The Jew in the Medieval World, 1963; The Dynamics of Emancipation; The Jew in the Modern Age, 1965; In Time and Eternity; A Jewish Reader, 1961.

JEWISH LEGENDS

448 Ginzberg, Louis. Legends of the Jews. Transl. from the German manuscript by H. Szold. Philadelphia, Jewish Publication Society of America, 1909-38. 7 vols.

Attempts to gather all Jewish legends from original sources such as the Talmudic-Midrashic literature, the Targumim, from the medieval Bible commentaries, the works of older Kabbalah, and various apocryphal pseudepigraphic sources. Vol. 7 consists of references to sources used, explanations of emandations of the Midrashim and the pseudepigraphics, and a comprehensive index.

HANDBOOKS AND SURVEYS

HISTORY--GENERAL

449 Baron, Salo Wittmayer. A Social and Religious History of the Jews, 2nd ed., rev. and enl. New York, Columbia Univ. Press, 1952-67 (1937).

A comprehensive survey that traces Jewish history from the beginning to A.D. 1200. Each volume contains bibliographic notes with references to sources.

450 Dimont, Max I. The Indestructible Jews; Is There a Manifest Destiny in Jewish History? New York, World Publ. Co., 1971 (New American Library Book). 374 p.

This passionately written popular book aims at presentation of an objective history of the Jews free of Jewish as well as Christian distortion. Contains a well selected bibliography and an index.

451 ______. Jews, Gods, and History. London, Allen, 1962. 463 p.

A popular presentation based on thorough knowledge of Jewish history and theology. A select bibliography and an index are provided.

452 Dubnov, S. M. History of the Jews, 4th rev. ed. Transl. from the Russian by M. Speigel. South Brunswick, N.J., T. Yoseloff, 1967- (in progress).

Translation of Istoriia evreĭskogo naroda na vostoke. This work is considered a classic of Jewish historiography. It is vast in scope, sound in scholarship and scientific in methodology, and applies a broad sociological approach, free of theological preconceptions. Information contained in this book is still reliable but should be up-dated with new materials, e.g. see no. 457. Contains a bibliography, but lacks an index.

453 Epstein, Isidore. Judaism: A Historical Presentation. Baltimore, Penguin Books, 1960 (1959) (Pelican Books A 440). 348 p.

An excellent introductory reading which presents Judaism as a distinctive religious way of life against its background of 4000 years of history from Bible times to the establishment of the Modern Jewish state. Bibliography and an index are provided.

454 Finkelstein, Louis, ed. The Jews, Their History, 4th ed. New York, Schocken Books, 1970-1 (1960). 2 vols.

A good scholarly work for advanced students which contains the first concise history of the Jews written by a group of specialists. It brings into focus various aspects of Jewish life and Judaism. Each chapter contains a bibliography. General index is included in vol. 2.

455 Margolis, Max, and A. Marx. History of the Jewish People. New York, Meridian Books, 1960 (1927). 752 p.

A well-organized study which traces the rise of Judaism in the major Jewish centers: Palestine--the eastern center; and Holland, Poland, Russia--the western. Contains bibliographic notes and an index.

456 Patai, Raphael. Tents of Jacob; The Diaspora Yesterday and Today. Englewood Cliffs, N.J., Prentice-Hall, 1971. 464 p.

Pt. 1 discusses major issues of the nature and phenomenology of the diaspora; pt. 2 surveys the Jewish communities in each country of the world. Bibliography and an index are provided. See also his The Jewish Mind (New York, Scribner, 1977. 624 p.).

457 The World History of the Jewish People. Ed. by E. A. Speiser, B. Mazar and others. New Brunswick, N.J., Rutgers Univ. Press, 1964- .

Provides a comprehensive coverage of the cultural, religious, and political developments from the beginning to the present times. Chapters are by such outstanding authorities as E. A. Speiser, Y. Yadin, H. L. Ginsbury, C. H. Gordon, Y. Aharoni, et al.

HISTORY OF RELIGION, THEOLOGY, PHILOSOPHY

458 Baeck, Leo. The Essence of Judaism, rev. ed. Rendition by I. Howe based on transl. from the German by V. Grubenwieser and L. Pearl. New York, Schocken Books, 1961 (1948). 287 p.

Translation of Das Wesen des Judentums. A presentation of Jewish religious philosophy based on thorough and meticulous scholarship. Includes bibliographic references, a guide to rabbinical quotations, and an index.

459 ______. This People Israel; The Meaning of Jewish Existence. Transl. and with an introd. note by Albert H. Friedlander. New York, Holt, 1965. 403 p.

Translation of Dieses Volk; jüdische Existenz. This scholarly work presents the essence of ethical and spiritual basis of Judaism. Pt. 1 deals with "the work of God": Exodus, journey from Canaan to Israel. Pt. 2 is divided into five sections, covers the Biblical period, the Jewish Middle Ages, and the recent developments. Contains bibliographic references in footnotes.

460 Blau, Joseph L. Judaism in America; From Curiosity to Third Faith. Chicago, University of Chicago Press, 1976 (Chicago History of American Religion). 156 p.

The author's attention is centered primarily in what has happened to Judaism in the United States. Bibliographic references in notes and a general index are supplied.

461 Bokser, Ben Zion. Judaism: Profile of a Faith. New York, Knopf, 1963. 293 p.

Presents an excellent explanation of the basic concepts of Judaism and the Jewish tradition. Bibliographical references are included in the footnotes. There is also an index.

462 Brasch, Rudolph. The Unknown Sanctuary; The Story of Judaism, Its Teachings, Philosophy, and Symbols. Sydney, Angus and Robertson, 1969. 399 p.

Contains a completely revised and up-dated combined edition of the author's previous works, The Star of David and The Eternal Flame. Provides an excellent survey of Jewish customs and symbols explaining their origin and their present day meaning. Index is included.

463 Buber, Martin. I and Thou; a New Translation with a Prologue "I and Thou" and notes by W. Kaufman. New York, Scribner's, 1970 (1937). 185 p.

The famous Jewish philosopher examines the distinctive formulations of Jewish religious thought.

464 ______. On Judaism. Ed. by N. Glatzer. New York, Schocken Books, 1967. 242 p.

Contains a collection of essays, including: Judaism and the Jews; Judaism and Mankind; Renewal of Judaism; The Spirit of the Orient and Judaism; Jewish Religiosity; Myth in Judaism; Judaism and Civilization; etc. Bibliographic references are included in the notes. No index is provided.

465 Cohon, Samuel S. Jewish Theology; A Historical and Systematic Interpretation of Judaism and its Foundations. Assen, van Gorcum, 1971. 481 p.
Presents a detailed scholarly review of Jewish philosophical schools with a well selected bibliography and an index.

466 ______. Judaism; A Way of Life. Cincinnati, Union of of American Hebrew Congregations, 1948. 423 p.
"Describes Judaism in its varied aspects of religious living, as ethical experience, as social justice, as prayer, as love of learning, as worship"--Preface. Contains a glossary of most important terms, a classified selective bibliography, and a useful subject index.

467 Commentary. The Condition of Jewish Belief; A Symposium. Comp. by the eds. of Commentary Magazine. New York, Macmillan, 1966. 280 p.
Comprises an interesting collection of papers which discuss the issues of the contemporary Jewish theology and Judaism.

468 Epstein, Isidore. Judaism: A Historical Presentation. Baltimore, Penguin Books, 1960 (1959) (Pelican Books A440). 348 p.
Provides an historical outline of the origin and development of Jewish religious and ethical teaching and practice, philosophical thought, as well as mystical doctrine. Contains a selected bibliography and an index.

469 Gordis, Robert. Judaism in a Christian World. New York, McGraw-Hill, 1966. 253 p.
Deals with Jewish tradition in the modern world, Jewish existence, the nature of Jewish identity, Judaism in the Christian world view, the Judeo-Christian tradition, American Jewish community, etc. Bibliography is included in the notes. An index is provided.

470 Guttmann, Julius. Philosophies of Judaism; The History of Jewish Philosophy from Biblical Times to Franz Rosenzweig. Transl. by D. Silverman. Introd. by Z. Werblowsky. Philadelphia, Jewish Publications Society of America, 1964 (1933). 464 p.
Provides information about the life, work, and teaching of every significant thinker from Philo of Alexandria to the rabbis of the Talmud, through the great mediaeval

thinkers to those of the 20th century. This classic is still called "the best history of Jewish philosophy to date." Contains a classified bibliography and a very detailed index.

471 Hardon, John A. American Judaism. Chicago, Loyola Univ. Press, 1971. 372 p.
A scholarly discussion and evaluation of Jewish history and law from Biblical times until today by a Christian theologian. Describes religious belief and practice among Orthodox, Conservative, and Reform Jews. Includes a selective bibliography, calendar of feast days, statistics of world and American Jewish population, a list of national Jewish organizations, and data on Jewish education in America.

472 Herberg, Will. Judaism and Modern Man; An Interpretation of Jewish Religion. New York, Farrar, Strauss, and Young, 1951. 313 p.
Provides an easy introduction to the principles of Jewish beliefs and customs. Pt. 1 discusses the nature of Jewish religion; Pt. 2 is devoted to a study of Juadism on three levels: God and man, God and history, and God and Israel. Contains bibliographic references in footnotes and an index.

473 Hertzberg, Arthur, ed. Judaism. New York, Braziller, 1961 (Great Religions of Modern Man). 256 p.
A popular work with useful bibliographic references.

474 Heschel, Abraham J. Between God and Man; An Interpretation of Judaism. From the Writings of A. J. Heschel, selected, ed. and introd. by F. A. Rothschild. New York, Harper, 1959. 279 p.
A selection which presents the author's views on faith, revelation, the divine concern, the illusion of human self-sufficiency, religion and law, etc. Contains an exhaustive bibliography of the writings of A. J. Heschel, including a brief selection of articles about him. Also includes bibliographical references in the notes. No index is provided.

475 Jacobs, Louis. Principles of the Jewish Faith. New York, Basic Books, 1964. 473 p.
A very thorough analysis of theological aspects of Judaism. The author chooses an opinion of a leading Jewish or non-Jewish thinker, philosopher, mystic, or scholar and examines its conformity with modern thought. Contains bibliographic references and an index of philosophers.

476 Kaplan, Mordecai M. The Greater Judaism in Making: A Study of the Modern Evolution of Judaism. New York, Reconstructionalist Press, 1960. 565 p.

"First comes a synoptic presentation of traditional Judaism before it encountered ... Western thought.... That is followed by a summary of medieval theology, both philosophic and mystical ... [and] then comes a brief description of the cultural revolution of the West..."--Preface. Bibliography is included in the notes, an index is also provided.

477 ________. Judaism as a Civilization; Towards a Reconstruction of American Jewish Life, enl. ed. New York, Reconstructionalist Press, 1957 (1934). 601 p.

"This book--written by the founder of the Reconstructionalist Movement--presents a program for 'a creative Judaism', a program that shall maintain the continuity of the traditional Jewish civilization in the face of such challenging conditions as those today"--Preface.

478 Kaufmann, Jecheskel. The Religion of Israel; From Its Beginnings to the Babylonian Exile. Transl. and abridged by M. Greenberg. Chicago, Univ. of Chicago Press, 1960 (1937). 486 p.

An abridgement of the Hebrew work in 8 vols.; Toldot haemunah ha-yisraelit. Presents an informative survey of ancient Judaism. It encompasses a wide range of relevant writings by anthropologists, linguists, and historians. Contains a double index of subjects and scripture passages.

479 Neusner, Jacob. The Way of Torah; An Introduction of Judaism. Belmont, Calif., Dickenson Pub. Co., 1970 (Religious Life of Man). 116 p.

A brief but informative introduction to basic issues that arise from the study of Judaism. Contains a well-selected bibliography of monographs and an index. Recommended for introductory reading.

480 Plaut, W. Gunther. The Rise of Reform Judaism. New York, New World Union for Progressive Judaism, 1963. 2 vols.

Forms a sourcebook of materials on the liberal movement in Judaism. Vol. 1 deals with the foundation of reform in Europe in 1780-1 as presented by fragments of original journals, books, manifestos and appeals. Each extract is supplied with biographical information on its author. Vol. 2 contains the history of American reform. Bibliography and an index are included.

481 Rosenzweig, Franz. Franz Rosenzweig: His Life and Thought, presented by N. N. Glatzer. New York, Farrar, Strauss and Young, 1953 (Schocken Book). 400 p.

Presents a substantial introduction in English to the works and ideas of this outstanding Jewish writer and theologian, who is one of the most original thinkers of modern times. The story is based mainly on Rosenzweig's own words. Especially interesting is the last part of the book, where the editor offers a cross-section of Rosenzweig's writings presenting his philosophy. Contains a list of Rosenzweig's writings, a selected bibliography, and an index.

482 Roth, Leon. Judaism; A Portrait. London, Faber and Faber, 1960. 240 p.
An excellent survey of Judaism which presents it as a prototype of the monotheistic religion. Index and a glossary are provided.

483 Rubenstein, Richard L. After Auschwitz; Radical Theology and Contemporary Judaism. Indianapolis, Bobbs-Merrill, 1966. 287 p.
A collection of essays which discusses various issues of significance in contemporary Judaism. Among other topics the authors review the ideas of Harvey, Cox, Arthur Cohen and Thomas Altizer. Bibliography included in footnotes.

484 Schechter, Salomon. Aspects of Rabbinic Theology. Introd. by L. Finkelstein. New York, Schocken Books, 1961 (1909). 384 p.
First edition published under the title, Some Aspects of Rabbinic Theology. A classic, which formulates major ideas of the Jewish religious consciousness regardless of sect or denomination. Includes a bibliography and an index.

485 Sharot, Stephen. Judaism; A Sociology. Vancouver, B. C., David & Charles, 1976. 224 p.
"The religious and cultural differences are analysed in relation to the socio-economic composition of the Jewish communities, to the dominant non-Jewish religious and cultural environments, and to the wider social structures..."--Introd. Bibliographic notes, glossary and an index are appended.

486 Silver, Abba H. Where Judaism Differed; An Inquiry into the Distinctiveness of Judaism. New York, Macmillan, 1963 (1956). 318 p.
Discusses basic differences of ideas in Judaism, Christianity, and Islam. Contains bibliographic references in notes and an index.

487 Silver, Daniel J. A History of Judaism. New York, Basic Books, 1974. 2 vol.
Provides a historical account of Judaism from the times of Abraham to the contemporary events in each volume. Glossary of Hebrew terms. Bibliographies in the form of essays. Index.

488 Steinberg, M. A Believing Jew: The Selected Writings of Milton Steinberg. Freeport, N.Y., Books for Libraries Press, 1971 (1951) (Essay Index Reprint Series). 318 p.
Presents a selection from writings by this outstanding Jewish philosopher on the idea of God; Judaism and the American Scene; Israel; and Judaism and the personal life. Lacks a bibliography and an index. Consult also the author's Basic Judaism (New York, Harcourt, 1947).

489 Trepp, Leo. Eternal Faith, Eternal People. Englewood Cliffs, N.J., Prentice-Hall, 1962. 455 p.
Provides a concise outline of Judaism with a well-selected classified bibliography and an index.

490 Weber, Max. Ancient Judaism. Transl. and ed. by H. H. Gerth and D. Martindale. Glencoe, Ill., Free Press, 1952 (1917). 484 p.
A classic which represents the author's socio-economic views of Judaism. Glossary and an index are provided.

491 Wolf, Arnold J., ed. Rediscovering Judaism; Reflections on a New Jewish Theology. Chicago, Quadrangle Books, 1965. 288 p.
A collection of essays which discuss such topics as Jewish revealed morality, the philosophical rational morality, individual and common prayer, man and sin, and relations between contemporary Judaism and Christianity. Includes bibliographical references.

SECTS

492 Blau, J. L. Modern Varieties of Judaism. New York, Columbia Univ. Press, 1966 (Lectures on the History of Religions. New ser. no. 8). 217 p.
An excellent survey which describes the three major branches in Judaism: Reform, Neo-Orthodox, and Conservative, as well as the Zionist movement. The style is dry and very matter-of-fact. Contains bibliographic references and an index.

493 Finkelstein, L. The Pharisees; The Sociological Background of Their Faith, 3rd ed. Philadelphia, Jewish Publications Society of America, 1962 (Morris Loeb Series). 2 vols.
This scholarly work describes the basic differences between the Saducees and the Pharisees in terms of the clash between urban and rural cultures. Bibliography and index are provided.

494 Roshwald, Mordecai. "Marginal Jewish Sects in Israel." International Journal of Middle East Studies, v. 4 (1973), p. 219-237, 328-354.

"The sects examined will be the Karaites, the Samaritans, and the Falashas"--Text. Bibliographic references are included in footnotes.

495 Simon, Marcel. Jewish Sects in the Times of Jesus. Transl. by J. Farley. Philadelphia, Fortress Press, 1967 (1960). 180 p.
Translation of Les Sectes juives en temps de Jesus. Presents a brief and informative study of Jewish sects. A well-selected classified bibliography is provided. Also contains a glossary of unfamiliar terms.

LITURGY

496 Idelsohn, Abraham Z. Jewish Liturgy and Its Development. New York, Schocken Books, 1971 (1932). 424 p.
Pt. 1 contains a history; Pt. 2 provides a description of the feasts, prayers, and services. There is also an appendix on the Jewish elements in early Christian liturgy.

497 Jews. Liturgy and Ritual. Hagadah. 1963/64. The Passover Haggadah, a New English Version by C. Roth. Ed. by B. Rothenberg. Tel Aviv, Lewim-Epstein, 1963/64.
A popular edition with parallel English and Hebrew Texts.

498 Levy, Isaac. The Synagogue, Its History and Function. London, Vallentine, 1963. 152 p.
Presents an informative survey with well selected bibliographic sources.

499 Millgram, Abraham E. Jewish Worship. Philadelphia, Jewish Publications Society of America, 1971. 673 p.
Reviews the growth of Jewish worship from its beginning to maturity. Bibliography is limited to books in English; the index, which includes foreign and technical terms, serves as a glossary. The very detailed contents table may be used as an easy access to selected topics.

500 Raphael, Chaim. A Feast of Liturgy; The Drama of Passover Through the Ages, with a New Translation of the Haggadah for Use at the Seder. London, Weidenfeld and Nicolson, 1972. 250 p.
A popular edition.

501 Sperling, Abraham I. Reasons for Jewish Customs and Traditions. Transl. into English by A. Maats. New York, Block, 1968. 310 p.
Explains the development of various Jewish customs and traditions on their historical and social background. Bibliographic notes and an index are included.

MYSTICISM

502 Scholem, G. G. Major Trends in Jewish Mysticism, 3rd rev. ed. New York, Schocken Books, 1961 (1954) (Schocken Paperbacks SB5). 460 p.
An informative account of Jewish mysticism which discusses the Merkaba, the Hassidim, the Kaballah, the Zohar, Isaac Luria and his school, the Sabbatai movement, etc. Bibliography and an index are included.

KABBALAH

503 Ponce, Charles. Kabbalah: An Illumination for the World Today. San Francisco, Straight Arrow Books, 1973. 297 p.
Attempts a presentation of the background and basic principles of Kabbalism. A select bibliography and an index are provided.

504 Scholem, Gershom. Kabalah. Jerusalem, Keter, 1974 (Library of Jewish Knowledge). 492 p.
Provides an excellent survey of issues in the study of Kabbalah. It deals with its historical development, basic ideas, and the influences of and research on Kabbalah. A glossary and a general index are added.

505 _______. "Kabbalah." Encyclopedia Judaica. New York, Macmillan, 1972. V. 10, p. 490-654.
See no. 414. An excellent survey which presents its historical development, its basic ideas, and the history of the research. A classified select bibliography is provided.

506 The Zohar. Transl. by H. Sperling and M. Simon. London, Soncino Press, 1931-34. 5 vols.
The Zohar, or The Book of Splendor is the central work of the Kabbalah. The excellent introduction explains its origins and literary values. Consult also Encyclopedia Judaica, V. 16, p. 1194-1215 (see entry above).

CALENDAR, FESTIVALS

507 Burnaby, Sherrad B. Elements of the Jewish and Muhammedan Calendars, with Rules and Tables and Explanatory Notes on the Julian and Gregorian Calendars. London, Bell, 1901. 554 p.
This classic is still of great help for learning the rules and conversion of dates.

508 Gaster, Theodor. Festivals of the Jewish Year; A Modern

Interpretation and Guide. New York, Sloane, 1953. 308 p.

Traces the evolution of each festival and compares the customs and ceremonies with those of other people. Contains a select bibliography of sources for each festival, fast and holy day. Also indexes are included.

509 Goldin, Hyman E. A Treasury of Jewish Holidays: History, Legends, Traditions. New York, Twayne, 1952. 308 p.

Provides a popular account of Jewish festive days.

JOURNALS

510 The American Jewish Historical Quarterly. New York, 1893- .

First published as American Jewish Historical Society. Publications, until vol. 50 (1960/61). Deals with Jewish history all over the world. Indexed: American History and Life; Hist. Abstr.

511 Hebrew Union College Annual. Cincinnati, 1924- .

Contains articles of Jewish scholarship from the scientific point of view. Articles in English, German, Hebrew, and French.

512 Israel Exploration Journal. Jerusalem, 1950- (quarterly).

Published by the Institute of Archaeology of the Hebrew University, the Dept. of Antiquities, and the Museum of the Ministry of Education and Culture. Text of articles in English and French. Provides good book reviewing service. Indexed: Bibliog. Hist. Sci.; Index to Jewish Periodicals.

513 The Jewish Journal of Sociology. London, 1959- (semiannually).

Published by the World Jewish Congress. Indexed: P.A.I.S.; Psychological Abstracts.

514 Jewish Quarterly Review. London, 1888-1908; Philadelphia, 1910- .

Contains book reviews, bibliography. Indexed: Rel. Theol. Abstr.

515 Jewish Social Studies. New York, 1939- (quarterly).

Published by the Conference on Jewish Social Studies. Contains papers and book reviews. Cumulated index is published every 15 years. Indexed: P.A.I.S.; Soc. Sci. Hum. Index.

516 Journal for the Studies of Judaism in the Persian, Hellenistic and Roman Period. Leiden, 1970- .
Periodical of importance for students of the Old and New Testament, Biblical archaeologists, classicists, and historians of religion.

517 Journal of Semitic Studies. Manchester, Eng., 1956- .
Contains current bibliographic information. Indexed: Br. Hum. Index.

518 Palestine Exploration Quarterly. London, 1859- .
Title varies: 1869-1936, Palestine Exploration Fund. Quarterly. Cumulated index is published every 2 years. Indexed: Br. Hum. Index.

Part Three--Judaism, Christianity, Islam (cont.)

II CHRISTIANITY

REFERENCE WORKS

DICTIONARIES AND ENCYCLOPEDIAS

519 Barker, William P. Who's Who in Church History. Old Tappan, N.J., Revell, 1969. 319 p.
Includes only names of prominent persons in the Christian community who influenced the ministry of the Church, and who are no longer living.

520 Bouyer, Louis. Dictionary of Theology. Transl. by C. Underhill Quinn. New York, Desclee, 1963. 470 p.
Provides a ready reference to the meaning of various theological terms.

521 A Catholic Dictionary of Theology. Ed. by H. F. Davis and others. Work projected with the approval of the Catholic Hierarchy of England and Wales. London, Nelson, 1962- (in progress; 4 vols. when completed).
Comprises an account of Roman Catholic theology in the form of articles arranged alphabetically. Articles, which vary in length, include references to sources and bibliographies.

522 Catholic Encyclopedia; An International Work of Reference on the Constitution, Doctrine, Discipline and History of the Catholic Church. Ed. by Charles G. Herbermann et al. New York, Appleton, 1907-12. 15 vols.
Consists of long signed articles with appended bibliographical references. Very useful for subjects in mediaeval literature, history, philosophy, arts, as well as biography. Should be used together with the New Catholic Encyclopedia, see no. 526.

523 Douglas, J. D., ed. The New International Dictionary of the Christian Church. Grand Rapids, Mich., Zondervan, 1974. 1074 p.
"The aim has been to steer a middle path between

academic textbook and popular introduction"--Preface. Includes brief articles with selected bibliographies.

524 Encyclopedia of Theology: A Concise Sacramentum Mundi. London, Burns and Oates, 1975. 1841 p.
Contains a selection of articles which provides the layman with essential information on the present-day understanding of the Christian faith, based on achievements of modern theological scholarship.

525 Harvey, Van A. A Handbook of Theological Terms. New York, Macmillan, 1964. 253 p.
Includes 300 articles which explain basic Catholic and Protestant theological terms. Doctrines and traditions of the Eastern Churches are touched upon, but in a less extensive manner.

526 New Catholic Encyclopedia. Prepared by an editorial staff at the Catholic University of America. New York, McGraw-Hill, 1967. 15 vols.
This completely new publication has no connection with the Catholic Encyclopedia (see no. 522). Takes into account latest reform movements within the church. Contains valuable bibliographies appended at the end of articles.

527 Ollard, S. L.; G. Croose; and M. F. Bond. A Dictionary of English Church History, 3rd ed. London, Mowbray, 1948. 698 p.
Limited to the English Church, the provinces of Canterbury and York. Articles are provided with short bibliographies.

528 The Oxford Dictionary of the Christian Church. Ed. by F. L. Cross. London, Oxford Univ. Press, 1974. 1518 p.
This new edition attempts to keep the dictionary up-to-date, especially in the bibliographical sections. Comprises numerous articles covering historical and doctrinal aspects, definitions of ecclesiastical terms and customs, biographies, etc.

529 Purvis, J. S. Dictionary of Ecclesiastical Terms. Toronto, Nelson, 1962. 204 p.
Provides definitions or explanations of basic terms. Rarely-used words have been excluded.

530 Rahner, Karl, and H. Vorglimler. Concise Theological Dictionary. Ed. by C. Ernst. Transl. by R. Strachan. London, Burns and Oates, 1965 (1961). 493 p.
Translation of Kleines theologisches Wörterbuch. Explains breifly the most important concepts of modern dogmatic theology.

531 Richardson, Alan. A Dictionary of Christian Theology. Philadelphia, Westminster Press, 1969. 394 p.
"It is with theological issues of today that this dictionary is primarily concerned"--Preface. Contains brief informative articles with basic bibliographic references.

532 Sacramentum mundi; An Encyclopedia of Theology. Ed. by Karl Rahner et al. Montreal, Palm Publishers, 1968-69. 6 vols.
A summary of modern Catholic ideas which reflect contemporary debates. Bibliographic references are appended to each article.

533 Smith, William, and Samuel Cheetham, eds. A Dictionary of Christian Antiquities, Comprising the History, Institutions and Antiquities of the Christian Church, from the Time of Apostles to the Age of Charlemagne. London, Murray, 1908. 2 vols.
"Treats of organization of the Church, its officers, legislation, discipline, and revenues; the social life of Christians; their worship and ceremonial, with the accompanying music, vestments, instruments, vessels, and insignia; their sacred places; their architecture and other forms of art; their symbolism; their sacred days and season..."--Preface. Contains references to sources. Should be used with caution because of the outdated scholarship.

534 ________, and Henry Wace, eds. Dictionary of Christian Biography, Literature, Sects, and Doctrines. London, Murray, 1877-87; reprint: New York, AMS Press, 1967. 4 vols.
Covers times to Charlemagne. Special attention is paid to England, Scotland and Ireland. Contains long signed articles with references to sources. Some information is outdated by modern scholarship, therefore should be used with caution.

535 Wace, Henry, and W. C. Piercy. A Dictionary of Christian Biography and Literature, to the End of the Sixth Century A.D., with an Account of Principal sects and Heresies. London, Murray, 1911. 1028 p.
Provides adequate accounts based on original sources. Special attention is given to English, Scottish and Irish Church history. It is an abridged edition of Smith and Wace's Dictionary of Christian Biography, see no. 534, but adds later references.

536 The Westminster Dictionary of the Church History. Ed. by Jerald B. Brauer. Philadelphia, Westminster Press, 1971. 887 p.
Presents accurate introductory definitions and descriptions of the major men, events, facts, and movements in

the history of Christianity. Bibliographies are appended to the longer articles. Pays special attention to the American Church scene.

BIBLIOGRAPHIES AND GUIDES

537 Case, Shirley J., et al., comps. A Bibliographical Guide to the History of Christianity. Chicago, Univ. of Chicago Press, 1951. (University of Chicago Publications in Religious Education. Handbooks of Ethics and Religion). 265 p.

A selective annotated bibliography which covers the Western Hemisphere, Asia, Africa, and the Pacific Islands. Contains numerous cross-references and author and subject indexes.

538 Chadwick, Owen. The History of the Church; A Selective Bibliography. London, Historical Association, 1962 (Helps for Students of History, no. 66). 52 p.

Comprises 700 entries most of them annotated. More comprehensive bibliographic information is often included in annotations. There is no index.

539 "[V.] Christianity." International Bibliography of the History of Religions. Leiden, Brill, 1954- .

See no. 27. Subjects are divided into: Origins; Patristic Literature; Apocrypha; Monasticism; Churches; Theology. The most comprehensive annual bibliography is published in Revue d'histoire ecclesiastique, see no. 778, it has international coverage and classified arrangement with author index.

540 McLean, George F., ed. Philosophy in the 20th Century: Catholic and Christian. New York, Ungar Pub. Co., 1967. 2 vols.

An annotated comprehensive bibliography; vol. 1: An Annotated Bibliography in Catholic thought, 1900-64; vol. 2: A Bibliography of Christian Philosophy and Contemporary Issues. Arranged alphabetically by author within each chapter. An index is provided.

541 Walsh, H. H., rev. by J. Pelikan. "Christianity." Adams, C. J. A Reader's Guide to Great Religions. 2nd ed. New York, Free Press, 1977 (1965), p. 345-406.

See no. 22. Provides an excellent survey of literature in the field.

INDEXES

542 Catholic Periodical Index; A Guide to Catholic Magazines. New York, Wilson, 1930- (quarterly with 2- and 5-year cumulations).

Covers all subjects and indexes about 200 periodicals including some European titles and the Revue de l'Université d'Ottawa.

543 Theological and Religious Index. Harrogate, Theological Abstracting and Bibliographical Services, 1971- .
Aims to index articles in "fringe" journals.

ATLASES

544 Freitag, Anton. The Universe Atlas of the Christian World; The Expansion of Christianity through the Centuries. London, Burns and Oates, 1963. 200 p.
Contains an excellent collection of maps and charts.

545 Jedin, Hubert; K. S. Latourette; and J. Martin, eds. Atlas zur Kirchengeschichte. (Atlas of the History of the Church); in: Geschichte un Gegenwart. Freiburg, Herder, 1970. 152 p.
A collection of maps and charts accompanied by a commentary. Bibliographical references are provided for each section. Detailed index is included.

HANDBOOKS AND SURVEYS

HISTORY

GENERAL WORKS

546 Albright, William F. From Stone Age to Christianity; Monotheism and the Historical Process, 2nd ed. with a new introd. Baltimore, Johns Hopkins Univ. Press, 1957. 432 p.
An excellent scholarly work which surveys the development of man's idea of God and relates it to historical and archaeological evidence. Exhaustive bibliographic references are included in footnotes. Also contains a very detailed index.

547 Anderson, R. T., and P. B. Fischer. An Introduction to Christianity. New York, Harper and Row, 1966. 234 p.
"The purpose of this book is to bring the doctrines of the major Christian faiths to an audience not necessarily familiar with any of them"--Preface. A brief list of books is added. Also contains a useful index.

548 Arberry, A. J., ed. Religions in the Middle East; Three Religions in Concord and Conflict. Cambridge, England, Cambridge Univ. Press, 1969. 2 vols.

Outstanding scholars in the field survey the three Middle Eastern religions: Judaism, Christianity, and Islam, and their relationship with each other in the last hundred years. The articles follow the interaction of ethnic, economic, political, social, and cultural factors as being essential for the understanding of the contemporary religious situation. Contains a well selected bibliography, a glossary, and an index in vol. 2.

549 Bainton, Roland H. *The Horizon History of Christianity*. Ed. by M. B. Davidson. New York, American Heritage Pub. Co., 1964. 432 p.

A very popular presentation of the evolution of the Christian faith and its institutions in two milleniums. It stresses its profound influence on Western civilization. "There is no denominational bias"--Publisher's note.

550 Barth, Karl. *Church Dogmatics*. Edinburgh, Clark, 1963- (in progress, 4 vols. published).

Provides a very scholarly treatment of the subject. Vol. 1 attempts to explain the task, theme, presuppositions, and methods both of theology and dogmatics; vol. 2 deals with the so-called doctrine of god; vol. 3, doctrine of creation; vol. 4 contains a discussion of the doctrine of reconciliation. Each volume includes a name-subject index. Also available in an abridged edition: Barth, Karl. *Church Dogmatics; A Selection*. Transl. and ed. by G. W. Bromiley.

551 Daniel-Rops, Henri. *The History of the Church of Christ.* 1963-68. 10 vols. are listed separately under their individual titles.

An outstanding comprehensive history of the Church, written by the renowned French scholar and writer, which covers the time of the Apostles, the Middle Ages, The Crusades, the Protestant Reformation, the development of republicanism and industrialism, and the ecumenical movement at the present. Each volume contains bibliographic references and an index.

552 ________. *The Church of the Apostles and Martyrs*. Transl. from the French by A. Butler. London, Dent, 1963 (1960) (History of the Church of Christ, v. 1). 623 p.

Translation of *L'Eglise des apôtres et martyrs.*

553 ________. *The Church in the Dark Ages*. Transl. from the French by A. Butler. London, Dent, 1959 (History of the Church of Christ, v. 2). 624 p.

Translation of *L'Eglise des temps barbares.*

554 ________. *Cathedral and Crusade; Studies in the Medieval Church, 1050-1350*. Transl. by J. Warrington. London, Dent; New York, Dutton, 1957 (History of the Church of

Christ, v. 3). 644 p.
Translation of L'Eglise de la cathédrale et de la croisade.

555 _______. The Protestant Reformation. Transl. from the French, by A. Butler. London, Dent; New York, Dutton, 1961 (History of the Church of Christ, v. 4). 560 p.
Translation of vol. 1, Une Revolution religieuse: la reforme protestante, of the work, L'Eglise de la renaissance et de la reforme.

556 _______. The Catholic Reformation. Transl. from the French by J. Warrington. London, Dent; New York, Dutton, 1962 (History of the Church of Christ, v. 5). 435 p.
Translation of vol. 2, Une Ere de renouvenu la reforme catholique, of the work, L'Eglise de la renaissance et de la reforme.

557 _______. The Church in the Seventeenth Century. Transl. by J. J. Buchingham. London, Dent, 1963 (History of the Church of Christ, v. 6). 466 p.
Translation of vol. 1, Le grand siècle des âmes, of the work, L'Eglise des temps classique.

558 _______. The Church in the Eighteenth Century. Transl. from the French by J. Warrington. Garden City, N.Y., Doubleday, 1966 (History of the Church of Christ, v. 7?).
Translation of vol. 2, L'Ere des grands craquements, of the work L'Eglise des temps classique.

559 _______. The Church in an Age of Revolution, 1789-1870. Transl. from the French by J. Warrington. London, Dent; New York, Dutton, 1965 (History of the Church of Christ, v. 8). 509 p.
Translation of vol. 1, En Face des nouveaux destins, of the work L'Eglise des révolutions.

560 _______. The Fight for God, 1870-1939. Transl. from the French by J. Warrington. London, Dent; New York, Dutton, 1966 (History of the Church of Christ, v. 9). 452 p.
Translation of vol. 2, Une combat pour Dieu, of the work L'Eglise des révolutions.

561 _______. Our Brothers in Christ, 1870-1959. New York, Dutton, 1968 (History of the Church of Christ, v. 10).
Translation of vol. 3, Ces Chrétiens nos frêres, of the work L'Eglise des révolutions.

562 Hughes, Philip. A History of the Church, rev. ed. London, Sheed and Ward, 1947- (1924-36). 3 vols.
A well-written comprehensive history which discusses in pt. 1: the Church and the world in which the Church was founded; pt. 2: the Church and world the Church created; pt. 3: the

Church and the revolt against it of the Church created world. Each volume contains bibliographic notes and an index.

563 Jedin, Hubert, and J. Dolan, eds. Handbook of Church History. Transl. from the 3rd rev. ed. New York, Herder, 1965- (in progress). 6 vols. when completed.
Translation of Handbuch der Kirchengeschichte. Presents a clear, well-organized, and well-translated scholarly history of the Church. Contains extensive updated bibliographies, and indexes in each volume.

564 Kerr, Hugh T. Readings in Christian Thought. Nashville, Abingdon Press, 1966. 382 p.
Contains an excellent selection of sources for all who are interested in the history and development of Christian thought from Justin the Martyr to contemporary theologians.

565 Latourrette, Kenneth S. A History of Christianity. London, Eyre and Spottiswoode, 1954. 1516 p.
Presents a scholarly summary of the entire history of Christianity from the time of Christ to the present. Selected chapter bibliographies and an index are provided.

566 Nicholls, William. Systematic and Philosophical Theology. Harmondsworth, England, Penguin, 1969 (Pelican Guide to Modern Theology, v. 1). 363 p.
Provides concise but informative introduction to 20th-century theology. Includes a selective bibliography and an index.

The Pelican History of the Church. 6 vols. Listed separately under their individual authors. See no. 578, 586, 597, 605, 610, 638.

567 Schaff, Philip. History of the Christian Church. Grand Rapids, Mich., Eerdmans, 1950-67 (1907-10). 8 vols.
This scholarly work presents a comprehensive history of the Church from the Apostolic Christianity to the end of the Reformation.

568 Tillich, Paul. Systematic Theology. Chicago, Univ. of Chicago Press, 1951-63. 3 vols.
"My purpose ... has been to present a method and a structure of a theological system written from the apologetic point of view and carried through in a continuous correlation with philosophy"--Preface. Each volume contains an index; numerous bibliographic references are included in footnotes. One should also read the critical study of this book--McKelway, A. J., The Systematic Theology of Paul Tillich.

569 Toynbee, Arnold. Christianity Among the Religions of the World. London, Oxford Univ. Press, 1958. 116 p.

A very brief and clear discussion of the essential values of Christianity and other religions.

570 Walker, Williston. A History of the Christian Church, rev. ed. New York, Scribner's, 1959 (1918). 585 p.
A new revision of this excellent classic textbook. Presents a concise history with valuable discussions of major theological issues. Selected bibliographic references are provided.

571 Welford, A. T. Christianity: A Psychologist's Translation. London, Hodder and Stoughton, 1971 (Knowing Christianity). 191 p.
A popular but solid presentation of Christianity in the light of modern experimental psychology. Extensive bibliographic references and an index are provided.

572 World Christian Handbook. London, 1949, 1952, 1957, 1968.
Each issue consists of survey articles on latest developments; statistical section including Catholic, Protestant and Jewish statistics; various directories. There is a general index.

EARLY CHURCH

573 Ayer, J. C., ed. The Source Book for Ancient Church History, from the Apostolic Period to the Close of the Concilliar Period. New York, Scribner's, 1930 (1913). 707 p.
A collection of standard sources for early Church history to A.D. 787 arranged by subject. Each selection is accompanied by a brief annotation on the authority of its sources.

574 Bainton, Roland H. Early Christianity. Princeton, N.J., Van Nostrand, 1960 (Anvil Original, 49). 192 p.
This popular book examines the first phase of Christian history. It combines narrative with source materials. Bibliography for further reading and an index are provided.

575 Bettenson, Henry S. The Early Christian Fathers. Oxford, Oxford Univ. Press, 1956. 424 p.

________. The Later Christian Fathers; The Selection from the Writings of the Fathers from St. Cyril of Jerusalem to St. Leo the Great. London, Oxford Univ. Press, 1970. 294 p.
In these two volumes the editor provides a small selection of some of the most important texts from the Patristic period. Constitutes an excellent introductory manual to the source material.

576 Bultmann, Rudolf K. Primitive Christianity in Its Primitive Contemporary Setting. Transl. by R. H. Fuller. London, Thames and Hudson, 1956. 240 p.

Translation of Das Urchristentum in Rahmen der antiken Religionen. The purpose of this scholarly work is to provide a new interpretation of the existing materials. Chapter bibliographies and subject and name indexes are included.

577 Cayré, F. Manual of Patrology and History of Theology. Transl. by H. Howitt. Paris, 1935-40. 2 vols.

Translation of vols. 1 and 2 of Patrologie et histoire de la théologie. Contains a thorough discussion of the Fathers, their lives, writings and doctrines associated with them; history of dogmas and positive theology; history and principles of spirituality. Selected bibliography in vol. 1, an index of authors studied or mentioned, and a doctrinal index are provided.

578 Chadwick, Henry. Early Church. Harmondsworth, England, Penguin, 1967 (Pelican History of the Church, v. 1). 304 p.

An excellent introductory history of the early Christian Church from the death of Christ to the papacy of Gregory the Great. "Makes use of the latest historical research to relate the story of emergent Christianity to the social and ideological context within which the young religion made its way"--Cover.

579 Fathers of the Church; A New Translation. Washington, D.C., Catholic Univ. of America Press, 1947- (in progress) 100 vols. when completed.

Newest Catholic presentation of the most complete critical translations of the Fathers.

580 Quasten, Johannes. Patrology. Utrecht, Spectrum, 1950-61. 3 vols.

An excellent work of detailed scholarship. Provides a general bibliographical introduction and essays on the history and background of the period and bio-bibliographical essays on each of the Fathers.

581 Wand, John W. C. A History of the Early Church to A.D. 500, 4th ed. London, Methuen, 1953 (1937). 290 p.

"The primary purpose of this brief popular history is to present the rise of Christianity as a society"--Preface. Contains a bibliography and an index.

MEDIEVAL CHURCH

582 Bainton, Roland H. The Mediaeval Church. Princeton, N.J., Van Nostrand, 1962 (Anvil original, 64). 191 p.

This popular presentation discusses the role of the Christian church in the formation of Western civilization. Each discussion is supported by citations from original sources newly translated by the author. Also contains a selected bibliography and an index.

583 Baldwin, Marshall W. The Mediaeval Church. Ithaca, N.Y., Cornell Univ. Press, 1953. (Development of Western Civilization; Narrative Essays in the History of Our Tradition from the Time of the Ancient Greeks and Hebrews to the Present). 124 p.

Presents the subject not only as a political organization in a struggle for power, but also as an all pervasive picture of medieval life. Selective bibliography and an index are included.

584 Deanesly, Margaret. A History of the Medieval Church, 590-1500. London, Methuen, 1971 (1954) (University Paperback). 283 p.

A popular brief history which gives some ideas of the medieval attitude toward life, religion, and the church, and of actual working of the church system. Contains a short bibliography and an index.

585 Russell, Jeffrey B. The History of Medieval Christianity: Prophesy and Order; An Investigation of Church History from Early Fourth Century to the Later Middle Ages. New York, Crowell, 1968. 216 p.

This book may serve as an excellent introduction to the history of the medieval church. It emphasizes its fundamental conflicts: the spirit of order and spirit of prophesy. Contains a list of significant popes and a selected chapter bibliographies. There is also an index.

586 Southern, R. W. Western Society and the Church in the Middle Ages. Harmondsworth, England, Penguin Books, 1970. (Pelican History of the Church, v. 2.) 376 p.

Presents an excellent popular introduction to the study of the social mechanisms of religious change in the medieval society. Covers the period from the 8th to the 16th century. Bibliographical references are included in footnotes. Also contains an index.

CRUSADES

587 Atiya, Aziz S. The Crusade: Historiography and Bibliography. Bloomington, Indiana Univ. Press, 1962. 170 p.

A very valuable survey bringing together all materials available in French, German, Italian, Spanish, Latin, Greek, Arabic, Turkish, and Slavonic languages. Stress is laid on the Oriental sources.

588 Mayer, Hans E. The Crusades. Transl. from the German by J. Gillingham. London, Oxford Univ. Press, 1972. 339 p.

Presents a brief survey of the crusades based on the findings of modern historical scholarship. Includes a well-selected bibliography and an index.

589 Runciman, Steven. A History of Crusades. Cambridge, England, Cambridge Univ. Press, 1953-4. 3 vols.

The most comprehensive survey. Covers the history of the movement from its beginning in the 11th century to its decline in the 14th century. Vol. 1: The First Crusade and the foundation of the Kingdom of Jerusalem; Vol. 2: The Kingdom of Jerusalem and the Frankish East; Vol. 3: The Kingdom of Acre and the later crusades. Each volume contains a selective classified bibliography and an index.

590 Setton, Kenneth M., ed. A History of Crusades, 2nd ed. Madison, Univ. of Wisconsin Press, 1969- [1955-].

A very comprehensive survey, being edited by a group of specialists in the field. Vol. 1 covers the first hundred years of the crusades; Vol. 2 reaches the beginning of the 14th century; Vol. 3 will be devoted chiefly to the 14th and 15th century; Vol. 5 will summarize the consequences, and also will provide genealogies and exhaustive bibliographies of sources and critical works.

REFORMATION AND COUNTER-REFORMATION

(BIBLIOGRAPHY)

591 Bainton, Roland H. Bibliography of the Continental Reformation; Materials Available in English, 2nd rev. and enl. ed. Hamden, Conn., Shoe String Press, 1972 (1935) (Archon Book).

Contains a bibliographic survey of English language publications on the Reformation.

592 Grimm, Harold J. The Reformation in Recent Historical Thought. New York, Macmillan, c1964 (American Historical Assoc. Service Center for Teachers of History, No. 54). 28 p.

Presents a brief but informative bibliographic survey of selected, important topics in the study of the Reformation.

593 International Committee of Historical Sciences. Commission International d'Histoire Ecclesiastique Comparée. Bibliographie de la Réforme, 1450-1648; ouvrages parus de 1940 à 1955. Leiden, Brill, 1958- .

This irregularly published bibliography lists monographs, dissertations, and periodical articles arranged by country indicated. An index of authors is provided.

(HANDBOOKS AND SURVEYS)

594 Bainton, Roland H. The Age of Reformation. Princeton, N.J., Van Nostrand, 1956 (1952) (Anvil Original, No. 13). 192 p.
Contains the most readily available collection of sources. Also includes a brief selective bibliography and an index.

595 _______. "Interpretations of the Reformation." American Historical Review, v. 66 (1960), p. 74-8.
Provides a scholarly review of various trends in the historiography of the Reformation. One should also read the author's collection of essays on the two major topics, Radical Reformation, and Luther: Studies on the Reformation.

596 _______. The Reformation of the Sixteenth Century. Boston, Beacon Press, 1963 (1952). 276 p.
One of the best interpretative histories of the Reformation, provided with an excellent selective bibliography listing monographs, encyclopedic articles, and papers published in journals. An index is included.

597 Chadwick, Owen. The Reformation. Baltimore, Penguin Books, 1964 (Pelican History of the Church, v. 3). 463 p.
This history of the Reformation treated in the popular manner deals with formative works of Erasmus, Luther, Zwingli, and Calvin, and includes also a discussion of special circumstances of the English Reformation, and the Counter-Reformation. Select bibliography and an index are provided.

598 Dolan, John P. History of the Reformation; A Conciliatory Assessment of Opposite Views. New York, Desclee, 1965 (American Library. Mentor Books). 417 p.
A very important book which introduces the reader to the current scholarly debate and evaluates the Catholic, Protestant and scholarly research. Contains an index but no bibliography.

599 Grimm, Harold J. The Reformation Era, 2nd ed. New York, Macmillan, 1973. 675 p.
Presents "the story of the rise of Protestantism and the Catholic reforms in their complete setting"--Preface. The last edition contains the fullest and most usefully detailed bibliography written in a form of essay. There is also a well-organized index.

600 Hillerbrand, Hans J. Christendom Divided; The Protestant Reformation. Philadelphia, Westminster Press; London, Hutchinson, 1971 (Theological Resources). 344 p.
A good scholarly work which presents basic disagreements on doctrines and life styles in the historical and

cultural context. Contains an excellent classified selected bibliography and an index.

601 Hughes, Philip. The Reformation in England, 5th ed. London, Hollis and Carter, 1952-4. 3 vols.
The best historical survey of the Reformation in England. Each volume contains a list of bibliographic sources and a detailed index.

602 The Social History of the Reformation. Ed. by L. P. Buck and J. W. Zophy. Columbus, Ohio State Univ. Press, 1972. 397 p.
Contains a collection of articles, written by outstanding scholars in the field, which "reflects a wide range of approaches to the social history of the Reformation"--Preface. Numerous bibliographic references are included in the notes. There is also an index.

603 Todd, John M. Reformation. Garden City, N.Y., Doubleday, 1971. 377 p.
The first chapter provides a detailed definition of the Reformation. The subject is then subdivided into three headings: 1) the place of the Bible and the history of Christianity in the centuries preceding the Reformation; 2) the revolution throughout Europe; 3) the outcome today. At the end, one finds bibliographic commentary on each chapter. Also contains a detailed index of subjects and names.

604 Williams, George H. The Radical Reformation. Philadelphia, Westminster Press, 1962. 924 p.
This scholarly work is a basic source of information about the radical movements in the Reformation, e.g. Anabaptists. Bibliographical footnotes and a good index are included.

MODERN CHURCH SINCE THE REFORMATION

605 Cragg, Gerald R. The Church and the Age of Reason, 1648-1789. Harmondsworth, England, Penguin Books; New York, Atheneum, 1966 (1960) (Pelican History of the Church, v. 4). 299 p.
A popular book which provides a background and an analysis of religious developments in the period. A well selected bibliography and an index are included.

606 Hardon, John A. Christianity in the Twentieth Century. Garden City, N.Y., Doubleday, 1971. 527 p.
A scholarly concise history of Christian thought and practice as it has been developing in the 20th century. Contains chapter bibliographies and an index.

607 Latourette, Kenneth S. Christianity in a Revolutionary Age; A History of Christianity in the Nineteenth and Twentieth Centuries. New York, Harper, 1958-62. 5 vols.
A comprehensive scholarly history of Christian Churches in the last two centuries with a select bibliography and an index.

608 Neill, Stephen C. Twentieth Century Christianity; A Survey of Modern Religious Trends by Leading Churchmen. London, Collins, 1961. 448 p.
Contains a collection of nine papers concerning the most important issues of the contemporary Christianity. There is a bibliography and an index.

609 Shinn, Roger L. Man; The New Humanism. Philadelphia, Westminster Press, 1968. 207 p.
Surveys the effects of recent development in the social sciences on Christianity. Bibliography and an index are provided.

610 Vidler, Alexander R. The Church in an Age of Revolution: 1789 to the Present Day. Harmondsworth, England, Penguin Books, 1961 (Pelican History of the Church, v. 5). 287 p.
A popular book which deals with developments in the Church after the French Revolution. Includes a select bibliography and an index.

611 Wand, John W. C. A History of the Modern Church from 1500 to the Present Day, 7th ed. rev. London, Methuen, 1955 (1930). 323 p.
This revised reprint of a classic history traces the rise of new attitudes toward the Christian life, the various conceptions of the faith and many ecclesiastical systems. Contains a select bibliography, a list of principal events: 1509-1921, and an index.

CREEDS AND DOCTRINES

612 Gerrish, Brian A., ed. The Faith of Christendom; A Sourcebook of Creeds and Confessions. Cleveland, World Pub. Co., 1963 (Living Age Book, LA 40; Meridian Book). 371 p.
Includes basic official statements of faith, with historical and explanatory comments. Covers the period from early Christianity through the Reformation up to the present. Some bibliographic references are provided.

613 Leith, John H., ed. Creeds of the Churches; A Reader in Christian Doctrine from the Bible to the Present. Chicago, Aldine Press, 1963. 589 p.
Presents the more important sources of the major

theological affirmations from the ancient faith of the Hebrews to the creed of Batak of 1951.

614 Schaff, Philip. Creeds of Christendom, 6th rev. ed. and enl. New York, Harper, 1877; Grand Rapids, Mich., Eerdmans, 1966 (Bibliotheca symbolica ecclesiae universalis). 3 vols.

Contains the most comprehensive collection of original texts with English translations. Comments and extensive references are provided.

ECUMENICAL MOVEMENT

615 Crow, Paul A. The Ecumenical Movement in Bibliographical Outline. New York, National Council of the Churches of Christ in the U.S.A., 1965. 79 p.

A comprehensive bibliography which primarily concentrates on literature published in English but which includes a selection of the more important French and German works. Periodical articles and theses are excluded. Supplements will be issued to update basic material.

616 Dollen, Charles, ed. Vatican II; A Bibliography. Metuchen, N.J., Scarecrow, 1969. 208 p.

Introduces both the student and the scholar to some 2500 entries, covering the decade 1959-1968, mainly materials available in English. Subject index is provided.

617 Hughes, Philip. The Church in Crisis; A History of General Councils, 325-1870. Garden City, N.Y., Hannover House; London, Burns and Oates, 1961. 342 p.

An authoritatively informative survey which reviews the background and achievements of 20 General Councils over 1500 years. Bibliographic appendix supplements the footnotes. Also contains an index.

618 Internationale ökumenische Bibliographie. International Ecumenical Bibliography. Bibliographie oecumenique internationale. Mainz, Matthias-Grunewald, 1962- .

An exhaustive current bibliography published annually. The content is divided into Churches and Theological questions. Indexes are provided.

619 Jedin, Hubert. Ecumenical Councils of the Catholic Church; An Historical Outline. Transl. by E. Graf. Freiburg, Herder, 1960. 253 p.

Translation of Kleine Konziliengeschichte. Contains a brief history of 20 ecumenical councils. Fullest treatment is given to Trent and Vatican I. A critical bibliography of history and sources is included.

620 Margull, Hans J., ed. The Councils of the Church; History

and Analysis. Philadelphia, Fortress Press, 1966. 528 p.
Translation of Die ökumenischen Konzile der Christenheit. Surveys the history of ecumenical councils and the most representative teachings about them. Index and bibliographic references are included.

621 Rouse, R., and S. C. Neill, eds. A History of the Ecumenical Movement, 2nd ed. with rev. bibliography. Philadelphis, Westminster, 1967-1970 (1954). 2 v.
Provides a survey of events of the movement striving for the unity of the Christian Church. A select bibliography, a glossary and explanatory notes, and an index are added.

622 Simonsen, C. The Christology of the Faith and Order Movement. Leiden, Brill, 1972 (Oekumenische Studien, 10). 189 p.
Provides "an examination of the career of Christology in Faith and Order Movement; and later, Commission"--Preface. A select bibliography and an index of names are included.

HERETICS

623 Nigg, Walter. The Heretics; A Comprehensive History of Heresy and of the Great Heretics. Ed. and transl. by Richard and Clara Winston. New York, Knopf, 1962. 411 p.
This scholarly book is an abridged translation of Das Buch der Ketzer. Contains bibliographic references in footnotes and an index.

624 Wakefield, W., and A. P. Evans, eds. Heresies of the Middle Ages. Selected sources transl. and annot. New York, Columbia Univ. Press, 1965. 865 p.
Comprises a collection of sources for the study of medieval heresies in English translation. Contains a valuable bibliography of works which have been referred to, and an index.

625 Wand, John W. C. The Four Great Heresies. London, Mowbray, 1955 (Lent Lectures, 1954). 139 p.
Presents a clear outline of the ideas behind the four great heresies: Arian, Apollinarian, Nestorian, and Eutychian. Neither bibliography nor index is provided.

LITURGY

626 Bumpus, John S. A Dictionary of Ecclesiastical Terms, Being a History and Explanation of Certain Terms Used in

Architecture, Ecclesiology, Liturgiology, Music, Ritual, Cathedral Constitution, etc. London, Werner Laurie, 1910; Detroit, Gale, 1969. 328 p.

Provides substantial definitions including bibliographic references in the text. When it is necessary, equivalent terms in foreign languages are given. Each entry consists of an etymological explanation and a brief history of the development of and changes in the particular word, name or phrase. The emphasis is on the Church of England.

627 Davies, J. G. A Dictionary of Liturgy and Worship. New York, Macmillan, 1972. 385 p.

Covers all major Christian denominations. To each sect or rite there is assigned an extended article describing the basic worship, liturgical books, rituals, prayers, etc. Although there are cross-references, it is not always simple to trace a subject to its hiding-place, e.g. penance is hidden under "absolution."

628 ________. A Select Liturgical Lexicon. London, Lutterworth Press, 1965. 146 p.

Provides simple explanations of terms used in liturgy. Bibliographic references are given for main entries.

629 Klauser, Theodore. A Brief History of the Liturgy. Minnesota, Liturgical Press, 1953. 32 p.

A remarkable, brief summary.

630 ________. A Short History of the Western Liturgy; An Account and Some Reflections. Transl. by J. Halliburton. London, Oxford Univ. Press, 1969. 236 p.

Provides an excellent scholarly survey of liturgy and ritual in the Christian Church. Includes a selective bibliography and an index.

631 Podhradsky, Gerhard. New Dictionary of the Liturgy, English edition ed. by L. Sheppard. London, Chapman, 1967 (1962). 208 p.

Translation of Lexikon der Liturgie. 'Deals with almost every liturgical topic likely to arise"--Foreword. Contains a valuable classified bibliography.

632 Thompson, Bard. Liturgies of the Western Church. Cleveland, Meridian Books, 1961 (Living Age Books, LA 35). 434 p.

"This book makes available ... the principal liturgies of Western Christianity.... Each text is supplied with an introduction that is meant to elucidate both the liturgy and the tradition in which it stands.... Bibliographies are appended to each chapter"--Introd. There is also an index.

MIRACLES

633 Brewers, E. C. A Dictionary of Miracles: Imitative, Realistic, and Dogmatic. Philadelphia, 1884; reprint: Detroit, Gale, 1966. 582 p.
In this unique work an attempt is made to collect impartial information on the subject. References to sources are included.

634 Lewis, Clive S. Miracles; A Preliminary Study. New York, Macmillan, 1968 (1947) (Macmillan Paperbacks). 192 p.
A popular study of Christian miracles. Contains an index but no bibliographic references.

MISSIONS

635 Latourette, Kenneth S. A History of the Expansion of Christianity. New York, Harper, 1937-45. 7 vols.
The most notable scholarly study of Christian missions from the earliest times up to the present. Covers Roman Catholic, Protestant, and Orthodox Churches. Each volume contains well selected chapter bibliographies and full indexes.

636 Mission Handbook: North American Protestant Ministers Overseas, prep. and ed. for the Missionary Research Library by Missions Advanced Research Communication Center, E. R. Dayton, ed. 10th ed. Monrovia, Calif., MARC, 1973. 645 p.
Provides the latest survey of North American world mission agencies and their activities. It contains listings of boards, societies, institutions, their statistical reports. A selective bibliography of monographs and periodicals is included, p. 643.

637 Neill, Stephen C. Christian Missions. Baltimore, Penguin Books, 1964 (Pelican History of the Church, v. 6). 622 p.
Provides a popular treatment of the subject with a well selected bibliography for further reading and an index.

638 ________. Colonialism and Christian Missions. New York, McGraw-Hill; London, Lutterworth, 1966. 445 p.
A well-balanced comprehensive account of a history of the relationship between the missionaries and contemporary political and economic interests. Represents a Protestant viewpoint. Contains a good selective bibliography and an index.

639 ________; G. H. Anderson; and J. Goodwin, eds. Concise Dictionary of the Christian World Missions. Nashville, Abingdon Press, 1971. 682 p.
Comprises names, places, and events of Christian

missionary history arranged alphabetically with numerous cross-references. Covers missionary activity from 1500 to the present. Each article is supplied with a brief bibliography.

MONASTICISM AND RELIGIOUS ORDERS

BIBLIOGRAPHY

640 Constable, Giles. Medieval Monasticism: A Select Bibliography. Toronto, Univ. of Toronto Press, 1976 (Toronto Medieval Bibliographies, 6). 171 p.
Provides a classified list of critical writings on Christian monasticism from its origins to the end of the Middle Ages in French, German, Italian, Latin, and Spanish. Index.

CRITICAL STUDIES

641 Canu, Jean. Religious Orders of Men. Transl. from the French by P. J. Hepburne-Scott. New York, Hawthorn Books, 1960 (Twentieth Century Encyclopedia of Catholicism, 85. Section 8: The Organization of the Church). London, Burns and Oates, 1960 (Faith and Fact Books, 84).
A brief popular account of monasticism. Contains a selected bibliography but no index.

642 Décarreux, Jean. Monks and Civilization; From the Barbarian Invasions to the Reign of Charlemagne. Transl. by C. Haldane. London, Allen and Unwin, 1964 (1962). 397 p.
Provides "an account of monastic institution in relation to Western civilization..."--Preface. Contains a well-selected bibliography and a full general index.

643 Montalambert, Charles Forbes René de Tryon. The Monks of the West, from St. Benedict to St. Bernard. Authorized translation.... Edinburgh, Blackwood, 1861-1879. 7 vols.
Translation of Les Moines d'Occident. An enthusiastic study and interpretation of religious orders. Extensive footnotes include numerous citations of sources. There is no index but the chronological order in the contents tables is of great help.

644 Nigg, Walter. Warriors of God; The Great Religious Orders and Their Founders. New York, Knopf, 1959. 353 p.
Translation of Vom Geheimnis der Mönche. Presents substantial individual studies of religious orders and those who founded them. Contains numerous citations from original documents. Also includes an index.

MYSTICISM

645 Graef, Hilda. The Story of Mysticism. London, Davies, 1966. 296 p.

"The book is meant to provide an introduction in a moderate size volume..."--Preface. The survey begins with a brief outline of non-Christian mysticism and continues with mysticism in the New Testament, the Age of the Martyrs, the Middle Ages, and the Reformation, and closes with modern times. A bibliography and an index are provided. See also pt. 1 in item no. 153.

MYTH AND SYMBOLISM

646 James, Edwin O. Christian Myth and Ritual; A Historical Study. Cleveland, Meridian Books, 1965 (Living Age Books, LA43). 345 p.

A popular book which reviews Christian myths and explains various rituals. Contains a useful select bibliography and an index.

647 Watts, Alan W. Myth and Ritual in Christianity. London, Thames and Hudson, 1954 (Myth and Man). 262 p.

A very well-written presentation which shows how the patterns of Christian ritual have evolved, and which analyzes the meaning of Christian symbols. One could, however, question its firmly stated assumption that there is a divergence between Christian and Hindu thought. Contains a glossary of terms and an index.

648 Webber, F. R. Church Symbolism; An Explanation of the More Important Symbols of the Old and New Testament, the Primitive, the Mediaeval, and the Modern Church, 2nd ed. rev. Cleveland, Jansen, 1938. 413 p.

Explains a wide variety of symbols, those commonly used both in Catholic and non-Catholic churches, as well as a number of Jewish symbols. A glossary of the more well known symbols is appended. Also contains a bibliography and an index.

PAPACY AND POPES

649 Carlen, Mary C., comp. Dictionary of Papal Pronouncements, Leo XIII to Pius XII (1878-1957). New York, Kennedy, 1958. 216 p.

Comprises all encyclical and other selected documents. The index contains in one alphabet all subjects and personal or corporate names. Also lists collections of papal documents. One should check the author's Guide to the Encyclicals of the Roman Pontiffs.

650 Gontard, Friedrich. The Popes. Transl. from the German by A. J. Peeler and E. F. Peeler. London, Barrie and Rockliff, 1964. (1959). 629 p.

Translation of Die Päpste. Provides an excellent interpretative history of the papacy. Contains a list of the popes and an index.

651 John, Eric, ed. The Popes; A Concise Biographical History. London, Burns and Oates, 1964. 496 p.

This historical survey of the popes is subdivided into seven parts. Each part contains an introductory essay and chronologically arranged biographies of popes. Contains an excellent bibliography and a general index.

652 Kühner, Hans. Encyclopedia of the Papacy. London, Owen, 1959. 248 p.

Translation of Lexikon der Päpste. Presents a chronological list of the popes from Peter to Pius XII. There is also an alphabetical list of the popes, the anti-popes, and the Ecumenical Councils, indicating the popes personally connected with each. A select bibliography and a general index are included.

653 Pastor, Ludwig. History of the Popes from the Close of the Middle Ages, 1305-1799; Drawn from the Secret Archives of the Vatican and Other Original Sources. London, Hodges, 1891-1953; Routledge and Paul, 1938-61. 40 vols.

This is the first history of the papacy based on original sources which were previously closed to scholars. Begins with the popes at Avignon, and concludes with the biography of Pius VI. Lengthy bibliographic references appear throughout the work, along with a general index in each volume.

SAINTS

654 Attwater, Donald. The Penguin Dictionary of Saints. Baltimore, Penguin, 1966 (1965) (Penguin Reference Books, R30). 362 p.

"This book is a work of quick reference to the lives and legends of the more important and interesting people among the saints.... Special attention has been paid to the saints of Great Britain and Ireland..."--Introd. Contains a short general bibliography and a glossary of special terms used in the text. Also lists some emblems and feast days.

655 The Book of Saints; A Dictionary of Servants of God Canonized by the Catholic Church, Extracted from the Roman and Other Martyrologies, 5th ed. rev. and enl. Comp. by the Monks of St. Augustin's Abbey, Ramsgate. New York, Macmillan, 1966. 740 p.

Contains brief and accurate biographical data about 2200

saints. Sources of information are documented.

656 Butler, Alan. Lives of the Saints. Ed., rev. and suppl. by H. Thurson and D. Attwater. New York, Kennedy, 1956. 4 vols.

This is an abridgment of the 18th-century masterpiece. It provides a short account of the saints in the calendar arrangement, with some critical commentary and bibliographical references. Individual indexes in each volume and a general index in vol. 4 are provided.

657 Holweck, F. G. A Biographical Dictionary of the Saints, with a General Introduction on Hagiology. St. Louis, Herder, 1924; reprint: Detroit, Gale, 1969.

Contains short articles on major saints arranged alphabetically. References to sources are included.

VESTMENTS AND ECCLESIASTICAL DRESS

658 Norris, Herbert. Church Vestments; Their Origin and Development. London, Dent, 1949. 190 p.

Presents the history of ecclesiastical dress up to the 15th century. Contains bibliography and an index.

CHRISTIAN CHURCHES AND SECTS

GENERAL

659 Corpus Dictionary of the Western Churches. Ed. by T. C. O'Brien. Washington, D.C., Corpus Publications, 1970 (Corpus Reference Work). 820 p.

While providing information on all the Churches that have developed throughout the history of Christianity, special attention is given to North American Churches in the Western tradition. Includes persons, explanation of terms, and a selected number of documents. Contains some 2200 entries with numerous cross-references. Bibliographic references are supplied.

660 Lehrburger, Egon. Strange Sects and Cults; A Study of Their Origins and Influence, by Egon Larsen. New York, Hart, 1972 (1971). 245 p.

A popular survey "of human folly and ferocity, extravaganza and gullibility..."--Introd. Deals only with the strangest sects from Western Europe, Far East, America, and Africa. There is a bibliography and an index.

661 Molland, Einer. Christendom: The Christian Churches, Their Doctrines, Constitutional Form, and Ways of

Worship. London, Mowbray, 1961 (1959). 418 p.
Translation of Konfesjonskunnskap. A survey of present churches including historical background, constitutions and ways of worship. Contains a well-selected bibliography and names and subject indexes with references to (1) Orthodox Church; (2) Other Oriental Churches; (3) Roman Catholic Church; (4) Old Catholics; (5) Catholic Apostolic Congregation (Iwingites); (6) Church of England and the Anglican Communion; (7) Church of South India; (8) Lutheran Church; (9) Moravians; (10) Reformed Church; (10a) Waldensian Church; (11) Methodist Church; (12) Congregationalist Churches; (13) Baptist Churches; (14) Disciples of Christ; (15) Pentacostalists; (16) Salvation Army; (17) Plymouth Brethren (Darbyites); (18) New Church, Church of New Jerusalem (Swedenborgians); (19) Adventists; (20) Society of Friends (Quakers); (21) Unitarianism; (22) Christian Science; (23) Jehovah's Witnesses; (24) Mormonism.

662 Niesel, Wilhelm. The Gospel of the Churches; A Comparison of Catholicism, Orthodoxy, and Protestantism. Transl. by D. Lewis. Philadelphia, Westminster Press, 1962 (1960). 384 p.
Translation of Das Evangelium und die Kirchen. "Attempts to give a brief and clear outline of problems involved, and to allow the sources to speak for themselves" --Foreword. There is a useful bibliography including references to: (1) Roman Catholic Church; (2) Eastern Orthodox Churches; (3) Lutheran Church; (4) Reformed and Presbyterian churches; (5) Anglican Church; (6) Congregationalism; (7) Baptists; (8) Methodism; (9) Society of Friends (Quakers).

663 Wilson, Bryan R. Religious Sects: A Sociological Study. London, Weidenfeld and Nicolson, 1970 (World University Library). 256 p.
In this study, sects are presented as movements of religious protest. The selected bibliography indicates important sociological works and some of the more important historical studies about movements discussed in the texts.

EASTERN ORTHODOX CHURCH

Dictionary

664 Demetrakopoulos, George H. Dictionary of Orthodox Theology; A Summary of the Beliefs, Practices, and History of Eastern Orthodox Church. New York, Philosophical Library, 1964. 187 p.
Provides concise explanations of the terms. No bibliographic references are provided.

Handbooks and Surveys

665 Attiya, Aziz S. A History of Eastern Christianity. London, Methuen, 1968 (1967). 486 p.

Outlines the history and the essentials of the Coptic, the Jacobite, the Nestorian, the Armenian, the St. Thomas Christians of South India, the Maronite; and the vanished churches of Carthage, Pentapolis, and Nubia. Includes a usefully selected bibliography and a full index.

666 Attwater, Donald. The Christian Churches of the East, rev. ed. Leominster, 1961 (1935). 2 vols.

Vol. 1 covers churches in accord with Rome; vol. 2 deals with those which do not recognize Rome's authority. Each volume contains a table of distribution of churches, a glossary of terms explained in the text, and a bibliography comprising reference books, monographs, and a list of periodicals. An index is also provided.

667 Benz, Ernst. The Eastern Orthodox Church; Its Thought and Life. Transl. by Richard and Clara Winston. Chicago, Aldine Pub. Co., 1963. 230 p.

Translation of Geist und Leben des Ostkirche. Includes a brief but authoritative study of the history, icons, liturgy and sacraments, constitution and law. Select bibliographies by chapter are supplied but no index.

668 King, Archdale A. Rites of Eastern Christendom. Rome, Catholic Book Agency, 1947-8; New York, AMS Press, 1972. 2 vols.

"The aim of this book ... is to provide a manual for those who wish to know something about the rites of Eastern Christianity"--Preface. Vol. 1 includes Syrian, Maronite, Syro-Malankara, Coptic, and Ethiopic rites, vol. 2--Byzantine with variant, Chaldean, Syro-Malabar, and Armenian rites. Each volume has a select bibliography and a general index.

669 Meyendorff, Jean. The Orthodox Church, Its Past and Its Role in the World Today. Transl. from the French by John Chapin. New York, Pantheon Books, 1962. 244 p.

Attempts to outline the historical development of the Orthodox Church from the apostolic times to the present. The basic dogmatic positions are explained, then certain doctrinal questions are discussed from the contemporary point of view. A select bibliography and an index are provided.

670 Pelican, Jaroslav. The Spirit of Eastern Christendom, 600-1700. Chicago, Univ. of Chicago Press, 1974. 329 p.

Surveys the development of doctrine from the time of christological controversies of the 7th century to the era of the symbolic confessions of faith in the orthodox East in the 17th century.

671 Ware, Kallistos. The Orthodox Church. Baltimore, Penguin, 1963 (Pelican Original A 592). 352 p.
Pt. 1 describes the history of Eastern Orthodoxy over the last 2000 years, and particularly its problems in 20th-century Soviet Union. Pt. 2 explains the principles of belief and worship of Orthodoxy today. Some ecumenical questions are discussed. Short bibliography and an index are included.

672 Zernov, Nicolas. Eastern Christendom; A Study of the Origin and Development of the Eastern Orthodox Church. New York, Putnam, 1961 (Putnam History of Religion). 326 p.
Contains extremely well-selected materials on the oldest, very important, branch of Christianity. Deals with its history, teaching, worship, and art. Chapter Bibliographies and an index included.

ROMAN CATHOLIC CHURCH

Dictionaries

673 Attwater, Donald. A Catholic Dictionary. New York, Macmillan, 1941. 576 p.
"General work of quick reference to the signification of words, terms, names and phrases in common use in the philosophy, dogmatic and moral theology, canon law, liturgy, institutions and organization of the Catholic Church."--Preface.

674 Gillow, Joseph. A Literary and Biographical History or Bibliographical Dictionary of the English Catholics from 1534 to the Present. London, 1885-1902; New York, Burt Franklin, 1962. 5 vols.
Includes martyrs, clergymen, artists, and other outstanding English Catholics with bibliographical references for each, entry and full annotated lists of works by author.

675 The Maryknoll Catholic Dictionary. Comp. and ed. by Albert J. Nevins. New York, Grosset and Dunlap, 1965. 710 p.
Provides useful and up-to-date information on all aspects of the Catholic Church. Incorporates the changes in liturgy, church discipline and organization that were introduced since Vatican II. Also contains a list of patron saints of occupations and professions and their feast days, international Catholic organizations, the popes, and biographies of deceased American and Canadian Catholics. The end papers contain statistical information on world religions, and a diagram of the principal Protestant sects of the West.

Guides

676 McCabe, James P. Critical Guide to Catholic Reference Books. Littleton, Colo., Libraries Unlimited, 1971. 287 p.
Includes more than 900 annotated titles in English and foreign languages dealing with various topics pertinent to the Catholic Church, and issues in the social sciences, literature, and the arts.

Handbooks and Surveys

677 Bullough, Sebastian. Roman Catholicism. Harmondsworth, England, Penguin Books, 1965 (1963). 332 p.
Presents a popular outline of the faith and practices of the Roman Catholic Church. Also provides a selected list of 80 books including more detailed information and an author-subject index.

678 The Christian Centuries; A New History of the Catholic Church. Ed. by Jean Daniélou and Henri Marrou. Transl. by V. Cronin. London, Darton, Longman, Todd, 1964- (in progress). 5 vols. when completed.
A well-balanced, scholarly account of the history of the Roman Catholic Church which covers both the Eastern and Western churches. Contains excellent chapter-by-chapter bibliographies with brief annotations, and two indexes: persons and places, and subjects.

679 Hales, Edward E. Y. The Catholic Church in the Modern World; A Survey from the French Revolution to the Present. Garden City, N.Y., Hanover House, 1958. 312 p.
Presents a critical interpretation of the history of the Catholic Church in the last two centuries. There is a select bibliography and an index.

680 Hughes, Philip. A Popular History of the Catholic Church. New York, Macmillan, 1957 (1947). 294 p.
An excellent introductory reading which encompasses the Church history from the apostolic times to 1946. Selective bibliography, chronological tables and a general index are provided.

681 Loewenich, Walther von. Modern Catholicism. Transl. by R. H. Fuller. New York, St. Martin's Press, 1959. 378 p.
Provides a critical examination of current developments in Catholicism. A select bibliography and an index are included.

682 Neill, Thomas P., and R. H. Schmandt. History of the Catholic Church. Milwaukee, Bruce, 1957. 684 p.

A useful introductory reading in the long history of the Church. Bibliographics references and an index are provided.

PROTESTANTISM--GENERAL

683 Curtis, C. J. Contemporary Protestant Thought. New York, Bruce, 1970 (Contemporary Theology Series). 225 p.
Provides a general reader with an introduction, written by a Protestant for Catholics, to the thought of the significant representatives of Protestant theology in the 20th century. Also includes an investigation of the Catholic thinker, P. Teilhard de Chardin, the Jewish philosopher Martin Buber, and a well-known Russian Orthodox spokesman, Nicolas Berdyaev. Bibliographic references in footnotes and a general index are included.

684 Dillinberger, John, and Claude Welch. Protestant Christianity Interpreted Through Its Development. New York, Scribner's, 1954. 340 p.
An interpretative presentation of the evolution of Protestant theology from the Reformation to the present.

685 A Handbook of Christian Theology; Definition Essays on Concepts and Movements of Thought in Contemporary Protestantism. Ed. by M. Halverson and A. A. Cohen. New York, Meridian Books, 1958 (Living Age Books). 380 p.
Contains 101 essays which present a summary of multiple trends in contemporary Protestant thought. Each essay is accompanied by a brief bibliography.

686 Léonard, Emile G. A History of Protestantism. Ed. by H. H. Rowley; transl. by J. M. H. Reid. London, Nelson, 1966-7. 2 vols.
Translation of Histoire générale du protestantisme. An outstanding scholarly work which surveys the history of the Protestant movement from its beginning in the medieval period to the present time. This work presents a controversial hypothesis that the Reformation was the final development of Catholicism. Contains extensive classified bibliographies and a detailed index.

687 Marty, Martin E. Protestantism. New York, Holt, Rinehart, and Winston, 1972 (History of Religion Series). 368 p.
This well-written survey covers the various denominations, rituals and doctrines of Protestantism presented both in historical perspective and in contemporary context. Annotated chapter bibliographies and a general index are included.

688 Weber, Max. The Protestant Ethic and Spirit of Capitalism. Transl. by T. Parsons. New York, Scribner's, 1958

(1904). 292 p.

Translation of Die protestantische Ethik und der Geist des Kapitaliamus. The remarkable essay written by the founder of the modern phase of the social sciences "... forms an excellent introduction to ... the sophisticated and refined analytical approach of the social sciences to problems of historical analysis and interpretation of society..." --Preface.

ANGLICAN AND EPISCOPAL

689 Dawley, P. M. The Episcopal Church and Its Work, rev. ed. Greenwich, Conn., Seabury Press, 1955 (Churches Teaching, v. 6). 310 p.

Presents a well documented survey of American churches of the Anglican Communion. There is a select bibliography.

690 Neill, Stephen C. Anglicanism, 3rd ed. Harmondsworth, England, Penguin Books, 1965 (1958) (Pelican Book A421). 468 p.

Provides "an explanation ... of the nature and working of the Anglican Communion, its relationship with other Christian groups, and its part in the movement for Christian union"--Cover. Contains two appendices: How the Church of England Is Governed and The Anglican Communion Today. Chapter-by-chapter bibliographies and a general index are provided.

691 Wand, J. W. C. Anglicanism in History and Today. New York, Nelson, 1962 (1961) (History of Religion). 265 p.

A popular explanation of the meaning and practices of the Anglican Church. It traces its history and the development of its "sister" churches in the Commonwealth, the United States, and other countries. Chapter bibliographies and a useful index are included.

BAPTISTS

Bibliography

692 Starr, Edward C. A Baptist Bibliography, Being a Register of Printed Material by and About Baptists, Including Works Written Against the Baptist. Rochester, N.Y., American Baptist Historical Society, 1947- (in progress, 18 vols. pub., A-P).

Contains about 4000 entries in a volume, arranged alphabetically. Each volume is provided with an index including authors, translators, Baptist publishers, distinctive titles, and subjects.

Handbooks and Surveys

693 Armstrong, O. K., and M. M. Armstrong. The Indomitable Baptists; A Narrative of Their Role in Shaping American History. Garden City, N.Y., Doubleday, 1967 (Religion in America Series). 392 p.
A popular presentation of the subject with bibliographic references for further reading, and an index.

694 Torbet, Robert G. A History of the Baptists, with a Foreword by K. S. Latourette. Philadelphia, Judson Press, 1963 (1950). 553 p.
Presents a denominational history which concentrates mainly on the American Baptists. It fails to place the movement in the context of universal Christian history.

CHRISTIAN SCIENCE

695 Eustace, Herbert W. Christian Science; Its Clear, Correct Teaching and Complete Writings. Berkeley, Calif., Lederer, Street and Zens Co., 1964. 1037 p.
This book is written "for the ... assistance ... of scholarly, consecrated Christian Scientists..."--Foreword.

696 Hoekema, Anthony A. The Four Major Cults: Christian Science, Jehovah's Witnesses, Mormonism, Seventh-Day Adventists. Grand Rapids, Mich., Eerdman, 1963. 447 p.
Provides a detailed analysis of doctrinal teachings based on an examination of the publishing done by the four denominations.

697 Judah, J. S. The History and Philosophy of the Metaphysical Movement in America. Philadelphia, Westminster Press, 1967. 317 p.
Attempts to compare and trace the similarities in thought and the common origins of such diverse metaphysical organizations as Christian Scientists, Rosicrucians, Spiritualists, and Theosophists. A general index and bibliographic references are included in footnotes.

CONGREGATIONAL CHURCH

698 Starkey, Marion L. The Congregational Way; The Role of the Pilgrims and Their Heirs in Shaping America. Garden City, N.Y., Doubleday, 1966 (Religion in America Series). 342 p.
A popularly presented history of the Congregationalists' movement with a selected bibliography in chapter-by-chapter arrangement.

EPISCOPAL see 689-691

JEHOVAH'S WITNESSES

See also no. 696.

699 Beckford, James A. The Trumpet of Prophecy: A Sociological Study of Jehovah's Witnesses. New York, Wiley, 1975. 244 p.
A thorough, scholarly study based on data from observation, interviews, questionnaires and secondary sources. Also contains a select bibliography and an index.

700 McKinney, George D. The Theology of the Jehovah's Witnesses. London, Marshall, Morgan, Scott, 1963 (1962). 131 p.
Contains a description of the theology and doctrine, as well as valuable criticisms and evaluation of the sect. Bibliography of primary and secondary sources including periodical articles, is provided. There is a general index.

701 Stroup, Herbert H. The Jehovah's Witnesses. New York, Russell and Russell, 1945. 180 p.
"The main basis of the work ... is observation..."--Preface. It deals with history and leaders, organization and finances, attitudes and relations. Contains a bibliography and an index.

LUTHERAN CHURCH

Encyclopedia

702 Bodensieck, Julius, ed. The Encyclopedia of the Lutheran Church. Minneapolis, Augsburg Pub. House, 1965. 3 vols.
About 3000 entries describe the doctrine and practices of the Luterans. Some interpretations are included. Includes numerous biographical articles, as well as places important for Lutherans. Short bibliographies are appended to articles.

703 Lutheran Cyclopedia. E. L. Lueker. St. Louis, Concordia, 1975. 845 p.
Deals with important aspects of the thought and life of the church. Includes the following areas: Bible interpretation, systematic theology, church history, life and worship in the church. Selected bibliographies are appended to the articles.

Handbooks and Surveys

704 Bergendorff, Conrad. The Church of the Lutheran Reformation; A Historical Survey of Lutheranism. Saint Louis, Concordia, 1967. 339 p.

A well presented denominational history with select bibliography for further readings.

705 Nelson, E. C. Lutheranism in North America, 1914-1970. Minneapolis, Augsburg Pub. House, 1972. 315 p.

A well-written interpretation of the development of the distinctive characteristics of the American Lutheranism. Bibliographic references are provided.

MENNONITES

Encyclopedia

706 The Mennonite Encyclopedia; A Comprehensive Reference Work on the Anabaptist-Mennonite Movement. Hillsboro, Kan., Mennonite Pub. House, 1955-59. 4 vols.

Deals with various topics concerned with the Anabaptist-Mennonite movement from the Reformation to the present. Includes articles on history, doctrines, and biography with appended bibliographies.

Bibliography

707 Hillerbrand, Hans J. A Bibliography of Anabaptism, 1520-1630. Elkhart, Ind., Institute of Mennonite Studies, 1962. 281 p. ____. ____ 1962-1974 [a sequel]. St. Louis, 1975.

"Designed to cover exhaustively the entire Anabaptist-Mennonite movement from the early 16th century to the present day"--Introd. Entries are arranged in Pt. 1 geographically and in Pt. 2 by topics. Indexes are included.

Handbooks and Surveys

708 Dyck, Cornelius J. The Introduction to Mennonite History; The Popular History of the Anabaptists and the Mennonites. Scottdale, Pa., Herald Press, 1967. 324 p.

"This is the history of Anabaptist-Mennonite life and thought from the 16th century to the present, written particularly for the young adult"--Preface. Bibliography is listed at the end of each chapter. Also contains an index.

709 Horsch, John. Mennonites in Europe, 2nd slightly rev. ed. Scottdale, Pa., Mennonite Pub. House, 1950 (Mennonite History, v. 1). 427 p.

"This is a handbook of Church history ... written in simple style, intended for members of the Church..."--Introd. Bibliography contains a selective list of monographs and periodical articles mainly in English. A general index is provided.

710 Mennonites and Their Heritage; A Handbook of Mennonite History and Beliefs, rev. ed. Scottdale, Pa., Herald Press, 1964 (1942). 148 p.
Presents a short popular history of the Mennonite movement in Europe and America. Lists various Mennonite branches and statistical data about them. Short bibliography is appended.

711 Wenger, John C. The Mennonite Church of America, Sometimes called Old Mennonites. Scottdale, Pa., Herald Press, 1966 (Mennonite History, v. 2). 384 p.
Continues no. 710. "Written on the request of the Historical and Research Committee of Mennonite General Conference"--Preface. This book presents the history of Mennonite life and experience in the United States and Canada. A select bibliography of reference books, monographs and periodicals is provided.

METHODISM

712 Davies, Rupert E. Methodism. Harmondsworth, England, Penguin Books, 1964 (1963) (Pelican Original). 224 p.
This popular book outlines the history of the Methodist Church since Wesley and discusses its present condition. Select bibliography and an index are provided.

713 Encyclopedia of World Methodism. Sponsored by the World Methodism Council and the Commission on Archives and History of the United Methodist Church. N. B. Harmon, gen. ed. Nashville, United Methodist Pub. House, 1974. 2 v.
Describes the doctrines and practices of the Methodists. Brings an excellent extensive bibliography and an index.

714 Ferguson, Charles W. Organizing to Beat the Devil; Methodists and the Making of America. Garden City, N.Y., Doubleday, 1971. 466 p.
Provides a well-written, rather popular history of the Methodist movement in America. Contributions of outstanding individuals are stressed. Bibliographic references are included in notes. There is a general index.

715 Sweet, William W. Methodists; A Collection of Source Materials. New York, Cooper Square Publishers, 1964 (1946) (Religion on the American Frontier). 800 p.
Comprises a good selection of various documents:

official conference minutes, personal journals and letters. A select bibliography and a general index are included.

MORMONS

See also no. 696.

716 Anderson, Nels. Desert Saints; The Mormon Frontier in Utah. Chicago, Univ. of Chicago Press, 1966 (1942). 459 p.

This is solid scholarly study devoted mainly to the sociological aspects of the Mormon family and community life. Bibliography comprises published and unpublished materials.

717 Hill, M. S., and J. B. Allen, eds. Mormonism in American Culture. New York, Harper and Row, 1972 (Interpretations of American History). 189 p.

A collection of essays discussing various topics of Mormon belief, practices, and life in American society. Bibliographic references are included.

718 O'Dea, Thomas F. The Mormons. Chicago, Univ. of Chicago Press, 1957. 288 p.

"A scholarly study of Mormons by a non-Mormon ... shows what Mormons believe and how they see the world, as well as the relationship of this world view to the conditions of life under which Mormonism originated and developed"--Preface. Abundant bibliographic references are included in the notes. An index is provided. A more popular presentation is to be found in: Bailey, P., The Armies of God (1968), which is provided with a good select bibliography, Jensen, Andrew, Encyclopedic History of the Church of Jesus Christ of Latter Saints (1941), which may be used as a source of quick reference; see also the authorized edition of The Book of Mormon (1948).

PENTECOSTALISM

719 Block-Hoel, Nils. The Pentacostal Movement; Its Origin, Development and Distinctive Character. Oslo, Universitetsforlaget, 1964. 255 p.

Translation of Pinsebevegelsen. Provides a critical study of the rise and expansion of the movement in the U.S. and Norway. Contains an analysis of doctrines, ethics, and worship. An extensive bibliography of monographs and periodical articles is appended.

720 Hollenweger, W. J. The Pentecostals; The Charismatic Movement in the Churches. Minneapolis, Augsburg Pub. House, 1972 (1969). 572 p.

Translation of Enthusiastisches Christentum. A scholarly survey of the Pentacostal movement. Pt. 1 traces its origin in North America and its spread in Brazil, South Africa, and Europe. Pt. 2 describes beliefs and practices. Lists a well selected bibliography.

PRESBYTERIANISM

721 "Presbyterianism." Corpus Dictionary of Western Churches. Washington, D.C., Corpus Publications, 1970, p. 617-19.
See no. 659. Provides a short history with selected bibliographic references, e.g. G. D. Henderson. Presbyterianism. (repr. 1956.)

QUAKERS (SOCIETY OF FRIENDS)

722 Bacon, Margaret H. The Quiet Rebels; The Story of the Quakers in America. New York, Basic Books, 1969. 229 p.
This book is a useful introduction to the history of the Society and its contributions from 1656 to the present. Contains a brief bibliography and an index.

723 Brinton, Howard. Friends for 300 Years; The History and Beliefs of the Society of Friends Since George Fox Started the Quaker Movement. New York, Harper, 1952. 239 p.
This thorough study "attempts to assess the value of Quaker principles and practices as they evolved through three centuries"--Introd. Bibliographic references are included in notes. Also an index is provided.

724 Trueblood, David E. The People Called Quakers. New York, Harper, 1966. 298 p.
An informative study which describes the development of Quakerism, its beliefs, and its contributions to religious thought.

SALVATION ARMY

725 Sandall, Robert. The History of the Salvation Army. London, Methuen, 1947- (in progress, 4 vols. publ.).
A comprehensive history with detailed indexes and bibliographies provided for each volume.

SHAKERS (UNITED SOCIETY OF BELIEVERS IN CHRIST'S SECOND APPEARING: MILLENNIAL CHURCH)

726 Andrews, Edward D. The People Called Shakers; A Search for the Perfect Society. New York, Oxford Univ. Press, 1953. 309 p.

This scholarly history presents the foundation of the Society in England in the 18th century, its expansion in America. There is a detailed index; and chapter-by-chapter bibliographies are included.

UNITARIAN CHURCH

727 Hewett, Austin P. An Unfettered Faith; The Religion of the Unitarian. London, Lindsey Press, 1958 (1955). 159 p.
The purpose of this book is to explain the fundamental principles of Unitarianism. Bibliographic references are included in the footnotes.

728 Mendelsohn, Jack. Why I Am a Unitarian Universalist. New York, Nelson, 1960. 214 p.
A prominent Unitarian minister defines the philosophy and practices of his Church.

CHRISTIANITY IN NORTH AMERICA

ATLAS

729 Gaustad, Edwin S. Historical Atlas of Religion in America, rev. ed. New York, Harper & Row, 1976. 1 v.
Presents a historical development of the major religions in America with special attention to geographical factors. Distinctive American religious groups such as the Mormons or Jehovah's Witnesses are given good treatment. Special section discusses religion among Indians, Negroes, Jews, and in Alaska and Hawaii.

CURRENT INFORMATION

730 Yearbook of American and Canadian Churches. Nashville, Abingdon Press, 1916- .
Contains the most complete and up-to-date information on churches of major faiths: Catholic, Protestant, Orthodox, and Jewish. Includes a calendar of religious observance, historical and statistical section, and a general index.

BIBLIOGRAPHIES AND GUIDES

731 Burr, Nelson R. A Critical Bibliography of Religion in America. Princeton, N.J., Princeton Univ. Press, 1961 (Religion in American Life). 2 vols.
Provides a general review of the history of religion in American life and thought. The historical, critical, and bibliographical references are combined in a continuous

text. It has a very detailed table of contents and a complete author index.

732 ________. Religion in American Life. New York, Appleton-Century-Crofts, 1971 (Golden Tree Bibliographies in American History). 171 p.
A selective bibliography with short annotations which "is intended for the use of graduate and advanced undergraduate students...." Materials on Judaism, Islam, Buddhism, Hindu cults, theosophy and spiritualism, as well as native Indian religions are included. Contains a very detailed table of contents and a general index.

733 Ellis, John T. A Guide to American Catholic History. Milwaukee, Bruce, 1959 (1921). 147 p.
A very careful compilation of literature dealing with various aspects of American Catholicism. Includes information on biographies and memoirs, religious communities, education, a list of periodicals and historical societies. A very detailed index is provided.

734 Gaustad, Edwin S. American Religious History. Washington, D.C., American Historical Association, 1966 (Service Center for Teachers of History, no. 65). 27 p.
Contains a brief informative bibliographic essay explaining how and where to find materials for research. Lists basic titles in American religious history. Of great interest are the author's: A Religious History of America (1966) and: Religious Issues in American Life (1968).

735 Jones, Charles E. A Guide to the Study of the Holiness Movement. Metuchen, N.J., Scarecrow, 1974. 918 p.
Covers research materials pertaining to the religious movement originated by Methodist Ministers.

736 Mode, Peter G. Source Book and Bibliographical Guide for American Church History. Boston, Canner, 1964. 735 p.
Lists "within a briefest possible space" the most significant documents for the entire field of American church history. There is a useful index.

737 Vollmar, Edward R. The Catholic Church in America; An Historical Bibliography. New York, Scarecrow Press, 1963. 354 p.
Contains a general bibliographic survey of the history of the Roman-Catholic Church in America. Lists monographs, periodical articles, master's theses, and doctoral dissertations covering the period 1850-1961.

HANDBOOK AND SURVEYS

738 Ahlström, Sydney E. A Religious History of the American People. New Haven, London, Yale Univ. Press, 1972. 1158 p.

This outstanding scholarly book presents a comprehensive survey of religions, sects, and spiritual movements from the earliest days to the present. Examines in detail Protestantism, Catholicism, Judaism, and Eastern Orthodoxy in the context of the social, political and intellectual aspects of American life. Includes an excellently selected topical bibliography and a detailed index.

739 Cavert, Samuel M. Church Cooperation and Unity in America; A Historical Review, 1900-1970. New York, Association Press, 1970. 400 p.

A scholarly survey of the situation in the American churches which traces the development of cooperation and unity in broad historical perspective. Canadian churches are included: check the index, p. 397. Contains an appendix: Chronology of Cooperation and Union, 1900-1970. A comprehensive bibliography by E. H. Lantero and a general index are provided.

740 Hudson, Winthrop S. Religion in America, 2nd ed. New York, Scribner's 1973 (1965) (Scribner's University Library). 463 p.

This is one of the most readable accounts of the development of religion in America from the colonial times to the present. It gives full attention to Protestant, Catholic, Orthodox, as well as Jewish religious groups. Bibliographic references are in the footnotes. Also a detailed index is provided.

CHRISTIANITY IN CANADA

BIBLIOGRAPHIES

741 "A Current Bibliography of Canadian Church History." Société canadienne d'histoire de l'église catholique. Study Sessions. Sessions d'étude. Toronto, 1964- (annually).

An exhaustive current bibliography which lists monographs and periodical articles arranged alphabetically by author in two separate sections. Local history and biography is arranged by subject, i.e. a place or person. Also includes particular communions: Adventists, Anglican, Doukhobor, Hutterite, Mennonite, Mormon, etc.

742 La Religion au Canada; Religion in Canada: Annotated Inventory of Scientific Study of Religion (1945-1972). Ed. by S. Crysdale and J. P. Montminy. Quebec, Presses de l'Université Laval, 1974. 189 p.

"This is the first bilingual inventory of scientific studies of a major social institution in this country..."--Foreword. Consult also: Religion in Canadian Society, ed. by S. Crysdale and L. Wheatcroft (Toronto, Macmillan of Canada, 1976, 498 p.).

743 Valk, Alphonse de, comp. Canadian Catholic Church. L'Eglise catholique canadienne. Saskatoon, St. Thomas More College at the Univ. of Saskatchewan, 1971 (History Collection. Catalogue no. 1).

This catalog comprises "two collections of historical material: (1) on Catholic education in English Speaking Canada; (2) on the history of the Catholic Church in English speaking Canada with special attention to western Canada"--Preface. Also includes a list of periodicals and newspapers.

HANDBOOKS AND SURVEYS

744 Clark, S. D. Church and Sects in Canada. Toronto, Univ. of Toronto Press, 1948. 458 p.

This scholarly work describes the history of Canadian religious life from the sociological point of view. Bibliographic references are included in footnotes. There is a good general index.

745 Cragg, G. R.; G. S. French; and J. W. Grant. Christianity and the Development of Canadian Culture. Hamilton, Ont., McMaster Divinity College, 1968 (McMaster Divinity College. Theological Bulletin, no. 3). 49 p.

An excellent collection of papers written by outstanding authorities in Canadian church history.

746 Grant, John W. Canadian Experience of Church Union. London, Lutterworth, 1967 (Ecumenical Studies in History, no. 8). 106 p.

Describes the creation and the four decades of the history of the United Church in Canada.

747 History of the Christian Church in Canada. Gen. Ed.: John W. Grant. Toronto, Ryerson Press, 1966-72. 3 vols.

This scholarly work, prepared by a group of specialists, provides the most comprehensive account of the history of Christian churches in Canada. Each volume contains a select bibliography of monographs and periodical articles. There is also a general index.

748 Moir, John S., ed. Church and State in Canada, 1627-1867; Basic Documents. Toronto, McClelland and Stewart, 1967. 274 p.

Brings together comprehensive collection of materials illustrating relations between the church and governments.

Each selection is accompanied by an explanation of its significance.

749 Walsh, Henry H. The Christian Church in Canada. Toronto, Ryerson, 1968. 355 p.
This scholarly presentation, free of any denominational presuppositions, describes the religious life in Canada and its history. Included are chapter-by-chapter select bibliographies and a general index.

CHRISTIANITY IN THE UNITED STATES

BIBLIOGRAPHY

750 Harrison, Ira. A Selected Annotated Bibliography on "Storefront" Churches and Other Religious Writing. Syracuse, N.Y., Syracuse Youth Development Center, 1963 (1962). 29 p.
Provides an annotated list of monographs and journal articles. Also "includes much literature which forms a body of knowledge called the sociology of religion"--Preface.

751 "Writing on the History of Religion in the United States." Manuscripta, 1957- .
A comprehensive listing of monographs and journal articles.

HANDBOOKS AND SURVEYS

752 Cavert, Samuel M. The American Churches in the Ecumenical Movement, 1900-1968. New York, Association Press, 1968. 288 p.
A well written historical study with abundant bibliographic references to documents and critical works.

753 Clark, Elmer T. The Small Sects in America, rev. ed. New York, Abingdon-Cokesbury Press, 1949. 256 p.
The sects under review are divided into seven groups: (1) Pessimistic or Adventist; (2) Perfectionist and Subjectivist; (3) Charismatic or Pentecostal; (4) Legalistic or Objectivist; (5) Egocentric or New Thought; (6) Communistic; (7) Esotetic or Mystic. Contains a select bibliography, index of religious bodies in the United States, and a general index.

754 Mayer, Frederick E., ed. The Religious Bodies of America. St. Louis, Concordia Pub. House, 1961 (1954). 598 p.
Provides an intelligent and sympathetic description of various denominations pointing out differences in doctrines and religious practices. Contains a general bibliography

and chapter-by-chapter bibliographies, a glossary of religious terms and statistics, as well as a general index.

755 Mead, Frank S. Handbook of Denominations in the United States, new 5th ed. Nashville, Abingdon Press, 1970. 265 p.

The latest data available on over 250 religious bodies in the United States are gathered into concise, convenient form. Includes facts about recent mergers among denominations. Arranged alphabetically, completely indexed.

756 Olmstead, Clifton E. History of Religion in the United States. Englewood Cliffs, N.J., Prentice-Hall, 1964 (1960). 628 p.

This scholarly work attempts "to set the story of American religion within a broad sweep of political, economic, social, and intellectual history"--Preface. Chapter-by-chapter select bibliographies and a general index are included.

757 Sontag, F., and J. K. Roth. The American Religious Experience: The Roots, Trends and Future of American Theology. New York, Harper and Row, 1972. 401 p.

A good scholarly interpretation of the "contributions made by major theologians and philosophers ... to the American tradition"--Preface. Contains a good select bibliography, but no index is provided.

JOURNALS

758 The American Benedictine Review. Atchison, Kan., 1950- (quarterly).

Published by the American Benedictine Academy. Indexed: Cath. Index.

759 Archiv für Reformationsgeschichte. Archive for Reformation History; An International Journal Concerned with the History of the Reformation and Its Significance in World Affairs. Stuttgart, 1903- (semi-annually).

Published by the Verein für Reformations-geschichte and the American Society for Reformation Research. Articles are in English, French, and German. Indexed: Rel. Per.; Rel. Theol. Abstr.

760 Canadian Church Historical Society. Journal. Toronto, 1950- (quarterly).

Published by the Dept. of History, Laurentian University, Sudbury.

761 Canadian Church Historical Society. Occasional Publications. Toronto, 1957- (irregularly).
Contains papers on miscellaneous topics in the Canadian Church history.

762 Canadian Journal of Theology. Toronto, 1955-70.
Text in English and French. Indexed: Rel. Per.; Rel. Theol. Abstr.

763 Catholic Historical Review. Washington, D.C., 1915- (quarterly).
Published by the American Catholic Historical Association and the Catholic University of America. Contains publication of documents important for Catholic history, informative book reviews, lists of new books and important periodical articles from other journals.

764 The Christian Century; An Ecumenical Weekly. Chicago, 1884- .
Until 1900 published under the title, Christian Oracle. Contains interesting editorials on current issues, church news, and brief book reviews.

765 Church History. New York, 1932- (quarterly).
Published by the American Society of Church History. Contains scholarly articles dealing with European and American church history, critical reviews of books. Each issue presents a bibliographical essay on a selected topic written by an expert.

766 Ecumenical Review; A Quarterly of the World Council of Churches. Geneva, 1948- .
An excellent source for news and views. Contains timely articles, chronicle of ecumenical events, and book reviews. Indexed: Rel. Per.; Soc. Sci. Hum. Index.

767 Harvard Theological Review. Cambridge, Mass., 1908- (quarterly).
Sponsored by the Faculty of Theology at Harvard University. Contains scholarly articles, excellent book reviews, and a list of new books received. Indexed: Rel. Theol. Abstr.; Soc. Sci. Hum. Index.

768 Huguenot Society of London. Proceedings. London, 1885- (6 times a year).
Contains material dealing in general with Huguenot history.

769 Huguenot Society of London. Publications. London, 1887- (irregularly).
Devoted mainly to publication of original documents and critical papers on the Huguenot movement.

770 International Review of Missions. Edinburgh, 1912- (quarterly).

Published under auspices of the World Council of Churches. Valuable source of information regarding missionary activities. Also contains book reviews and bibliographic information about new publications. Indexed: Br. Hum. Index; Rel. Per.; Soc. Sci. Hum. Index.

771 The Journal of Ecclesiastical History. New York, 1950- (quarterly).

Includes papers of high scholarly standard, and dependable book reviews. Indexed: Br. Hum. Index; Rel. Per.; Rel. Theol. Abstr.

772 The Journal of Theological Studies. London, 1950- (semiannually).

Comprised of scholarly articles and bibliographic news. Indexed: Br. Hum. Index; Rel. Per.; Rel. Theol. Abstr.

773 Laval théologique et philosophique. Québec, 1945- .

Text of articles in English and French.

774 The Month; A Review of Christian Thought and World Affairs. London, 1864- (monthly).

Supersedes Herder Correspondence. Provides a popular presentation of current events, new book announcements and reports of church news. Indexed: Br. Hum. Index; Cath. Ind.

775 Recherches de théologie ancienne et mediévale. Louvain, 1929- (semiannually).

Its scholarly articles are in English, French, and German.

776 Recusant History; A Journal of Research in Post-Reformation Catholic History in the British Isles. Kent, 1951- (3 times a year).

Published by the Catholic Record Society. First three vols. called Biographical Studies.

777 Religion in Life; Christian Quarterly of Opinion and Discussion. New York, 1932- .

Indexed: Rel. Theol. Abstr.; Soc. Sci. Hum. Index.

778 Revue d'histoire écclesiastique. Louvain, 1900- (quarterly).

This outstanding French journal is published by the Université Catholique de Louvain. It is known for its international coverage, exhaustive bibliography of over 7000 monographs and periodical articles on church history and related topics. Entries in classified arrangement contain brief annotations and references to book reviews.

779 Scottish Journal of Theology. Edinburgh, 1948- (quarterly).
Includes contributions of major theological and philosophical interest. Regularly carries articles in Biblical and applied theology, and valuable book reviews. Indexed: Rel. Per.; Rel. Theol. Abstr.

780 Société canadienne d'histoire de l'église catholique. Study Sessions. Toronto, 1966- (annually).
Contains papers on various topics in the history of the Canadian Catholic Church. Carries an annual bibliography See no. 741.

781 Studia Liturgica; An International Ecumenical Quarterly for Liturgical Research and Renewal. Rotterdam, 1962- .
Text in English, French and German with English summaries. Indexed: Rel. Per.

782 Theological Studies. New York, 1940- (quarterly).
Each issue is devoted to a selected topic. Contains book reviews. Indexed: Cath. Ind.; Rel. Theol. Abstr.

783 Theology Today. Princeton, 1944- (quarterly).
An excellent scholarly journal presenting neo-reformation American opinions. Contains reliable book reviews and biographical information. Indexed: Rel. Per.; Rel. Theol. Index.

III GNOSTICISM

784 Grant, Robert M. "Gnosticism." *Dictionary of the History of Ideas*. New York, Scribner's, 1973. V. 2, p. 326-31.
See no. 10. Provides an excellent brief survey of this religious movement which existed among Christianity and Judaism during the first three centuries of the Christian era. Discusses available sources to some gnostic systems. A bibliography of the most important writings is provided.

785 ________. *Gnosticism; A Source Book of Heretical Writings from the Early Christian Period*. New York, Harper, 1961. 254 p.
Contains a discussion of the oldest gnostic systems, an analysis of some gnostic documents, Basilides and Isadore, Valentinus and his school, selections from the hermetic writings, etc. A glossary, select bibliography and an index are provided.

786 Groningen, G. van. *First Century Gnosticism; Its Origins and Motifs*. Leiden, Brill, 1967. 209 p.
Provides an objective survey of all the materials at hand explaining the major gnostic systems. A well selected bibliography and an index are provided.

787 Jonas, Hans. *The Gnostic Religion: The Message of the Alien God and the Beginning of Christianity*, 2nd rev. ed. Boston, Beacon Press, 1963 (1958) (Beacon Paperback). 355 p.
Attempts a reconstruction of gnostic systems based on the gnostic writings. Contains an excellent select bibliography and an index.

Part Three--Judaism, Christianity, Islam (cont.)

IV BIBLICAL STUDIES

ENGLISH TRANSLATIONS, REFERENCE WORKS

INTRODUCTIONS

788 Bruce, F. F. The English Bible: A History of Translations from the Earliest English Versions to the New English Bible, new rev. ed. New York, Oxford Univ. Press, 1970 (1961). 262 p.

"It traces the history of the English Bible from its beginning in the seventh century to the present time"--Preface. Bibliographic references in footnotes. Index is provided.

789 May, Herbert. Our English Bible in the Making: The Word of Life and Living Language, rev. ed. Philadelphia, Publ. for the Cooperative Publication Assoc. by the Westminster Press, 1965. 163 p.

A brief popular survey of the subject which presents information concerning biblical manuscripts and translations into English. Bibliographic references are included in the text. There is also a section of suggestions and questions for discussion, additional bibliographic notes, and an index of names and subjects.

790 Price, Ira M. The Ancestry of Our English Bible: An Account of Manuscripts, Text, and Versions of the Bible, 3rd rev. ed. by W. A. Irwin, and A. P. Wikgren. New York, Harper, 1956. 363 p.

A very valuable introduction to the textual study of the Bible which discusses the Old Testament Hebrew text and its ancient versions; the New Testament text, manuscripts and ancient versions; and the history of the English Bible. There is a useful index and a bibliography of some 350 items arranged by subject.

PRINCIPAL VERSIONS IN ENGLISH TRANSLATION

791 Bible. English. Anchor Bible. Garden City, N.Y.,

Doubleday, 1964- (in progress).
A joint publication of Catholic, Jewish, and Protestant scholars which provides new translations, introductions, and informative commentaries.

792 ________. ________. 1953. Authorized. The Holy Bible, Containing the Old and New Testaments ... Authorized (King James) Version, Self-pronouncing Reference Edition. Philadelphia, Gideon, 1953. 990, 303 p.
The version in use among the Protestants.

793 ________. ________. 1952. Revised Standard. The Holy Bible. Revised Standard Version Containing the Old and New Testaments ... Being the Version Set Forth A.D. 1611 ... Revised 1952. New York, Nelson, 1952. 997, 293 p.
Presents a modern translation which was prepared by a group of outstanding American scholars.

794 ________. ________. Douay. 1914. The Holy Bible, Translated from the Latin Vulgate ... with Annotations, References, and a Historical and Chronological Table. Baltimore, Murphy, 1914. 1086, 306 p.
The Douay Bible is used by the Catholics. It differs in number and order of the books since the Apocrypha are recognized as canonical and included with other books.

795 ________. ________. 1966. Jerusalem Bible. Gen. ed. A. Jones. Garden City, N.Y., Doubleday, 1966. 1547, 498 p.
Based on La Bible de Jérusalem prepared at the Ecole Biblique de Jérusalem. Translations are done directly from original languages. Contains introductory essays, marginal references, and numerous footnotes. An index of biblical themes is provided.

796 ________. ________. Moffatt. 1937. A New Translation of the Bible, Containing the Old and New Testaments, by J. Moffatt. New York, Harper, 1935. 2 vols. in 1.
Presents a modern translation.

797 ________. ________. Catholic Biblical Association of America. 1971. The New American Bible. Translated from the Original Languages with Critical Use of All the Ancient Sources.... Chicago, Catholic Press, 1971 (1970). 828, 238 p.
Presents a successful rendition of the biblical text into contemporary English prepared by a group of outstanding American specialists in the field.

798 ________. ________. New English. 1961. The New English Bible. New York, Oxford Univ. Press, 1961-70. 3 vols.
Provides "a faithful rendering of the best available Greek texts into current speech of our times"--Introd.

799 _______. _______. Revised Standard. The New Oxford Annotated Bible, with the Apocrypha. Revised Standard Version. Ed. by H. G. May and B. M. Metzger. New York, Oxford Univ. Press, 1973. 1 v.

Contains the original 1965 edition of the Oxford Bible and the Oxford Annotated Apocrypha. An index to commentaries is provided.

800 _______. O. T. English. 1963. Jewish Publications Society. The Torah, the Five Books of Moses. Philadelphia, Jewish Publication Society of America, 1963.

See no. 440.

DICTIONARIES AND ENCYCLOPEDIAS

801 Bauer, Johannes, ed. Encyclopedia of Biblical Theology. London, Sheed and Ward, 1970 (1967). 3 vols.

Translation of the 3rd ed. of Bibeltheologisches Wörterbuch; the American edition is called Sacramentum verbi. This is a work of cooperation between the Catholic and Protestant scholars. Articles vary in length and value. Useful bibliographic references are attached to each article, and at the end of vol. 3 there is a supplementary bibliography. Also contains an analytical index of articles with cross-references, index of biblical terms in Hebrew and Greek, and Biblical references.

802 Comay, Joan. Who's Who in the Old Testament, Together with the Apocrypha. London, Weidenfeld & Nicolson, 1973 (1971). 448 p.

A popularly presented list of some 3000 persons who appear in the Old Testament: patriarchs, kings, warriors, prophets and sages, heroes and villains.

803 Cornfeld, Gaalyahu, ed. Pictorial Biblical Encyclopedia; A Visual Guide to the Old and New Testament. New York-London, Macmillan, 1964. 712 p.

Popular work which attempts at "a concise and authoritative account of the results of Biblical research since World War I presented in terms of readable scholarship"--Introd. General index provided but no bibliographic references.

804 Corswant, W. A Dictionary of Life in the Bible Times. Transl. from the French by A. Heathcote. Foreword by A. Parrot. London, Hodder and Stoughton, 1960 (1956). 308 p.

"Every ... aspect of the personal, social, and religious life of the Israelites and early Christians is treated together with such associated topics as the fauna, flora, and minerals of Palestine. Political history and geography are excluded, along with directly theological and literary questions"--Preface. Provides references to the biblical text.

805 Encyclopedic Dictionary of the Bible. A transl. and adaptation of A. van den Born's Bijbels woordenboek. 2nd rev. ed. by L. F. Hartman. New York, McGraw-Hill, 1963. 2634 cols.
Contains articles dealing with historical, archeological, linguistic and literary matters. Brief bibliographies are provided at the end of each article.

806 Gehman, Henry S., ed. The New Westminster Dictionary of the Bible, New ed. Philadelphia, Westminster Press, 1970. 1027 p.
Contains authoritative and scholarly articles. As a rule, bibliographic references have been omitted but some lesser known works are mentioned. Entries refer to Revised Standard version, American Standard version, and the Jewish version.

807 Hastings, James, ed. Dictionary of the Bible, rev. ed. by F. C. Grant and H. H. Rowley. New York, Scribner's, 1963. 1059 p.
A new edition of a reference work which has been in use for over 60 years. Every entry was read, and a number of them were rewritten to ensure the accuracy and currency of the information. Entries are based on the Revised Standard version.

808 The Interpreter's Dictionary of the Bible; An Illustrated Encyclopedia Identifying and Explaining All Proper Names and Significant Terms and Subjects in the Holy Scriptures, Including the Apocrypha, with an Attention to Archaeological Discoveries and Researches into the Life and Faith of Ancient Times. New York, Nashville, 1962. 4 vols.
____. ____. (Suppl.) 1976.
Provides a scholarly presentation of all topics for modern biblical studies. Select bibliographies are provided.

809 McKenzie, John L. Dictionary of the Bible. Milwaukee, Bruce, 1965. 954 p.
"A one-volume dictionary ... for general use..."--Preface. Contains a list of books which were used in the preparation of articles.

810 Miller, M., and J. L. Miller. Encyclopedia of Bible Life. New York-London, Harper, 1955 (1944). 493 p.
A compact reference book which includes information about agriculture, animals, apparel, arts and crafts, homes, jewelry, social structures, worships, etc. Also contains additional Bible references, a select bibliography and a general index with cross-references.

811 Payne, J. B. Encyclopedia of Biblical Prophecy: The Complete Guide to Scriptural Predictions and Their Fulfillment. New York, Harper & Row, 1973. 745 p.

Presents a popular guide with footnotes leading to more detailed exegetical studies, primarily in English. Also includes an excellent select bibliography and indexes: (1) The Biblical predications; (2) Selective passages not properly predictive; (3) Subjects; (4) Biblical words and phrases; (5) Passages discussed in the introduction, with scattered references to other significant discussions.

812 Pfeiffer, Charles F., ed. The Biblical World; A Dictionary of Biblical Archaeology. Grand Rapids, Mich., Baker, 1966. 612 p.

"Deals with the lands of eastern Mediterranean and the Fertile Crescent--the areas in which the Biblical history took place.... Geography, history, and literature, art--all come within the scope of Biblical archaeology..."--Introd. Major archaeological terms are explained. Brief bibliographic references are provided at the end of more important articles.

813 Rowley, Harold H. Dictionary of Bible Place Names. Old Tappan, N.J., Revell Co., 1970. 173 p.

Lists each place name which is mentioned in the Revised Standard Version including the Apocrypha, as well as some variants from the Jerusalem Bible. See no. 795.

814 ________. Short Dictionary of Bible Personal Names. New York, Basic Books, 1968. 168 p.

Includes each personal name mentioned in the text of the Revised Standard Version. See also the author's Short Dictionary of Bible Themes (1968).

815 Smith, William. The New Smith's Bible Dictionary. Completely rev. by R. G. Lemmons et al. Garden City, N.Y. Doubleday, 1966 (1900). 441 p.

An excellent reference work. Revisions include recent archaeological research, linguistic advances, changes in chronology, etc.

816 Theological Dictionary of the Old Testament. G. J. Botterweck, and H. Ringgren, eds. Transl. by J. T. Willis. Grand Rapids, Mich., Eerdmans, 1973- .

A new reference work which explains the elements of the Hebrew Bible, the Septuagint, and Qumran texts, and relates them to other ancient Near Eastern literatures. Bibliographic references are provided.

817 The Zondervan Pictorial Encyclopedia of the Bible. ed. M. C. Nenney. Grand Rapids, Mich., Zondervan, 1975. 5 v.

"The scope of this encyclopedia is intended to cover directly or indirectly all persons, places, objects, customs, and historical events and major teaching of the Bible.... It is intended to include a larger body of material, and to supply more detail for scholarly study"--Preface. Selected bibliographic references are appended at the end for each article.

BIBLIOGRAPHIES, GUIDES, INDEXES

818 Ackroyd, Peter A. Bible Bibliography, 1967-1973; Old Testament. Oxford, Blackwell, 1974 (Book Lists of the Society for Old Testament Study, 1967-1973). 505 p.
Contains an alphabetically arranged list of books with informative signed annotations. An author index is added.

819 Brock, S. P.; C. T. Fritsch; S. Jellicoe, eds. A Classified Bibliography of the Septuagint. Leiden, Brill, 1973 (Arbeiten zur Literatur und Geschichte des Hellenistischen Judentums). 217 p.
Contains a selective listing of critical studies up to 1969 arranged by subject. An author index is added.

820 The Cambridge History of the Bible. Cambridge, England, University Press, 1963-70. 3 vols.
An excellent work of reference which covers the entire history of the Bible. It traces essential features of the process by which the Bible came into being. Separate sections are designed to be read independently. There is a useful bibliography for each section of the book. Also contains a general subject index and an index of biblical quotations.

821 Danker, Frederick W. Multipurpose Tools for Bible Study, 2nd rev. ed. St. Louis, Concordia, 1966 (1960). 295 p.
A useful guide which presents a systematic survey of tools available for Bible research. Bibliographical references are accompanied by brief annotations. Separate subject and author indexes are provided.

822 Elenchus bibliographicus Biblicus. Pontificio Instituto Biblico, 1920- (annually).
First appeared as a quarterly selective bibliography in Biblica; see no. 987. v. 1-48, 1920-67; v. 49, 1968- is published separately as an annual supplement which covers all aspects of scholarly biblical studies. A detailed table of contents, an author index are provided. Dissertations are included.

823 Glanzman, George S., and J. A. Fitzmyer, eds. An Introductory Bibliography for the Study of Scripture. Westminster, Md., Newman Press, 1962 (Woodstock Papers: Occasional Papers for Theology, no. 5). 135 p.
Provides a selective list of publications in various

disciplines of biblical studies; includes both the Old and New Testaments. Covers works in English, French, and German.

824 Langevin, Paul-E. Bibliographie biblique; Biblical Bibliography, 1930-70. Québec, Presses l'Université Laval, 1972. 935 p.
Contains references to articles from 70 Catholic periodicals in English, French, German, Italian, Spanish, and Portuguese. The content is divided into five sections, and further into more than a thousand precise headings. There is an index of authors and subjects in both English and French. Another volume, which will cover non-Catholic writers, is being prepared.

825 Peterson, Kenneth G. A Bibliography of Bible Study for Theological Students. Berkeley, Calif., Pacific Lutheran Seminary, 1964. 41 p.
"The Bibliography follows a classified arrangement with books grouped into four main categories: biblical, historical, theological, and functional; within these categories items are listed alphabetically. A list of recommended periodicals has been also included..."--Introd.

826 Saint John's University. Library. Index to Biblical Journals. Collegeville, Minn., St. John's Univ. Press, 1971.
Contains a list of references to articles from major biblical journals, including: Biblica, Harvard Theological Review, Journal of Biblical Literature, New Testament Studies, etc. Articles are indexed by subject with frequent cross-references under related topics.

827 Society for Old Testament Study. Eleven Years of Bible Bibliography, the Book List, 1946-1956. Indian Hills, Colo., Falcon's Wing Press, 1957. 804 p.
An annotated list of monographs chronologically arranged by the date of publication. Annotations indicate the subject with which the book deals and provide a critical evaluation. See sequel, no. 826.

828 ________. A Decade of Bible Bibliography, 1957-1966. Ed. by G. W. Anderson. Oxford, Blackwell, 1967. 706 p.
A sequel to no. 825. A classified list of monographs chronologically arranged with annotations. An author index is provided.

829 L'Université de Montréal. Facultés de Théologie et de Philosophie. Bibliographie biblique. Montréal, 1958. 398 p.
Contains some 9000 references to articles in English, French, Latin from selected Catholic periodicals and collections of essays. An index of subjects is provided.

COMMENTARIES

830 Bible. English. 1964. Anchor Bible. Garden City, N.Y., Doubleday, 1964- (38 vols. when completed).
See no. 791.

831 Black, Matthew, ed. Peake's Commentary on the Bible. Gen. ed. and New Testament ed., M. Black; Old Testament ed. H. H. Rowley. London, Nelson, 1964 (1962). 1126 p.
Provides a commentary to the Revised Standard Version. This new edition is brought up to date taking into account the modern excavations and discoveries.

832 Broadman Bible Commentary. Ed. by C. J. Allen. London, Marshall, Morgan & Scott, 1970- .
A cooperative venture of leading Baptist scholars who attempt to make use of the best tools for scholarly research in the study of the biblical text.

833 Brown, R. E., and R. E. Murphy, eds. The Jerome Biblical Commentary, with a foreword by Augustin Cardinal Bea. Englewood Cliffs, N.J., Prentice-Hall, 1968. 2 vols.
Prepared by the Catholic Association of America. It discusses all the books of the Bible, with an informative introduction to each book and verse-by-verse commentary. Some articles deal with general subjects, e.g., history of Israel, modern criticism, etc. There is an elaborate but clear system of cross-references. Also contains chapter bibliographies and an index.

834 Cambridge Bible Commentary. Cambridge, England, Univ. Press, 1963- .
A series of commentaries which cover both testaments, based on the New English Bible. Comprises excellent general introductory volumes to the background of the Testaments, and commentaries to each biblical book.

835 Fuller, Reginald, ed. A New Catholic Commentary on Holy Scripture, new and fully rev. ed. London, Nelson, 1969 (1953). 1377 p.
Contains commentaries on the biblical text paragraph by paragraph. A useful index is provided.

836 International Critical Commentary on the Holy Scriptures of the Old and New Testament. New York, Scribner's, 1896- (45 vols. already pub.).
Contains commentaries on both testaments written by outstanding scholars. Emphasis is critical and philological. The quality of particular volumes is uneven, and some of them need up-dating.

837 The Interpreter's Bible; The Holy Scripture ... with General Articles and Introduction, Exegesis, Exposition for Each Book of the Bible. Editorial board: G. A. Buttrick. New York, Abingdon-Cokesbury Press, 1951-57. 12 vols.
A guide and commentary to the Bible which presents the Protestant point of view. Covers both Testaments. The King James and Revised Standard versions are placed in parallel columns. In the center one finds the exegesis, and at the bottom, the exposition. Contains extensive essays on the background of the biblical writings in vols. 1 and 7 with useful bibliographical references. Indexes and maps are provided.

838 The Interpreter's One-Volume Commentary on the Bible: Introduction and Commentary for Each Book of the Bible, Including the Apocrypha, with General Articles. Ed. by C. M. Laymon. Nashville, Abingdon Press, 1971. 1386 p.
Contains general articles explaining various approaches to biblical interpretation: historical, literary, linguistic, geographical, archeological, theological, etc. A separate discussion on each biblical book is provided. Also includes information on chronology, measures and money, maps, and an index of subjects.

839 Neil, William. Harper's Bible Commentary. New York, Harper & Row, 1962. 544 p.
British edition of this work is entitled, One Volume Bible Commentary. A concise companion to the Revised Standard Version.

COMPANIONS

840 Manson, Thomas W. The Companion to the Bible, new ed. by H. H. Rowley. Edinburgh, Clark, 1963. 468 p.
A useful reference work by a professor of biblical criticism and exegesis at the University of Manchester. Provides informative introductions to various topics with bibliographic references.

841 Neil, William, ed. The Bible Companion; A Complete Pictorial and Reference Guide to the People, Places, Events, Background and Faith of the Bible. London, Skeffington, 1959. 468 p.
This popular guide presents the Protestant standpoint on biblical studies. Includes a section on archeology, and alphabetical glossaries of people, places, plants, animals. Also contains information on the arts, social life, books and writers of the Bible. Chapter bibliographies are provided.

CONCORDANCES

842 Cruden, Alexander. Cruden's Complete Concordance of the Old and the New Testaments. Ed. by A. D. Adams, C. H. Irvin, and S. A. Walters. Notes and Biblical Proper Names under One Alphabetical Arrangement. Philadelphia, Universal Book and Bible House, 1949 (1737). 783 p.
One of the oldest concordances reprinted in various editions which is still valuable for its 250,000 entries arranged A-Z by English word. Information is accurate but needs up-dating.

843 Ellison, John W., comp. Nelson's Complete Concordance of the Revised Standard Version of the Bible. New York, Nelson, 1957. 2157 p.
This is a first attempt to use a computer for compilation of concordances. It lists all the principal words in the Revised Standard Version with references to passage where they appear.

844 Gant, William J. The Moffatt Bible Concordance; A Complete Concordance to the Bible, [in the] New Translation by J. Moffatt. New York, Harper, 1950. 550 p.
Contains a complete listing of proper names and key words used in the Moffatt translation of the Bible of 1913-1929.

845 Strong, James. The Exhaustive Concordance of the Bible ... of the Common English Version of the Canonical Books, and Every Occurrence of Each Word.... A Comparative Concordance of the Authorized and Revised Versions.... Nashville, Abingdon Press, 1943 (1890). 1 vol.
Lists some 400,000 entries. Also contains a Hebrew, Assyro-Akkadian, and Greek glossary.

846 Young, Robert. Analytical Concordance to the Bible on an Entirely New Plan Containing about 311,000 References, Subdivided under the Hebrew and Greek Originals with the Literal Meaning and Pronunciation of Each; ... also Index Lexicons to the Old and New Testaments, Being a Guide to Parallel Passages and a Complete List of Scripture Proper Names Showing Their Modern Pronunciation. The Canon of Scripture, by R. K. Harrison, and E. F. Harrison. New York, Funk & Wagnalls, 1970 (1879). 1090 p.
The 1956 edition contains the famous essay by W. F. Albright on new archeological discoveries.

SUBJECT GUIDES

847 Garland, George F. Subject Guide to Bible Stories. Westport, Conn., Greenwood, 1968. 365 p.
"The purpose of this concordance [sic] is to suggest

where to find a story that makes a desired point.... It locates biblical comment on a number of familiar topics, but, because of its compactness it cannot include all possible subjects..."--Introd. Consists of two parts: Subject guide, and Character guide.

848 Joy, Charles R. Harper's Topical Concordance, rev. and enl. ed. New York, Harper & Row, 1962. 628 p.
Contains 25,000 extracts of biblical passages which are listed under 2100 topics with abundant cross-references.

HANDBOOKS AND CRITICAL WORKS

INTRODUCTIONS

849 Davidson, R., and A. R. C. Leaney. Biblical Criticism. Harmondsworth, England, Penguin, 1970 (Pelican Guide to Modern Theology, v. 3). 392 p.
Provides the general reader with a useful introduction to some of the main issues in contemporary biblical studies. Bibliographic references and a general index are included.

850 Watts, Harold H. The Modern Reader's Guide to the Bible, rev. ed. New York, Harper, 1959 (1949). 544 p.
This popular reference book points out the most important facts about the biblical books. Bibliography and index are provided.

CHRONOLOGY

851 Finegan, Jack. Handbook of Biblical Chronology; Principles of Time Reckoning in the Ancient World, and Problems of Chronology in the Bible. Princeton, N.J., Princeton Univ. Press, 1964. 338 p.
Presents an informative study of the chronological problems in biblical times. Part one explains the principles of Babylonian and Assyrian, Egyptian, Hebrew, Greek, and Roman chronology. Part two examines modern theories and interpretations of chronology in both the Old and New Testaments. Contains also bibliographic references and a general index.

BIBLICAL GEOGRAPHY--ATLASES

852 Baly, D., and A. D. Tushingham. Atlas of the Biblical World. Consultants R. de Vaux and others. New York, World Pub. Co., 1971. 208 p.

One of the best biblical atlases--the result of cooperation between a geographer and an archeologist. It contains extensive information about political and historical geography. Also describes physical characteristics of the land, plant life, and climate. Of special interest is the part on recent excavations carried out by K. Kenyon. Select bibliography, indexes to the text and maps are included.

853 Grollenberg, Luc H. Atlas to the Bible. Transl. and ed. by J. M. H. Reid and H. H. Rowley. Foreword by W. F. Albright and H. H. Rowley. Preface by R. de Vaux. London, Nelson, 1956 (1954). 165 p.

Translation of Atlas van de Bijbel. A well produced English translation with excellent maps and illustrations and informative explanations. Includes a full index.

854 May, Herbert G.; R. W. Hamilton; and G. N. S. Hunt. Oxford Atlas to the Bible. London, Oxford Univ. Press, 1962. 144 p.

Comprises a well-selected collection of historical and archeological maps accompanied by brief citations of the appropriate passages from the Bible. Also includes maps of vegetation, rainfall, and temperature. A gazetteer of biblical names is provided.

855 Wright, George E., and F. V. Filson. Westminster Historical Atlas to the Bible, with an Introductory Article by W. F. Albright, rev. ed. London, SCM Press, 1956. 130 p.

Presents new interpretations of the Hebrew conquest and political history of Palestine. Also includes sections on the rise of Jewish sects in the Maccabean and Herodian periods. Indexes to the text and the maps are provided.

BIBLICAL GEOGRAPHY--SURVEYS

856 Baly, Denis. Geographical Companion to the Bible. Toronto, Ryerson Press, 1963. 196 p.

Describes geographical features of Mesopotamia, Syria, Palestine, and Egypt, placing a strong emphasis on the natural boundries of regions of settlement, rivers, ridges, etc. There is also a section on strategic geography. Bibliographical references are included in the notes. An index is provided.

857 ________. Geography of the Bible; A Study in Historical Geography. London, Lutterworth, 1957. 303 p.

Provides a well-informed description of the ecology of life in Palestine and Syria. A selective bibliography for further reading is most useful.

858 Pfeiffer, C., and H. F. Vos. The Wycliff Historical Geography

of Bible Lands. London, Oliphant, 1967. 588 p.
Comprises a brief geographical outline and an historical survey of all the lands mentioned in the Bible. There is a general index, a scripture index, an index of maps, and a short selective bibliography.

859 Simon, Jan J. Geographical and Topographical Texts of the Old Testament; A Concise Commentary. Leiden, Brill, 1959 (Studia Francisci Schotten memoriae dedicata, v. 2). 613 p.
A guide to various problems presented by the analysis and interpretation of the geographical texts in the Old Testament. Bibliographic references are included in the footnotes. Also contains an index of biblical texts, a list of biblical and extra-biblical names, and a gazetteer to the maps.

860 Smith, George A. The Historical Geography of the Holy Land, 25th ed. Introd. by H. H. Rowley. New York, Harper and Row, 1966 (1894) (Harper Torchbooks). 512 p.
A fascinating classic which presents old and new geographical materials pertaining to Palestine, its place in the history of the world, its geographical features, climate, etc. There is a general index, and an index of maps. Bibliographic references are included in the notes, and a special bibliography for eastern Palestine is provided.

BIBLICAL ARCHEOLOGY/HISTORICAL SURVEYS

861 Albright, William F. Archeology and Religion of Israel. Baltimore, Johns Hopkins Press, 1956 (1941) (Ayer Lecture of the Colgate Rochester Divinity School, 1941). 246 p.
Presents archeological and linguistic evidence that the ideas of Judaic monotheism reach much earlier times than is generally assumed.

862 ______. Yahweh and the Gods of Canaan; A Historical Analysis of Two Contrasting Faiths. Garden City, N.Y., Doubleday, 1968 (Jordan Lecture, 1965). 294 p.
Describes the Canaanite, Phoenician and Israelite religion; and then attempts to trace foreign influences in the development of the Jewish religious outlook. Provides an index of names and subjects, and bibliographical references in the footnotes. See also no. 546.

863 Encyclopedia of Archaeological Excavations in the Holy Land. Ed. by M. Avi-Yonah. London, Oxford Univ. Press, 1976- .
Provides the most up-to-date source of information on various aspects of biblical archeology.

864 Fohrer, Georg. History of Israelite Religion. Transl. by

D. Green. Nashville, Abingdon Press, 1972. 416 p.
Translation of Geschichte der israelitischen Religion. An informative guide to almost every significant aspect of the Old Testament scholarship. Information on the religions of Israel's neighbors are included. Also provides a selected bibliography.

865 Frank, Harry T. Bible, Archaeology, and Faith. Nashville, Abingdon Press, 1971. 352 p.
Together with G. E. Wright's Biblical Archaeology (1962) (see also no. 882), comprises a basic survey of the subject. It reviews the newest discoveries of the last decade including Masada, Hazor, Gezer, Arad, Mt. Gerazim, and Jerusalem. Bibliographic references. Scriptural index, and a name index are provided.

866 Freedman, David, and G. E. Wright, eds. The Biblical Archaeologist Reader. Garden City, N.Y., Doubleday, 1961-70 (Anchor Books). 3 vols.
Contains a selection of articles published by the American Schools of Oriental Research. Some of the articles have been revised.

867 Heaton, Eric W. Everyday Life in Old Testament Times. New York, Scribner's, 1956. 240 p.
A popular guide-book which attempts a reconstruction of the daily life of the people who have left almost no pictorial records. Some bibliographic references are included in footnotes. There is also an index. See also Wiseman, Donald J., ed., People of the Old Testament Times (London, Oxford Univ. Press, 1973).

868 Kenyon, Kathleen M. Archaeology in the Holy Land, 3rd ed. London, Benn, 1970 (1960). 328 p.
An excellent handbook for the advanced student which surveys up-to-date archeological findings in Palestine. The appendix contains a listing of the archeological sites, together with a bibliography and the names of the excavators. An index is provided.

869 ________. Royal Cities of the Old Testament. London, Barrie and Jenkins, 1971.
A popular book which presents an informative survey of the cities known since the Salomon's times: Jerusalem, Hazor, Megiddo, Gezer, Samaria. Contains excellent illustrations, maps, and plans in the text. A useful select bibliography and an index are included.

870 Lapp, Paul W. Biblical Archaeology and History. New York, World Publ. Co., 1969. 129 p.
Contains four lectures delivered by an outstanding specialist in the field. Deals with the sources of history, the Bible and history, the Bible and archeology, and the

search for biblical connections. A useful bibliography is provided in the notes.

871 Mould, Elmer W. K.; H. N. Richardson; and R. F. Berkey. Essentials of Bible History, 3rd rev. ed. New York, Ronald Press, 1966 (1950). 842 p.

Provides a survey of major historical events from 2000 B.C. to A.D. 100. Also contains informative colored maps, a genealogy of the English Bible, and a glossary of technical terms. A select bibliography and an index are also included.

872 New Directions in Biblical Archaeology. Ed. by D. N. Freedman and J. C. Greenfield. Garden City, N.Y., Doubleday, 1969. 191 p.

A collection of essays by some of the best-known American and Israeli specialists in the field concerned with the newest excavations and discoveries. It contains the famous survey by W. F. Albright, "Impact of Archaeology on Biblical Research--1966." Chronological tables, a glossary, and a general index are provided. One finds also useful bibliographical references to monographs, and to a broad range of reports and periodical articles.

873 Oesterley, William O. and T. H. Robinson. The Hebrew Religion; Its Origin and Development. London, SPCK, 1961 (1930). 400 p.

Two outstanding authorities in the field present a comprehensive survey of the background of Hebrew religious tradition. Pt. 1 describes its animistic and polytheistic stages in the nomadic period; Pt. 2 traces the development of religious beliefs and institutions up to the fall of Jerusalem; Pt. 3 deals with established monotheistic religion covering the period of exile, the Persian period, and the Greek period. Contains bibliographic references in footnotes and an index.

874 Orlinsky, H. M. Understanding Bible Through History and Archaeology. New York, KTAV, 1972. 292 p.

A popular introduction to biblical history, archeology and literature.

875 Pritchard, J. B., ed. The Ancient Near Eastern Texts Relating to the Old Testament. Princeton, N.J., Princeton Univ. Press, 1955. 3 vols.

See nos. 288 and 289.

876 Renckens, Henricus. The Religion of Israel. Transl. by N. B. Smith. New York, Sheed and Ward, 1966 (1962). 370 p.

Translation of De godsdienst van Israel. Provides an informative "guide to the study of the Bible, God's purpose in the Old Testament, and in particular of his present purpose, in the life today"--Preface. Contains a selective bibliography of monographs and journal articles. Also a subject index is included.

877 Ringgren, Helmer. Israelite Religion. Transl. by D. E. Green. Philadelphia, Fortress Press, 1966 (1963). 391 p.

Provides an orientation in "a jungle of diverse scholarly opinions and dogmatically conditioned judgements"--Foreword. Special emphasis is placed on the developments during the period of monarchy. Bibliographic references are included in footnotes. Contains an index.

878 Thomas, David W. Archaeology and Old Testament; Jubilee Volume of the Society for Old Testament Study, 1917-1967. Oxford, Clarendon Press, 1967. 493 p.

Attention is directed to discoveries made both in Palestine and surrounding lands: Mesopotamia and Syria. Chronological charts, an index of biblical citations, and a general index are provided.

879 ________. Documents from Old Testament Times, Translated with Introductions and Notes by Members of the Society for Old Testament Study. London, Nelson; New York, Harper, 1965 (1958). 302 p.

"The documents are ... grouped together on a basis of the script and language"--Preface. They are provided with a brief annotation and explanation of the way in which they are related to the Old Testament. A chronological table is included. Contains numerous bibliographic references and a useful general index.

880 Vaux, Roland de. Ancient Israel; Its Life and Institutions. New York, McGraw-Hill, 1961. 592 p.

Translation of Les Institutions de l'Ancient Testament. Vol. 1 discusses social institutions; vol. 2 deals with religious institutions. Select bibliography and an index are included.

881 ________. The Bible and the Ancient Near East. Transl. from the French by D. McHugh. London, Darton, Longman, Todd, 1972 (1967). 284 p.

"A collection of essays which is cutting into the Bible at different angles and reaching down to different strata (history, comparative religion, and theology).... The author makes clear that no understanding of the Bible is possible unless one reads it in the setting of Near Eastern history... "--Introd. Contains numerous bibliographic references in the footnotes. No index is provided.

882 Williams, Walter G. Archaeology in Biblical Research. Nashville, Abingdon Press, 1965. 223 p.

Pt. 1 explains the essence of biblical archeology; Pt. 2

analyzes various aspects of archeology; Pt. 3 presents the world in which the Bible was written. Contains numerous footnotes, well selected chapter bibliographies, and an excellent general list of references to periodical articles and monographs. See also no. 865.

883 Wright, George E. Biblical Archaeology, new rev. ed. Philadelphia, Westminster Press, 1962 (1957). 291 p.
Provides a comprehensive survey of all the archeological discoveries connected with the biblical texts. It both is accurate and careful in conclusions. Index is subdivided into sections listing modern names, biblical names, biblical places, and biblical references. Bibliographic references are provided. For more up-to-date information one should consult also Frank, Harry T., Bible, Archaeology, and Faith (1971)--see no. 865.

884 Yamauchi, Edwin M. The Stones and the Scriptures. Philadelphia, Lippincott, 1972 (Evangelical Perspectives). 207 p.
A popularly presented history of the biblical times based on the biblical text documented with archeological evidence. Contains a helpful select bibliography of monographs and periodical articles, and indexes of names, places, subjects, and biblical references.

TEXTUAL AND LITERARY CRITICISM

885 Auzou, Georges. The Formation of the Bible; History of the Sacred Writings of the People of God. The English version by J. Thornton. St. Louis, Mo., Herder, 1963 (1957). 462 p.
Translation of La tradition biblique. Contains a review of research on the composition of biblical writings including the Apocrypha, and some Pseudepigrapha which are presented in their historical context. Bibliographic references in footnotes are provided. Arranged to aid students and the non-expert.

886 Bratton, Fred G. A History of the Bible; An Introduction to the Historical Method. Boston, Beacon, 1959. 382 p.
A popular presentation which provides a wide-ranging survey emphasizing the relationship of the Bible to other religious writings of the Near East. It traces the formation of the Testaments, with their subsequent translations and editions to present time.

887 Campenhausen, Hans von. The Formation of the Christian Bible. London, Black, 1972 (1968). 342 p.
Translation of Die Entstehung der christlichen Bibel. An authoritative scholarly study by an outstanding early church history specialist. It presents the Christian point of view on the development of the canon. Bibliographic

references and an index are included.

888 Colwell, Ernest C. The Study of the Bible, rev. ed. Chicago, Chicago Univ. Press, 1964 (1945). 202 p.
Provides a well-written account on the history of the biblical text and its transmission through the centuries. It explains the principles of historical and literary criticism. Bibliographic references are included.

889 Dougherty, John J. Searching the Scriptures. Garden City, N.Y., Doubleday, 1959. 239 p.
Contains a popular presentation of Old and New Testament history which deals with the textual problems, archeology, and geography of the biblical lands. Also includes an interesting discussion of the Dead Sea scrolls. Some bibliographic information is provided.

890 Eissfeldt, Otto. The Old Testament; Including the Apocrypha and Pseudepigraphica, and also the Works of Similar Type from Qumran. The History of the Formation of the Old Testament. Transl. by P. R. Ackroy. Oxford, Blackwell, 1966 (1934). 861 p.
This scholarly and up-to-date work is recognized as the best summary of biblical research. The first section deals with the pre-literary stage, and this is followed by a detailed analysis of the individual books of the Bible and the development of the canon. The discussion is closed at the point when the biblical text appears to have reached an established form. Contains extensive bibliographic references up to 1964. A reference index and an index of authors are supplied.

891 Goodspeed, Edgar J. The Story of the Bible. Chicago, Univ. of Chicago Press, 1957 (1936). 159 p.
Provides a basic introduction to critical studies of the biblical texts. Bibliographic references and index are included. An excellent reading source for beginners.

892 Gros Louis, Kenneth R. R., et al. Literary Interpretations of Biblical Narratives. Nashville, Abingdon, 1974 (Bible in Literature Courses). 352 p.
This book is designed to meet the needs of teachers and students of both secondary and undergraduate level. It introduces innovative approaches to the study of biblical stories as literary texts. Some bibliographic references are included in notes. Lacks an index.

893 Henn, Thomas R. The Bible as Literature. New York, Oxford Univ. Press, 1970. 270 p.
A scholarly study which defines similarities of styles and images appearing in the biblical text and other literary works outside the Bible. Special attention is given to the Book of Job, the Psalms, the Canticles, and the Song of

Deborah. A select bibliography and an index are provided.

894 Herclots, Hugh G. G. How the Bible Came to Us: Its Texts and Versions. Harmondsworth, England, Penguin Books, 1959 (1954) (Pelican Book). 190 p.
A popular book which traces the literary history of the Bible. The main emphasis is on the New Testament. Includes a section on the Dead Sea scrolls. Bibliographic references and an index are added.

895 Hornsby, Samuel. "Style in the Bible: A Bibliography." Style, v. 7:3 (fall 1973), p. 349-74.
"The bibliography deals specifically with the English Bible and includes only secondary material available in English"--Text.

896 Kenyon, Frederick G. Our Bible and the Ancient Manuscripts, rev. by A. W. Adams, London, Eyre and Spottiswoode, 1965 (1958). 350 p.
This valuable critical work presents the history of transmission of the biblical text. It discusses all the variations of the text, the English Bibles, etc. Contains a general index, and an index of biblical passages.

897 Koch, Klaus. The Growth of the Biblical Tradition; the Form-critical Method. Transl. from the 2nd German ed. by S. M. Cupitt. New York, Scribner's, 1969 (Scribner Studies in Biblical Interpretation). 233 p.
Translation of Was ist Formgeschichte? "It is intended ... as a guide for the student, as an introduction to form-critical research, the evidence for which has gradually accumulated in innumerable articles on the Old Testament, some of them almost unobtainable..."--Introd. Contains an index of biblical literary types and their elements, and an index of biblical references.

898 MacGregor, Geddes. The Bible in the Making. Philadelphia, Lippincott, 1959. 447 p.
Presents a comprehensive account of opinions on the development and transmission of the Bible. Contains a concise and informative chapter on translations into English. Also includes appendices which list manuscripts, versions, and an essay evaluating the place of the Bible in Western World to-day. An index is provided.

899 ______. A Literary History of the Bible, from the Middle Ages to Present Day. Nashville, Abingdon Press, 1968. 400 p.
A useful textbook which presents many facts about biblical scholarship. It shows how advances in archeology and linguistics promote efforts to make the biblical text available in a clear modern language. As an example, it

selects a biblical passage and presents it in fifty translations from the Middle Ages to the Jerusalem Bible of 1966. Bibliographic references are provided in footnotes. There is also a general index.

900 McKnight, Edgar V. What Is Form Criticism? Philadelphia, Fortress Press, 1969 (Guides to Biblical Scholarship). 86 p.
Presents a survey of the written gospels back to the early Christian era. It points out how the tradition was transmitted from an oral stage to its written form of the canonical gospels. It is a useful introductory text which contains a list for additional readings.

901 Polzin, Robert M. Biblical Structuralism: Method and Subjectivity in the Study of Ancient Texts. Philadelphia, Fortress Press, 1976 (Semeia Supplements).
Contains a survey of new approaches to the study of biblical texts with selected bibliographical references and an index.

902 Rast, Walter. Tradition, History, and the Old Testament. Philadelphia, Fortress Press, 1971 (Old Testament Series: Guides to Biblical Scholarship). 82 p.
A popular paperback which explains various methods of literary criticism as applied to the study of the biblical text and its traditions. It takes into account the contemporary political and social motives and forces. Contains a glossary and a useful select bibliography. No index is provided.

903 Schwartz, Werner. Principles and Theories of Biblical Translation; Some Reformation Controversies and Their Background. Cambridge, Cambridge Univ. Press, 1955. 224 p.
This scholarly and instructive book is an historical study of the theories which have guided translators in the past. Contains useful indexes and extensive bibliographic references.

904 Wegener, Gunther S. 6000 Years of the Bible. Transl. by M. Shenfield. New York, Harper & Row, 1963 (1958). 352 p.
Translation of 6000 Jahre und eine Buch. A popular review which "presents the story of the Bible from its Hebrew origins to the English Bible"--Preface.

OLD TESTAMENT STUDIES

905 Anderson, Bernhard W. Understanding the Old Testament, 3rd ed. Englewood Cliffs, N.J., Prentice-Hall, 1975 (1957). 649 p.
A popular introduction to various subjects encountered

in the Old Testament. The reader will find references to other more serious critical works, and a useful classified bibliography.

906 Anderson, George W. A Critical Introduction to the Old Testament. London, Duckworth, 1959 (Studies in Theology). 250 p.
Provides a clear critical review of studies done on the subject. It discusses the canon, and then presents a critical analysis of individual books. A bibliography is provided.

907 Beebe, H. Keith. The Old Testament. Belmont, Calif., Dickenson, 1970. 505 p.
A well organized guide to the study of biblical topics for beginners. Contains a general select bibliography, and chapter bibliographies. There is also a general index.

908 Bewer, Julius A. The Literature of the Old Testament, 3rd ed. completely rev. by E. G. Kraeling. New York, Columbia Univ. Press, 1962 (1922). 496 p.
An excellent introduction aimed at the more serious student. It presents an historical survey of biblical events. Includes a select bibliography and a general index.

909 Fromm, Erich. You Shall Be as Gods; A Radical Interpretation of the Old Testament and Its Tradition. New York, Holt, 1966. 240 p.
A controversial work which presents "a non-theistic" interpretation of the Old Testament, the Talmud, and the Hasidic masters.

910 Goldingay, John. Old Testament Commentary Survey. London, Theological Students Fellowship, 1975. 37 p.
Provides an annotated list of selected tools for the study of the Old Testament.

911 Gottwald, Norman K. A Light of the Nations; An Introduction to the Old Testament. New York, Harper, 1959. 615 p.
Reviews the Old Testament against the historical background supported by new archeological evidence. "There has been an attempt to integrate the literature, history, and religion"--Introd. Contains a glossary of basically important names and technical terms. Bibliographic references are included.

912 Jellicoe, Sidney. The Septuagint and Modern Study. Oxford, England, Clarendon Press, 1968. 423 p.
A scholarly handbook for studies in the Old Testament in Greek. It surveys the older theories and discusses also new interpretations. An excellent bibliography, subject and author indexes are provided.

913 Moore, George F. The Literature of the Old Testament, 2nd ed., rev. by L. H. Brocklington. London, Oxford Univ. Press, 1948 (1913) (Home University Library of Modern Knowledge, 84). 232 p.

A classic written over 60 years ago which is presented with minor changes and additions. The opening chapters discuss the questions of sources and chronology, and then are followed by an analysis of each of the five books.

914 Oesterley, William O. E., and T. H. Robinson. An Introduction to the Books of the Old Testament. London, S. P. C. K.; New York, Macmillan, 1960 (1934). 454 p.

For a long time this book has been a standard textbook for biblical studies in English. It presents a critical study of the background of individual biblical books.

915 Pfeiffer, R. H. Introduction to the Old Testament. New York, Harper, 1948. 909 p.

A monumental scholarly work. The chapters on the canon, the text and versions, and the legal codes are still of great value. Contains a useful bibliography of older works. See also Roberts, Bleddyn J., The Old Testament Text and Versions: The Hebrew Text in Transmission, and the History of the Ancient Versions (Cardiff, Univ. of Wales Press, 1951).

916 Scott, Robert B. Y. The Way of Wisdom in the Old Testament. New York, Macmillan, 1971. 238 p.

Provides a general introduction to Old Testament studies, with bibliographic information for further studies in footnotes. Contains separate indexes for subjects, authors, and biblical references.

917 Weiser, A. The Old Testament: Its Formation and Development. New York, Association Press, 1968 (1961). 492 p.

Translation of Einleitung in das Alte Testament. This scholarly book surveys the history of each book separately. It deals also with the history of the text and the formation of the canon. Bibliographic references are included in footnotes. General index, and an index of biblical and post-biblical passages are provided.

NEW TESTAMENT STUDIES

Bibliographies

918 France, R. T., ed. A Bibliographical Guide to the New Testament Research, Cambridge, England, Tyndale Fellowship for Biblical Research, 1974 (1968) 45 p.

Provides a guide to sources of information for the study of the New Testament.

919 Hurd, John C. A Bibliography of New Testament Bibliographies. New York, Seabury, 1966. 75 p.

Provides an extensive annotated list of bibliographies which appeared in monographs and periodicals. Foreign language studies are included. A section containing individual bibliographies of outstanding scholars is included. There is no author index.

920 Mattil, A. J. and M. B. Mattil. A Classified Bibliography of Literature on the Acts of the Apostles. Leiden, Brill, 1966. 513 p.

Contains a listing of 6646 items including monographs and periodical articles. An author index is provided.

921 Murphy, Harold S. and P. Schubert, eds. Working Bibliography for the New Testament. New Haven, Conn., Yale Divinity School, 1950. 64 p.

Prepared for the students of the Yale University Divinity School. May be used as a general guide but should be up-dated with newer works.

922 Scholer, David M. A Basic Bibliographic Guide for New Testament Exegesis, new rev. ed. South Hamilton, Miss., Gordon-Conwell Book Center, 1973 (1971). 56 p.

The arrangement is by form--i.e. concordances, dictionaries, etc.--and by subjects.

Dictionaries and Guides

923 Brownrigg, Ronald. Who's Who in the New Testament. London, Weidenfeld and Nicolson, 1971. 448 p.

Lists all the people mentioned by name in the New Testament. Includes also some political and religious groups. It is based on the Revised Standard Version but lists also some variants from the King James Version. The Old Testament names are excluded.

924 Guy, Harold A. Who's Who in the Gospels. London, Macmillan; New York, St. Martin's Press, 1966. 152 p.

This popular and fairly reliable biographical dictionary lists people, places, and institutions which appear in the text of the New Testament.

925 Kittel, Gerhard. Theological Dictionary of the New Testament. Transl. and Ed.: G. W. Bromiley. Grand Rapids, Mich., Eerdmans, 1964- (8 vols. when completed).

A full authorized English translation of the famous Theologisches Wörterbuch zum Neuen Testament. Contains extensive scholarly articles on all aspects of the New Testament theology. Bibliographic references are provided.

Companion

926 Harvey, Anthony E. *The New English Bible: Companion to the New Testament.* Cambridge, England, Univ. Press, 1970. 850 p.

Presents the cultural, historical, literary, and theological background to the Gospels, the Letters of Apostles, the Acts, and the Revelation of John. It is arranged as a commentary to the text, line by line. An index provides a subject approach.

Abstracts

927 *New Testament Abstracts.* Weston, Mass., Weston College of the Holy Spirit, Fall 1956- (3 issues a year).

Published by the Weston College Theological Faculty. Contains an index of references to the scriptural text, and an index of authors.

Handbooks and Critical Works

928 Batey, Richard A., ed. *New Testament Issues.* New York, Harper & Row, 1970. 241 p.

This collection is comprised of papers by outstanding specialists in the field, e.g. N. Perrin, R. Bultmann, S. Sandmel, J. A. T. Robinson, etc. Bibliographic references are included.

929 Briggs, R. C. *Interpreting the Gospels: An Introduction to Methods and Issues in the Study of the Synoptic Gospels.* Nashville, Abingdon Press, 1969. 188 p.

Provides a clear and concise presentation of the problems one encounters in biblical research and the methods which are used to solve them. There are some bibliographic references included.

930 Bruce, Frederick F. *New Testament History.* London, Nelson, 1969 (Library of Theology). 434 p.

An historian presents a well-documented scholarly survey of events of the New Testament times. Contains a select bibliography, an index of authors, index of historical persons, and an index of places.

931 Colwell, Ernst C. *Studies in Methodology in Textual Criticism of the New Testament.* Leiden, Brill, 1969 (*New Testament Tools and Studies*, v. 9). 183 p.

This collection is comprised of 11 essays which explain various methods applied in the research of the New Testament texts. Numerous bibliographic references to both periodical articles and monographs are included. There is also a name index.

932 Davies, W. D. Invitation to the New Testament: A Guide to Its Main Witnesses. Garden City, N.Y., Doubleday, 1966. 540 p.

Presents a popular interpretation of the main issues in New Testament studies. It provides a general review of the field, and deals with the first three gospels, Paul, and, on its own, the fourth gospel. Contains a select bibliography, and an index of biblical citations.

933 Filson, Floyd V. A New Testament History; the Story of the Emerging Church. Philadelphia, Westminster, 1964. 435 p.

"Provides a clear and connected account of the crucial three hundred years of history that are involved"--Preface. Also contains bibliographic references mainly to English materials, a general index, and colored maps.

934 Finegan, Jack. The Archeology of the New Testament, the Life of Jesus and the Beginning of Early Church. Princeton, N.J., Princeton Univ. Press, 1969. 273 p.

A useful handbook which investigates the remains of places mentioned in the New Testament. Each site is discussed in connection with the tests. A chronological list of ancient places, bibliographies, an index of scriptural references, and a general index are provided.

935 Grant, Frederic C. The Gospels, Their Origin and Their Growth. London, Faber and Faber, 1957. 216 p.

A scholarly study which discusses the origin and development of the gospels. A select bibliography and an index of subject, persons, and texts are included.

936 Grant, Robert M. The Formation of the New Testament. London, Hutchinson, 1965 (University Library; Religion). 196 p.

A popular introduction which explains the historical circumstances surrounding the formation of the New Testament tradition. Select bibliography and an index are provided.

937 ________. An Introduction to the New Testament. London, Collins, 1963. 447 p.

A scholarly study which deals with the theory of interpretation, the canon, the New Testament literature, etc. Also contains a discussion of the New Testament chronology. An index is included.

938 Harrison, Everett F. Introduction to the New Testament. Grand Rapids, Mich., 1964. 480 p.

This is a useful guide to "the various lines of investigation that are germaine to the approach to the New Testament..."--Preface. Brief bibliographies at the end of each chapter and a general bibliography are provided. There is also an index of subjects, authors, and scriptural references.

939 Henshaw, Thomas. New Testament Literature in the Light of Modern Scholarship. London, Hodder and Stoughton, 1963. 454 p.

A popular introduction to the study of the New Testament which presents a reliable summary of achievements of modern scholarship. A select bibliography and an index are included.

940 Jeremias, Joachim. New Testament Theology. London, SCM, 1971- (New Testament Library).

A significant study which accepts the reliability of the synoptic gospels as giving an essentially authentic picture of the historical events. Contains frequent references to other important critical works, e.g. of Karl Barth, Rudolph K. Bultmann.

941 Kee, H.; F. W. Young; and K. Froelich. Understanding the New Testament, 2nd ed. Englewood Cliffs, N.J., Prentice-Hall, 1965 (1957). 490 p.

The British edition is known under the title: The Living World of the New Testament. An excellent textbook for beginners which combines historical, theological, and literary studies for presentation of the historical setting and sequence of events in the development of early Christianity. Contains a well selected and annotated bibliography.

942 Kümmel, Werner G. The New Testament: The History of the Investigation of Its Problems. Transl. by S. MacLean Gilmour and H. Clark Kee. London, SCM, 1973 (New Testament Library). 510 p.

This exhaustive survey, now revised and up-dated, sorts out the major movements and prevailing ways in which historical problems relating to the New Testament and its background have been defined and investigated. Bibliographic references and an index are included.

943 McKnight, Edgar V. What Is Form Criticism? Philadelphia, Fortress Press, 1969 (Guides to Biblical Scholarship). 86 p.

A brief popular explanation of modern critical methods used in biblical scholarship. A short bibliography is included.

944 Metzger, Bruce M. The Text of the New Testament, Its Transmission, Corruption, and Restoration, 2nd ed. New York, Oxford Univ. Press, 1968 (1964). 284 p.

The most comprehensive and up-to-date handbook for advanced students. It outlines the origins and transmission of ancient manuscripts which contain the most important evidence of the authenticity of the New Testament text. It also deals with the history of textual criticism as reflected in the printed editions of the Greek Testament. Contains a check-list of the Greek papyri of the New

Testament. A select bibliography and an index are included.

945 Neill, Stephen C. The Interpretation of the New Testament, 1861-1961. London, Oxford Univ. Press, 1964 (Firth Lectures, 1962). 360 p.

Excellent reading for the non-specialist; traces the history of New Testament textual criticism and discusses the problem of the historical Jesus. There are some bibliographic references in the footnotes.

946 Perrin, Norman. What Is Redaction Criticism? London, S. P. C. K., 1970 (Guides to Biblical Scholarship). 85 p.

A well-written popular explanation of the modern critical methods used in biblical scholarship. A short bibliography is provided.

947 Pfeiffer, R. H. History of the New Testament Times, with an Introduction to the Apocrypha. New York, Harper, 1949. 561 p.

The sequel and completion of the author's Introduction to the Old Testament--see no. 915. Provides an informative survey of opinions on the political, religious, and literary history of the period. Contains an extensive select bibliography.

948 Price, James L. Interpreting the New Testament, 2nd ed. New York, Holt, Rinehart, and Winston, 1971 (1961). 624 p.

This excellent book outlines the background of the entire New Testament giving special attention to the intellectual values created by the people of the Hellenistic period. One should note chapters on "the historical Jesus" which present the most recent developments in the field. A select bibliography and an index are provided. Contains a well-selected collection of illustrations.

949 Pritchard, John P. A Literary Approach to the New Testament. Norman, Univ. of Oklahoma Press, 1972. 355 p.

Presents a summary of the endless variety of interpretations of the development of the form and content of the New Testament. It explains in detail who was the author of each book, when it was written, to whom it was addressed, and the motives involved. Contains a glossary of literary and biblical terms, an excellent selective bibliography and an index.

950 Spivey, Robert A., and D. Moody Smith. Anatomy of the New Testament. London, Macmillan, 1969. 510 p.

A popular work which takes into consideration the new discoveries, new approaches and methodologies used in the New Testament research. It takes each of the books and examines its structure, content, and theological focus.

Contains a glossary of terms, general select bibliography, name and subject index, and a biblical index.

951 Wikenhauser, Alfred. New Testament Introduction. Transl. by J. Cunningham. New York, Herder & Herder, 1958 (1956). 579 p.
Translation of the 2nd rev. and enlarged edition of Einleitung in das Neue Testament. It is recognized as one of the best introductory texts to the study of the subject. Bibliographic references are included in footnotes. Contains also an index of persons and subjects.

JESUS STUDIES

Dictionary

952 Hastings, James. Dictionary of Christ and Gospels. New York, Scribner's, 1908. 2 vols.
"The purpose of this dictionary is to give an account of everything that relates to Christ, his person, life, work, and teaching... [and] it includes everything that the Gospels contain..."--Preface. An old but still useful reference work; information should be supplemented with more recent data.

Index to Periodicals

953 Metzger, Bruce M., ed. Index to Periodical Literature on Christ and the Gospels. Grand Rapids, Mich., Eerdmans, 1962 (New Testament Tools and Studies, v. 6). 602 p.
Contains citations to articles from some 160 periodicals in 16 languages. An author index is provided.

Critical Studies

954 Anderson, Charles C. Critical Quests of Jesus. Grand Rapids, Mich., Eerdmans, 1969. 208 p.
Contains a review of various historical approaches to the question of the "historical Jesus" since the beginning of the 19th century up to the early 1960s. A well-selected bibliography and separate indexes for names and subjects are included.

955 Anderson, Hugh. Jesus and Christian Origins; A Commentary on Modern Viewpoints. New York, Oxford Univ. Press, 1964. 265 p.
This scholarly study aims at the explanation of modern understanding of the "Jesus of history" and "Christ of faith" issues. A select bibliography, and an index are included.

956 Bornkamm, Günther. Jesus of Nazareth. Transl. by Irene and Fraser McLuskey with J. M. Robinson. New York, Harper, 1960 (1956). 239 p.

Reviews the state of knowledge in the field of Jesus' studies. Also contains a bibliography, an index of subject, and an index of names.

957 Cohn, Haim. The Trial and Death of Jesus. New York, Harper & Row, 1972. 419 p.

An outstanding Israeli lawyer investigates the judicial proceedings against Jesus. Contains an extensive classified bibliography of monographs and periodical articles, and a general index.

958 Connick, C. M. Jesus; The Man, the Mission, and the Message, 2nd ed. Englewood Cliffs, N.J., Prentice-Hall, 1974. 464 p.

The aim of the book is to provide a balanced and up-to-date account about Jesus. Also contains suggestions for further reading, an index of biblical references, and a subject index.

959 Daniel-Rops, Henri. Jesus and His Times. Transl. from the French by R. Millar. New York, Dutton, 1954. 615 p.

In this well written popular book a respected French Catholic theologian reviews the contemporary knowledge of Jesus based on historical and theological interpretations. A chronological table is included.

960 Hayes, John H. Son of God to Superstar: Twentieth Century Interpretations of Jesus. Nashville, Abingdon, 1976. 255 p.

Contains a survey of selected treatments of the life of Jesus from the late 19th and 20th centuries. There are no critical or evaluative comments. A list of works employed is added.

961 Kähler, Martin. The So-Called Historical Jesus and the Historic Biblical Christ. Transl., ed., and with an Introd. by Carl E. Braaten. Foreword by P. J. Tillich. Philadelphia, Fortress Press, 1964 (1961) (Seminar Editions). 153 p.

Translation of Der sogennante historische Jesus (1961). Presents the problem of "historical Jesus" on the background of scholarly research into the sources. Bibliography in footnotes and an index are provided.

962 Kee, Howard C. Jesus in History; An Approach to the Study of Gospels. New York, Harcourt, Brace, 1970. 280 p.

Reviews the critical methods that have been used in the study of the gospels. Bibliographic references in footnotes, and an index are included. Also contains a classification system for the synoptic tradition.

963 McArthur, Harvey K., ed. In Search of Historical Jesus. London, S.P.C.K., 1970. 284 p.
Contains extracts from papers by the most outstanding specialists published in periodicals in the last thirty years.

964 Machoveč, Milan. Marxist Looks at Jesus. With an Introd. by P. Hebblethwaite. Philadelphia, Fortress Press, 1976. 231 p.
Translation of Jesus für Atheisten. Provides a Marxist analysis of problems pertaining to the studies of Jesus. Useful indexes and additional readings are provided.

965 Peter, James. Finding the Historical Jesus; A Statement of the Principals Involved. London, Collins, 1965. 222 p.
Presents the "state of knowledge" concerning Jesus as presented by the New Testament and historiography. It contains also an evaluation of contributions made by the "school of demythologizing." Bibliographic notes and an index arc provided.

966 Schweizer, Eduard. Jesus. London, SCM, 1971 (New Testament Library). 200 p.
Contains a fairly orthodox exposition of personal convictions concerning Jesus and his place in the faith of the early church. Some bibliographic notes, an index of modern scholars, and a selective index of New Testament references are supplied.

PAULINE STUDIES

Index to Periodicals

967 Metzger, Bruce M. Index to Periodical Literature on the Apostle Paul. Leiden, Brill, 1960 (New Testament Tools and Studies, v. 1). 183 p.
Contains citations to articles from some 135 periodicals in 14 languages. Coverage is up to the end of 1957; there is also an author index.

Critical Studies

968 Bornkamm, Günther. Paul. Transl. by D. M. G. Stalker. London, Hodder & Stoughton, 1971. 259 p.
Translation of Paulus (1969). The introductory chapters present the life and work of Paul. The core of the book analyzes basic elements of the Pauline theology. It stresses the continuity between the messages of Jesus and Paul. Contains an index and a select bibliography.

969 Deissmann, Adolph. Paul; A Study in Social and Religious History. Transl. by W. E. Wilson. New York, Harper and Row, 1957 (1912; rev. ed. 1925) (Harper Torchbook. Cloister Library).

A well-written popular discussion of basic problems of "Pauline Studies." Contains some bibliographic notes, and an index.

STUDIES IN APOCRYPHA

970 Brockington, L. H. A Critical Introduction to the Apocrypha. London, Duckworth, 1961 (Studies in Theology). 170 p.

The introductory chapter presents a survey of research and draws an historical background of the stories of the Apocrypha. It is followed by chapters which discuss each book separately. The last chapter attempts to evaluate their importance in one's understanding of the biblical texts. Also includes a select bibliography, an index of biblical references, and a general index.

971 Torrey, Charles C. The Apocryphal Literature: A Brief Introduction. New Haven, Conn., Yale Univ. Press, 1948 (1946). 151 p.

Presents a concise and informative survey of the political, religious, and literary history of the period when the text of the Apocrypha was in the formative stage. Contains also some bibliographic information.

QUMRAN [DEAD SEA SCROLLS] STUDIES

General Survey

972 Sanders, James A. "The Dead Sea Scrolls; A Quarter Century of Study." The Biblical Archaeologist, v. 36:4 (Dec. 1973).

Provides a detailed account and evaluation of research with extensive bibliographic references to monographs, field reports, and periodical articles within the text.

Texts of Scrolls in English Translation

973 Dead Sea Scrolls. English. The Dead Sea Scriptures in English Translation with Introduction and Notes, by T. H. Gaster. Rev. and enl. ed. Garden City, N.Y., Doubleday, 1964 (1954) (Anchor Books). 420 p.

"The purpose of this book is to provide a complete and reliable translation.... This book is addressed to laymen" --Preface. Contains a list of sources, an analytical index, and biblical quotations and parallels. Bibliographic references are provided.

974 Fitzmyer, Joseph A. The Dead Sea Scrolls: Major Publications and Tools for Study. Missoula, Mont., Scholars Press, 1975 (Sources for Biblical Studies, 8). 171 p.

This well-designed bibliographic tool "includes not only the list of sites where the texts have been found and the full bibliographical titles of the major publications, but also guides for further materials: bibliographies of the Dead Sea scrolls, survey articles, other attempts to list the materials, concordances and dictionaries for the study of the texts, secondary collections of Qumran texts, translations in modern languages..."--Preface.

Bibliographies

975 "Bibliographie." Revue de Qumran, 1958- .

Each issue brings a current, exhaustive listing of monographs, essays in collections, and periodicals. See no. 986.

976 Jongeling, B. A Classified Bibliography of the Finds in the Desert of Judah, 1958-1969. Leiden, Brill, 1971 (Studies on the Texts of the Desert of Judah, v. 7). 140 p.

Continues no. 977 but some pre-1958 publications are included, especially periodical articles. Also a number of 1970 publications is recorded. An author index is supplied.

977 LaSor, William S. Bibliography of the Dead Sea Scrolls, 1948-1957. Pasadena, Calif., Fuller Theological Seminary Library, 1958 (Fuller Library Bulletin, no. 31; Theological Seminary Bibliographical Series, no. 2). 92 p.

Lists some 2982 items arranged in three main groups: general works, the texts of Qumran, and the interpretation of the Qumran literature. There are useful cross-references, a complete index of authors, and a subject index. Continued by no. 976.

Handbooks and Critical Works

978 Cross, Frank M. An Ancient Library of Qumran and Modern Biblical Studies, rev. ed. Garden City, N.Y., Anchor Books, 1961 (Haskell Lectures, 1956-57). 260 p.

Presents a systematic interpretation of the facts available at the time the lectures were delivered. Deals with the discoveries, the Essenes, the "righteous teacher," the Old Testament in Qumran, the question of Essenes and the primitive church, etc. Some bibliographic references are given in footnotes. There is also a general index.

979 Driver, G. R. The Judean Scrolls: The Problem and the Solution. New York, Schocken Books, 1966. 624 p.

One of the most comprehensive discussions of the scrolls. It relates the scrolls to the Jewish revolt against Rome in A.D. 66-73 making them contemporary to the events described in the New Testament, and as such considering them as the most important documents for the understanding of New Testament history. Extensive bibliographic references and a general index are provided.

980 Dupont-Sommer, A. The Essene Writing from Qumran. Transl. by G. Vermès. Cleveland, World Pub. Co., 1962 (1959) (Meridian Book). 428 p.

Translation of Les Escrits esséniens découverts près de la Mer Morte. "The book constitutes a corpus of the Qumran writings, and, in addition, sums up all the problems raised by the new texts. The latter are provided with the introductions and explanations necessary for placing them, as far as possible, within their time and environment"--Preface. Contains a bibliography, an alphabetical index of the translated Qumran writings, an index of biblical references and an index of authors.

981 LaSor, William S. The Dead Sea Scrolls and the New Testament. Grand Rapids, Mich., Eerdmans, 1972. 281 p.

Present an excellent survey of the Qumran studies with a classified bibliography, and separate indexes of subjects and authors.

982 Mansoor, Menahem. The Dead Sea Scrolls; A College Textbook and a Study Guide. Grand Rapids, Mich., Eerdmans, 1964. 210 p.

Outlines the most important works done in the field. It presents materials on the Jewish sects, and evidence relating to the Bar Kochba's uprising. Contains a list of topics for further study, a glossary of terms and proper names, a list of main scrolls, a recommended bibliography, a chronological table for the intertestamental period, and a general index.

983 Qumran and the History of the Biblical Text. Ed. by Cross, F. M. and S. Talmon. Cambridge, Mass., Harvard Univ. Press, 1975. 415 p.

Selects 17 previously published articles which discuss various critical issues of the Qumran texts. Bibliographic references are included in notes. Lacks an index.

984 Vermès, Géza. Discoveries in the Judean Desert. New York, Desclee, 1956. 237 p.

This is the first scholarly attempt to summarize the discoveries and theories about the provenance of the scrolls. Contains a review of circumstances of the discovery, comments on the texts, and their first interpretation. There is a new theory by the author added. Select bibliography and an index are included.

985 Yadin, Yigael. The Message of the Scrolls. New York, Grosset and Dunlap, 1962 (1957). 191 p.
Israeli archeologist's popular account of Dead Sea scrolls; Index is supplied, but no bibliographic references.

Journal

986 Revue de Qumran. Paris, 1958- .
Its papers--in English, French, German, Italian, or Latin--are completely devoted to the field. Contains feature articles, book reviews, and a comprehensive current bibliography. Indexed: Rel. Per.; Rel. Theol. Abstr.

JOURNALS

987 Biblica; Rome, 1920- (quarterly).
Published by the Pontificio Istituto Biblico. Papers in English, German, French, Italian, Latin, and Spanish. Contains book reviews and lists new acquisitions. Indexed: Rel. Per.; Rel. Theol. Abstr.

988 Biblical Archaeologist. Cambridge, Mass., 1938- (quarterly).
Published by the American School of Oriental Research. Contains a long feature article, news reports, and brief bibliographic information. Indexed: Art Index; Rel. Per.; Rel. Theol. Abstr.

989 Biblical Research. Amsterdam, 1957- (irregularly).
Published by the Chicago Society of Biblical Research. Indexed: Rel. Per.

990 Journal of Biblical Literature. Philadelphia, 1882- (quarterly).
Published by the Society of Biblical Literature, University of Montana, Missoula. Indexed: Index of Jewish Periodicals; New Testament Abstracts; Rel. Theol. Abstr.; Soc. Sci. Hum. Index.

991 New Testament Studies; An International Journal. Cambridge, England, 1954- (quarterly).
Published under auspices of the Studiorum Novi Testamenti Societas. Articles in English, French, and German. Indexed: Rel. Per.; Rel. Theol. Abstr.

992 Novum Testamentum; An International Quarterly for New Testament and Related Studies Based on International Cooperation. Leiden, Brill, 1956- (15 vols. per year).

993 Textus; Annual. Jerusalem, 1960- .
Published by the Hebrew University Bible Project.

994 Zeitschrift für die Alttestamentliche Wissenschaft. Berlin, 1881- (3 issues a year).
One of the most important journals in the field, containing articles in English, French or German by leading archeologists, linguists, psychologists, experts in comparative religion, historians, and others. An extensive book and periodical review section is provided. Indexed: Rel. Per.; Rel. Theol. Abstr.

Part Three--Judaism, Christianity, Islam (cont.)

V ISLAM

REFERENCE WORKS

DICTIONARIES AND ENCYCLOPEDIAS

995 Encyclopedia of Islam. New ed. by H. A. R. Gibb, J. H. Kramers, E. Lévi-Provençal, J. Schacht ... under the patronage of the International Union of Academies. Leiden, Brill; London, Luzac, 1954- (1st ed. 1911-38, 4 vols.).

This is the fundamental Western compendium of Islamic knowledge. Contains signed articles, with bibliographies, on biography, history, geography, religious beliefs, institutions, manners and customs, tribes, industries, sciences. Articles on geography include information on places where Islam has been of importance. The new edition gives more emphasis on political, social and economic aspects; there is also more information on Islamic arts. The use of the work is somewhat difficult because the entries are given in the appropriate Arabic term, e.g. the article on the mosque is found under its Arabic name, masdjid. One might find helpful a register of subjects in English with their Arabic equivalents in the Shorter Encyclopedia of Islam, p. 663-5 (see no. 1001). Until the new edition is completed the older one of 1911-38 must be still used.

996 Encyclopedia of the Middle East. Ed. M. Hawryluk. Detroit, Publishing Center, Inc., 1976. 20 v.

Lists some 10,000 signed articles, many pertaining to religious problems. An excellent index volume with over 4000 references; a bibliography volume and an annual volume are provided.

997 Heravi, Mehdi, ed. Concise Encyclopedia of the Middle East. New York, Public Affairs Press, 1974. 336 p.

"The purpose of this book is to provide the reader with a convenient source of essential information about the Middle East, its nations, its institutions, its problems, and its personalities"--Foreword.

998 Hughes, Thomas. A Dictionary of Islam, Being a Cyclopedia of the Doctrines, Rites, Ceremonies, and Customs, Together with the Technical and Theological Terms of the Muhammedan Religion. London, Allen, 1885. 750 p.
This old but still useful work contains articles on a variety of the subjects that concern Islamic doctrines, rites, ceremonies, customs, etc. However, information must be carefully interpreted and up-dated.

999 Ibn Khallikan. Biographical Dictionary. Transl. from the Arabic by Mac Guckin de Slane. New York, Johnson Reprints, 1961 (1842-71). 4 vols.
This work, originally completed in 1256 (!), contains a compilation of biographies of some 1000 distinguished Muslims from the formative period of Islam. Each volume is provided with an index of biographies included.

1000 Ronart, S., and N. Ronart. Concise Encyclopedia of Islamic Civilization; The Arab East. New York, Praeger, 1959 (Books that Matter). 2 vols., suppl. in preparation.
Covers the Arabian Peninsula, Egypt, Iraq, Jordan, Lebanon, and Syria. Biographies are included. There is also a brief list of bibliographic references.

1001 Shorter Encyclopedia of Islam. Ed. on behalf of the Royal Netherlands Academy by H. A. R. Gibb and J. H. Krammer. Leiden, Brill, 1953. 671 p.
Contains a selection of articles from the 1st ed. of the Encyclopedia of Islam, with a number of new additions. Bibliographies are up-dated. There is a register of subjects in English with their Arabic equivalents which aids in finding the proper Arabic entry of an article.

BIBLIOGRAPHIES AND GUIDES

1002 Adams, Charles J. "Islam." A Reader's Guide to the Great Religions. 2nd ed. New York, Free Press, 1977 (1965), p. 407-466.
See no. 22. A bibliographic essay which reviews all aspects of Islamic studies: the pre-Islamic background, prophet and the Qur'an, tradition, philosophy, theology, Islamic institutions, mysticism, modern developments. A list of periodicals is provided.

1003 Atiyeh, George N. The Contemporary Middle East, 1948-1973; Selective and Annotated Bibliography. Boston, G. K. Hall, 1975. 664 p.
"This is basically a social sciences bibliography...." It "introduces by annotation significant publications bearing directly on the contemporary Middle East"--Introd.

Of special interest are the sections, D. Religion, and E. Law and Islamic Law, p. 63-76. Author and subject indexes are appended.

1004 Bacharach, Jere L. A Near East Studies Handbook, Rev. ed. Seattle, Univ. of Washington Press, 1976 (1974). 158 p.
Contains dynastic and genealogical tables, a historical atlas, and conversion calendar, a glossary of foreign terms, a chronology of important historical events, and other miscellaneous data.

1005 Bijlefeld, Willem A. "Introducing Islam; A Bibliographical Essay." Muslim World, v. 63:3 (July 1973), p. 171-184.
Presents an informative survey of the literature for studies of Islam and its civilization.

1006 Ettinghausen, Richard, ed. A Selected and Annotated Bibliography of Books and Periodicals in Western Languages Dealing with the Near and Middle East, with Special Emphasis on Medieval and Modern Times. (Completed Summer 1951, with a Supplement 1953.) Washington, D.C., Middle East Institute, 1952. 137 p.
Contains a detailed table of contents. One should note the sections Pre-Islamic Arabia, p. 29; Islamic Civilization to Early 1800's, p. 31; and Modern Islam, p. 63. A useful general bibliography with annotations.

1007 Fiegenbaum, J. W. "A Bibliography of the Islamic Tradition." Choice, v. 9:10 (1972) p. 1268-74.
Contains a list of monographs divided into four categories: (1) basic introductory reading; (2-3) more advanced studies; (4) materials for more complex research on the undergraduate level.

1008 Geddes, Charles L. Analytical Guide to the Bibliographies on the Arabian Peninsula. Denver, American Institute of Islamic Studies, 1974 (Bibliographic series, no. 4). 50 p.
An annotated bibliography of bibliographies on Islam and the Muslim world. Lists some 70 bibliographies in Western languages.

1009 ______. Books in English on Islam, Muhammad, and the Qur'an: A Selected and Annotated Bibliography. Denver, American Institute of Islamic Studies, 1976 (Bibliographic Series, 5). 68 p.
Lists some 135 books of value selected for the English reading student and non-specialist. Arranged by subject with annotations. A general index of authors, subjects and titles is provided.

1010 Hopwood, Derek, and D. Grimwood-Jones. Middle East and Islam; A Bibliographical Introduction. Foreword by J. D.

Pearson. Zug, Switzerland, Inter-Documentation Co., 1972 (Middle East Library Committee. Bibliotheca asiatica, 9). 368 p.

This bibliography was compiled from lists prepared for a conference held in Cambridge in 1970. Its aim is to establish a list of items for a basic research collection; this list will be kept up-to-date by annual supplements.

1011 "Islam." McCasland, S. V. Religions of the World. New York, Random House, 1969. p. 313-43; 351-2.

An informative introduction which deals with religious beliefs in pre-Islamic Arabia, Muhammad and the Qur'an, Muslim law, theology, and mysticism. Also discusses the basic issues of the contemporary Islam. Contains a select bibliography of monographs.

1012 Kuwait. University. Libraries Department. Select Bibliography on Arab Islamic Civilization and Its Contributions to Human Progress. Kuwait, University, 1971 (Its Bibliographical Series, no. 3). 152 p.

Its scope is limited to non-Arabic sources, predominantly English, French, and German.

1013 McNeil, W. K., ed. A Bibliography of Middle East Folklore. Bloomington, Ind., Folklore Institute, 1972 (Folklore Forum; A Communication for Students of Folklore; Bibliographic and Special Series, no. 9).

Is comprised of materials on peoples; cultures and customs; drama, epic, and romance; proverbs and riddles; magic; superstition; medicine; sufism; and philosophy. An author index and an area index are added.

1014 Pearson, J. D., ed. Arab Islamic Bibliography: The Middle East Library Committee Guide. Based on Gabrieli's Manuale di bibliografia musulmana. Hassocks, Sussex, Harvester, 1976.

Provides a series of bibliographic essays by outstanding specialists. Deals with reference books in general, bibliographies, periodicals, manuscripts, Festschriften, and the publications of expeditions.

1015 Zuwiyya, Jalal, ed. The Near East (South-West Asia and North Africa): A Bibliographic Study. Metuchen, N.J., Scarecrow Press, 1973. 392 p.

Includes a selection of some 3600 titles written in the European languages, arranged alphabetically by author. Of special interest is the section: Philosophy, Religion, Mythology, p. 72-111.

INDEXES AND ABSTRACTS

1016 Abstracta islamica; supplément à la Revue des études islamiques. Paris, 1927- (annually).
Lists monographs and periodical articles. The content is divided into: historical studies, geography, ethnography, sociology, language, literature and folklore, reformism and nationalism of contemporary Islam, etc. An author index is added.

1017 Pearson, James D., comp. Index islamicus; A Catalogue of Articles on Islamic Subjects in Periodicals and Other Collective Publications. Cambridge, England, Mansell, 1958- (now quarterly).
Formerly published annually in paperbound supplements with five-year cumulations. A comprehensive classified index to nearly all scholarly articles published in the field since 1905. 1977-on, published quarterly.

GEOGRAPHICAL WORKS AND ATLASES

1018 Hazard, Harry W. Atlas of Islamic History. Maps executed by H. L. Cooke, and J. McA. Smiley. 3 rev. and corrected ed. Princeton, N.J., Princeton Univ. Press, 1954 (Princeton Oriental Studies, v. 12).
Contains information on the development of the Islamic countries from A.D. 622 to the present. Provides summaries of the important historical events in Europe, Africa, and Asia on the page opposite each map. At the end one finds a conversion table of Christian and Moslem calendars. There is also an index of places shown on the maps.

1019 LaStrange, Guy, ed. Palestine under the Moslems; A Description of Syria and the Holy Land from A.D. 650 to 1500. Translated from the Works of the Mediaeval Arab Geographers ... with a new Introduction by W. Khadily. Beirut, Khayyat., 1965 (1890) (Khayyat Oriental Reprints, no. 14). 604 p.

1020 ________. The Lands of the Eastern Caliphate: Mesopotamia, Persia, and Central Asia from the Moslem Conquest to the Time of Timur. London, Cass, 1966 (1905). 536 p.
The editor and translator presents the most complete collection of original geographical materials of the medieval Muslims concerning the most important regions in the development of Islamic civilization.

1021 Planhol, Xavier de. The World of Islam. Ithaca, N.Y., Cornell Univ. Press, 1959 (1957).

Discusses the geographical aspects in Islamic history and society.

1022 Roolvink, R., comp. and others. Historical Atlas of the Muslim Peoples. Cambridge, Mass., Harvard Univ. Press, 1957. 40 p.
The best atlas of its kind. It contains clear, well-produced maps covering the period from A.D. 622 to the present. Especially good coverage is provided for the middle ages.

CHRONOLOGY

1023 Bosworth, Clifford E. The Islamic Dynasties; A Chronological Handbook. Edinburgh, Univ. Press, 1967 (Islamic Surveys, V. 5). 245 p.
Lists some 82 Islamic dynasties in all parts of the Islamic world, from the beginning of Islam to the present day. Each genealogical table is accompanied by a brief informative history of a dynasty. Consult also: Lane-Poole, S. The Muhammedan Dynasties (New York, Unger, 1965 (1893)).

QUR'AN [KORAN]

TESTS IN ENGLISH TRANSLATION

1024 Koran. English and Arabic. The Message of the Qur'an Presented in Perspective, by Hashin Amir-Ali. Rutland, Vt., Tuttle, 1974. 1 v.
Provides a new rendition of the text with parallel text in Arabic. Also contains some interesting critical comments. Presents the Indian viewpoint.

1025 _______. English. The Koran Interpreted, by Arthur J. Arberry, combined in one volume. New York, Macmillan, 1955, 358 p.
This is the best of recent translations; uses rhythm patterns to express the power of the original Arabic version. In addition, it includes a review of precious English translations. An index of subjects and names is provided.

1026 _______. _______. The Qur'an; translated with critical re-arrangement of the Surahs by Richard Bell. Edinburgh, Clark, 1937. 2 vols.
An excellent translation which presents the results of contemporary critical studies of the text. Contains a bibliography. Should be used together with the author's

Introduction to the Qur'an (see no. 1034).

1027 _______. _______. The Koran; a New Translation by N. J. Dawood. Harmondsworth, England, Penguin, 1956.
Translation is accompanied by explanatory notes based on classical authorities. The surahs are rearranged to create a better literary effect.

1028 _______. _______. al-Qur'an. Rendered into English by Syed Abdul Lalif. Hyderabad, Academy of Islamic Studies, 1969. 579 p.

1029 _______. _______. The Holy Qur'an; The Text, Translation, and Commentary; rev. ed. by Maulana Muhammad 'Ali. Lahore, Ahmadiyyah Anjuman Isha'at Islam, 1951. 1254 p.
The two cited above items present examples of modern translations by Indian Muslims.

1030 _______. _______. The Qur'an. Translated and with an introduction by E. H. Palmer. Oxford, Clarendon Press, 1880 (World Classics. Sacred Books of the East, ed. by Max Muller, v. 6, 9). 2 vols.
Follows the traditional arrangement of surahs. This is an example of an older translation resembling the language of the English Bible.

1031 _______. _______. The Meaning of the Glorious Koran; An Explanatory Translation, by Marmaduke Pickthall. London, Allen & Unwin, 1930. 464 p.
A modern translation by an English Muslim which renders clearly the meaning of the verses. One should be cautious when reading the author's explanatory notes.

1032 _______. _______. 1975. The Holy Qur'an; English Translation and Explanatory Notes. Ed. Abdul Hameed Saddiqui. Lahore, Islamic Book Centre, 1975- .
Arabic text runs parallel with the English translation. Contains detailed footnotes to obscure words and detailed explanation of passages.

GUIDE

1033 Watt, William M. Companion to the Qur'an, Based on the Arberry transl. London, Allen and Unwin, 1967. 355 p.
Provides extensive background information for the understanding and appreciation of the Koran in translation. It is arranged by surahs. Contains an index to the proper names appearing in the Qur'an and an index to the commentary.

CRITICAL WORKS

1034 Bell, Richard. Introduction to the Qur'an, rev. and enl. by W. M. Watt. Edinburgh, Univ. Press, 1970 (Islamic Surveys, v. 8). 190 p.

A remarkably concise but comprehensive discussion of the Qur'an and its scholarship. It offers answers to many specific problems posed by the Qur'an as a religious scripture and literary work. Includes also a summary of research on the prophet. Contains a table of surahs, an index to the Qur'an, and a general index.

1035 Cragg, Kenneth. The Event of the Qur'an: Islam in Its Scripture. London, Allen and Unwin, 1971 (Bross Lectures, 1968). 208 p.

The first four chapters discuss various aspects of the prophetic ministry, the idea of scripture, and the concept of god. The subsequent sections deal with geography and society, as well as with the information about Muhammad's career as it is reflected in the Qur'an. Bibliographic references are given in the footnotes. See also the author's The Mind of the Qur'an (London, Allen and Unwin, 1973, 209 p.).

1036 Gätje, Helmut. The Qur'an and Its Exegesis; Selected Texts with Classical and Modern Muslim Interpretations. Transl. and ed. by A. T. Welch. Berkeley, Univ. of California Press, 1976 (Islamic World). 327 p.

Contains key passages selected from the Arberry translation with their classical and modern commentaries.

1037 Izutsu, Toshihiko. Ethico-Religious Concepts of the Qur'an, rev. ed. Montréal, McGill Univ. Press, 1966 (1959) (McGill Islamic Studies, 1). 284 p.

Originally published under the title, The Structure of the Ethical Terms in the Koran. Presents one of the most illuminating studies of fundamental Qur'anic concepts based on the linguistic analysis of the text. Numerous bibliographic references are included. One should also be acquainted with the author's God and Man in the Qur'an (Tokyo, Keio Univ. Inst. of Cultural and Linguistic Studies, 1964).

1038 Jeffery, Arthur. The Qur'an as Scripture. New York, Moore, 1952. 103 p.

Explains the unique features of the Muslim concept of scripture showing major differences from other known religious scriptures. Some bibliographic references are included. See also the author's The Foreign Vocabulary of the Qur'an (Baroda, Oriental Institute, 1938); and Materials for the History of the Text of the Qur'an (Leiden, Brill, 1937).

1039 Rahbar, Daud. God of Justice; A Study of the Ethical Doctrine of the Qur'an. Leiden, Brill, 1960.
This scholarly work surveys new developments in the critical studies of the Qur'anic text. The author maintains that the original meaning of the Qur'an has been obscured by interpretations made during the ages, especially those which were influenced by Greek thought. Contains a select bibliography.

1040 Stanton, Herbert U. W. The Teaching of the Qur'an, with an Account of Its Growth and a Subject Index. London, S.P.C.K., 1969 (1919).
An old but still useful presentation of the essential religious ideas of the Qur'an. Contains an up-dated bibliography.

MUHAMMAD

1041 'Abd al-Malik Ibn Hisham. The Life of Muhammad; A Translation of Ishaq's "Sirat rasul Allah," with Introd. and Notes by A. Guillaume. London, Oxford Univ. Press, 1955. 813 p.
Presents an excellent scholarly reconstruction of Muhammad's biography based on the most important single source handed down from the times shortly after the prophet's death.

1042 Andrae, Tor. Mohammed, the Man and His Faith. Transl. by T. Menzel. London, Allen & Unwin, 1956 (1936). 196 p.
A short biography which tends to take a psychological approach. It makes particular use of the early Christian sources from Syria.

1043 Gabrieli, Francesco. Muhammad and the Conquest of Islam. New York, McGraw-Hill, 1968 (1965). 256 p.
Translation of Mahomet. Contains a popular presentation of Muhammad's life with no emphasis on dates or historical background. Selected bibliographic references are included.

1044 Glubb, John B. The Life and Times of Muhammad. London, Hodder & Stoughton, 1970. 416 p.
Provides an excellent, popularly presented survey of events which took place in the life of Muhammad. The first three chapters present an informative description of the pre-Islamic Arabia. Next four chapters deal with the beginning of the prophecy. The following sections discuss the period in Medina. The study closes with a brief review of religious wars and conquests. A select bibliography and an index are included.

1045 Muir, William. Life of Mohammed from Original Sources, new and rev. ed. by T. H. Weir. Edinburgh, Grant, 1923 (1861). 556 p.
An out-dated but still useful work which is based on the studies of Islamic tradition.

1046 Watt, William M. Muhammad: Prophet and Statesman. London, Oxford Univ. Press, 1961. 250 p.
Presents a popular biography with special attention to the social and economic conditions of Arabia at the time of the rise of Islam. It is comprised essentially of abridgments of the author's Muhammad at Mecca (London, Oxford Univ. Press, 1953) and Muhammad at Medina (Oxford, England, Clarendon Press, 1956). Bibliographic references are included.

TRADITION (HADITH)

1047 Ali, Muhammad Maulana. A Manual of Hadith, 2nd ed. Lahore, Ahmadiya Anjuman Ishaat Islam, 19 . 408 p.
A collection which "contains 690 hadith, out of which 513 ... have been taken from the Buhari"--Preface.

1048 Doi, A. R. I. Introduction to the Hadith; The Tradition of the Prophet Muhammad. Lagos, Nigeria, Islamic Publications Bureau, 1971. 155 p.
An eminent scholar from Nigeria presents a simple introduction to the Islamic tradition for the general reader. Some select bibliographic references are cited. Also get acquainted with the author's Introduction to the Qur'an (Lagos, Islamic Pub. Bureau, 1972).

1049 Goldziher, Ignaz. Muslim Studies. Ed. by S. M. Stern, and transl. from the German by C. R. Barber and S. M. Stern. London, Allen and Unwin, 1966; Chicago, Aldine, 1967 (1889-90). 2 vols.
Translation of Muhammedanische Studien (1888). This great classic by a pioneer in Islamic studies presents an excellent comparison of the world view of the Qur'an and of the pre-Islamic bedouin. Vol. 2 contains a fundamental critical study of the hadith literature based on the original sources.

1050 Guillaume, Alfred. The Traditions of Islam; An Introduction to the Hadith Literature. Beirut, Khayyats, 1966 (1924) (Khayyats Oriental Reprints, 13). 184 p.
An excellent brief introduction which examines the doctrines and practices in historical context. Contains some bibliographic references.

1051 al-Hakim al-Nisaburi, Muhammad ibn 'Abd Allah. An Introduction to the Science of Tradition. Transl. by J. Robson.

London, Royal Asiatic Society of Great Britain and Ireland, 1953. 54 p.
Explains basic problems which are encountered in the studies of Islamic tradition.

JESUS IN ISLAM

1052 Wismer, Don. The Islamic Jesus; an Annotated Bibliography of Sources in English and French. Chicago, Garland, 1976. 325 p.
Considers the Qur'an, the Hadith literature, early and medieval Muslim writers, and modern Muslim commentaries from the 18th century to the present.

ANTHOLOGIES OF TEXTS IN ENGLISH TRANSLATION

1053 Arberry, Arthur J., ed. Aspects of Islamic Civilization as Depicted in the Original Texts. London, Allen and Unwin, 1964. 408 p.
Contains a selection of Islamic texts from the 7th century to the present outlining the development of Islam as seen by the participants. Translated fragments are arranged by subject. Also includes a selected bibliography.

1054 Jeffery, Arthur, ed. Islam: Muhammad and His Religion ... with an Introduction.... New York, Liberal Arts Press, 1958 (Library of Religion, no. 6). 252 p.
This excellent anthology is comprised of selections from the orthodox Muslim teachings. Modern interpretations are excluded.

1055 ________. A Reader on Islam; Passages from Standard Arabic Writings Illustrative of the Beliefs and Practices of Muslims. 's Gravenhage, Mouton, 1962. 678 p.
Presents an introduction to Islamic studies through translations of original texts. A selected bibliography is provided.

1056 Kritzeck, James, ed. Anthology of Islamic Literature; From the Rise of Islam to Modern Times. New York, Holt, Rinehard and Winston, 1964. 379 p.
Presents a useful introduction to classical Islamic literature through 40 selections from the Qur'an, essays, poetry, and proverbs on the favorite Islamic themes of love, beauty, death, god, etc. Texts are translated mainly from Arabic and Persian, with a few Turkish examples. It is continued by item 1057.

1057 ______. Modern Islamic Literature from 1800 to the Present, with an Introd. and Commentaries. New York, Holt, Rinehart and Winston, 1970. 310 p.
A sequel to item 1056. Provides a broader coverage including a wider geographical area, from West Africa to Indonesia.

1058 Williams, John A., ed. Islam. New York, Braziller, 1961 (Great Religions of Modern Man). 256 p.
A well-selected anthology from the Qur'an and classical Islamic writings which is connected by informative introductions. It presents Islam as seen by its followers. Includes some bibliographic references.

1059 ______. Themes of Islamic Civilization. Berkeley, Univ. of California Press, 1971. 382 p.
Presents the religious system of Islam through carefully selected extracts from English translations of the most important sources. Each selection is accompanied by informative introduction. There are six themes which are taken into consideration: the community, the perfect ruler, the will of god, the expected deliverer, the struggle, and the friends of god. Select bibliography.

HANDBOOKS AND CRITICAL WORKS

GENERAL INTRODUCTIONS

1060 Ali, Muhammad Maulana. The Living Thoughts of the Prophet Muhammad. London, Cassell, 1947 (Living Thoughts Library). 142 p.
An interesting survey presented by an outstanding Muslim scholar. Consult also the author's The Religion of Islam; A Comprehensive Discussion of Sources, Principles and Practices of Islam (Lahore, Ahmadiyyah Anjuman Isha'at Islam, 1950).

1061 Arberry, Arthur J., ed. Religion in the Middle East: Three Religions in Concord and Conflict. Cambridge, England, Univ. Press, 1969. 2 vols.
See no. 548. Contains a collection of essays by noted specialists on Judaism, Christianity, and Islam with excellent bibliographic references and indexes.

1062 Arnold, Thomas W., and A. Guillaume, eds. The Legacy of Islam. London, New York, Oxford Univ. Press, 1931. 416 p.
An excellent popular introduction for the layman which contains essays by outstanding specialists on such subjects as history, geography, economics, art and architecture, literature, religion, etc. Recently appeared in its 2nd

edition: Schacht, Joseph and C. E. Bosworth, eds., The Legacy of Islam (London, Oxford Univ. Press, 1973).

1063 Azzam, Abdel R. The Eternal Message of Mohammad. Transl. from the Arabic by C. E. Farah. New York, Devin-Adair Co., 1964. 297 p.
Modern Islam; bibliographic footnotes.

1064 Calverley, Edwin E. Islam; An Introduction. Cairo, American University, 1974 (1956) (American University at Cairo. School of Oriental Studies. C. C. Adams Memorial Studies). 97 p.
Brief, informative, for beginners; 12 essays; a few bibliographic notes; no index.

1065 The Cambridge History of Islam. Ed. by P. M. Holt. Cambridge, England, Univ. Press, 1970. 2 vols.
An excellent comprehensive introduction to the entire civilization of Islam: 51 essays by experts survey religious, philosophical, economic, military, scientific, artistic aspects to ca. 1950. Vol. 1: The Central Islamic Lands; Vol. 2: The Further Islamic Lands; Islamic Society and Civilization. Bibliography (mostly in European languages), glossary, detailed index.

1066 Christopher, John B. The Islamic Tradition. New York, Harper & Row, 1972. 185 p.
Popular, aimed at beginners; 13 short chapters, focus Western understanding. Brief history up to 1258; select bibliography.

1067 Cragg, Kenneth. The Call of the Minaret. New York, Oxford, Oxford Univ. Press, 1956. 376 p.
Informative introduction to Islam centered around lines of the Muslim call to prayer. Also discusses Muslim-Christian relations; selective bibliography, useful index.

1068 _______. The House of Islam, 2nd ed. Encino, Calif., Dickenson, 1975. 145 p.
Brief popular interpretation of Muslim understanding of god and his relation to man and the world, Muhammad and the Qur'an, etc.; useful glossary, brief selective bibliography.

1069 Farah, Cesar E. Islam: Beliefs and Observances. New York, Barron, 1970 (Barron's Educational Series). 306 p.
Various aspects in social and cultural context.

1070 Gardet, Louis. Mohammedanism. Transl. from the French by W. Burridge. New York, Hawthorn Books, 1961 (1958) (Twentieth Century Encyclopedia of Catholicism. Section 15: Non-Christian Beliefs). 176 p.
Translation of Connaître l'Islam; survey of Islam as

religion and civilization; covers contemporary issues; brief bibliography.

1071 Gibb, Hamilton A. R. Mohammedanism; An Historical Survey, 2nd ed. London, Oxford Univ. Press, 1964 (1953) (Home University Library of Modern Knowledge, 197).
Best introductory reading for beginners; helpful bibliographic guide; index.

1072 Guillaume, Alfred. Islam, 2nd ed. Harmondsworth, England, Penguin Books, 1956. 209 p.
Popular; some bibliographic references.

1073 Hasan, Hassan Ibrahim. Islam: a Religious, Political, Social, and Economic Study. Beirut, Dar al-Maaref, 1967. 586 p.
Comprehensive; includes the Shi'ites, the Kharijites, and the Mu'tazilites; extensive bibliography.

1074 Hitti, Philip K. Islam; a Way of Life. Minneapolis: Univ. of Minnesota Press, 1970. 198 p.
Religion, state, and culture covered for advanced students. Includes the Prophet and the Qur'an, history of Islamic empires, and something of post-Ottoman times; short bibliography.

1075 Klein, F. A. The Religion of Islam. New York, Curzon Press, 1971 (1906). 241 p.
Great deal on Islam not easily available elsewhere; large number of Arabic terms makes the text difficult.

1076 Morgan, Kenneth, ed. Islam the Straight Path; Islam Interpreted by Muslims. New York, Ronald, 1958. 453 p.
Collection of essays; some bibliographic references, glossary, index.

1077 Nasr, Hossein. Ideals and Realities of Islam. New York, Praeger, 1972 (1963). 184 p.
Discusses the Qur'an, the Prophet, the law, sufism, Sunnism and Shi'ism; annotated bibliographies and index.

1078 ______. Science and Civilization of Islam. Cambridge, Mass., Harvard Univ. Press, 1968. 384 p.
Islamic intellectual evolution in the Middle Ages: natural sciences, physics, mathematics, astronomy, medicine, psychology, alchemy, theology, philosophy; select bibliography is inadequate and out-dated.

1079 Rahman, Fazlur. Islam. London, Weidenfeld & Nicolson, 1967. 271 p.
Discusses Muhammad, the Qur'an, hadith and Sunna, Islamic law, theology, sufi organization, and sect

development; also, education and reform movements. Select bibliography, index.

1080 Savory, R. M., ed. Introduction to Islamic Civilization. Cambridge, England, Univ. Press, 1976. 204 p.
Essays by recognized authorities on history of Pre-Islamic world; theology, philosophy, law; literature (Arabic, Turkish, Persian); art; science; borrowing by West; modern developments. Annotated bibliography.

1081 Sourdel, D. Islam. Transl. from French by D. Scott. New York, Walker, 1963 (1961) (Sun Book: Religion and Mythology). 155 p.
Translation of L'Islam; brief popular introduction to Muhammad and the Qur'an, to 19th century, Islamic law, sectarian movements, sufism and philosophy, intellectual and artistic life, and newest developments. Brief bibliography.

1082 Tritton, Arthur S. Islam; Beliefs and Practices. London, Hutchinson, 1951 (University Library). 200 p.
Popular, concise; short bibliography.

1083 Von Grunebaum, Gustave E. Islam: Essays in the Nature and Growth of a Cultural Tradition, 2nd ed. London, Routledge and Kegan, 1961. 260 p.
Three fundamental problems dealt with: growth among Muslims of a culture consciousness; unity of Muslim literary, political, scientific civilization; and interaction with other civilizations. Contains bibliographic references, index.

1084 Watt, William M. What Is Islam? New York, Praeger, 1968 (Arab Background Series). 256 p.
Contains a general introduction to Islamic studies historical in approach with emphasis on the religious world view. Useful for a reader who is already familiar with the field. There is a brief bibliography and two indexes.

HISTORY--GENERAL

1085 Arnold, Thomas W. The Preaching of Islam; A History of the Propagation of the Muslim Faith. Lahore, Ashraf, 1965 (1896). 508 p.
Provides an account of the rise of Islam and its expansion until the 19th century. Contains an extensive bibliography of older works.

1086 Brockelmann, Carl. History of the Islamic Peoples. Transl. by J. Carmichael and M. Perlman from the German. London, Routledge and Kegan Paul, 1949 (1939).

566 p.
Translation of Geschichte der islamischen Völker. One of the most detailed general histories of the Muslim peoples, especially political history. Excludes post-medieval Muslim India, Indonesia, and central Asia. Impossible for continuous reading, but good for quick reference. Extensive bibliographic references are provided.

1087 Dunlop, D. M. Arab Civilization to A.D. 1500. London, Longman; Beirut, Librarie du Liban, 1971 (Arab Background Series). 368 p.
Begins with the history of the Arabs before the formation of Islam, and then surveys major events in the history of the Caliphate. Deals also with literature, historians, travelers, philosophers, and the history of medicine. Lacks a discussion of religious life and law. Bibliographic references and an index are provided. Aimed at the scholars and advanced students who are acquainted with the problems of research in Islamic history and civilization.

1088 Gabrieli, Francesco. The Arabs; A Compact History. Transl. by S. Attanasio. New York, Hawthorn Books, 1963 (1957). 215 p.
Translation of Gli Arabi. "The aim of this modest volume is to give a summary ... as accurate and up-to-date as possible ... of the Arab people from their beginnings up to the present day"--Preface. Contains a brief bibliography and an index.

1089 Glubb, John. A Short History of the Arab Peoples. London, Hodder and Stoughton, 1969. 318 p.
Presents a concise history of Muslim peoples including Arabs, Turks, Mongols, and Berbers from the beginning to the mid-20th century with the accent on political and military developments. A select bibliography is included. The index is substantial and helpful.

1090 Hitti, Philip K. History of the Arabs, from the Earliest Times to the Present, 7th ed. London, Macmillan, 1960 (1956). 822 p.
The best available general survey which presents the political, economic, and cultural aspects of the life of the Arabs from the earliest times to the present. It has been subjected to criticism for its overly factual treatment of the sources, lack of broad interpretation, and sketchy coverage of the last centuries. Numerous bibliographic references are given in footnotes. Also contains a detailed index.

1091 Hodgson, Marshall G. S. The Venture of Islam: Conscience and History in the World Civilization. Chicago, Univ. of

Chicago Press, 1975. 3 v.
Presents the best interpretative history of the Muslim civilization from the 7th century to the contemporary developments. Vol. 1, The Classical Age of Islam; vol. 2, The Expansion of Islam in the Middle Periods; vol. 3, The Gunpowder Empires and Modern Times. Also contains a well-selected bibliography, a glossary and an index.

1092 Lewis, Bernard. The Arabs in History, 4th ed. London, Hutchinson, 1966 (University Library: History). 200 p.
A brief but very informative interpretative history with special emphasis on social issues. It describes the role of the Arabs in the region where they lived and flourished and in the development of the world history as a whole. Contains a chronological table, a select bibliography for further reading, and an index.

1093 ________. Islam in History; Ideas, Men, and Events in the Middle East. London, Alcove Press, 1973. 349 p.
Contains a selection of scholarly articles which cover all the facets of Islamic studies: ideologies, sources and aspects of history and historiography, etc. A selective bibliography and an index are provided.

1094 ________, ed. The World of Islam: Faith, People, Culture. London, Thames and Hudson, 1976. 360 p. 490 illus.
Provides a popular survey of the Western knowledge of Islam, its religious aspects, astonishing expansion in Asia, India, and the Mediterranean, the quality of life in Islamic cities, and the achievement in art, architecture, music, literature and science, from the age of Muhammad to the present day. A list of books for further reading and an index are supplied.

1095 Peters, Frank E. Allah's Commonwealth; A History of Islam in the Near East, 600-1100 A.D. New York, Simon & Schuster, 1973. 800 p.
"A comprehensive, scholarly, detailed, but eminently readable history of the first 500 years of Islamic community with special emphasis upon its intellectual and religious development.... It is especially remarkable for its success in setting Islamic trends in the wider context of Near Eastern political and intellectual life..."--reviewer. Also includes a chronology, a glossary, an annotated bibliography, and an index.

1096 Spuler, Bertold. The Muslim World; An Historical Survey. Transl. from the German by F. R. C. Bagley. Leiden, Brill, 1960- (Manuals of Oriental Studies, v. 6).
Translation of Geschichte des Islamischen Länder. A selection from works by B. Spuler and other scholars which presents a survey of historical events of the lands

in which the religion and civilization of Islam are or have been predominant. In four parts when the translation is completed: Pt. 1. The Age of Caliphs (7th to mid-13th centuries); Pt. 2. The Mongol Period (the 13th century); Pt. 3. The Last Great Muslim Empires: Ottoman Empire, Iran, Central Asia, Moghul India). Pt. 4. Modern Times, since end of the 18th century. Includes an extensive classified bibliography and two indexes, persons, families, tribes, and religious communities; and names of places, nations, and languages.

HISTORY--EARLY ISLAM

1097 Bravmann, Meir M. The Spiritual Background of Early Islam; Studies in Ancient Arab Concepts. Leiden, Brill, 1972. 336 p.

Contains a collection of 14 papers presenting various aspects of early Islam.

1098 O'Leary, de Lacy Evans. Arabia Before Muhammad. New York, AMS Press, 1974 (1927). 234 p.

Presents a survey of pre-Islamic history of Arabia. It should be borne in mind that there is no satisfactory history of the subject written in English. Some bibliographic references are provided.

1099 Shaban, M. A. Islamic History, A.D. 600-700 (A.H. 132). Cambridge, England, Univ. Press, 1971. 196 p.

_______. Islamic History, A.D. 750-1055 A.H. (132-448); A New Interpretation. Cambridge, England, Univ. Press, 1976. 221 p.

This two-volume interpretative history presents cultural and military events from the rise of Islam to the Abbasid era. Explains selected events and movements in terms of socio-political structures and forces. Bibliographic references and indexes are included in each volume.

1100 Von Grunebaum, Gustave E. Classical Islam; A History, 600-1258. Transl. by K. Watson. Chicago, Aldine Press, 1970 (1963). 243 p.

Translation of Islam in seiner klassischen Epoche. It deals with pre-Islamic Arabia, Muhammad, the 'Umayyads, the Abbasids, the Fatimids, the Tulunids, and the Arab West. It also discusses some selected topics in theology, philosophy, mysticism, literature, etc. Contains chronological tables, a select classified bibliography, mostly of English works, and an index. Especially helpful for beginners.

1101 Watt, W. M. The Formative Period of Islamic Thought.

Edinburgh, University Press, 1973. 424 p.
Begins the formative period with the murder of 'Uthman and ends it with Ash'ari's codification of theology, around 950.

1102 ______. The Majesty That Was Islam; The Islamic World, 661-1110. New York, Praeger, 1974 (Great Civilization series). 276 p.
Provides a lucid account of theological developments on the background of the history of dynasties and political events from the death of 'Ali to the Seljuqs. Also contains a select bibliography and an index.

HISTORY--MEDIEVAL ISLAM

1103 Von Grunebaum, Gustave E. von. Medieval Islam; A Study of Cultural Orientation, 2nd ed. Chicago, Univ. of Chicago Press, 1953 (Oriental Institute Essay). 378 p.
Presents the best existing description of medieval Islamic society in any European language. Some bibliographic references are included in footnotes.

HISTORY--MODERN ISLAM

1104 Cragg, Kenneth. Counsels in Contemporary Islam. Edinburgh, Univ. Press, 1965 (Islamic Survey, v. 3). 255 p.
Presents a survey of contemporary thinkers and their ideologies in Islamic India, Turkey and North Africa. Contains a very extensive bibliography and an index.

1105 Gibb, Hamilton A. R. Modern Trends in Islam. Chicago, Univ. of Chicago Press, 1947 (Haskell Lectures in Comparative Religion, 1945).
"The great virtue of this book is exhibited in the author's ability to set the central concerns of modernism against the background of the entire historical tradition of Islamic thought and experience"--C. Adams. Also contains a number of bibliographic notes.

1106 Hourani, Albert H. Arabic Thought in the Liberal Age, 1798-1939. New York, Oxford Univ. Press, 1962. 403 p.
Presents an excellent study of Arab intellectual history under the influence of French and English liberal ideas. The style of the book is lively and engaging. Bibliographic references are included.

1107 Rosenthal, Erwin I. J. Islam in the Modern National State. Cambridge, England, Univ. Press, 1965. 416 p.
A thorough and competent study, with special reference

to India, Pakistan, Malaya, Iran, Turkey, Tunisia, and Morocco. It surveys the development of political ideas emphasizing the unity of religion and politics. A select bibliography and an index are provided.

1108 Smith, Wilfred C. Islam in Modern History. Princeton, N.J., Princeton Univ. Press, 1957. 317 p.
Presents the best analysis of modern Islamic problems in the light of their historical development. It covers the Arabs, the Turks, and the Muslims of India and Pakistan.

1109 Von Grunebaum, Gustave E. Modern Islam: The Search for Cultural Identity. Berkeley, Univ. of California Press, 1962. 303 p.
A collection of papers published previously in periodicals, with bibliographic references provided in footnotes.

1110 Watt, William M. Islamic Revelation in the Modern World. Edinburgh, Univ. of Edinburgh Press, 1969. 143 p.
Contains a collection of brief lectures which seek to establish the basis for Christian-Muslim understanding. The book is useful for advanced students.

ISLAMIC ART AND ARCHITECTURE

Bibliography

1111 "Arts and Crafts, Architecture, and Science." Birnbaum, Eleazer. Books on Asia, from the Near East to the Far East. Toronto, Univ. of Toronto Press, 1971; p. 105-112.
Contains a selective list of monographs in classified arrangement: (1) General works; (2) Painting, miniatures, and book arts; (3) Architecture; (4) Ceramics, metalwork, and mosaics; (5) Carpets; (6) Other arts and crafts.

1112 Cresswell, Keppel A. C. Bibliography of the Architecture, Arts, and Crafts of Islam. Cairo, American Univ. at Cairo Press, 1961. ____. ____. Supplement, 1973.
An extensive bibliography of monographs and periodical articles. It covers every branch of Muslim art and architecture. Architecture is subdivided geographically; the arts and crafts section is arranged alphabetically by subjects. Includes references to book reviews. An index of authors is included.

Critical Works

1113 Burckhardt, Titus. Art of Islam: Language and Meaning. Transl. by J. P. Hobson. Foreword S. H. Nasr. Leiden,

Brill, 1976 (World of Islam Festival). 204 p.; color plates.

Presents a popular survey of Islamic arts, with a select list of readings and an index.

1114 Ettinghausen, Richard. Arab Painting. Cleveland, World Pub. Co., 1962. 208 p.

Presents an excellent survey of the subject from the 7th to the 14th centuries. It covers frescoes, and painting on wood, parchment, paper, glass, stone mosaics, and pottery painting. It is accompanied by a well-selected classified bibliography. Also includes a general index.

1115 Grabar, Oleg. The Formation of Islamic Art. New Haven, Conn., Yale Univ. Press, 1973. 233 p.

Presents all of the artistic, political, religious and social currents that influenced the formation of this rich and complex art. A selected bibliography is included.

1116 Grube, Ernst. The World of Islam. New York, McGraw-Hill, 1967 (Landmarks of the World's Art). 176 p.

Presents an informative description of Islamic arts, with excellent illustrations.

1117 Hill, Derek. Islamic Architecture and Its Decoration, A.D. 800-1500. A photographic survey by Derek Hill, and an introd. text by O. Grabar. London, Faber and Faber, 1967. 88 p., 535 plates.

Contains photographs taken in Iran, Turkey, Afganistan and Soviet Central Asia.

1118 Kühnel, Ernst. Islamic Art and Architecture. Transl. from the German by K. Watson. London, Bell, 1966. 200 p., plates, plans, tables.

A good handbook which covers the history of Islamic art from its beginning to the present day. It is especially useful for subjects on applied arts and crafts. Contains excellent illustrations. Some bibliographic references are included.

1119 New York. Metropolitan Museum of Art. A Handbook of Muhammedan Art, by M. S. Dimand. 2nd ed. rev. and enl. New York, Hartsdale House, 1947 (1930). 347 p.

A standard survey of all fields of Islamic arts, with helpful bibliographic references.

1120 Rice, David T. Islamic Art, rev. ed. London, Thames & Hudson, 1976. 288 p.

The best popular introduction to the varieties of Islamic art. Deals both with historical development, and geographical spread. Examples cover almost every medium, e.g. architecture, painting, metal work, etc.

1121 ______. Islamic Painting; A Survey. Edinburgh, Edinburgh Univ. Press, 1971. 185 p.

A useful survey which brings together scattered information on the subject. It discusses the place of figural painting in the Islamic world, the Byzantine influences during the 'Umayyads, and the development of the art under the Abbasides. One will also find chapters devoted to Egypt, North Africa, Spain, Mesopotamia, Persia, and Turkey. Contains a select bibliography of monographs and periodical articles, and valuable illustrations. No index is provided.

1122 Schimmel, Annemarie. Islamic Calligraphy. Leiden, Brill, 1970 (State University, Gronningen. Iconography of Religions. Section 22: Islam, fasc. 1). 80 p.

This brief study contains an excellent introduction, with a select bibliography, and a collection of 48 plates with informative explanations.

CALENDAR

1123 Freeman-Grenville, G. S. P. The Muslim and Christian Calendars. New York, Oxford Univ. Press, 1963. 87 p.

Provides an equivalent of any date or day in either calendar, from the first year of the Hijra to the Christian year A.D. 2000. Contains tables for: the Hijra year and the Christian year, the Muslim months and days of the year, the Christian months and days of the year, perpetual calendar of the days of the week in the Christian year, the principal Muslim festivals, the principal Christian fixed festivals, movable Christian festivals. One should also get acquainted with Wüstenfeld, H. F. Vergleichungs-Tabellen zur Umrechnung Orient-Christlichen Ären (Wiesbaden, Deutsche Morgenländische Gesellschaft, 1961). See also no. 1018.

ETHICS

1124 Donaldson, Dwight M. Studies in Muslim Ethics. London, S. P. C. K., 1953. 304 p.

Contains a useful survey of Islamic ethics, with selected bibliographic references.

ISLAMIC INSTITUTIONS (SOCIAL/POLITICAL)

1125 Arnold, Thomas W. The Caliphate, with a concluding chapter by S. G. Haim. London, Routledge, 1965 (1924). 267 p.

A well-presented study which discusses the status of the office of caliph in Islamic political system. The additional chapter provides an analysis of the abolition of the institution and its consequences. Bibliographic references to older works are included.

1126 Gaudefroy-Demombine, Maurice. Muslim Institutions, 2nd ed. Transl. from the French by J. P. MacGregor. London, Allen & Unwin, 1954 (1921). 216 p.

Translation of Les Institutions musulmanes. Presents a useful introduction to the social and political studies of various Islamic institutions. Some bibliographic references are included.

1127 Goitein, Solomon D. F. Study in Islamic History and Institutions. Leiden, Brill, 1966. 391 p.

Contains well-presented studies on the nature and development of Islam, Islamic religious and political institutions, and Islamic social history. It is accompanied by numerous bibliographic footnotes, and a select bibliography for further reading at the end of the book.

1128 Levy, Reuben. The Social Structure of Islam, 2nd ed. Cambridge, England, Cambridge Univ. Press, 1957 (1931). 536 p.

First ed. of 1931 was titled, Sociology of Islam. "The purpose of this book is an endeavour to investigate the effects of the religious system of Islam on the life and organization of the societies and acknowledge it.... Here the basic principles of Islam are examined, and an attempt is made to ascertain how Muslems of different periods and climes have adopted their way of life to them"--Preface. Contains a good bibliography and an index.

1129 Watt, William M. Islam and the Integration of Society. London, Routledge & Paul, 1961 (International Library of Sociology and Social Reconstruction). 293 p.

This scholarly book attempts to answer a number of sociological questions, e.g.: the place of economic and social factors, the role of ideation, the will to unity and disunity, the integration of the political life, the integration of intellectual life and the psyche, etc. Contains useful bibliographic references in footnotes and an index.

ISLAMIC LAW (FIKH, SHARI'A)

Bibliography

1130 Stern, W. B. "A Bibliography of Books and Articles on Mohammedan Law in the English Language." Law Library Journal, V. 43 (1950), p. 16-21.

Contains a selective list of bibliographical references to the older materials.

Critical Works

1131 Anderson, James N. D. Islamic Law in the Modern World. New York, New York Univ. Press, 1959. 106 p.
Contains a collection of five papers which describe the traditional Islamic law and contemporary trends towards its secularization. Includes some bibliographic references.

1132 Coulson, Noel J. A History of Islamic Law. Edinburgh, Edinburgh Univ. Press, 1964 (Islamic Surveys, v. 2). 264 p.
Presents a concise but informative introduction to Islamic law in the modern world based on references to a wide range of substantive legal rules and institutions. Also discusses issues of legal reform on the background of the entire legal history. Contains a select bibliography and an index.

1133 Fyzee, Asaf A. A. Outlines of Muhammedan Law, 3rd ed. London, Oxford Univ. Press, 1964. 509 p.
A textbook of Islamic law for Indian students which attempts to cover the major Sunni and Shi'ite legal practices, with emphasis on the traditional Hanafi school of Islamic law. Also contains a well-selected bibliography and an index.

1134 Schacht, Joseph. An Introduction to Islamic Law. Oxford, England, Clarendon Press, 1964. 304 p.
A useful concise introduction to the problems and practice of Islamic law, with selected bibliographic references.

LITERATURE OF ISLAMIC PEOPLES

1135 Lang, David M., ed. A Guide to Eastern Literatures. London, Weidenfeld and Nicolson, 1971. 500 p.
Includes brief but informative survey articles on the Arabic, Persian, Turkish, Indian, Pakistani, etc., literatures. Useful select bibliographies are provided at the end of each article.

1136 Najib Ullah. Islamic Literature; An Introductory History with Selections. New York, Washington Square Press, 1963. 441 p.
"The author has given a clear and simple introduction to the history of Arabic, Persian, and Turkish.... And he has included biographies of the most important authors ... along with translations from their most memorable works"--Cover. Also contains a list of selected readings and an index.

ARABIC LITERATURE

1137 Gibb, Hamilton A. R. Arabic Literature; An Introduction, 2nd ed. Oxford, England, Clarendon Press, 1963 (1933). 182 p.

The best brief introduction for beginners. It surveys all varieties of Arabic writing up to the 18th century. Also contains a good bibliography of Arabic works available in English translation. The most comprehensive coverage is provided in: Brockelmann, Carl, Geschichte der arabischen Literatur (Leiden, Brill, 1943-).

1138 Nicholson, Reynold A. A Literary History of the Arabs. Cambridge, England, Cambridge Univ. Press, 1969 (1907). 506 p.

A useful introduction for more advanced students. It presents the history of classical Arabic literature to the 14th century. Contains bibliographic references for further reading.

PERSIAN LITERATURE

Bibliography

1139 Storey, C. A. Persian Literature; A Bio-Bibliographical Survey. London, Luzac, 1927- .

A comprehensive survey of Persian literature subdivided into sections devoted to particular branches of literature. Within each section works are arranged chronologically. There are indexes at the end of each section.

Critical Works

1140 Browne, Edward G. A Literary History of Persia. Cambridge, England, Cambridge Univ. Press, 1928. 4 vols.

An old but still valuable standard critical study of the entire field of Persian literature. It contains an excellent review of materials on the religious system of Shi'ah. Also includes numerous selections of literary texts in translation. The coverage is to 1924. Bibliographic references and an index are provided.

1141 Rypka, Jan, ed. History of Iranian Literature, written in collab. with O. Klima and others. Dordrecht, Reidel, 1968 (1956). 929 p.

Translation of Dejiny perské a tadžicke literatury. This masterpiece of collective scholarship examines the entire span of the history of Iranian literature, from the very first traces of evidence to the present. It brings together views of specialists from both East and West. Some interpretations are done from the Marxist point of view. There is also a chapter dealing with the folk literature. Includes a well selected bibliography and a useful index.

TURKISH LITERATURE

1142 Hofman, H. F. Turkish Literature; A Bio-Bibliographical Survey. Pub. by the Library of the Univ. of Utrecht, under the auspices of the Royal Asiatic Soc. of Great Britain and England. Leiden, Brill, 1969- .

A detailed review of all available material for the study of Turkish literature which follows the pattern of the work by C. A. Storey (see no. 1139).

MYSTICISM (SUFISM)

1143 Arberry, Arthur J. Sufism; An Account of the Mystics of Islam. London, Allen & Unwin, 1950 (Ethical and Religious Classics of East and West). 141 p.

The best existing history of Sufism, illustrated by well selected fragments from mystical literature. Bibliographic references are included in notes.

1144 Brenner, Louis. "Separate Realities: A Review of Literature on Sufism." The International Journal of African Historical Studies, v. 5:4 (1971), p. 637-58.

Presents a critical review of 10 recent books on the subject.

1145 Nicholson, Reynold A. The Mystics of Islam. London, Routledge and Paul, 1970 (1914). 178 p.

Contains a well-presented brief introduction to Islamic mysticism, with numerous extracts from mystic writings in English translation. Some bibliographic references are included. An excellent reading for beginners.

1146 _______. Studies in Islamic Mysticism. Cambridge, England, Cambridge Univ. Press, 1967 (1921). 282 p.

A scholarly work which presents various aspects of sufism. One will find numerous bibliographic references.

1147 Schimmel, Annemarie. Mystical Dimensions of Islam. Chapel Hill, Univ. of North Carolina Press, 1975. 506 p.

Covers the development of Sufism from its origins through the 19th century. Especially valuable are chapters on Persian and Turkish mystic poetry. Also contains two appendices: Letter Symbolism in Sufi Literature and The Feminine Element in Sufism. Exhaustive bibliography and several indexes are added.

1148 Smith, Margaret. Readings from the Mystics of Islam; Translations from the Arabic and Persian, Together with a Short Account of the History and Doctrines of Sufism and Biographical Notes on Each Sufi Writer. London, Luzac, 1950. 144 p.

This is an excellent anthology of Islamic mystical writings. Selected bibliography is provided.

1149 ________. The Sufi Path of Love; An Anthology of Sufism. London, Luzac, 1954. 154 p.

Materials for this collection are drawn from both the Sufis themselves and their commentators. It traces the nature of Sufism and its principal doctrines. An extensive bibliography serves as a guide to the existing English translations.

1150 Trimmingham, John S. The Sufi Orders in Islam. Oxford, Clarendon Press, 1971. 333 p.

Presents a scholarly study which covers the history, development, and organization of the Sufi orders. It also analyzes the political and social implications of the orders on Islamic societies throughout the history. Especially interesting is the chapter on the Sufi orders in contemporary Islamic society. Contains a comprehensive bibliography which lists most of the available books and articles on the subject in both European and oriental languages.

PHILOSOPHY (FALSAFAH)

(see also THEOLOGY, immediately following)

1151 Boer, Tjitze J. de. The History of Philosophy of Islam, 2nd ed. Transl. by E. R. Jones. New York, Dover Pub., 1967 (1903). 216 p.

This is a reprint of an older work which in spite of all new research still provides a useful framework for study of major medieval systems. Contains translations of writings preserved in Syria.

1152 Fakhry, Majid. A History of Islamic Philosophy. New York, Columbia Univ. Press, 1970 (Studies in Oriental Culture, no. 5). 427 p.

The only comprehensive history, in English, modern in approach, based on primary sources. It covers the origins, the great medieval philosophers like Ibn Rushd and Mulla Sadra, early modern representatives like Abduh and al-Afgani, and a few 20th-century Arab philosophers. Also discusses the interaction of Islamic theology and sufism with philosophy. Contains a brief but well selected bibliography and an index.

1153 Sharif, M. M., ed. A History of Muslim Philosophy, with Short Accounts of Other Disciplines and the Modern Renaissance in Muslim Lands. Wiesbaden, Harrasowitz; London, Luzac, 1963-66. 2 vols.

An excellent presentation of the subject by a group of outstanding specialists in Islamic studies. They discuss the most important issues of the Qur'an, literature, architecture, and arts. There are numerous footnotes and chapter bibliographies.

1154 Watt, William M. Islamic Philosophy and Theology. Edinburgh, Univ. Press, 1962 (Islamic Surveys, 1). 196 p.

An informative survey which presents the development of philosophical and theological ideas within the context of social and political changes. Contains excellent annotated bibliographies at the end of chapters. There is also a useful index.

THEOLOGY

(see also PHILOSOPHY, immediately preceding)

1155 Arberry, Arthur J. Revelation and Reason in Islam. London, Allen and Unwin, 1957 (Forwood Lectures, 1956). 122 p.

Presents many aspects of Islamic thought, including the mystical and philosophical. It covers a wide range of orthodox supporters, those who were influenced by Hellenistic philosophy, the esoteric school of Isma'ili, and the Sufis.

1156 Macdonald, Duncan B. Development of Muslim Theology, Jurisprudence, and Constitutional Theory. New York, Russell & Russell, 1966. 386 p.

The most useful work in English which presents the origins, history, and theory of law in Islam in a concise examination of the complex subject. A select bibliography is provided.

1157 Nasr. Hossein. An Introduction to Islamic Cosmological Doctrines: Conceptions of Nature and Methods Used for Its Study by Ikhwan al-Safa, al-Biruni, and Ibn Sina. Cambridge, Mass., Belknap Press of Harvard Univ. Press, 1964. 312 p.

This comprehensive and scholarly study presents a particular view of Islamic thought as it developed in the first seven centuries of Islamic history. Contains a list of symbols of the planets and the divisions of the Zodiac. An excellent select bibliography and an index are provided.

1158 Wensinck, A. J. The Muslim Creed. London, Cass, 1965

(1952). 304 p.

A comprehensive study of the historical development of Muslim dogmas and beliefs consisting of translations and commentaries. Bibliographic references to older works are provided.

1159 Wolfson, H. A. The Philosophy of the Kalam. Cambridge, Mass., Harvard Univ. Press, 1976.

Provides an explication of the schools and texts of Muslim philosophy. Also includes bibliographical references and an index.

WORSHIP

1160 Lammens, Henri. Islam: Beliefs and Institutions. Transl. from the French by E. D. Ross. London, Cassells, 1958 (1941) (Islam and the Muslim World, no. 6). 256 p.

Provides a substantial introduction sufficiently nontechnical to be useful for beginners. A select bibliography is included.

1161 Padwick, Constance E. Muslim Devotions: A Study of Prayer Manuals in Common Use. London, S.P.C.K., 1961. 313 p.

Contains a presentation of Islamic devotional formulas and prayers, other than the prescribed ones, in use by Muslims in different countries. The translations are provided with useful explanations. Bibliographic references in footnotes and an index are included.

1162 Von Grunebaum, Gustave E. Muhammedan Festivals. London, Abelard, 1958. 107 p.

"The presentation here has been concerned with the essential and typical elements of Islamic ritual ... [and] it hopes to contribute to a portrayal of the typical Muslim as practicing believer by showing him at prayer, on pilgrimage, or in the act of honoring his saints"--Preface. Bibliographic references are included in notes. There is also an index.

ISLAM AND THE WEST

1163 Daniel, Norman. Islam and the West; The Making of an Image. Edinburgh, Univ. Press, 1960. 443 p.

Provides a well-documented review of understanding of Islam and its civilization in medieval Europe. An extensive bibliography is appended, subdivided into (1) Direct Sources to 1350, (2) Writers on Islam of the Period 1350-1850, and (3) Modern Sources. An index is supplied. Continued by item 1164.

1164 ________. Islam, Europe, and Empire. Edinburgh, Univ. Press, 1969 (Edinburgh University Publications: Language and Literature, ser. no. 15). 619 p.
A sequel to item 1163. It surveys the attitude of 19th-century Europe towards Islam and its civilization. Contains an extensive bibliography of works referred to in the text, and a useful index.

1165 Hitti, Philip. Islam and the West; A Historical Cultural Survey. Princeton, N.J., Van Nostrand, 1962 (Anvil Original). 192 p.
A popularly presented basic outline of the subject, with some bibliographic references, and an index.

ISLAM IN AFRICA

1166 Fisher, Humphrey J. Ahmadiyyah: A Study in Contemporary Islam on the West African Coast. London, Oxford Univ. Press, 1963. 206 p.
Pt. 1 describes Islam in its West African setting; Pt. 2 explains the basic issues of the Ahmadiyyah doctrines; Pt. 3 surveys the history of the movement in West Africa; Pt. 4 presents the organization of Ahmadiyyah. Contains an index and bibliographic references in the footnotes.

1167 Hampson, Ruth M. Islam in South Africa; A Bibliography. Cape Town, Univ. of Cape Town School of Librarianship, 1964. 55 p.
Arranged by subject and then alphabetically by author. Contains a list of Islamic periodicals. An author index is added.

1168 Julien, C. A. History of North Africa: Tunisia, Algeria, Morocco, from the Arab Conquest to 1830. Ed. and rev. by R. LeTourneau; transl. by J. Petrie. New York, Praeger, 1970 (1951). 446 p.
Translation of vol. 2 of Histoire de l'Afrique du nord (1951). Presents a standard general history. Includes an extensive annotated bibliography and an index.

1169 Kritzeck, James, and W. H. Lewis, eds. Islam in Africa. Contrib.: J. S. Trimingham and others. New York, Van Nostrand-Rinehold, 1969. 339 p.
Contains a collection of papers by outstanding specialists divided into three parts. Pt. 1: Historical Perspectives--traces the origins and growth of Islamic influence and the forces which have facilitated its spread in tropical Africa. Pt. 2: Aspects of African Islam--discusses the factors and the institutions which have established Islam in this area. Pt. 3: Some Regional Developments--deals with the internal influence of Islam in countries and

regions. Each section has a select bibliography, and there is also an index.

1170 Nimtz, August H., Jr. "Islam in Tanzania; An Annotated Bibliography." Tanzania Notes and Records, No. 72 (1973), p. 51-74.
"The following compilation is intended to fill the bibliographic hiatus ... since publication of C. H. Becker's "Materialen zur Kenntnis des Islam in Deutsch-Ostafrika" (Der Islam, v. 2 (1911). p. 1-48).

1171 Trimmingham, J. S. The Influence of Islam upon Africa. New York, Praeger, 1968. 159 p.
This excellent scholarly study describes the penetration of Islam into the African continent, interpreting the implications of this still unfinished process on the life and thought of Africa. Also contains a select bibliography and an index. Note the author's Islam in East Africa, A History of Islam in West Africa (1962); Islam in Ethiopa, and Islam in the Sudan (1949).

ISLAM IN NORTH AMERICA

1172 Lovell, Emily K. "A Survey of the Arab-Muslims in the United States and Canada." Muslim World, v. 63:2 (1973), p. 139-54.
This brief article contains an analysis of a questionnaire sent out by the Federation of Islamic Associations in the United States and Canada (FIA) to all the Islamic centers, mosques, and individuals. Bibliographic references are included in the footnotes.

1173 Williams, Ethel, and C. F. Brown. Afro-American Religious Studies: A Comprehensive Bibliography with Locations in American Libraries. Metuchen, N.J., Scarecrow Press, 1972. p. 201-5.
See no. 1781. Section b. Black Muslims contains references to monographs and periodical articles.

ISLAM IN PERSIA (IRAN)

1174 Cambridge History of Iran. Ed. by W. B. Fisher. Cambridge, England, Univ. Press, 1968- (8 vols.).
A chronologically arranged survey of Iranian history. Vol. 4 deals with the history of religious, philosophical, political, economic, scientific, and artistic elements in Iranian civilization, with special emphasis on geographical and ecological factors. Vol. 8 contains a well-selected bibliography, a survey of research, and a comprehensive index.

1175 Donaldson, Dwight M. The Shi'ite Religion; A History of Islam in Persia and Irak. London, S. P. C. K., 1953 (1935). 304 p.

Presents a considerable number of traditional materials about the imāms, and excerpts from accepted Shi'ah authorities. Also contains a review of great shrines in Iraq and Persia and describes rites associated with pilgrimage to them. An excellent classified bibliography is included.

1176 Tabataba'i, A. S. M. H. Shi'ite Islam. Transl. from Persian with introd. and notes by S. H. Nasr. Ed. by E. yar-Shater. Albany, State Univ. of New York Press, 1975.

The most revered living religious figure of Iran presents the history of the Shi'i branch of Islam, its doctrine and practice. It is authoritative because of its source, but lacks scholarly depth.

1177 Wickens, G. M., and R. M. Savory. Persia in Islamic Times: A Practical Bibliography of Its History, Culture, and Language. Ed. by W. J. Watson. Montreal, McGill Univ. Inst. of Islamic Studies, 1964. 57 p.

"This bibliography is intended as a basic desiderata list for both undergraduate and early graduate work"--Preface. Contains critical works on Persian texts and their translations, and poetry.

ISLAM IN THE SOVIET UNION

1178 Benningsen, Alexandre, and C. Lemercier Quelquejay. Islam in the Soviet Union. Transl. from the French by G. E. Wheeler, and H. Evans. New York, Praeger, 1967. 272 p.

A survey sponsored by the Central Research Centre, London. The authors based their research on Russian and other original source materials, and compiled into a well-presented and comprehensive survey. Bibliography of selected studies and an index are included.

ISLAM IN SPAIN

1179 Watt, William M. A History of Islamic Spain, with Additional Sections on Literature, by Pierre Cachia. Edinburgh, Univ. Press, 1965 (Islamic Surveys, v. 4). 210 p.

An excellent historical survey which covers the period from 711 to 1492. Also contains special chapters dealing with literature and philosophy. A well-selected bibliography for further readings and an index are included.

ISLAM IN TURKEY

1180 Birge, John K. Guide to Turkish Area Study. Washington, D.C., American Council of Learned Societies, 1949. 240 p.
A well-designed guide to various aspects of Turkish history and culture. Bibliography is limited mainly to English language publications.

1181 Itzkowitz, Norman. Ottoman Empire and Islamic Tradition. New York, Knopf, 1972 (Studies in World Civilization). 117 p.
"This book provides the student with an introduction to the historical development of the Ottoman Empire ... social structure, and intellectual foundations"--Preface. In the bibliography one will find references to general survey works since there is as yet no comprehensive history of the Ottoman Empire available in English.

ISLAM IN THE INDIAN SUBCONTINENT

1182 Aziz Ahmad. An Intellectual History of Islam in India. Edinburgh, Univ. Press, 1969 (Islamic Surveys, v. 7). 226 p.
Presents the main cultural and religious aspects of Islam in South Asia. Also discusses the architecture, painting, and music. A select bibliography and an index are provided.

1183 ________. Islamic Modernism in India and Pakistan, 1857-1964. London, Oxford Univ. Press, 1967. 294 p.
One of the best studies of the subject; it presents the progress of modernist religious thought on the background of the political developments, and in comparison with Islamic modernism in other lands. Contains a select bibliography and an index.

1184 Smith, Wilfred C. Modern Islam in India: Social Analysis, rev. ed. London, Gollancz, 1963 (1946). 344 p.
An informative account of modern developments in India. Presents a Marxist analysis of movements and trends from the last years of the 19th century until the partition of the subcontinent. Some bibliographic references for further reading are included.

ISLAM IN INDONESIA

1185 Noer, Deliar. The Modernist Muslim Movement in Indonesia 1900-1942. London, Oxford Univ. Press, 1973. 390 p.
This scholarly study surveys the origin and growth of the modern Muslim movement, on its social and political

background. Also contains a glossary, a bibliography including newspapers and periodical articles, and an index. Note also: Nieuwenhuijze, C. A. O. van, Aspects of Islam in Post-colonial Indonesia, and Boland, B. J., The Struggle of Islam in Modern Indonesia (1971).

THE BAHA'I

1186 Miller, William M. The Baha'i Faith. South Pasadena, Calif., W. Carey, 1974. 443 p.
Provides a historical survey of the Bahai movement from 1844 to the contemporary developments in North America. Also includes some bibliographic references at the end of each chapter, translations of al-Kitab al-Agdas, some additional documents, and an index.

JOURNALS

1187 Ars Orientalis; The Arts of Islam and the East. Washington, D.C., 1954- .
Continues Ars Islamica, v. 1-14, 1934-51. Published by the Freer Gallery of Art, the Smithsonian Institution, and the Dept. of Arts of the University of Michigan. Includes articles on the art of both Near and Far East. Indexed: Index Islamicus.

1188 International Journal of Middle East Studies. Cambridge, England, 1970- (quarterly).
Published on behalf of the Middle East Studies Association of America. Papers cover the countries of the Arab world, Iran, Turkey, Afganistan, Israel, India, Pakistan, etc. Deals with history, political science, economics, anthropology, sociology, philology and literature, folklore, comparative religion, theology, law, and philosophy. Indexed: P.A.I.S.; Index Islamicus.

1189 Der Islam; Zeitschrift für Geschichte und Kultur des islamischen Orients. Berlin, 1910- (quarterly).
Official publication of the Deutsche Morgenländische Gesellschaft. Articles in English, German, French. Especially valuable for its articles on the modern Near East. Indexed: Index Islamicus.

1190 Islam and the Modern Age; Quarterly Journal. New Delhi, 1970- .
Contributes articles on modern interpretations of Islamic teaching. Indexed: Index Islamicus.

1191 Islamic Culture; An English Quarterly. Hyderabad, 1927- .
Published by the Islamic Culture Board, Hyderabad, India. Mainly devoted to the Indian Muslim developments. Articles are of very uneven quality. Indexed: Index Islamicus.

1192 Islamic Quarterly; A Review of Islamic Culture. London, 1954- .
Published by the Islamic Cultural Centre, London. Indexed: Index Islamicus.

1193 Islamic Studies. Karachi, 1962- (quarterly).
Published by Islamic Research Institute. Indexed: Index Islamicus.

1194 Middle Eastern Affairs. London, 1958- (monthly).
Published by the Council for Middle Eastern Affairs. Indexed: Index Islamicus.

1195 Middle Eastern Studies. London, 1964- (3 issues a year).
Indexed: Br. Hum. Index; Index Islamicus.

1196 Muslim World; A Quarterly of Islamic Study with Special Attention on the Contemporary Muslim World. Hartford, 1911- .
Contains useful articles on religious and social subjects in the medieval and modern Near East. Indexed: Hist. Abstr.; Modern Language Abstracts; Rel. Per.; Rel. Theol. Abstr.

1197 Studia Islamica. Paris, 1953- (irregularly).
Papers in English and French by specialists in the vast field of Islamic studies. Indexed: Index Islamicus.

1198 Die Welt des Islams. The World of Islam. Le monde de l'Islam. Bd. 1-27; New Series, Leiden, 1951- .
Papers in English, French, or Arabic. Indexed: Index Islamicus.

Part Four

ASIAN RELIGIONS

I GENERAL INTRODUCTION

REFERENCE WORKS

BIBLIOGRAPHIES AND GUIDES

1199 Asia: A Guide to Paperbacks. Rev. ed. by A. T. Embree and others. New York, Asia Society, 1968. 178 p.
Provides an annotated list of paperbacks currently available for studies of Asian countries. Arrangement is by subject within each geographical and cultural area. Author and title indexes are included.

1200 Bibliography of Asian Studies. Ann Arbor, Mich., 1956- .
Published as an annual supplement to The Journal of Asian Studies (see no. 1238). Originally, 1941-55, known under the title Far Eastern Bibliography. Each issue contains a listing of several thousand monographs and periodical articles in Western languages which appeared during the preceding year. A very detailed table of contents is provided, subdivided geographically, and then by subject. Pertinent materials are listed in the Philosophy and Religion sections. Cumulations in two parts, authors and subjects, are provided.

1201 Birnbaum, Eleazar. Books on Asia, from the Near East to the Far East; A Guide for the General Reader. Toronto, Univ. Press, 1971. 341 p.
This selective bibliography covers both popular and more specialized works. Of special interest are sections III. India, South and South East Asia; and IV. Far East. References are accompanied by brief annotations.

1202 Chicago. University. College. Introduction to Civilization of India, South Asia: An Introductory Bibliography. Ed. by M. L. P. Patterson and R. B. Inden. Chicago, Univ. Press, 1962. 412 p.
"Provides an outline guide to humanistic and social

science fields ... [and] contains a built-in reference chronology, and also affords an overview of the units of Indian civilization"--Preface. Especially important are the sections Religion and Philosophy, p. 287-324, and Literature, Sciences, and the Arts, p. 325-72.

1203 Embree, J. F., and L. O. Dotson. Bibliography of the Peoples and Cultures of Mainland Southeast Asia. New Haven, Conn., Yale Univ. Southeast Asia Studies, 1950. 821 p.
Lists monographs and periodical articles dealing with the peoples and cultures of the area. A section on religion is included in each geographical area. No index is provided.

1204 McCasland, S. V. Religions of the World. New York, Random House, 1969, p. 353-737.
See no. 16. Of special interest are Part IV. Religions of India; and Part V. Religions of East Asia. Provides a brief popular introduction discussing the Indian background, Vedic religion, Hindu tradition, the Jains, the Sikhs. A selective bibliography for further reading is provided.

1205 Silberman, Bernard S. Japan and Korea; A Critical Bibliography. Tucson, Univ. of Arizona Press, 1962. 120 p.
"Provides for the student and non-specialist a selected annotated and graded guide to the most authoritative and available works on Japan and Korea..."--Foreword. Each section contains a chapter on religion and philosophy: Japan, p. 29-39; Korea, p. 105-7. An index is provided.

1206 Smith, William M. "The Religions of Asia: A Bibliographical Essay." Choice, v. 10:5-6 (July-Aug. 1973), p. 723-44.
A survey article which "suggests those areas that ought to be covered to achieve a balanced library collection on Eastern religion." Reviews basic materials for the study of Hinduism, Buddhism, Jainism, Sikhism, Chinese, and Japanese religions.

1207 Southeast Asia: A Bibliography for Undergraduate Libraries. D. C. Johnson, area ed., et al. Williamsport, Pa., Bro-Dart, 1970. 59 p.
Contains a list of basic monographs arranged by country, and then by subject including the section: Philosophy and Religion.

DICTIONARIES AND ENCYCLOPEDIAS

1208 Encyclopedia of East Asia. Ed. W. J. Bifolck. Harperwoods, Mich., Publishing Center, 1976. 30 vols.

Covers China, Japan, Korea. Includes two volumes devoted to religion and philosophy. A bibliography and an index volume are added.

1209 Parrinder, E. Geoffrey. Dictionary of Non-Christian Religions. Amersham, Bucks., England, Huton, 1971. 320 p.
See no. 18. Covers religions of Indian origin, as well as of China, Japan, Tibet, etc. Brief selected bibliographies are appended to the articles.

1210 Zaehner, R. C. The Concise Encyclopedia of Living Faith. London, Hutchinson, 1964 (1959), p. 225-401; Bibliography: p. 421-23.
See no. 21. Consists of informative essays on Hinduism, Jainism, Buddhism: Theravada and Mahayana, Shinto, Confucianism, Taoism. Select bibliography and a useful index are included.

SCRIPTURAL COLLECTIONS IN ENGLISH TRANSLATIONS

1211 Harvard Oriental Series. Ed. with the cooperation of various scholars by C. R. Lanman. Cambridge, Mass., Harvard Univ. Press, 1943- .
Contains critical editions of original texts and their translations with informative commentaries. Some of the volumes are comprised of critical works.

1212 Sacred Books of the East. Ed. by F. Müller. Oxford, England, Clarendon Press, 1879-1910. 50 vols.
This monumental collection contains excellent translations of basic religious texts. Vol. 50 contains a detailed index.

ANTHOLOGIES

1213 De Bary, William T., Wing-Tsit Chan, and B. Watson. Sources of Chinese Tradition. New York, Columbia Univ. Press, 1963 (1960). 2 vols.
This excellent book is comprised of selected translations from the major writings of India and China. Bibliographic references include monographs and periodical articles. An index is provided.

1214 Frazier, Allie M., ed. Readings in Eastern Religious Thought. Philadelphia, Westminster Press, 1969. 2 vols.
Vol. 1: Hinduism; Vol. 2: Buddhism. It brings together both interpretative essays on the Hindu and Buddhist traditions and carefully chosen selections from their sacred literature. Contains glossaries of unfamiliar terms and bibliographic references for further reading.

Aimed at the beginner.

1215 Great Asian Religions: An Anthology. Riverside, N.J., Macmillan, 1969. 412 p.

Contains a collection of contemporary translations from the major Asian religious writings into English. A brief bibliography for further reading is provided.

1216 Lin, Yutang, ed. The Wisdom of China and India. New York, Random House, 1942. 1104 p.

Contains selections from the most outstanding Hindu and Chinese writings. Each selection is preceded by an informative introduction. Pt. 1 includes hymns from the Rigveda, the Upanishads, the Ramayana, and the Buddhist writings; Pt. 2 consists of fragments from Chinese mystics, Mencius, Motse, the Aphorisms of Confucius, etc. A glossary of Hindu words, the rules for pronunciation of Chinese names, and a table of Chinese dynastics are provided. The book is aimed at the general reader.

CRITICAL WORKS

1217 Baird, Robert, and A. Bloom. Indian and Far Eastern Religious Traditions. New York, Harper & Row, 1972 (Religion of Man). 306 p.

Provides a description of the principal religions of India, China, and Japan encompassing their development, cultural influences, current practices, and influence on each other. A glossary, bibliographic references, and an index are included.

1218 Bancroft, Anne. Religions of the East. London, Heinemann, 1974. 256 p.

This popularly presented book deals with Tibetan Buddhism, Zen Buddhism, Taoism and, surprisingly, the ideas of the Sufis originally from Persia where the Hindu influences were strong. A list of books for more extensive reading, a glossary and an index are at the back of the book.

1219 Eliot, Charles N. E. Hinduism and Buddhism; An Historical Sketch, new ed. New York, Barnes and Noble, 1954 (1921). 3 vols.

Provides an unusually well-presented Western interpretation of the two major religions of Asia. Notes a great number of religious sects in their historical sequence, and describes the 20th-century status of religion. Bibliographic references are given in footnotes. The index serves as a complete source for looking up new words, strange titles and definitions of terms.

1220 Kitagawa, Joseph M. Religions of the East. Philadelphia, Westminster Press, 1960. 319 p.

Attempts "to give special attention to the modern development of Eastern religions, especially with reference to the encounter of Eastern religious communities and modernity"--Foreword. Contains an analysis of Chinese religions and the family system, Hinduism and the caste system, Buddhism and the Sangha, etc. Also provides a select bibliography, a subject index, and an author index.

1221 Morgan, Kenneth. Asian Religions: An Introduction to the Study of Hinduism, Buddhism, Islam, Confucianism, and Taoism. New York, Macmillan, 1964 (Service Center for Teachers of History. Pub. no. 55). 30 p.

Provides a general survey of the subject with bibliographical references.

1222 Nakamura, Hajime. Ways of Thinking of Eastern Peoples: India, China, Tibet, Japan, rev. English transl. ed. by P. P. Wiener. Honolulu, East-West Center Press, 1964 (1960). 712 p.

This "book was the basis of conferences held at the East-West Center, in 1962-63.... It analyzes, with vigor and objectivity, the characteristic thought-patterns of Asian peoples as these are revealed in their languages, their logic, and their cultural product"--Foreword. "...Likely for a long time to be a source of judgments on the nature of Asian civilizations"--Journal of the History of Ideas. Extensive bibliographic references are included in the notes. Also provides a useful index.

1223 Parrinder, Edward G. An Introduction to Asian Religions. London, S.P.C.K., 1958 (1957). 138 p.

A popular presentation of the study of major Asian religions. Bibliographic references and an index are included.

1224 Quale, G. R. Eastern Civilizations. New York, Appleton-Century-Crofts, 1966. 509 p.

"Provides the reader with a basic knowledge of the historical growth of the major Eastern civilizations.... Contains the civilizations of the Islamic Middle East, the Indo-Pakistan subcontinent, the traditionally Chinese-dominated world of East Asia, their distinctive social, political, religious, philosophic, and literary traditions" --Preface. Classified bibliographies are provided at the end of each chapter. A useful index is included.

1225 Religion and Change in Contemporary Asia. Ed. by R. F. Spencer. Minneapolis, Univ. of Minnesota Press, 1971. 172 p.

Contains a collection of eight essays by outstanding specialists on various problems of modern religious life in China, Japan, Vietnam, India, Burma, Pakistan, and Indonesia. Each essay is supplied with useful bibliographic notes. There is also a general index.

1226 Sinor, Denis, ed. Orientalism and History. Bloomington, Indiana Univ. Press, 1970. 123 p.

The principal aim of this book is to inform the non-specialist of materials available for studies of the Ancient Near East, India and its cultural heritage, China and central Asia. References are included in annotated bibliographic notes at the end of each essay. No index is enclosed.

1227 Steadman, John M. The Myth of Asia. New York, Simon & Schuster, 1969. 353 p.

This popular book gives the historical background for the understanding of the cultural complex of Asia, its philosophy and religion, arts and esthetics, and political life. A select bibliography and an index are provided.

1228 Stroup, Herbert H. Four Religions of Asia; A Primer. New York, Harper & Row, 1968. 212 p.

An informative introduction for the beginner, with a useful list for further reading.

1229 Welty, Paul T. The Asians, Their Heritage, and Their Destiny, 3rd ed. Philadelphia, Lippincott, 1970 (1963). 351 p.

An introductory text for beginners which provides some understanding of the social and economic environment, as well as of the Asian cultural traditions. Contains a well selected bibliography and an index.

JOURNALS

1230 Acta Asiatica; Bulletin of the Institute of Eastern Culture. Tokyo, Toho Gakkai, 1960.

Contains highly valued scholarly articles. Indexed: Bibliog. As. St.

1231 Acta Orientalia. Budapest, Akadémiai Kiado, 1950- (3 issues annually).

Published by the Hungarian Academy of Sciences. Includes articles in English, French, German, or Russian. Also contains a large number of brief book reviews. Indexed: Bibliog. As. St.

1232 Acta Orientalia. Copenhagen, Munsgaard, 1922- .

Articles in English, French, or German. Also includes reviews. Indexed: Bibliog. As. St.

1233 American Oriental Society. Journal. Boston, 1843- .
Indexed: Soc. Sci. Hum. Index.

1234 Archiv orientalní. Praha, Československa Akademia Věd, Orientalní Ustav, 1929- .
Contains articles in English, French, or German, book reviews. Indexed: Bibliog. As. St.; Int. Bibliog. Hist. Rel.

1235 Asia Major; A British Journal of Far Eastern Studies. London, 1924-35; new ser. 1944- (2 issues a year).
Includes articles on history, religious problems, literature, etc. Also contains a section of signed book reviews. Indexed: Br. Hum. Index; Bibliog. As. St.

1236 Asian Affairs; Journal of the Royal Central Society. London, 1903- (3 issues a year).
Continues: Royal Central Society, London, Journal. Articles discuss various topics in history, literature, religious life, etc. Also contains reliable book reviews. Indexed: Br. Hum. Index; Bibliog. As. St.

1237 Asian Perspectives; A Journal of Archaeology and Prehistory of Asia and Pacific. Tuscon, 1957- .
Indexed: Bibliog. As. St.

1238 Central Asiatic Journal; International Periodical for the Languages, Literature, History, and Archaeology of Central Asia. Wiesbaden, Harrassowitz, 1955- .
Indexed: Bibliog. As. St.; Int. Bibliog. Per. Lit.

1239 East and West; Quarterly. Rome, 1950- .
Published by the Istituto Italiano per il Medio ed Estremo Oriente. Indexed: Int. Bibliog. Hist. Rel.

1240 Harvard Journal of Asiatic Studies. Cambridge, Mass., Harvard Yenching Institute, 1936- .
Contains excellent articles on broad range of subjects in history, literature, religions, etc. Also includes informative signed book reviews. Indexed: Soc. Sci. Hum. Index.

1241 Journal of Asian History. Wiesbaden, 1967- .
Articles in English, French, German, or Russian. Also provides useful book reviews. Indexed: Bibliog. As. St.

1242 Journal of Asian Studies. Ann Arbor, Mich., 1941- (quarterly).
Published by the Association for Asian Studies. Covers research in all the disciplines of the social sciences and humanities on the countries of East, Southeast, South Asia, from Japan to Pakistan. Also includes an

annual supplement: Bibliography of Asian Studies (see no. 1200). Indexed: Soc. Sci. Hum. Index; Bibliog. As. St.; P. A. I. S.

1243 Journal of Oriental Research. Madras, India, 1927- .
Published by Kuppusswami Satri Research Institute. Indexed: Bibliog. As. St.

1244 Journal of Oriental Studies. Hong Kong, Univ. Press, 1954- .
Articles in English or Chinese. Also contains some useful book reviews. Indexed: Int. Bibliog. Per. Lit.; Bibliog. As. St., Hist. Abstr.

1245 Journal of Southeast Asian Studies. Singapore, McGraw-Hill Far Eastern Publishers, 1970- .
Supersedes: Journal of Southeast Asian History. Indexed: Bibliog. As. St.

1246 London. University. School of Oriental and African Studies. Bulletin.
Indexed: Br. Hum. Index; Bibliog. As. St.

1247 Monumenta Serica; Journal of Oriental Studies. Tokyo, 1936- .
Contains scholarly articles on various topics in history, literature, religions, etc. Also includes book reviews. Indexed: Bibliog. As. St.

1248 Oriens Extremus; Zeitschrift für Sprache, Kunst und Kultur der Länder des Fernen Ostens (Far East; Journal of Language, Art and Culture). Wiesbaden, Harrassowitz, 1954- (2 issues a year).
Indexed: Int. Bibliog. Per. Lit.; Bibliog. As. St.

1249 Philosophy East and West; A Quarterly of Asian and Comparative Thought. Honolulu, Univ. of Hawaii, 1951- .
Contains specialized articles on Asian philosophies, and studies relating philosophy to the arts, literature, science, and social practices of Asian civilizations. Also includes reliable book reviews. Indexed: Bibliog. As. St.

1250 Royal Asiatic Society of Great Britain and Ireland. Journal. London, 1834- .
Indexed: British Hum. Index; Bibliog. As. St.

1251 T'Oung Pao; Archives concernant l'histoire, les langues, la geographie, l'ethnographie, et les arts de l'Asie orientale (Archives concerning studies in history, languages, geography, and arts in Asia). Leiden, Brill, 1890- .
Articles in English, French, or German. Covers East and Southeast studies area. Indexed: Bibliog. As. St.

Part Four--Asian Religions (cont.)

II INDIA AND HINDUISM

INDIAN BACKGROUND OF ASIAN RELIGIONS

BIBLIOGRAPHIES

1252 Instituut Kern, Leiden. Annual Bibliography of Indian Archaeology. Leiden, Brill, 1926- .
Contains a systematically arranged list of all monographs and periodical articles on history, art, geography, and other fields related to Indian archaeology. Also includes informative introductory surveys.

1253 Mahar, J. M. India; A Critical Bibliography. Tucson, Univ. of Arizona Press, 1964. 119 p.
Provides a selected list of works, mainly in English, that deal with traditional and modern India. Entries are arranged by subject. Of special interest is the section, Religion and Philosophy, p. 75-97.

DICTIONARIES AND ENCYCLOPEDIAS

1254 Balfour, Edward. The Cyclopedia of India and of Eastern and Southern Asia. Graz, Akademische Druck- und Verlagsanstalt, 1967 (1885). 3 vols.
Alphabetically arranged articles provide still useful information on geography, history, religious life, ethnography, etc. Some bibliographic information is included.

1255 Bhattacharya, S. A Dictionary of Indian History. Calcutta, University, 1967. 833 p.
Contains some 3000 entries, arranged alphabetically, including names of persons, places, and significant events in the development of Indian history. No bibliographic references provided.

1256 Garret, John. A Classical Dictionary of India, Illustrative of the Mythology, Philosophy, Literature, Antiquities, Arts, Manners, Customs.... Graz, Akademische

Druck- und Verlagsanstalt, 1971 (1871). 793, 160 p.
Provides information on all the Hindu deities, and all the mythical personages and objects which appear in the studies of Hindu literature, various terms of Brahmanical and Buddhic theology and ritual, and of the Indian philosophical schools.

1257 Mani, Vettam. Puranic Encyclopedia: A Comprehensive Dictionary with Special Reference to the Epic and Puranic Literature. Delhi, Barnasidass, 1975. 922 p.
Presents a ready reference work to the ideas and ideologies as embodied in the contents of the Puranas. Numerous references to the texts are included.

CRITICAL WORKS

INDIAN CIVILIZATION

1258 Basham, Arthur L. The Wonder That Was India; A Survey of the History and Culture of the Indian Sub-continent Before the Coming of the Muslims, 3rd rev. ed. New York, Taplinger, 1968 (1954). 527 p.
This basic work is the best available introduction to the development of classical Indian culture from the Indus Civilization to A.D. 1000. Provides excellent reading for the beginner. Well-selected chapter bibliographies are included at the end. There is also a useful general index.

1259 The Cambridge History of India. Cambridge, England, Cambridge Univ. Press, 1922- (6 vols. and suppls. already published).
Provides a comprehensive survey of all aspects of Indian history, including religious life, from the earliest times to 1947. Each volume contains extensive bibliographic references and a detailed index. Supplementary volumes: M. Wheeler, The Indus Civilization.

1260 Conference on Oriental Civilizations in General Education. Approaches to Asian Civilizations. Ed. by W. T. De-Bary and A. T. Embree. New York, Columbia Univ. Press, 1964. 294 p.
Includes papers dealing with historical, political, economical, sociological, and anthropological aspects in the development of Asian civilizations.

1261 The Cultural Heritage of India. Calcutta, the Ramakrishna Mission, 1953. 4 vols.
This collection is comprised of outstanding essays by a group of Hindu scholars who look at Indian history and culture "from the inside." Vol. 4 contains studies on various religious topics. Selected bibliographic references

are included in each volume. A detailed index is provided.

1262 East-West Philosophers' Conference. The Indian Mind: Essentials of Indian Philosophy and Culture. Ed. by C. A. Moore. Honolulu, Univ. of Hawaii Press, 1967. 485 p.
Contains a collection of papers, dealing with various aspects of Indian religious philosophy, delivered at the University of Hawaii. Bibliographical references are included in notes; an index is provided. There is also an appendix: Who's Who of Participants.

1263 Edwardes, Michael. A History of India from the Earliest Times to the Present Day. London, Thames and Hudson, 1961. 444 p.
Attempts "to give a view of the life of the people of India within a framework of political events. Discussion of each period contains a section on religious life"--Preface. A selective bibliography and an index are provided.

1264 History and Culture of the Indian People. Eds.: R. C. Majumdar, A. D. Pusalkar. London, Allen & Unwin, 1952- .
Prepared under the auspices of the Bharatiya Itihāsa Samiti (Academy of Indian History). Provides a detailed survey of Indian history. Each volume contains a section on religious life of the described period. Selected bibliography contains monographs, and periodical articles in classified arrangement. Also contains a detailed index and historical maps.

1265 Macdonnel, Arthur A. India's Past: A Survey of Her Literatures, Religions, Languages and Antiquities. Varanasi, Motilal Banarsidass, 1956 (1927). 300 p.
This old but still very useful work provides a summary of India's cultural heritage. Each chapter concludes with a select bibliography. There is also an index.

RELIGIONS OF INDIA--GENERAL

1266 Banerjee, Priyatosh. Early Indian Religions. Delhi, Vikas, 1973. 241 p.
"The book aims at presenting a historical account of some aspects of India's religious life of the post-Madrian period, i.e. 185 B.C. to A.D. 300..."--Preface. A list of ancient Indian texts, and a select bibliography of modern critical works is supplied. Also a subject index is included.

1267 Berry, Thomas M. Religions of India: Yoga, Buddhism. New York, Bruce, 1971. 226 p.

Contains a brief informative survey with a select bibliography, glossary and an index.

1268 Conference on Religion in South Asia, Berkeley, Calif., 1961. Religion in South Asia. Ed. by E. B. Harper. Seattle, Univ. of Washington Press, 1964. 199 p.
This collection is composed of papers from the conference. Bibliographic references are appended at the end of each article.

1269 Gonda, Jan. Change and Continuity in Indian Religion. The Mouton, 1965 (Disputationes Rheno-Trajectinae, 9). 484 p.
"This book is a series of essays or monographs rather than a complete and systematic presentation of the problems connected with change and continuity in Indian history.... The book addresses itself ... to historians, archaeologists, and historians of religion"--Preface. Numerous bibliographic references are included in footnotes. Also contains indexes: of names, other terms, Sanskrit and other words, and text-places.

1270 Konow, Sten, and P. Tuxen. The Religions of India. Copenhagen, Gad, 1949 (1948). 214 p.
Provides a popular introduction to the historical development and ideas of Hinduism, Jainism, and Buddhism. Select bibliography is included; no index.

1271 Renou, Louis. Religions of Ancient India. London, Athlone, 1953 (Jordan Lectures in Comparative Religion, 1). 139 p.
Presents a brief and solid introduction to the ancient religious tradition of Vedism, Hinduism and Jainism. Bibliographic references in footnotes and an index are provided.

1272 Weber, Max. The Religions of India: The Sociology of Hinduism and Buddhism. Transl. and ed. by H. H. Gertz and D. Martindale. Glencoe, Ill., Free Press, 1958 (1921). 392 p.
A classic work in the sociological study of religion. It attempts to analyze Indian religions in relation to a general sociological problem. The author considers the Indian religious value to be in conflict with the rational development of capitalistic institutions. Bibliographic references and an index are included.

1273 Younger, Paul. The Indian Religious Tradition. Varanasi, Bharatiya Vidya Prakashan, 1970. 138 p.
Presents a brief and informative discussion on the background, formulation, consolidation and survival of the Hindu religious and philosophical tradition. Also contains a glossary of terms, selected bibliography and

a general index.

1274 ________. Introduction to Indian Religious Thought. Philadelphia, Westminster, 1972. 142 p.

This book is specifically designed for those who "had fallen in love with India but badly needed guidance if their love was to mature"--Preface. The author points out that this new love relationship with India is a Western not an Indian phenomenon. A glossary is supplied, but neither bibliography for further reading nor index is added.

FESTIVALS; PILGRIMAGE

1275 Bhardwaj, Surinder M. Hindu Places of Pilgrimage in India: A Study in Cultural Geography. Berkeley, Univ. of Calif. Press, 1973 (University of California, Berkeley. Center for South and Southeast Asia Studies). 258 p.

This excellent scholarly study surveys the literature on places of pilgrimage in India. An exhaustive bibliography contains published and unpublished works, both monographs and periodical articles. An index is provided.

1276 Thomas, Paul. Festivals and Holidays of India. Bombay, Taraporeda, 1971. 115 p.

Describes in detail all the important festivals and holidays, both religious and secular, and the places of pilgrimage and shrines of all religious groups in India. Also provides a list of important annual festivals and holidays, a list of shrines, and a glossary of terms. An index is included.

INDIAN ART

1277 Banerjea, Jitendra. The Development of Hindu Iconography, 2nd rev. ed. Calcutta, Univ. of Calcutta Press, 1956 (1941). 653 p.

Presents the history of the origin and development of Hindu cult images and the inter-related iconographic principles. Bibliography includes original textual sources, archeological documentation, and secondary critical readings. Comprehensive index of proper names and terms is included. Illustrations are abundantly used.

1278 Gopinatha, Rao T. A. Elements of Hindu Iconography, 2nd ed. New York, Paragon, 1968 (1914). 2 vols. in 4.

Contains an exhaustive survey of Hindu iconography with references to sources and illustrative materials. Bibliographic references are provided. Each volume contains an index of presentations.

1279 Gupta, R. S. Iconography of the Hindus, Buddhist and Jains. Bombay, Taraporevala, 1972. 201 p.

This is a first attempt to cover the iconographies of the three important Indian religions in their entirety. Information is given in tabular form. There is an index but no bibliography.

MYTHOLOGY

Dictionary

1280 Dowson, John. A Classical Dictionary of Hindu Mythology and Religion, Geography, History, and Literatures, 8th ed. London: Routledge and Paul, 1968 (1879) (Trübner's Oriental Series). 411 p.

Includes names of gods, personal and geographical names, as well as subjects.

Critical Works

1281 Bhattacharji, Sukumari. The Indian Theogony: A Comparative Study of Indian Mythology from the Vedas to the Puranas. Cambridge, England, Univ. Press, 1970. 397 p.

"A most complete collection of Indian mythology ... a mass of raw materials like a card index"--review. Presents the entire mythology of the Indian gods and the course of its development from Rigveda to the Puranic literature based on detailed textual studies. Selected bibliography is comprised of monographs and periodical articles. An index is provided.

1282 Ions, Veronica. Indian Mythology. London, Hamlyn, 1967. 141 p.

Presents a popular survey of Indian myths including early and Vedic deities, the Brahmanic age, as well as the Buddhist tradition. Numerous illustrations, bibliographies, and an index are supplied.

1283 Zimmer, Heinrich R. Myths and Symbols in Indian Arts and Civilization. Ed. by J. Campbell. New York, Harper, 1962 (Bollingen Series, 6). 248 p.

Deals with myths of eternity and time, the Vishnu tradition, myths related to the guardian of life, the cosmic delight of Siva, and the goddess. Bibliographic references in footnotes and an index are included.

HINDU RELIGIOUS TRADITION

BIBLIOGRAPHIES AND GUIDES

1284 Boyce, M. "Hinduism." Bleeker, C. J. Historia Religionum. Leiden, Brill, 1969, p. 237-345.
See no. 38. Provides a brief and informative survey with some bibliographic listing.

1285 "Classics in the Indian Tradition." Columbia University. Columbia College. A Guide to Oriental Classics. Ed. by W. T. DeBary and A. T. Embree. 2nd ed. New York, Columbia Univ. Press, 1975. p. 49-133.
Contains a classified bibliography of monographs and periodical articles.

1286 Dandekar, Ramchandra N. Vedic Bibliography; An up-to-date Analytically Arranged Register of All Important Work Done Since 1930 in the Field of the Veda and Allied Antiquities Including Indus Valley Civilization. Bombay, Karnatak, 1946-61. 2 vols.
This bibliography continues Renou, L. Bibliographie vedique, see no. 1289. It provides "an exhaustive analytical register of all significant writings which were not included in Renou's work..."--Preface; plus some 9000 new publications. It follows basically the Renou arrangement. Contains an index of authors and an index of subjects.

1287 Hein, N. J. "Hinduism." Adams, C. J., ed. A Reader's Guide to the Great Religions. 2nd ed. New York, Free Press, 1977 (1965), p. 106-155.
See no. 22. An excellent bibliographic essay which surveys works on the entire religious tradition, collections of religious literature in translation, the Harappa culture, Vedic religion, the Karma-Marga, the way of knowledge, the Sādhu, the philosophies of Jnana-Marga, the way of devotion, Sāktism, modern forms of Hinduism, etc. Bibliographic references are included within the text.

1288 "Hinduism." International Bibliography of the History of Religions. Leiden, Brill, 1954- .
See no. 27. An annual bibliography which lists monographs and periodical articles.

1289 Renou, Louis. Bibliographie védique. Paris, Librairie d'Amérique et d'Orient, 1931- (irregularly).
Published periodically, this bibliography provides a comprehensive coverage of materials. Entries are arranged by subject. Also contains an index of authors and of subjects.

DICTIONARY

1290 Walker, Benjamin. Hindu World; An Encyclopedic Survey of Hinduism. London, Allen & Unwin, 1968. 2 vols.
This excellent reference book attempts to cover all aspects of the Hindu tradition. Entries are arranged alphabetically. Selected bibliographic references are appended to each article. Vol. 2 contains a detailed subject index with numerous cross references.

SCRIPTURAL WRITINGS

CRITICAL SURVEY

1291 Farquhar, John N. An Outline of the Religious Literature of India. Delhi, Motilal Banarsidas, 1967 (1920). 451 p.
This exhaustive survey is arranged by systems and schools within their historical periods to show the stages of Indian religious development. It serves as an invaluable guide to the content and chronology of Hindu, Buddhist, and Jain ideas, from the Vedic period to ca. A.D. 1800. Classified bibliography and a detailed index are supplied.

SCRIPTURAL COLLECTIONS IN ENGLISH TRANSLATIONS

1292 Emeneau, Murray B. A Union List of Printed Indic Texts. New York, Kraus Reprint, 1967 (1935) (American Oriental Series). 540 p.
A useful source for locating translations as well as texts in American libraries. An author index, and a subject index in Sanskrit order are provided. See also no. 1211, 1212, and The Sacred Books of the Hindus (Allahabad, Panini Office, 1909-37).

ANTHOLOGIES

1293 DeBary, William T., et al. Sources of Indian Tradition. New York, Columbia Univ. Press, 1958 (Records of Civilizations). 961 p.
A balanced and comprehensive selection from Hindu scriptures illustrating intellectual and spiritual traditions. Informative introductions place selected texts in history and evaluate their meaning in the Hindu tradition. Selected bibliographies contain information on monographs and periodical articles. An index is provided.

1294 Embree, Ainslie T., ed. The Hindu Tradition. New York, Random House, 1966 (Readings of Oriental Thought). 363 p.

This anthology is comprised of selections from sources in English translation, divided into a five-part chronology, which convey the essential meaning of the Hindu tradition. Sources of selections are provided. Also contains some bibliographic references in footnotes, and an index.

1295 Macnicol, Nicol, ed. Hindu Scriptures: Hymns from the Rigveda, Five Upanishads, the Bhagavadgita. London, Dent, 1938 (Everyman's Library: Theology and Philosophy, no. 944). 293 p.

Still one of the best collections including R. Griffith's translation of some 30 Rigvedic hymns, M. Müller's version of five Upanishads, and L. Barnett's rendition of the Bhagavadgita.

1296 Zaehner, Robert C. Hindu Scriptures. London, Dent, 1966 (Everyman's Library, no. 944). 312 p.

A useful anthology of Indian religious texts including selections from the Rigveda, the Atharvaveda, the Upanishads, and the Bhagavadgita.

THE VEDAS

Complete Texts in English Translation

See no. 1211 and 1212.

1297 Vedas. Rigveda. English. Hymns of the Rigveda. Transl. with a popular commentary by R. T. H. Griffith. 4th ed. Varanasi, Chowkamba Sanskrit Series Office, 1963 (Chowkamba Sanskrit Series). 2 vols.

This is a new edition of the only complete English translation of the Rigveda. Has been criticized for some inaccuracies, and therefore should be used with caution. Indexes of hymns and names are included.

Anthology

1298 Macdonell, Arthur A. A Vedic Reader for Students, Containing Thirty Hymns of Rigveda in the Original Samhita and Pada Texts, with Transliteration, Translation, Explanatory Notes, Introduction, Vocabulary. Madras, Oxford University Press, 1965 (1917). 263 p.

Contains a selection of 30 hymns from the Rigveda presented in the original text with English translations. Brief introduction and numerous explanatory notes are provided. There is also an index.

Concordance

1299 Bloomfield, Maurice. A Vedic Concordance, Being an Alphabetic Index to Every Line of the Published Vedic Literature and to Liturgical Formulas, Thereof, That is an Index to the Vedic Mantras, Together with an Account of Their Variations in the Different Vedic Books. Cambridge, Mass., Harvard Univ. Press, 1906 (Harvard Oriental Series, v. 10). 1078 p.

This monumental work contains a universal word index to the Vedas. It also serves as an index of subjects and ideas. An explanation of the use of the concordance, and a bibliography of works cited, is provided.

Critical Studies

1300 Keith, Arthur B. The Religion and the Philosophy of the Vedas and Upanishads. Cambridge, Mass., Harvard Univ. Press, 1925 (Harvard Oriental Series, v. 31-32). 2 vols.

A classic which provides a scholarly review of the Vedic tradition in relation to other non-vedic religions, and other Indo-European civilizations. Bibliographic references are given in footnotes. An index is included.

1301 Macdonell, Arthur A. The Vedic Mythology. Varanasi, Indological Book House, 1971. 189 p.

Contains discussions on Vedic conceptions, gods, mythical priests and heroes, animals and inanimate objects, demons and fiends, and eschatology. A Sanskrit index and a general index are provided.

1302 Miller, Jeanine. The Vedas: Harmony, Meditation and Fulfilment. London, Rider, 1974. 240 p.

I: Mythology and the Vedic myth; II: Vedic meditation; III: Vedic eschatology; IV: Selected hymns which illustrate subjects discussed. A select list of books and an index are provided.

1303 Pannikar, Raimundo. The Vedic Experience; Mantramanjart: An Anthropology of the Vedas for Modern Man and Contemporary Celebration. Berkeley, Univ. of Calif. Press, 1976. 800 p.

Contains a selection of texts newly translated into contemporary English.

THE UPANISHADS

Text in English Translations

1304 Chitrita Devi. Upanisads for All. New Delhi, Chand, 1973.

380 p.

Edited in popular style, this selection of texts with informative introductions aims at preparing the reader to understand the somewhat cryptic language. Includes some bibliographic references and a general index.

1305 Upanishads. English. The Thirteen Principal Upanishads. Transl. by R. E. Hume, with a list of recurrent and parallel passages by G. C. O. Haas. London, Oxford Univ. Press, 1962 (1921). 587 p.

This excellent translation of 13 Upanishads is accompanied by interesting remarks concerning the translations, methods and arrangement, and their philosophy. One finds also a select classified bibliography with annotations, a Sanskrit index, and a general index.

1306 _______. _______. The Principal Upanishads. Ed. with introd. text, transl. and notes by S. S. Radhakrishnan. London, Allen & Unwin, 1953 (Muirhead Library of Philosophy). 958 p.

The editor, a devout Hindu and a highly respected scholar, presents an accurate and literary translation of the text accompanied by an informative introduction dealing with the chronology, and authorship, and their relations to the Vedas. There is also a selected bibliography listing other English translations, and critical works. An index is provided.

1307 _______. _______. The Upanishads. Transl. from the Sanskrit with Introductions Embodying a General Survey and the Metaphysics and Psychology of the Upanishads, and with Notes, and Explanations Based on the Commentary of Sri Sankarāchār--the Great Ninth Century Philosopher and Saint. New York, 1949-56. 3 vols.

Contains: vol. 1. Katha, Iśa, Kena, Murdaka; vol. 2. Svetāśvatara, Praśna, Mandrikya with Gaudapāda's Karika; vol. 3. Aitareya and Brihadāranyaka. Each volume includes an introductory discussion and a glossary. Some bibliographic reference are provided in the footnotes.

Concordance

1308 Jacob, George A. A Concordance to the Principal Upanishads and Bhagavadgita. Delhi, Motilal Banarsidass, 1963. 1083 p.

Cites words from some 56 published Upanishads.

Critical Studies

1309 Deussen, Paul. The Philosophy of the Upanishads. Transl.

by A. S. Geden. New York, Dover, 1966 (1906). 429 p.
An old but still reliable and comprehensive study of the fundamental philosophic ideas of the Upanishads. Some bibliographic references are included in the footnotes. An index is provided.

1310 Ranade, Ramchandra D. A Constructive Survey of Upanishadic Philosophy, Being an Introduction to the Thought of the Upanishads. Bombay, Bharatiya Vidya Bhauan, 1968. 340 p.
A useful introductory reading with some bibliographic references and an index.

See also no. 1300.

THE MAHABHARATA

Text in English Translation

1311 The Mahabharata. English. The Mahabharata. Transl. and Ed. J. A. B. van Buitenen. Chicago, Univ. Press, 1974- .
This new scholarly translation of the Mahabharata is based in the Poona edition of 1933-66. It contains an informative introduction and a summary. A useful glossary and an index of names are also included.

1312 ________. ________. Mahabharata. Transl. from the Sanskrit of Vyasa by P. Lal. Calcutta, Writer's Shop, 1968- (some 50 vols. already published).
Contains a complete translation of the text "sloka by sloka." Notes on characters, terms, and proper names are added at the end of each volume.

1313 ________. ________. Selections. The Mahabharata; An English Version Based on Selected Verses. Transl. by Chakravarthi V. Narasimhan. New York, Columbia Univ. Press, 1965 (Records of Civilization: Sources and Studies). 254 p.
"The purpose of the present work is to give a straightforward narrative account of the main theme of the epic: the rivalry between the Pandavas and the Kauravas.... It is essentially a condensation of the main story..."--Preface. A useful introduction and a glossary are provided. There is also an index of alternative names.

1314 ________. Bhagavadgita. English. The Bhagavad Gita with a Commentary Based on the Original Sources. Oxford, England, Clarendon Press, 1969. 480 p.
Includes transliteration of the original Sanskrit text with an excellent introduction on the philosophical background and the teaching of the Gita. An index of passages

cited, and a general index are provided.

1315 _______. _______. Sanskrit and English. The Bhagavad-gita. Transl. by S. Radhakrishnan. 2nd ed. London, Allen & Unwin, 1948. 388 p.
Presents an accurate scholarly translation with an informative introduction explaining the philosophical and historical background of the epic. Brief bibliography and an index are provided.

1316 _______. _______. _______. Bhagavadgita. Transl. by F. Egerton. Cambridge, Mass., Harvard Univ. Press, 1972 (1944). 2 vols.
Provides a well-rendered translation with an introduction explaining the author's interpretation and placing it historically and philosophically within the frame of Indian civilization. Some bibliographic references are supplied.

Concordance

1317 Jacob, George A. A Concordance to the Principal Upanishads and Bhagavadgita. Delhi, Motilal Banarsidass, 1963. 1083 p.

See no. 1308.

1318 Khair, Gajanan S. Quest for the Original Gita. Bombay, Somaiya, 1969 (Critical Study of Bhagavadgita). 248 p.
Discusses various problems encountered in the study of the Gita. It surveys the methods and tools for investigation, authors and their personalities, etc. It includes a chapter on the meaning of the Gita and the modern age. There is a bibliography of relevant books and an index.

1319 Lal, Rajendra B. The Gita in the Light of Modern Science. Bombay, Somaiya, 1970. 315 p.
"Takes a fresh look at the Gita and tries to establish how far the fundamental doctrines are consistent with logic, common sense and the findings of science"--Preface. Contains a select bibliography and an index.

THE RAMAYANA

Texts in English Translation

1320 Valmiki. The Ramayana. Transl. by H. P. Shastri. 2nd rev. ed. London, Shanti Sadan, 1962-70. 3 vols.
The standard English translation of the most famous Indian epic about a struggle between the forces of good and evil. Each volume contains a glossary.

1321 Valmiki. Ramayana Critically Edited for the First Time. Board of Eds. J. M. Metha, et al. Baroda, Oriental Institute, 1960- (6 vols. already pub.).
A new attempt to render a scholarly critical edition of the text.

CRITICAL STUDIES

PHILOSOPHICAL SYSTEMS--GENERAL

Bibliography

1322 Potter, Karl H. Bibliography of Indian Philosophies. Delhi, Motilal Banarsidass, 1970 (Encyclopedia of Indian Philosophies). 811 p.
Published for the American Institute of Indian Studies. Has been up-dated by the "First Supplement" (Journal of Indian Philosophy, v. 2:1 (1972), p. 65-112). Contains in Pt. 1-2: Sanskrit Texts, Pt. 3: Secondary Literature. Also provides an index of names, an index of titles, and a topic index.

Anthology

1323 Radhakrishnan, S. S., and C. A. Moore. A Source Book in Indian Philosophy. Princeton, N.J., Princeton Univ. Press, 1967. 683 p.
Contains selections from the major philosophical texts of India, presenting religious writings of Hinduism, Buddhism, Carvaka, Jainism, and includes the Bhagavadgita and Dhammapada. The introductions to each section provide useful information. Selected bibliography includes periodical articles and an index.

Critical Studies

1324 Dasgupta, Surendra N. A History of Indian Philosophy. Cambridge, Eng., Cambridge Univ. Press, 1952 (1932). 5 vols.
Presents a comprehensive survey of principal schools and systems. Each volume contains numerous bibliographic references in footnotes. Some useful indexes are supplied. A 1969 abridged edition is also available.

1325 Radhakrishnan, S. S. Indian Philosophy. New York, Macmillan, 1940. 2 vols.
Provides an accurate survey of the Indian philosophical traditions in the context of Western philosophical developments. Numerous bibliographical references and

an index are included. Recommended for the beginner.

1326 Sharma, Chandradhar D. A Critical Survey of Indian Philosophy. London, Rider, 1960. 414 p.
A brief and clear introduction to the major Indian philosophical concepts. Also contains a selective topical bibliography and an index.

1327 Smart, Ninian. Doctrine and Argument in Indian Philosophy. London, Allen & Unwin, 1964 (Muirhead Library of Philosophy). 255 p.
This popular book presents an analytical exposition of the various schools, describing their religious and philosophical determinants. Includes a glossary, a brief history of the schools, a selected bibliography, and a biographical information. An index is provided.

VEDANTA

Dictionary

1328 Wood, Ernest. Vedanta Dictionary. London, Owen, 1964 (1963). 225 p.
A useful reference work for finding the names and terms which appear in Western works on Vedanta.

Texts and Critical Studies

1329 Badarayana. The Brahma Sutra; The Philosophy of Spiritual Life. Transl. with an Introd. by S. S. Radhakrishnan. New York, Greenwood Press, 1968 (1960). 606 p.
Pt. 1 presents an excellent introduction discussing the tradition of the Brahma Sutra, commentators, reason and revelation, the nature of reality, the status of the world, the individual self, the way to perfection; Pt. 2 contains the text, its translation, and critical notes. A selected bibliography, a glossary of Sanskrit terms, and an index are included.

1330 Deutsch, Eliot, and J. A. B. van Buitenen. A Source Book of Advaita Vedanta. Honolulu, Univ. of Hawaii Press, 1971. 335 p.
Contains English translations of the major Sanskrit writings of the most important Vedantic philosophers. Some bibliographic notes included.

1331 Ranade, Ramchandra D. Vedanta, the Culmination of Indian Thought. Bombay, Bharatiya Vidya Bhavan, 1970. 234 p.
"Outcome of the Basu Mallik lectures on Vedanta philosophy delivered ... in 1929 at the Calcutta University"--Preface. Contains discussions on cosmology, metaphysics,

logic, epistomology, problem of god, self, etc. Also provides a list of sources, bibliographic notes, and an index.

YOGA

Dictionary

1332 Rai, Ram Kumar. Encyclopedia of Yoga. Varanasi, Prachya Prakashan, 1975 (Indological Reference Series, no. 1). 421 p.
Contains a comprehensive guide to yoga practices with a bibliography to basic philosophical works.

1333 Wood, Ernest. Yoga Dictionary. New York, Philosophical Library, 1956.
Lists alphabetically all basic information on Yoga tradition drawn from many different schools. No bibliographic information is provided.

Critical Surveys

1334 Eliade, Mircea. Yoga: Immortality and Freedom. Transl. from the French by W. R. Trask. 2nd ed. Princeton, N.J., Princeton Univ. Press, 1969 (Bollingen Series, no. 56). 536 p.
Presents an introduction to the principles of Yoga for Westerners. Deals with the doctrines of Yoga, techniques for autonomy, Yoga and Brahmanism, Yoga and Tantrism, etc. Also contains excellent explanatory notes with bibliographic references, an extensive list of periodical articles and monographs cited, and an index of subjects and names.

1335 Wood, Ernest. Yoga. Harmondsworth, Penguin, 1969 (1959) (Pelican Book). 271 p.
This book contains a popular explanation of the Yoga philosophy and practices including a description of Yoga exercises for Westerners. One finds numerous references to sources, e.g. Patanjali, Yoga Sutra, transl. by J. Wood (1966). A glossary, a list of Sanskrit titles, a selected bibliography of books on Yoga in English, and an index are provided.

GENERAL STUDIES ON HINDUISM

1336 Bloomfield, Maurice. The Religion of the Veda, the Ancient Religion of India (from Rig-veda to Upanishads). New York, Putnam, 1908 (American Lectures on the History of Religions, 7th ser.). 300 p.

A recognized classic which traces the development of religious life of the Aryans from the Vedas to the Upanishads. Bibliographic references may serve as an example of thoroughness of the author's research.

1337 Bouquet, Alan C. Hinduism, 3rd rev. ed. London, Hutchinson, 1966 (Hutchinson Univ. Library: Religion). 175 p.
A popular presentation of various aspects of Hindu religious ideas on their historical background.

1338 Brent, Peter L. Godmen of India. London, Allen Lane, 1972. 346 p.
A well-designed popular book which assists the reader to gain a better understanding of the Indian outlook on the universe. Glossary is provided but there is neither bibliography nor index.

1339 Chatterjee, S. The Fundamentals of Hinduism: A Philosophical Study. Calcutta, Das Gupta, 1950. 177 p.
Presents a fine introductory survey of Hindu doctrinal teachings. A brief list of books for further reading is included.

1340 Dandekar, Ramchandra N. Some Aspects of the History of Hinduism. Poona, Univ. of Poona, 1967 (Centre for Advanced Studies in Sanskrit. Publications, Class B, no. 3). 142 p.
Contains five lectures dealing with protohistoric Hinduism, the Vedic period, classical Hinduism, and Hinduism in modern times. Some bibliographic references are included; no index is provided. See also the author's God in Hindu Thought, Poona, 1968.

1341 Danielou, Alain. Hindu Polytheism. New York, Bollingen Foundation; dist. by Pantheon Books, 1964 (Bollingen series, 73). 491 p.
Presents a thorough description of the numerous gods of India based on the study of the texts. Selected bibliography is divided into Sanskrit texts, and modern works. An index is provided.

1342 Hinduism. Contrib.: K. R. Sundararajan, et al. Patiala, Punjabi University, 1969 (Guru Nanak Quincentenary Celebration Series). 128 p.
Contains a collection of papers by outstanding Hindu specialists. Bibliographic references are listed at the end of each paper.

1343 Hopkins, Thomas J. The Hindu Religious Tradition. Encino, Calif., Dickenson Pub. Co., 1971 (Religious Life of Man). 156 p.
Presents a popular analysis of the complex issues of Hinduism. Also contains an outline of the development

of Vedic writings, a schematic diagram of the Hindu Religious tradition, a list of selected readings, and an index.

1344 Mahadevan, T. M. P. Outlines of Hinduism, with a Foreword by S. Radhakrishnan. 2nd ed. Bombay, Chetana, 1960. 312 p.
An introductory survey which deals not only with doctrinal teachings but also with the discussion of scriptures, rituals, cults, and personalities of traditional Hinduism. Some bibliographic references are cited in the text. An index is included.

1345 Morgan, Kenneth W., ed. The Religion of the Hindus, Interpreted by the Hindus. New York, Ronald, 1953. 434 p.
Contains seven articles by religious leaders of outstanding authority on various aspects of Hindu beliefs and practices. Includes a glossary of Hindu terms and a map of sacred places. The last chapter, an anthology of Hindu scriptures, is valuable as an indication of what is esteemed and actually used today. A select bibliography and an index are provided.

1346 Nirvedananda, Swami. Hinduism at a Glance, 4th ed. enl. Calcutta, Ramakrishna Mission, 1969. 271 p.
A popularly presented outline of the teachings and ideals of Hinduism, directed to the layman. A glossary and an index are provided.

1347 Organ, Troy W. The Hindu Quest for the Perfection of Man. Athens, Ohio Univ. Press, 1970. 439 p.
Contains a discussion of a number of selected quests in Hinduism, e.g. quest for reality, spirituality, liberation, perfected man, etc. Also includes an extensive bibliography, p. 348-419, and an index.

1348 Sarma, Dittakavi S. Hinduism Through the Ages. Bombay, Bhatariya Vidya Bhavan, 1961 (Bhavan's Book University, 37). 284 p.
A scholarly historical survey which is a revised and abridged version of the author's 1944 publication, Renaissance of Hinduism.

1349 Sen, Kshiti M. Hinduism. Harmondsworth, England, Penguin Books, 1961. 160 p.
The author, a practicing Hindu, explains to Westerners the basic principles of Hinduism. A brief bibliography and an index are included.

1350 Stroup, Herbert H. Like a Great River; An Introduction to Hinduism. New York, Harper and Row, 1972. 200 p.
A popular work which makes accessible the complex world of Hindu mythology, history, religion, and social

structures. Also provides an annotated bibliography for more extensive reading, name and subjects indexes, and a glossary of unfamiliar terms.

1351 Zaehner, Robert C. Hinduism. London, Oxford Univ. Press, 1968. 272 p.
Contains excellent introductory reading for the beginner with a well-selected and partly annotated bibliography and an index.

MODERN RELIGIOUS MOVEMENTS

1352 Ashby, Philip. Modern Trends in Hinduism. New York, Columbia Univ. Press, 1974. 143 p.
This book is comprised of a series of lectures given in 1968-69. It contains a discussion on the nature of Indian religion, popular esoteric religion, Radha Saomi Satsang, and the role of religion and cultural traditions in Indian politics. Also includes a chronological chart, a glossary, and an index. Some bibliographic references are supplied in footnotes.

1353 Farquhar, John N. Modern Religious Movements in India. Delhi, Munshiram Manoharlal, 1967 (1913) (Hartford-Lamson Lectures on the Religions of the World). 471 p.
A fundamental work for the study of religious developments after 1800. New Movements are classified and described according to their degree of being open to Western influences. Some attention is given to the nationalistic and reform movements. Includes some bibliographic information in footnotes. A glossary and an index are provided.

SECTS

1354 Chattopadhyaya, Sudhakar. Evolution of Hindu Sects. New Delhi, Munshiran Manoharlal, 1970. 216 p.
Describes the Vaisnavas, the Saivas, the Saktas, and the Sanras. A select bibliography and an index are added.

1355 Gonda, Jan. Visnavaism and Sivaism: A Comparison. London, Athlone, 1970 (Jordan Lectures in Comparative Religion, 1969). 228 p.
Surveys materials illustrating the character and interactions of the cults of the great Hindu gods Visnu and Siva. Bibliographic references are included in notes, an index is provided.

1356 Wilson, Horace H. Religious Sects of the Hindus, 2nd ed. Ed. by E. R. Rost. Calcutta, Susil Gupta, 1958. 221 p.

Originally published under the title, A Sketch of the Religious Sects of the Hindus. Contains a monumental survey of the most known sects. Some bibliographic references are included, and there is also an index.

JOURNALS

1357 Indian Horizon. New Delhi, Indian Council for Cultural Relations, 1952- (quarterly).
Continues Indo-Asian Culture. Indexed: Hist. Abstr.; Bibliog. As. St.

1358 Indian Studies: Past and Present. Calcutta, 1959- .
Feature articles are of uneven value. Often carries translations of original texts. Indexed: Bibliog. As. St.

1359 Indo-Iranian Journal. Leiden, Brill, 1956- .
Recognized as a publication of highly scholarly standard. Articles are in English, French, or German. Indexed: Int. Bibliog. Per. Lit.

1360 Journal of Indian History. Trivandrum, India, 1921- .
Indexed: Bibliog. As. St.

1361 Journal of Indian Philosophy. Dordrecht, Reidel, 1970- .
Indexed: Bibliog. As. St.; Philosopher's Index.

1362 Mother India: Monthly Review of Culture. Pondicherry, Ashram Press, 1949- .
A popular magazine which contains feature articles, English translations of ancient writings, and book reviews.

1363 The Visvabharati Quarterly. Calcutta, 1923- .
Deals mainly with philosophical and religious topics.

Part Four--Asian Religions (cont.)

III JAINISM, SIKHISM, TIBETAN RELIGIONS

JAINISM

BIBLIOGRAPHIES AND GUIDES

1364 Basham, A. L. "Jainism." Zaehner, R. C. The Concise Encyclopedia of Living Faiths. London, Hutchinson, 1964 (1954), p. 261-6, p. 421.
See no. 21. Provides a very concise survey of our knowledge of the Jains, with a brief list of books for further reading.

1365 Casa, Carlo della. "Jainism." Bleeker, C. J. Historia religionum. Leiden, Brill, 1969, p. 346-71.
See no. 38. A brief survey dealing with the essence of Jainism, its history, eternal cosmic law and transitory divinities, and a short history of research in Jainism. Selected bibliography is divided into texts and their translations, and modern critical works.

1366 "The Jains." McCasland, S. V. Religions of the World. New York, Random House, 1969, p. 485-97, 519-20.
See no. 16. A brief introductory survey for the beginner with well-selected bibliographic references.

SCRIPTURES IN ENGLISH TRANSLATIONS

1367 Siddhanta. Selections. English from Prākrit. Jaina Sutras. Transl. by H. G. Jacobi. Delhi, Motilal Banarsidass, 1964 (1884-95) (Sacred Books of the East, v. 22, 45. UNESCO Collection of Representative Works: Indian Series). 2 vols.
Contains: Akaranga sutra, Kalpa sutra, Uttaradhyayna, Sutrakritanga.

CRITICAL STUDIES

1368 Gopalan, S. Outlines of Jainism. New York, Wiley, 1973. 205 p.

Presents an informative and comprehensive survey of Jainism. It traces the whole Jaina tradition from its ancient beginnings to present-day developments. The book is directed to advanced students.

1369 Kalghatgi, T. G. Jaina View of Life. Sholapur, Jaina Samskrti Samraksaka Sanga, 1969 (Jivaraja Jaina granthamala, no. 20). 200 p.

Contains a collection of articles discussing various aspects of Jainism.

1370 Stevenson, Margaret. The Heart of Jainism. New Delhi, Munshiram Manoharlal, 1970 (1915). 336 p.

An older work which is still useful for its scholarly survey of the historical background, philosophy, mythology, as well as Jaina art and architecture. A list of older books and an index are provided.

1371 Tatia, Nathmal. Studies in Jaina Philosophy. Banaras, Jain Cultural Research Society, 1951. 327 p.

This scholarly study discusses the non-absolutistic attitude of the Jainas, the epistemology of the Agamas, the problem of Avidya, the Jaina doctrine of Karman, and the Jaina Yoga. Numerous bibliographic references to sources and critical works are included in the footnotes. Also has indexes: authors cited; works quoted; general subjects; and Sanskrit, Prākrit, and Pāli words.

SIKHISM

BIBLIOGRAPHIES AND GUIDES

1372 Barrier, N. G. The Sikhs and Their Literature: A Guide to Books, Tracts, and Periodicals, 1849-1919. Delhi, Manohar Book Service, 1970. 143 p.

This excellent reference work lists some 1240 entries including original Sikh publications. Also contains a select bibliography on Sikh history and literature, a subject-title index, and a general index.

1373 Navalani, K. "Towards a Bibliography of the Sikhs and the Punjab." Comparative Librarianship. Delhi, Vikas, 1973. p. 151-61.

A bibliographic essay which reviews major sources of information on the Sikhs and their history.

1374 "The Sikhs." McCasland, S. V. Religions of the World. New York, Random House, 1969, p. 501-14, 520.
See no. 16. Includes a concise discussion of the historical background, scriptures, doctrines, and the Sikhs in the contemporary world. A bibliography is provided.

1375 Singh, Ganda. A Select Bibliography of the Sikhs and Sikhism. Amritsar, Sikh Itihas Research Board, 1965. 432 p.
This bibliography includes a selective list of materials available in Indian and other foreign languages. No index is provided.

SCRIPTURES IN ENGLISH TRANSLATION

1376 Adi-Granth. English. Selections. Selections from the Sacred Writings of the Sikhs. Transl. by T. Singh, et al. Rev. ed. by G. S. Fraser. Introd. by S. S. Radhakrishnan. Foreword by A. Toynbee. London, Allen & Unwin, 1960 (UNESCO Collection of Representative Works: Indian Series). 288 p.
An excellent critical edition of the text. Glossary of unfamiliar terms and an index are provided.

1377 Nanak. Hymns of Guru Nanak. Transl. by K. Singh. London, Orient Longmans, 1969 (UNESCO Collection of Representative Works: Indian Series). 192 p.
Contains a critical edition of 97 hymns. Some bibliographic references are included.

CRITICAL STUDIES

1378 Archer, John C. The Sikhs in Relation to Hindus, Moslems, Christians, the Ahmadiyyas: A Study in Comparative Religion. Princeton, N.J., Princeton Univ. Press, 1946. 353 p.
An excellent comparative study analyzing the relations of the Sikhs to other religious groups of northern India. Bibliographic references in footnotes, a glossary, and a general index are provided.

1379 Gupta, Hari R. History of the Sikh Gurus. New Delhi, Kapur, 1973. 320 p.
Provides biographies of the Sikh gurus with historical background. Abundant bibliographic references are given at the end of each chapter. An index is provided.

1380 Macauliffe, Max A. The Sikh Religion: Its Gurus, Sacred Writings and Authors. Oxford, Clarendon Press, 1909. 6 vols. in 3.
Contains translations of the Granth Sahib, the sacred

book of the Sikhs. Bibliographic references in footnotes refer to older works. Also includes an index.

1381 McLeod, W. H. Guru Nanak and the Sikh Religion. Oxford, Clarendon Press, 1968. 259 p.
Contains an interesting presentation of the man, his life, faith, and teachings. Also provides a glossary, a biographical index, a doctrinal index, and a general index. Some bibliographic materials are included.

1382 Ray, Nihar-ranjan. The Sikh Gurus and the Sikh Society; A Study in Social Analysis. Patiala, Punjabi Univ., 1970. 204 p.
Contains a collection of three lectures on the milieu, message, and mission of the gurus. A selected bibliography of monographs and periodical articles, and an index are included.

1383 Singh, Gopal. The Religion of the Sikhs. New York, Asia Publishing House, 1971. 191 p.
A popularly presented survey of the Sikh religious principles and history, with admirable translations of prayers and hymns. Lacks bibliographical references, but an index is added.

1384 Singh, Krushwant. The History of the Sikhs. London, Oxford Univ. Press, 1963-66. 2 vols.
Presents a "panoramic view" of the history of the Sikhs from the birth of Nanak, a founder of Sikhism, in 1469 to the death of Nehru in 1967. The study is based on original sources in Gurmukhi, Persian, and English. Bibliographic references are included in footnotes. An index is provided.

1385 Singh, Teja. Sikhism: Its Ideals and Institutions, new rev. ed. Bombay, Orient Longmans, 1951. 142 p.
Contains a collection of essays "on the different essential features of Sikhism..."--Preface.

JOURNAL

1386 Sikh Review; A Socio-cultural and Religious Monthly. Calcutta, 1953- .
Provides information on the history and current events of the Sikh community.

TIBETAN RELIGIONS [for Tibetan Buddhism, see nos. 1474-80]

BIBLIOGRAPHY

1387 Chudhuri, Sibadas. Bibliography of Tibetan Studies, Being a Record of Printed Publications Mainly in European Languages. Calcutta, Asiatic Society, 1972. 232 p.
Contains an alphabetical listing of selected monographs, essays, and periodical articles. Entries related to the subject may be found through the subject index, in the section: Philosophy and Religion, p. 169-76.

TEXTS IN ENGLISH TRANSLATION

1388 gZi-brjid. The Nine Ways of Bon. Excerpts from gZi-brjid. Ed. and transl. by D. L. Snellgrove. London, Oxford Univ. Press, 1967. 312 p.
First presentation of religious ideas of Bon through original accounts in English translation. Also provides an informative introduction with numerous bibliographic citations in footnotes, and a glossary of Tibetan terms.

1389 ________. A Treasury of Good Sayings: A Tibetan History of Bon. Ed. and transl. by S. G. Karmay. London, Oxford Univ. Press, 1972 (London Oriental Series, v. 26). 365 p.
Contains a partial translation of the Tibetan text: Legs-bshad-mdzod. The text is preceded by an informative introduction dealing with genealogies and historical background. A glossary of Tibetan terms and indexes are provided.

CRITICAL STUDIES

1390 Ekvall, Robert B. Religious Observances in Tibet: Patterns and Function. Chicago, Univ. Press, 1964. 313 p.
"Attempts to bring to life the religion of Tibet as a subjective response expressed in a pattern of behaviour which makes sense in the context of their world view, as an answer to personal and social needs..."--Preface. Contains an excellent selected bibliography, and a detailed index.

1391 Nebesky-Wojkowitz, Rene de. Oracles and Demons of Tibet: The Cult and Iconography of the Tibetan Protective Deities. 's-Gravenhage, Mouton, 1956. 666 p.
Pt. 1 deals with the iconography, classification, appearance and attributes of the protective deities. Pt. 2 describes their cults. Contains a list of Tibetan sources, and an index of names and classes of deities, an index

of general Tibetan expressions, an index of Sanskrit terms, an index of authors, and an index of subjects. Bibliographic references are included in footnotes.

1392 Stein, Rolf A. Tibetan Civilization. Transl. by J. E. S. Driver. Stanford, Calif., Stanford Univ. Press; London, Faber & Faber, 1970 (1962). 333 p.

Translation of La Civilisation tibetaine. Presents an excellent introduction for the non-specialist. Discusses the habitat and inhabitants, surveys the historical events from the ancient monarchy to the modern times, analyzes the structure of the Tibetan society, and deals with religious life and customs including Lamaism and Bon. Selected bibliography refers to Tibetan sources, and to modern critical studies.

Part Four: Asian Religions (cont.)

IV BUDDHISM

REFERENCE WORKS

BIBLIOGRAPHIES AND GUIDES

1393 Bibliographie bouddhique (Buddhist Bibliography). Paris, Librairie d'Amerique et d'Orient, 1930- (Buddhica).
A current annotated bibliography including monographs and periodical articles relevant to Buddhist studies.

1394 "[VIII.] Buddhism." International Bibliography of the History of Religions. Leiden, Brill, 1954- .
See no. 27. An annual bibliography listing monographs and periodical articles.

1395 Hanayama, Shinsho. Bibliography on Buddhism. Tokyo, Hokuseido Press, 1961. 869 p.
Includes Western language studies up to 1932. Entries are listed alphabetically by author. A subject index is provided.

1396 Reynolds, F. E. "Buddhism." Adams, C. J., ed. A Reader's Guide to the Religions. 2nd ed. New York, Free Press, 1977 (1965). p. 156-222.
Contains an informative bibliographic essay reviewing materials available for studies of Buddhism.

1397 Wayman, A. "Buddhism." Bleeker, C. J. and G. Widengren. Historia religionum. Leiden, Brill, 1969. p. 372-464.
See no. 38. Presents a brief systematic survey dealing with essence of Buddhism, conception of deity, worship, conception of man, present religious situation, and a short history of the study of Buddhism. Selected bibliography includes monographs and periodical articles.

1398 Yoo, Yushin. Books on Buddhism: An Annotated Subject Guide, with a Foreword by E. C. Strohecker. Metuchen, N.J., Scarecrow Press, 1976. 25 p.
A conveniently arranged list of selected English

language monographs. The table of contents provides a detailed outline of topics. Also contains indexes of authors, editors and translators, and titles.

DICTIONARIES AND ENCYCLOPEDIAS

1399 A Dictionary of Buddhism. Introd. by T. O. Ling. New York, Scribner's, 1972. 277 p.
Contains entries selected from S. G. F. Brandon's Dictionary of Comparative Religion (see no. 100). Some brief bibliographic references are listed.

1400 Encyclopedia of Buddhism. Ed. by G. P. Malalasekara. Colombo, Ceylon Gov. Press, 1961- .
Sponsored by the Buddhist Council of Ceylon [now Sri Lanka]. Includes articles on all aspects of Buddhist thought, history, and civilization, personal and place names, literary titles, and especially religious and moral concepts. Bibliographic references are cited within the text, or appended at the end.

1401 Hôbôgirin; dictionnaire encyclopedique du bouddhisme [Encyclopedic Dictionary of Buddhism] d'après les sources chinoises et japonaises, sous le haut patronage de l'Academie imperiale du Japan et sous la direction de S. Levi ... et J. Takakusu. Redacteur ... P. Demieville. Tokyo, Maison franco-japonaise, 1929- (3 vols. pub.).
Still not completed. Explains Buddhist terms used in Chinese and Japanese writings.

1402 Humphreys, Christmas. A Popular Dictionary of Buddhism. London, Arco Publications, 1962. 223 p.
"Attempts to cover the entire field of Buddhism ... explaining terms ... chosen from seven languages spoken in ten countries in at least ten major schools of Buddhism"--Preface.

1403 Japanese-English Buddhist Dictionary. Tokyo, Daito Shupansha, 1965. 383 p.
Transliterated terms are arranged alphabetically. An index of Japanese words is provided.

1404 Nyanatiloka, Bhikku. Buddhist Dictionary; Manual of Buddhist Terms and Doctrines, 2nd rev. ed. Colombo, Ceylon, Frevin, 1956. 197 p.
Provides definitions and explanations of canonical and post-canonical terms and doctrines, based on Sutta, Abhidhama, and Commentaries.

1405 Soothill, William E. A Dictionary of Chinese Buddhist Terms, with Sanskrit and English Equivalents, and a Sanskrit-Pali Index. London, Paul, Trench, Trubner,

1937. 510 p.
The entries are arranged according to the number of strokes.

INDEX

1406 Yoo, Yushin. Buddhism; A Subject Index to Periodical Articles in English, 1728-1971. Metuchen, N.J., Scarecrow Press, 1973. 162 p.
Contains an international directory of Buddhist Associations, a list of periodicals indexed, a title index, and an author-subject index. Provides a well-organized handy reference guide to articles published in popular magazines, as well as to those which appeared in learned journals. The last part gives a brief summary of basic principles of Buddhism.

SCRIPTURAL COLLECTIONS AND ANTHOLOGIES

COLLECTIONS

1407 Sacred Books of the Buddhist. London, Luzac for the Pali Text Society, 1895- .
This excellent series is comprised of critically edited translations with remarkable exposition and analysis or many important points. Each volume contains an exhaustive bibliography of primary and critical works. Includes: the Gatakamala, Dialogues of the Buddha, Further Dialogues of the Buddha, Book of the Discipline, Sutta-Nipata, Mahavastu, Milinda's Questions.

See also nos. 1211 and 1212.

ANTHOLOGIES

1408 Allen, George. The Buddha's Philosophy: Selections from the Pali Canon and an Introductory Essay. Foreword by A. L. Basham. London, Allen and Unwin, 1959. 194 p.
A popular selection from major Buddhist writings with informative explanations.

1409 Burtt, Edwin. Buddhist Meditation. London, Allen and Unwin, 1956 (Ethical and Religious Classics of the East and West, no. 13). 183 p.
Contains a selection of texts illustrating philosophical concepts and techniques of meditation. The introduction provides some explanation of contemporary psychotherapy. Glossary of technical terms is provided.

1410 ________. The Teachings of the Compassionate Buddha. New York, Mentor Books, 1955. 247 p.

A source-book of readings in Buddhist Mahayana and Theravada scriptures, with reliable introductory essays on the history and religious practices. Also includes some information on Chinese sects.

1411 Conze, Edward, ed. Buddhist Texts Through the Ages, Newly Translated from the Original Pali, Sanskrit, Chinese, Tibetan, Japanese and Apabhramsa. New York, Harper & Row, 1964 (1954). 322 p.

A well balanced selection designed as a companion volume to the author's Buddhism, Its Essence and Development (see no. 1419). Bibliography includes sources. Glossary of technical terms with their Sanskrit equivalents are included. Also consult another editor's selection from both Theravada and Mahayana texts: Buddhist Scriptures (Baltimore, Penguin Books, 1959).

1412 DeBary, William T., ed. The Buddhist Tradition in India, China, and Japan. Ed. by W. T. DeBary with the collaboration of Y. Hakeda and P. Yampolsky, and with contrib. by A. L. Basham, L. Hurvitz, and R. Tsunoda. New York, Vintage Books, 1972 (1969). 417 p.

This excellent collection is comprised of excerpts from the major writings of Buddhist thinkers with informative commentaries. Also contains a selected bibliography of monographs and periodical articles, and an index.

1413 Goddard, Dwight, ed. The Buddhist Bible. Introd. by H. Smith. Boston, Beacon, 1970 (1932). 677 p.

A popular anthology which includes selections from Pali, Sanskrit, Chinese, Tibetan, as well as modern writings. Each section is preceded by an informative comment. Neither index nor bibliography is added.

1414 Hamilton, Clarence H. Buddhism; A Religion of Infinite Compassion. New York, Liberal Arts Press, 1952 (Library of Religion, v. 1). 189 p.

A topically arranged sourcebook of Buddhist teachings with a very helpful introduction. It includes Pali sources on the life and teachings of Buddha, and other sources from China, Japan, and Tibet. A selected bibliography, and a glossary included; no index.

1415 Humphreys, Christmas. The Wisdom of Buddhism. London, Rider, 1960. 280 p.

A popularly presented selection from major Buddhist writings with informative introductions. Also contains a list of sources, a glossary, and an index.

1416 Stryk, Lucien, ed. World of the Buddha; A Reader. Ed. with Introd. and Commentaries. Garden City, N.Y.,

Doubleday, 1968. 423 p.
Presents chronologically arranged selections from the most revered Buddhist writings. Aimed at a newcomer to Buddhism. Lacks a bibliography and an index.

CRITICAL STUDIES

GENERAL

1417 Banerjee, Anukul C. Buddhism in India and Abroad. Calcutta, World Press, 1973. 263 p.
Pt. 1 deals with religious and cultural aspects of Buddhism in India; Pt. 2 presents the story of Buddhism in neighbouring countries: its introduction, expansion, ramification into different schools and sects, literature, etc. Bibliographic references are included in footnotes. Also an index is added.

1418 Bapat, P. V. 2500 Years of Buddhism. Foreword by S. Radhakrishnan. New Delhi, Govt. of India Press, 1956. 503 p.
Contains a collection of papers by outstanding scholars in the field of Buddhist studies. Chapter bibliographies are added at the end. An index is provided.

1419 Bhuddhasa, Bhikku. Towards the Truth. Ed. by D. Swearer. Philadelphia, Westminster, 1971. 189 p.
This interesting collection is comprised of provocative essays by an outstanding Thai Buddhist scholar. Bibliographic references are given in notes. Also contains a glossary of Pali terms.

1420 Conze, Edward. Buddhism, Its Essence and Development. Oxford, Cassirer; New York, Harper, 1958 (1952). 212 p.
A standard comprehensive introduction to world Buddhism providing a clear chronological study of the major concepts of Buddhism in its historical development. Includes a selected bibliography. Should be used together with the author's Buddhist Texts Through the Ages (see no. 1411).

1421 _______. A Short History of Buddhism. Bombay, Chetana, 1960 (Buddhist Library, 1). 117 p.
Presents a brief historical outline of Buddhism. It discusses basic doctrines, sects, and its expansion. A selected bibliography is provided but lacks an index.

1422 _______. Thirty Years of Buddhist Studies; Selected Essays. Columbia, Univ. of South Carolina Press, 1968. 274 p.

This important collection is comprised of papers by an outstanding American authority in the field of Buddhist studies; some of them are unobtainable from other sources. It is divided into two surveys: the first illustrates the revolutionary changes of approach to Buddhism in 1940-60, the second deals with various topics of Mahayana Buddhism. Some bibliographic references, and an index are included.

1423 Donath, Dorothy C. Buddhism for the West. Theravada, Mahayana, and Vajrayana; A Comprehensive Review of Buddhist History, Philosophy, and the Teachings from the Time of the Buddha to the Present Day. New York, Julian, 1971. 146 p.

A Western follower of Buddhism presents its principal ideas in an easy way. A selected bibliography and an index are provided.

1424 Eliot, Charles, N. E. Hinduism and Buddhism; an Historical Sketch, new ed. New York, Barnes and Noble, 1954. 3 vols.

See no. 1219. A standard historical survey.

1425 Fozdar, Jamshed. The God of Buddha. New York, Asia Pub. House, 1973. 184 p.

Presents a popular study of the principal doctrines of Buddhism based on the Pali and Sanskrit sources. Also contains a selected bibliography, a glossary and an index.

1426 Glasenapp, Helmuth von. Buddhism; A Non Theistic Religion, with a Selection of Buddhist Scriptures. Ed. by H. Bechert. London, Allen and Unwin, 1970 (1954). 208 p.

Translation of Buddhismus und Gottesidee. "Introduces an aspect of Buddhism which is perhaps foreign to our way of thinking yet crucial to an understanding of the subject--a religiosity of a non-theistic religion"--Foreword. Bibliographic references are included in notes. There is also an index, and a glossary of terms.

1427 Humphreys, Christmas. Buddhism, 3rd ed. Baltimore, Penguin, 1962 (Pelican Books A228). 256 p.

A popularly presented survey which deals with the life of the Buddha, the spread of Buddhism, Theravada, Mahayana, and issues of contemporary Buddhism. A glossary, a selected bibliography, and an index are provided.

1428 ________. A Buddhist Student's Manual. London, Buddhist Society, 1956. 279 p.

An easy exposition of basic Buddhist principles aimed at the Buddhist movement in the West. Also contains an elaborate glossary, an analysis of the scriptures, and a selected bibliography.

1429 Mizuno, Kogen. Primitive Buddhism. Transl., annot. and comp. by K. Yamamoto. Oyama, Karin Bunko, 1969. 295 p.

"Introduction for beginners for general reading"--Preface. A selected bibliography is included.

1430 Morgan, Kenneth W., ed. The Path of Buddha; Buddhism. Interpreted by Buddhists. New York, Ronald, 1956. 432 p.

This collection is comprised of essays discussing doctrines and practices of both Theravada and Mahayana schools by outstanding Buddhist scholars from India, Burma, Ceylon, Tibet and Japan. A select bibliography and an index are provided.

1431 Pande, Goving C. Studies in the Origins of Buddhism. Allahabad, Univ. of Allahabad, 1957 (Ancient History Research Series, 1). 600 p.

Pt. 1 deals with the early Buddhist sources; pt. 2 discusses the historical and cultural background of early Buddhism; pt. 3 analyzes early Buddhist doctrines. Some bibliographic references are included.

1432 Perdue, Peter A. Buddhism; A Historical Introduction to Buddhist Values and the Social and Political Forms They Have Assumed in Asia. New York, Macmillan, 1971 (1968). 203 p.

Presents basic information on Buddhist history and teachings, with an examination of the relationship between Buddhist values and the diverse cultural, social, and political forms in India, China, Southeast Asia, Tibet and Japan. Also includes a select bibliography and an index.

1433 Robinson, Richard H. The Buddhist Religion; A Historical Introduction. Belmont, Calif., Dickenson Pub. Co., 1970 (Religious Life of Man). 136 p.

An informative introduction which explains basic religious concepts, forms of worship, spiritual practices, and social institutions of Buddhism. Also contains a list of selected readings with annotations, and an overview of Buddhist scriptures. Aimed at the college student.

1434 Saddhatissa, H. The Buddha's Way. London, Allen & Unwin; New York, Braziller, 1972 (1971). 139 p.

Pt. 1 describes the life and teachings of the Buddha; pt. 2 explains Four Noble Truths forming the foundation of Buddhist philosophy; pt. 3 outlines the significance of meditation. Also includes some selected texts from the Pali scriptures. A selected bibliography, a glossary, and an index are included.

1435 Swearer, Donald K. Buddhism in Transition. Philadelphia, Westminster, 1970. 160 p.
This brief popular book "shows the changing emphases and their probable consequences for Asia and the West"--Cover note. Some bibliographic references are included.

1436 Takakusu, Junjro. The Essentials of Buddhist Philosophy. Ed. by Wing-Tsit Chan and C. A. Moore. 3rd ed. Honolulu, Office Appliance Co., 1956. 221 p.
This collection of essays contains selections from the lifetime work of the outstanding Japanese Buddhologist. Bibliographic references and an index are included.

1437 Thomas, Edward J. The History of Buddhist Thought. London, Routledge & Kegan Paul, 1951 (1933). 316 p.
Contains information on the development of Buddhist philosophy from its origins. Also includes some bibliographic references to sources, and modern critical works. An index is provided.

1438 Varma, Vishvanath P. Early Buddhism and Its Origins. Delhi, Manoharlal, 1973. 505 p.
Presents an analysis of economic, political, social, and anthropological aspects of early Buddhism. A selected bibliography of sources and critical studies is supplied. There is also a useful index.

1439 Welbon, Guy R. The Buddhist Nirvana and Its Western Interpreters. Chicago, Univ. of Chicago Press, 1968. 320 p.
Reviews the attempts of Western Indologists to determine and explain the original meaning of the concept of nirvana in Buddhism. It traces the historical evolution of the translation and exegesis of the Pali and Sanskrit texts. Contains a carefully selected bibliography, and a thorough index.

1440 Zürcher, Erik. Buddhism, Its Origin and Spread in Words, Maps and Pictures. London, Routledge & Kegan Paul, 1962 (Concise Histories of World Religions). 96 p.
Presents a brief elementary survey of basic information on Buddhism. List for further reading is provided.

LIFE OF BUDDHA

1441 Foucher, Alfred C. A. The Life of Buddha, According to the Ancient Texts and Monuments of India. Abridged transl. by S. B. Boas. Middletown, Conn., Wesleyan Univ. Press, 1963 (1949). 272 p.
Translation of La Vie du Buddha. This collection of

biographical information is composed of various traditional writings and documents. Some bibliographical references are provided. There is no index.

1442 Thomas, Edward J. The Life of Buddha as Legend and History, 3rd ed. London, Paul, 1931 (History of Civilization). 297 p.
An older but still useful biography which attempts to integrate the legends and facts of the Buddha's life with their historical situation. A selection of bibliographical references to sources and older critical works is included. An index is provided.

MAHAYANA BUDDHISM

Anthology

1443 Buddhist Mahayana Texts. Oxford, Univ. Press, 1894. 2 vols. in 1.
This is an older selection from the most important Mahayana writings.

Critical Studies

1444 Dutt, Nalinaksha. Mahayana Buddhism. Calcutta, Mukhopadhyay, 1973. 304 p.
Revised edition of the author's Aspects of Mahayana Buddhism and Its Relation to Hinayana. Outlines some principal ideas such as the conception of Trikaya, exposition of truths, conception of the truths and absolute. Bibliographic references are given in footnotes. An index is provided.

1445 Murti, Tirupattur R. V. The Central Philosophy of Buddhism. London, Allen & Unwin, 1955. 372 p.
This scholarly study deals with the Madhyamika School of the early Mahayana system. Provides some bibliographic references in footnotes. A glossary and an index are included.

1446 Robinson, Richard H. Early Madhyamika in India and China. Madison, Univ. of Wisconsin Press, 1967. 347 p.
Contains an excellent scholarly review of existing opinions on the subject of the Madhyamika texts. Bibliographic references include monographs and periodical articles. An index is added.

1447 Suzuki, Beatrice L. Mahayana Buddhism, with an Introd. by D. T. Suzuki, and a Foreword by C. Humphreys. London, Allen & Unwin, 1948 (1939). 146 p.
A popular presentation of the Mahayana school of

Buddhism, its history and doctrines. Also contains some extracts from Mahayana sutras. A selected list of books, and short glossary are included.

1448 Suzuki, Daisetz T. On Indian Mahayana. Ed. with an Introd. by E. Conze. New York, Harper, 1968. 284 p.
Contains selected essays discussing various issues of the Mahayana school by an outstanding Japanese scholar. Also includes bibliographical notes on sources and an index.

ZEN BUDDHISM

REFERENCE WORKS

Bibliography

1449 Vessie, Patricia A. Zen Buddhism: A Bibliography of Books and Articles in English, 1892-1975. Ann Arbor, Mich., Univ. Microfilms, 1976. 81 p.
"This work is published under the aegis of the East Asia Library, University of Washington, which deems it a significant contribution to scholarship."

Dictionary

1450 Wood, Ernest. Zen Dictionary. London, P. Owen, 1963 (1957). 165 p.
Explains elementary terms. Entries are arranged alphabetically. There is also a brief list of books for further reading.

Anthologies

1451 Briggs, William, ed. Anthology of Zen, with a Foreword by W. Barrett. London, Evergreen; New York, Grove, 1961.
Includes selections from major Zen writings. There is also a brief section on Zen in the West and Buddhist meditation. Some bibliographic references are given in footnotes. No index is provided.

1452 Hoffman, Yoel. The Sound of the One Hand. 281 Zen Koans with Answers. Transl. with a commentary by Y. Hoffmann. Foreword by Zen Master Hirano Sojo. Introd. by B. A. Scharfstein. New York, Basic Books, 1975. 322 p.
Attempts an explanation of the Zen koan teachings as revealed by the Zen masters. A select bibliography is added.

1453 Luk, Charles, ed. Ch'an and Zen Teaching. Ed., Transl. and Explained by Lu K'uan Yu (C. Luk). London, Rider, 1960. 3 vols.

This collection is comprised of selections from basic Ch'an and Zen teachings, preceded by introductions giving useful information about the origins and meaning of the work from which the fragments are cited. Each volume contains a glossary of Chinese and Sanskrit names, terms, and places, as well as an index.

CRITICAL STUDIES

Beginnings of Zen in China

1454 Tao-yüan, Shih. Original Teachings of Chan Buddhism, Selected from the Transmission of the Lamp. Transl. with introductions by Chang Chung-yuan. New York, Pantheon Books, 1969. 333 p.

Includes selections from 19 masters representing the five schools of Ch'an Buddhism, as well as from the teachings of the earliest Ch'an masters. A chart showing the eminent Ch'an masters is added. Also provides a list of works cited in the text, and an index.

General Studies

1455 Blyth, Reginald H. Zen and Zen Classics. Tokyo, Hokuseido, 1960- (5 vols. when completed).

Presents a systematic survey of the history of Zen and its principal writings. Each volume contains a detailed index. A few bibliographic references are included.

1456 Chang, Ch'eng-chi. The Practice of Zen. New York, Harper & Row, 1959 (Perennial Library). 256 p.

Popular presentation of Zen for the enthusiasts in the West. It discusses the nature of Zen, the four and five Zen masters, and the practice of meditation. Also supplies a selected bibliography and an index.

1457 Dumoulin, Heinrich. A History of Zen Buddhism. Transl. by P. Peachey. New York, Pantheon, 1963 (1959). 385 p.

Translation of the author's Zen. "This book is of historical nature and is intended to give to the reader a faithful account of the historical development of Zen as far as it is possible at the present time"--Preface. Includes a selected bibliography of monographs and periodical articles, and an index.

1458 Fromm, Erich; D. T. Suzuki; and R. DeMartino. Zen Buddhism and Psychoanalysis. New York, Harper, 1960. 180 p.

This book is comprised of papers by the three most prominent authorities in the field of Buddhist studies and social sciences. Contains a select bibliography and an index.

1459 Humphreys, Christmas. Zen; A Way of Life. London, English Univ. Press, 1962. (Teach Yourself Books). 199 p.
A popular introduction aimed at the reader interested in Zen, with a list of books for further reading. A glossary and an index are provided.

1460 ______. Zen Buddhism. London, Allen & Unwin, 1961 (1958). 175 p.
Contains a popular explanation of basic principles of Zen "for the West." A brief select bibliography and an index are added.

1461 Kapleau, Philip, ed. The Three Pillars of Zen, Teaching, Practice and Enlightment. New York, Harper & Row, 1966 (1965). 384 p.
Presents a step-by-step exposition of Zen training methods and a rational approach to this religion. Includes a glossary and an index.

1462 Ross, Nancy W. The World of Zen: An East-West Anthology. New York, Random House, 1960. 362 p.
Contains a collection of articles preceded by an informative introduction.

1463 Suzuki, Daizetz T. Essays in Zen Buddhism. London, Rider, 1971-2. Series 1-3.
Includes a collection of essays attempting to explain ideas of Zen to the Westerners. Each volume contains some bibliographic references and an index.

1464 ______. Manual of Zen Buddhism. London, Published for the Buddhist Society.
Describes the daily life and practices of a Zen monk. Also supplemented by selections from important Zen texts.

1465 ______. Zen and Japanese Culture. New York, Pantheon Books, 1959 (1938) (Bollingen Series, 64). 478 p.
Originally published under the title Zen Buddhism and Its Influence on Japanese Culture. Presents the author's reflections on Zen and the various aspects of Japanese culture, e.g. Zen and Haiku, Zen and the Art of Tea, Love of Nature, etc. Also contains a selected bibliography and an index.

1466 Watts, Alan W. The Spirit of Zen: A Way of Life, Work, and Art in the Far East. New York, Grove Press, 1960 (1936) (Wisdom of the East). 128 p.
Presents a popular introduction discussing the origins of Zen, its secret, technique, life in the Zen community,

and its place in the civilization of the Far East. Contains a glossary of terms, a select bibliography; no index is added.

1467 ______. The Way of Zen. London, Thames and Hudson, 1958.
Provides a survey of history, principles, and practice of Zen. Select bibliography is divided into original sources, and critical studies in European languages. A useful index is added.

ZEN AND WESTERN CULTURE

1468 Blyth, Reginald H. Zen in English Literature and Oriental Classics. Tokyo, Hokuseido, 1942. 446 p.
A scholarly study surveying influence of Zen ideas on the prominent Western writers, e.g. Cervantes, Shakespeare, Wordsworth, etc. No bibliographic references are included, but there is an index.

1469 Thich, Thien-An. Zen Philosophy, Zen Practice. Emeryville, Calif., Dharma Publishing, 1975. 179 p.
A popular handbook for people who "are seeking personal religious experiences through oriental meditations and rituals"--D. R. Barker.

THERAVADA BUDDHISM

Anthology

1470 Nyanatiloka, Bhikku. The Word of the Buddha: An Outline of the Teaching of the Buddha in the Words of the Pali Canon, 13th rev. ed. Kandy, Buddhist Publ. Society, 1959 (1907). 97 p.
Contains a detailed exposition of the Theravada Buddhist system based on original documents.

1471 Warren, Henry C., ed. Buddhism in Translations: Passages Selected from the Buddhist Sacred Books ... from the Original Pali. London, Atheneum, 1970 (1896). 496 p.
An old but still useful selection from the Theravada texts arranged according to the three jewels: Buddha, Doctrine, and Sangha. A detailed table of contents should be consulted.

Critical Studies

1472 Lester, Robert C. Theravada Buddhism in Southeast Asia. Ann Arbor, Univ. of Michigan Press, 1973. 201 p.
"This book is intended to communicate the major

features of the present-day practice of Theravada Buddhism in Southeast Asia in the perspective of scripture and history"--Preface. Contains a select bibliography divided into A. Scriptures in Translation; B. General; C. Burma; D. Cambodia; E. Laos; F. Thailand. An index is provided.

1473 Rahula, Walpola. What the Buddhas Taught. Belford, G. Fraser, 1959. 103 p.
Presents a clear-cut Theravada exposition. Bibliography is included in footnotes, an index is provided.

BUDDHISM IN TIBET AND THE TANTRIC TRADITION

1474 Agehananda, Bhatari S. A Tantric Tradition. London, Rider, 1966 (1966). 350 p.
Deals with the philosophical content of Tantra, its terminology, India and Tibet in Tantric literature, polarity symbolism in Tantric doctrine and practice. A selection of bibliographic references to monographs and periodical articles is included. There is also a useful index.

1475 Anuruddha, R. P. An Introduction to Lamaism, the Mystical Buddhism of Tibet. Hoshiarpur, Vishveshvaranand Research Institute, 1959. 212 p.
Provides a survey of basic features of Lamaism, its history, Tantricism and Iconography. A list of books for further study is included. Also contains an index which makes the study useful for quick reference.

1476 Bell, Charles A. The Religion of Tibet. Oxford, England, Clarendon Press, 1931. 235 p.
This older but still valuable work "attempts to describe how Buddhism, in a late and strange form, came to Tibet and was there developed to suit the needs of an exceptional country and people"--Preface. Contains some bibliographic references in footnotes. An index is provided.

1477 Blofeld, John E. C. The Tantric Mysticism of Tibet; A Practical Guide. New York, Dutton, 1970. 257 p.
Pt. 1: Background and Theory, deals with the Vajrayana, the Mahayana, the essence of the Tantric method, psychic and material symbols. Pt. 2: Practice, discusses the aspiration, the preliminaries, general practice, the Sadhanas, and the advanced practice, etc. Also contains a glossary, a list of useful books containing materials on Tantric Buddhism, and an index.

1478 Dasgupta, Shashibhushan. Introduction to Tantric Buddhism,

2nd ed. Calcutta, Univ. of Calcutta, 1958. 211 p.
Originally delivered as a graduate thesis in 1931, this is a well presented scholarly study for advanced students, but with some already outdated bibliographic references.

1479 Govinda, Anagarika B. Foundations of Tibetan Mysticism, According to the Esoteric Teachings of the Great Mantra: Om Mani Padme Hum. London, Rider, 1969 (1959). 311 p.
Translation of Grundlagen tibetanischer Mystik. An excellent study aimed at advanced students, with useful bibliographic references and an index.

1480 Hoffmann, Helmut. The Religions of Tibet. Transl. by E. Fitzgerald. London, Allen & Unwin, 1961 (1956).
A thorough historical survey, excellent as a reference guide with a detailed index, but not for light reading nor quick study. A selected bibliography is added.

See also nos. 1387-1392.

BUDDHISM IN CHINA

1481 Ch'en, Kenneth K. S. Buddhism in China: A Historical Survey. Princeton, N.J., Princeton Univ. Press, 1964 (Princeton Studies in the History of Religions). 560 p.
Presents one of the best systematic and chronological surveys of the history, beliefs, and practices of Chinese Buddhism. It deals with its early development and spread in South and North, Chinese Buddhist schools, the Tripitaka and modern changes. Contains a useful glossary of Buddhist terms, a list of Chinese names and titles. A select bibliography includes monographs and periodical articles. An index is added.

1482 ________. The Chinese Transformation of Buddhism. Princeton, N.J., Princeton Univ. Press, 1973. 345 p.
A thorough, scholarly study which investigates the role of Buddhism in the ethical, political, economic, literary, educational and social life in China. Bibliography is divided into primary and secondary sources. Also contains a list of Chinese and Japanese words, and a detailed index.

1483 Overmyer, Daniel L. Folk Buddhist Religion: Dissenting Sects in the Late Traditional China. Cambridge, Mass., Harvard University Press, 1976. 285 p.
Provides an excellent scholarly study with an extensive bibliography and an index.

1484 Reichelt, Karl L. Truth and Tradition in Chinese Buddhism; A Study of Chinese Mahayana Buddhism. Transl. from the Norwegian by K. van Wagenen Bugge. 2nd ed. New York, Paragon, 1968 (1928). 330 p.

Translation of Fra østens religiøse liv. An older work containing still valuable observations of Buddhist life. A few bibliographic footnotes and an index are included.

1485 Welch, Holmes. Buddhism under Mao. Cambridge, Mass., Harvard Univ. Press, 1971 (Harvard East Asian Series, 69). 666 p.

"It attempts to give the fullest answer so far to the question: what happens to religion in a Communist state?"--Preface. It brings together all available sources in English, Chinese, and Japanese, as well as interviews with refugees and visitors to China. An excellent bibliography and an index are included.

1486 ______. The Buddhist Revival in China. Cambridge, Mass., Harvard Univ. Press, 1968 (Harvard East Asian Series, 33). 385 p.

Examines the rapid changes in Chinese Buddhism of the mid-20th century. Some very interesting photographic documentation is included. Also contains a selected bibliography and an index.

1487 ______. The Practice of Chinese Buddhism. Cambridge, Mass., Harvard Univ. Press, 1967 (Harvard East Asian Studies, 26).

This interesting study traces the developments in Chinese Buddhism through the first half of the 20th century. Also describes the life in the Buddhist monasteries and some doctrinal matters. Includes a select bibliography and an index.

1488 Wright, Arthur F. Buddhism in Chinese History. Stanford, Calif., Stanford Univ. Press, 1959 (Stanford Studies in the Civilization of Eastern Asia). 144 p.

Presents an historical survey of Buddhism in China with an assessment of its impact on the development of Chinese civilization. Contains an annotated list of books for further reading, and an index.

1489 Zürcher, Erik. The Buddhist Conquest of China; The Spread and Adaptation of Buddhism in Early Medieval China. Leiden, Brill, 1959 (Sinica leidensia, v. 11). 2 vols.

"The present study is an attempt to describe the main aspects of the particular type of Buddhism which developed in Southern and Central China in the 4th and early 5th century A.D."--Introd. Bibliography includes only works mentioned in the text, and is divided into Chinese and other language works. There is also an index of Chinese names and terms.

BUDDHISM IN INDIA AND SRI LANKA [CEYLON]

1490 Conze, Edward. Buddhist Thought in India: Three Phases of Buddhist Philosophy. London, Allen & Unwin, 1962. 302 p.

"This book sets out to discuss and interpret the main themes of Buddhist thought of India"--Preface. It deals with the archaic Buddhism, the Sthaviras, and the Mahayana. Contains some bibliographic references in notes at the end of the book. An index is supplied.

1491 Evers, Hans D. Monks, Priests and Peasants; A Study of Buddhism and Social Structure in Central Ceylon. Leiden, Brill, 1972 (Monographs in Social Anthropology and Theoretical Studies in Honor of N. Anderson). 136 p.

"This book is written for a specialist, either the sociologist and anthropologist of religion or the student of Buddhism and its cultural history in Ceylon and Southeast Asia"--Preface. A select bibliography, a glossary of terms, and a useful index are provided.

1492 Keith, Arthur B. Buddhist Philosophy in India and Ceylon. Oxford, Clarendon Press, 1923. 339 p.

One of the earliest systematic studies of Buddhist philosophical ideas. Some sections, however, must be up-dated due to the discovery of new materials. Bibliographic footnotes and an index are provided.

1493 Ling, Trevor O. The Buddha: Buddhist Civilization in India and Ceylon. London, Temple Smith, 1973 (Makers of New Worlds). 287 p.

Provides an excellent popular presentation of Buddhism dealing with its historical background, ideology, and modern developments. A select bibliography and an index are included.

1494 Rahula, Walpola. History of Buddhism in Ceylon: the Anuradhapura Period, 3rd Century B.C.-10th Century A.D. Colombo, Ceylon, Gunasena, 1956. 351 p.

Presents a detailed scholarly study based on materials drawn from almost all available sources. It investigates the Indian background, years of development, the monastic life, the social and religious life of the people, ceremonies and festivals, and education. Also contains a list of Pali, Singalese and Sanskrit sources; their translations into English; as well as a list of selected modern critical works.

1495 Warder, Anthony K. Indian Buddhism. Delhi, Motilal Banarsidaas, 1970. 622 p.

Presents a historical development of Buddhism from the 6th century B.C. to A.D. 1200. Each new development is discussed on a broad background drawn from various Tripitaka texts, mainly Pali and Sanskrit. It also deals with the cultural and religious heritage from which Buddhism emerged. An extensive bibliography is limited to primary sources. A detailed index may be used as a glossary.

BUDDHISM IN JAPAN

Bibliography

1496 Bando, Shojun, and others. A Bibliography of Japanese Buddhism. Tokyo, Cultural Interchange Institute for Buddhist Press, 1958. 180 p.
Contains a list of monographs and articles, some published in obscure periodicals or collections, arranged by sects. An index is provided.

General Studies

1497 Eliot, Charles N. E. Japanese Buddhism. London, Routledge & Paul, 1959 (1935). 449 p.
Provides a detailed study of the history of Japanese Buddhism. A large section of the book is devoted to the five major sects. Bibliographic footnotes cite mainly original sources and older critical surveys. Also an index is added.

1498 Kidder, Jonathan E. Early Buddhist Japan. New York, Praeger; London, Thames and Hudson, 1972 (Ancient People and Places, v. 78). 212 p.
A popular presentation for the beginner with some bibliographic references for further reading.

1499 Reischauer, August K. Studies in Japanese Buddhism. New York, Macmillan, 1971 (1917). 316 p.
An older but still useful overview of Japanese Buddhism. Some bibliographic information and an index are included.

1500 Saunders, Ernest D. Buddhism in Japan, with an Outline of Its Origins in India. Philadelphia, Univ. of Pennsylvania Press, 1964. 328 p.
"Provides an historical framework based on noteworthy points of departure for further reading.... Pt. 1 gives the general outlines of the doctrine that evolved in India. Pt. 2 presents more detailed treatment according to sects of Buddhism in the Japanese Islands from earliest times until the twentieth century"--Foreword. Also contains a select bibliography, statistics, chronologies, glossary of Indian terms with their Japanese equivalents, and an Index.

1501 Shoko, Watanabe. Japanese Buddhism; A Critical Appraisal, rev. ed. Tokyo, Kokusai Bunka Shin Kokai, 1968 (Japanese Life and Culture Series). 174 p.

Presents a survey of the mainstreams of Japanese Buddhism with some new observations. Also includes a table of the most important sects, and statistical information on temples, teachers, and parishioners.

1502 Visser, Marinus W. de. Ancient Buddhism in Japan: Sutras and Ceremonies in Use in the Seventh and Eighth Centuries A.D. and their History in Later Times. Paris, Geuthner, 1928-35 (Buddhica. Documents et travaux pour l'etude du bouddhisme ... 1 ver.: Memoires, t. 3-4). 2 vols.

This excellent scholarly study presents a systematic survey of sources for study of Buddhist tradition. Information must be, however, up-dated. Numerous bibliographic footnotes are included in the text. A detailed index is included in vol. 2.

Sects

1503 Armstrong, Robert C. An Introduction to Japanese Buddhist Sects. Ed. by K. W. Armstrong. Private printing, 1950. 350 p.

Outlines the development of Buddhism in Japan, the introduction of Mahayana teachings, and the ancient sects of Japan. Contains a selected bibliography of critical studies in English, and an index.

1504 Brannen, Noah S. Sōka Gakkai: Japan Militant Buddhists. Richmond, Va., Knox, 1968. 181 p.

Attempts to describe in some detail the case of Sōka Gakkai, their theory, doctrine, and faith. A selected list of works in English is enclosed. No index is supplied.

1505 Murata, Kiyoaki. Japan's New Buddhism; An Objective Account of Sōka Gakkai. Foreword by D. Ikeda. New York, Walker & Weatherhill, 1969. 194 p.

This is an interesting analysis by a journalist who "seems to have endeavored to free himself from prejudices and preoccupations in order to understand the doctrines of Nichiren, Shoshu and the true nature of Sōkagakkai"--Foreword. Chronological tables, a select bibliography of monographs and periodical articles, a glossary of terms, and an index are provided.

1506 Steinilber-Oberlin, Emile, and K. Matsuo. The Buddhist Sects of Japan, Their History, Philosophical Doctrines and Sanctuaries. Transl. by M. Loge. London, Allen & Unwin, 1938 (1930). 303 p.

Translation of the author's Les Sectes bouddiques japonaises. Presents an unsurpassed survey of the history and theology of a great number of Japanese Buddhist sects. A classified bibliography of older studies is included. There is no index, instead a very detailed table of contents should be consulted.

1507 Suzuki, Daisetz T. Shin Buddhism. New York, Harper & Row, 1970. 93 p.
Contains a collection of fine lectures by the famous Japanese buddhologist on the principles of Shinshu teachings. Neither index nor bibliographic notes included.

BUDDHISM IN SOUTHEAST ASIA

1508 Nhat-Hanh, Thich. Vietnam: Lotus in a Sea of Fire, with a Foreword by T. Merton. New York, Hill and Wang, 1967. 115 p.
Presents a Vietnamese monk's view of Buddhism in Vietnam on a background centered mainly on recent events in Vietnam.

1509 Sarkisyanz, E. Buddhist Background of the Burmese Revolution. The Hague, Nijhoff, 1965. 248 p.
Presents a scholarly analysis of the Buddhist traditions in Burma in the social and political framework. Numerous bibliographic references in footnotes, and an index are included.

1510 Schecter, Jerrold. The New Face of Buddha; Buddhism and Political Power in Southeast Asia. New York, Coward-McCann, 1967. 330 p.
Provides a popular presentation of the contemporary changes in the life of Buddhists in Southeast Asia against the background of political, social, and economic developments. A selected bibliography subdivided geographically by country, and an index are included.

1511 Spiro, Melford E. Buddhism and Society; A Great Tradition and Its Burmese Vicissitudes. New York, Harper & Row, 1970. 510 p.
Presents an anthropological study of Burmese Buddhism in which religion is studied in relation to Burmese society as a whole. Also contains a bibliography of works cited, and an index. One should also become acquainted with the author's Burmese Supernaturalism (Englewood Cliffs, N.J., Prentice Hall, 1967).

1512 Wells, Kenneth E. Thai Buddhism, Its Rites and Activities. Bangkok, 1960 (1939). 320 p.
The only historical analysis of Buddhism in Thailand. Bibliographic references and an index are included.

JOURNALS

1513 Bodhi Leaves. Kandy, Ceylon, 19 - (irregularly).
Published by the Buddhist Publication Society. Contains translations of Buddhist writings, and some critical discussions.

1514 Buddhist Review. London, 1909- .
Published by the Buddhist Society of Great Britain and Ireland.

1515 The Eastern Buddhist; An Unsectarian Journal Devoted to an Open and Critical Study of Mahayana Buddhism in All of Its Aspects. Kyoto, 1921- (semiannually).
"An unsectarian journal devoted to an open and critical study of Mahayana Buddhism in all of its respects..." --blurb. Published by the Eastern Buddhist Society, Otani University, Kyoto. Contains discussion articles, translations of unpublished documents, and valuable book reviews.

1516 Maha Bodhi; A Monthly Journal of International Buddhist Brotherhood. Calcutta, 1892- (monthly).
Carries articles on various aspects of Buddhism, and English translations of Buddhist writings. Indexed: Bibliog. As. St.

1517 Wheel. Kandy, Ceylon, 1959- (irregularly).
Published by the Buddhist Publication Society. Also called The Wheel Publication. Each issue has a distinctive title.

V CHINESE RELIGIONS [for Chinese Buddhism, see nos. 1481-1489]

REFERENCE WORKS

BIBLIOGRAPHIES AND GUIDES

1518 "[IX.] Chinese Religions." International Bibliography of the History of the Religions. Leiden, Brill, 1954- .
See no. 27. Lists annually a broad selection of monographs and periodical articles.

1519 "Classics of the Chinese Tradition." Columbia University. Columbia College. A Guide to Oriental Classics. Ed. W. T. De Bary and A. T. Embree. 2nd ed. New York, Columbia Univ. Press, 1975. p. 145-215.
Lists the most important classics, their editions in translation, selections, and some critical studies about them.

1520 Dobson, W. A. C. H. "The Religions of China (Excepting Buddhism)." Adams, C. J., ed. A Reader's Guide to the Great Religions. 2nd ed. New York, Free Press, 1977 (1965), p. 90-105.
See no. 22. Provides the beginner with introductory information on bibliography for studies of Chinese religions. Bibliographical references are cited within the text.

1521 Hucker, Charles O. China; A Critical Bibliography. Tucson, Univ. of Arizona Press, 1962. 125 p.
An annotated listing of books, articles, and individual chapters for study of both traditional and modern China. Designed to be of use equally to introductory and advanced research. Chapter 4: Intellectual and Aesthetic Patterns, includes sections on religion and philosophy.

1522 Thompson, Laurence G. Studies in Chinese Religion: Studies of Chinese Religion: A Comprehensive and Classified Bibliography of Publications in English, French, and German Through 1970. Encino, Calif., Dickenson, 1976.

169 p.
It is arranged in three parts: Bibliography and General Studies, Chinese Religion Exclusive of Buddhism, and Chinese Buddhism. Lacks annotations.

ENCYCLOPEDIA

1523 Couling, Samuel. The Encyclopedia Sinica. Tapei, Ch'eng Wen, 1967 (1917). 632 p.
Provides information on history, geography, literature, arts, religions, institutions, biography, etc. Some bibliographic references are included.

CRITICAL STUDIES

HISTORY OF CHINESE CIVILIZATION

1524 Eichhorn, Werner. Chinese Civilization: An Introduction. New York, Praeger, 1969 (1964). 360 p.
Translation of the author's Kulturgeschichte. China's. "Its emphasis is principally on the intellectual aspect of Chinese civilization.... Provides the beginner with a chronologically arranged survey of the most important basic features, and a delineation of Chinese civilization in its historical development"--Foreword. Each section contains a presentation of religious life in the discussed period. A select bibliography and an index are provided.

1525 Fitzgerald, C. P. China; A Short Cultural History. New York, Praeger, 1961 (1935). 624 p.
Presents a balanced outline of China's 3000-year history with a greater stress on cultural conditions, the development of religion, literature and arts. The early relations with the Roman Orient and the Middle East is fully treated. Some bibliographic references are given in footnotes. Also contains an index.

1526 Meskill, John, ed. An Introduction to Chinese Civilization. New York, Columbia Univ. Press, 1973. 699 p.
"This book consists of a brief history of China and ten essays on major aspects of Chinese civilization. It is meant to be an introduction, primarily for undergraduates"--Preface. Of special interest is the essay by C. K. Yang, "The Role of Religion in Chinese Society," p. 643-86. Contains some bibliographic references in footnotes, and an index.

1527 Watson, Burton. Early Chinese Literature. New York, Columbia Univ. Press, 1962. 304 p.

"This book is intended to answer some of the questions a general reader might be expected to have concerning early Chinese Literature, its major forms, its themes, its particular characteristics, and its works of distinction"--Preface. A brief list of suggested readings and an index are included.

RELIGIOUS HISTORY

1528 Groot, Jan J. M. The Religion of the Chinese. New York, Macmillan, 1912 (Hartford-Lamson Lectures on the Religions of the World). 230 p.
Contains a collection of studies which examine the universalistic animism and polydemonism, ancestral worship, Confucianism, Taoism, and Buddhism. An index is supplied.

1529 ________. The Religious Systems of China; Its Ancient Forms, Evolution, History and Present Aspects, Manners, Customs, and Social Institutions Connected Therewith. Taipei, Literature House, 1964 (1892-1901). 6 vols.
This excellent survey is based entirely on the original Chinese sources. Some of the interpretations are outdated but the factual materials are still reliable.

1530 Hughes, Ernest, and K. Hughes. Religion in China. London, Hutchinson, 1950 (Hutchinson University Library: World Religion, no. 39). 151 p.
A brief survey of the history and creeds of Confucianism, Taoism, Buddhism, Islam, and Christianity in China, with a concluding chapter about the religious conditions in the 20th century. Also contains a list of suggestions for further reading, and an index.

1531 Legge, James. The Religions of China; Confucianism, and Taoism, Described and Compared with Christianity. London, Hodder, 1880. 310 p.
An older but still valuable collection of lectures. Neither index nor bibliographic references provided.

1532 Smith, David H. Chinese Religions. London, Weidenfeld & Nicolson, 1968. 221 p.
The best existing survey of the historical development of Chinese religions from the early Shan dynasty to the present day. Selected bibliographies for each chapter are listed at the end of the book. A glossary of Chinese terms, and an index are also included.

1533 Soothill, William E. The Three Religions of China, 3rd ed. London, Oxford Univ. Press, 1929. 271 p.
Examines the interrelationship of Confucianism, Taoism,

and Buddhism in Chinese life and thought. It deals with the idea of god, cosmological ideas, moral ideas, the official cult, private religion, etc. Some bibliographic references are given in footnotes. An index is provided.

1534 Thompson, Laurence. Chinese Religion: An Introduction. Belmont, Calif., Dickenson, 1969. 119 p.

Presents a brief introductory survey comprised of discussions on native traditions; introduction, assimilation, and dominance of Buddhism; renaissance of native traditions; dominance of neo-Confucianism; disruption of tradition by Western "imports." Each chapter contains selected readings. An index is provided.

1535 ________. Chinese Way in Religion. Encino, Calif., Dickenson, 1973 (Religious Life of Man).

An anthology which contains excerpts from the writings representing the ancient native tradition, Taoism, Buddhism, religion of the state, family religion, popular religion, and religion under Communism. Some bibliographic references and an index are provided.

1536 Van Over, Raymond. Chinese Mystics. New York, Harper & Row, 1973. 183 p.

Provides a solid selection of readings in Chinese mysticism aimed at the general reader.

1537 Weber, Max. The Religion of China: Confucianism and Taoism. Transl. and Ed. by H. H. Gerth. Glencoe, Ill., Free Press, 1955 (1912). 308 p.

Translation of the author's essay: Konfucianismus und Taoismus. It "discusses the impact of Confucianism and Taoism on Chinese society as reinforcing traditionalism because of the conservative, humanistic character of China's main culture bearers, the literati. Weber sees traditionalism as a major deterrent to capitalistic development"--Nottingham. Has to be used with great caution since the great sociologist tended to interpret all religions according to his still disputed sociological theories. A glossary of terms and an index are provided. Also contains some bibliographic information in notes at the end.

1538 Yang, Chin-Kun. Religion in Chinese Society. Berkeley, Univ. of California Press, 1961. 473 p.

This sociological study explains the functions of religion in contemporary Chinese society. A list of books for further reading is added.

MODERN RELIGIOUS LIFE

1539 Bush, Richard C. Religion in Communist China. Nashville, Abingdon Press, 1970. 432 p.

Presents a survey of the religious situation in China in the years since the Communist revolution. Bibliographic references are given in footnotes. An index is included.

1540 Chan, Wing-tsit. Religious Trends in Modern China. New York, Columbia Univ. Press, 1953 (Haskell Lectures in Comparative Religion, 1950). 327 p.

Includes five lectures dealing with the significant trends in Confucianism, Buddhism, popular religions--mainly Taoism, Islam, and the "intellectual religions" in the first half of the 20th century. Also includes a selected bibliography of Western language monographs and periodical articles, major writings in Chinese, and a list of Chinese periodicals. A detailed index is provided.

1541 Haglund, Åke. Contact and Conflict: Studies in Contemporary Religious Attitudes among Chinese People. Lund, Gleerup, 1972. 248 p.

A scholarly study exploring recent developments in the religious life of China. Some bibliographic references are provided.

FESTIVALS

1542 Burkhardt, Valentine R. Chinese Creeds and Customs. Hong Kong, South China Morning Press, 1966 (1954). 3 vols.

Describes origins, locality, and recent expressions of the more important customs and festivals. An index is provided. Lacks bibliographic notes.

1543 Eberhard, Wolfram. Chinese Festivals. New York, Schuman, 1952 (Great Religious Festivals Series). 152 p.

Presents a brief survey of the religious festivals of traditional China with comments made from a sociological point of view. Some bibliographic references are given in the notes. An index is added.

MYTHOLOGY

Dictionary and Encyclopedia

1544 Werner, Edward T. C. A Dictionary of Chinese Mythology. Introd. by H. Kublin. New York, Julian Press, 1961 (1932). 627 p.

This dictionary is derived from personal observations

of the author. It includes information concerning the Chinese "otherworld." Also contains an index of myths, a table of Chinese dynasties, and a select bibliography.

1545 Williams, C. A. S. Encyclopedia of Chinese Symbolism and Art Motives; An Alphabetical Compendium of Legends and Beliefs as Reflected in the Manners and Customs of the Chinese Throughout the History. Introd. by K. W. Kato. New York, Julian Press, 1960. 468 p.

An excellent reference work which should be approached simultaneously through its detailed table of contents and subject index.

Critical Survey

1546 Werner, Edward T. C. Myths and Legends of China. London, Harrap, 1956 (1922). 453 p.

This is the only existing systematic study of Chinese myths. First, it provides a sociological background to the understanding of the basic ideas and emotions of the Chinese, and secondly, presents a survey of specific myths arranged in groups, e.g. myths of the stars, fire, epidemics, etc. Some bibliographic references are given in the footnotes. A combined glossary-index is provided.

CHINESE PHILOSOPHIES

Bibliography

1547 Chan, Wing-tsit. An Outline and an Annotated Bibliography of Chinese Philosophy. New Haven, Conn., Yale Univ. Far Eastern Publications, 1969 (1959) (Sinological Series). 127 p.

Contains an annotated list of monographs and periodical articles arranged by topic.

Anthologies

1548 Baskin, Wade. Classics in Chinese Philosophy. New York, Philosophical Library, 1972. 737 p.

"Provides the reader with practical means of familiarizing himself with the most important documents of the cultural heritage of China ... from the Confucian Analects to the theoretical statements of Mao Tse-tung"--Preface. Each selection is preceded by a brief biographic note. Some bibliographic references are given in the footnotes.

1549 Chan, Wing-tsit. A Source Book in Chinese Philosophy. Princeton, N.J., Princeton Univ. Press, 1969 (1963).

856 p.

Presents chronologically arranged selections from the most important Chinese philosophical writings. Also contains a glossary of Chinese characters, an extensive bibliography including monographs and periodical articles, and a detailed index.

1550 Li, Dun J. The Essence of Chinese Civilization. Princeton, N.J., Van Nostrand, 1967. 476 p.

"This is a book about traditional China, presented in translations of Chinese authors.... The authors range from such famous men as Confucius and Lao-tsu to the comparatively more obscure"--Preface. Of special interest is Pt. 1, Philosophy and Religion, which includes a discussion of Confucianism, "Hundred Schools," Taoism, Buddhism, neo-Confucianism and its aftermath, etc. Each section is preceded by a brief explanation. Some bibliographic references are included in footnotes. An index is added.

1551 Waley, Arthur. Three Ways of Thought in Ancient China. London, Allen & Unwin, 1956 (1939). 275 p.

Contains selections from Chuang-tzu, Mencius, and Han Fei-tzu.

Critical Studies

1552 Creel, Herrlee G. Chinese Thought, from Confucius to Mao Tse-Tung. New York, New American Library, 1964 (1953) (Mentor Book, MP 498). 240 p.

"This book is a non-technical account of the main outlines of the history of Chinese thought, from the earliest times ... to the present day"--Preface. Bibliography of monographs and periodical articles and an index are included.

1553 Fêng, Yü-lan. A History of Chinese Philosophy, with Introduction, Notes, Bibliography, and Index. Transl. by D. Bodde. Peiping, Vetch, 1966 (1948). 2 vols.

This extensive survey for Westerners presents a detailed historical development of Chinese philosophical schools, pointing out the interplay among them. Also contains a chronological table of the classical period, an extensive bibliography of monographs and periodical articles, and an index. An abridged edition of this book is also available: A Short History of Chinese Philosophy, 1966 (1948).

1554 ________. The Spirit of Chinese Philosophy. Transl. by E. R. Hughes. London, Paul, Trench, Trubner, 1947. 224 p.

Provides a brief outline of Chinese philosophical

schools: Confucius and Mencius, Yang Chu and Mo Ti, Lao Tzu and Chuang Tzu, the Han scholars, the mystical school, the Inner-Light School of Buddhism, the neo-Confucian philosophy, etc. Some bibliographic references are given in footnotes. An index is added.

1555 Moore, Charles, ed. The Chinese Mind: Essentials of Chinese Philosophy and Culture. Honolulu, East-West Center Press, 1967. 402 p.
This is a selection of papers presented at the East-West Philosophers' Conferences held at the University of Hawaii. Some bibliographic notes and an index are added.

1556 Wright, Arthur F. Studies in Chinese Thought. Chicago, Univ. of Chicago Press, 1953. 317 p.
Contains a selection of nine essays by outstanding experts in the field of Chinese studies.

THE "FIVE CLASSICS" AND THE "FOUR BOOKS"

COMPLETE "FIVE CLASSICS"

1557 Legge, James. The Chinese Classics, with a Translation, Critical and Exegetical Notes, Prolegomena, and ... Indexes, 2nd rev. ed. Hong Kong, Univ. Press, 1960 (1893-5). 6 vols.
Includes complete translations of the Analects, Mencius, the Shu ching (Book of History), the Shih ching (Book of Odes), the I ching (Book of Changes), the Ch'un-ch'iu (Spring and Autumn), and the Li chi (Book of Rituals). English translations are parallel with original Chinese text. This excellent rendition is recognized as a standard reference for scholarly purposes. See also the author's Sacred Books of China: The Texts of Confucianism (Oxford, England, Clarendon Press, 1882-99).

THE SHU CHING [Book of History]

1558 Shu ching. The Book of Documents. Transl. by B. Karlgren. Stockholm, Museum of Far Eastern Antiquities, 1950. 81 p.
This is an accurate and highly valued recent translation. See also Shu ching, or the Chinese Historical Classic, transl. by W. G. Old (London, Theosophical Pub. Soc., 1904), and entry no. 1557.

THE SHIH CHING [Book of Odes]

1559 Granet, Marcel. Festivals and Songs of Ancient China. London, Routledge, 1932 (1929). 281 p.
Translation of the author's Fêtes et chansons anciennes de la Chine. The poems are placed in their context of festival and ritual.

1560 Shih ching. The Book of Odes. Transl. by B. Karlgren. Stockholm, Museum of Far Eastern Antiquities, 1950. 270 p.
Contains a more recent translation of the text.

1561 _______. The Book of Songs. Transl. by A. Waley. 2nd ed. New York, Grove, 1960 (Evergreen book, E 209). 358 p.
Presents a collection of some 300 folk songs, religious hymns, court songs, ballads of the great Chou dynasty rendered in a readable style.

THE I CHING [Book of Changes]

Introductory Study

1562 Hook, Diana F. The I Ching and You. London, Routledge and Kegan Paul, 1973. 149 p.
"This is a guidebook to I Ching. It is therefore necessary to have a copy of I Ching to which to refer..."--Preface. Also includes an explanation of terms, a selected bibliography and an index.

Text in English Translations

1563 I ching. English. Book of Changes. Transl. by J. Legge ... with Study Introd. and Study Guide. New Hyde Park, N.Y., University Books, 1964 (1876). 448 p.
Presents an older translation with an excellent discussion of the origins, structure, concepts, and philosophy. Some bibliographic references are included.

1564 _______. _______. The I Ching, or Book of Changes. The R. Wilhelm's Translation Rendered into English by C. F. Baynes. Foreword by C. G. Jung, 3rd rev. ed. Princeton, N.J., Princeton Univ. Press, 1967 (Bollingen Series, 19). 740 p.
The translation is accompanied by an informative introduction discussing the use of the I Ching, its history, and the methods applied in translation of the intricate text. Some bibliographic references are included in footnotes. An index is added.

1565 Siu, Ralph G. H. The Man of Many Qualities: The Legacy of I Ching. Cambridge, Mass., MIT Press, 1968. 463 p.

Contains a clearly rendered scholarly translation, preceded by an informative comment. Useful bibliographic references are included. An index is provided.

THE CH'UN-CHIU [Spring and Autumn]

J. Legge's 19th-century translation is still the only available; see no. 1557.

THE LI CHI [Book of Rituals]

1566 Li Chi: Book of Rites; An Encyclopedia of Ancient Ceremonial Usages, Religious Creeds, and Social Institutions. Transl. by J. Legge. Ed. with Introd. and Study Guide by Ch'u Chai and Weinberg Chai. New Hyde Park, University Books, 1967. 2 vols.

The informative introduction discusses the formation of the Li Chi, its title and content, authorship, and significance in Chinese culture. The translation is accompanied by useful critical annotations, and bibliographic notes.

THE "FOUR BOOKS"

1567 Ssŭ Shu. The Four Books: Confucian Analects, the Great Learning, the Doctrine of the Mean, and the Works of Mencius. Ed. and transl. by J. Legge. New York, Paragon Books, 1966 (1870). 1014 p.

Contains: the Lu-Yu (Analects), the Meng-Tzu (Mencius), Ta-Hsueh (Great Learning), Chung Yung (Doctrine of the Mean), with the original Chinese text and its parallel English translation accompanied by critical notes.

CONFUCIANISM

ANTHOLOGIES

1568 Chai, Ch'u, and W. Chai, eds. and transl. The Sacred Books of Confucius and Other Confucian Classics. New Hyde Park, N.Y., University Books, 1965. 384 p.

A well-selected anthology aimed at the general reader presenting excerpts from the up-to-date translations of Hsun Tsu, Ta Hsueh, Chung Yung, Hsiao Ching, Li Chi, and Tung Chung-Shu. The texts are preceded by an informative introduction. A selected bibliography is included in the footnotes. A glossary and an index are supplied. The anthology was also published under the title The Humanist Way in Ancient China: Essential Works on Confucianism (New York, 1965).

1569 Kenney, Edward H. A Confucian Notebook, by Edward Herbert [pseud.], with a Foreword by A. Waley. New York, Grove, 1960 (Wisdom of the East, WP5). 89 p.
"Represents an attempt to give not a description but an impression of Confucianism by selecting certain facets of it, which have a special significance or interest"--Preface. A brief bibliography and an index are included.

CRITICAL WORKS

1570 Fairbanks, John K., ed. Chinese Thought and Institutions: A Study of Confucian State or Impact of Confucianism on Chinese State. Chicago, Univ. of Chicago Press, 1957. 438 p.
Presents a collection of papers dealing with various aspects of state Confucianism. Bibliographic references are given in the notes. An index is provided.

1571 Liu, Wu-chi. A Short History of Confucian Philosophy. New York, Dell, 1955. 226 p.
"Presents a systematic account of Confucianism from its origins to contemporary times, bringing into clear perspective its place in Chinese thought and history"--cover. Selected bibliography for each chapter is given at the end. An index is supplied.

1572 Nivison, David S., and F. Wright, eds. Confucianism in Action. Stanford, Calif., Stanford Univ. Press, 1959 (Stanford Studies in the Civilization of Eastern Asia, v. 3). 390 p.
Contains 11 papers by outstanding experts in Chinese studies dealing with the influence of Confucianism on the family and on the formation of bureaucracy in China. Some bibliographic references are included in notes. An index is provided.

1573 Shryock, John K. The Origin and Development of the State Cult of Confucius; An Introductory Study. New York, Paragon Books Reprint, 1966 (1932). 298 p.
Presents an historical survey of the development of the Confucian school from the death of Confucius to the Republic. A bibliography of older monographs and periodical articles in Chinese, Japanese, and Western languages is supplied, and an index provided.

WORKS OF CONFUCIUS

1574 Confucius. The Analects of Confucius. London, Allen & Unwin, 1948 (1938). 268 p.

An excellent modern translation, with critical textual and historical annotations and authoritative introductory discussions of some of the most important terms and ideas that appear in the text. Some bibliographic references are provided.

CRITICAL STUDIES OF CONFUCIUS

1575 Creel, Herrlee G. Confucius; The Man of the Myth. New York, Day, 1949. 363 p.

Also published under the title Confucius and the Chinese Way (New York, Harper, 1960). Provides a concise presentation of major figures of Chinese philosophical schools designed for the general reader. It discusses the life and times of Confucius, his ideas and their transformation into a state doctrine, and its influence in modern times both in China and the West. The work was criticized for overemphasizing the democratic qualities of Confucianism. Includes a selected bibliography of monographs and periodical articles, and an index.

1576 Do-dingh, Pierre. Confucius and Chinese Humanism. Transl. by S. L. Markmann. New York, Funk & Wagnall, 1960 (1950). 217 p.

A popularly presented survey which contains the biography of Confucius, a discussion of his doctrine, an outline of sects and schools, and highlights of the 2500-year history. Also contains a comparative chronological table of Chinese and Western history, a bibliographical sketch, and a useful index.

1577 Smith, David H. Confucius. New York, Scribner's, 1973 (Makers of New Worlds). 240 p.

Attempts "to provide the general reader with a reliable and trustworthy account of the life, teaching, and influence of Confucius... "--Preface. Includes a well-selected bibliography and an index.

1578 Wright, Arthur. The Confucian Persuasion. Stanford, Calif., Stanford Univ. Press, 1960 (Stanford Studies in the Civilization of the Eastern Asia, v. 4). 390 p.

Explains the ways in which Confucianism influenced the life, art, and literature of the Chinese people. Provides some bibliographic references in notes, and an index.

1579 ________, and D. Twitchett, eds. Confucian Personalities. Stanford, Calif., Stanford Univ. Press, 1962 (Stanford

Studies in the Civilization of Eastern Asia, v. 5). 411 p. Includes biographies of 12 great Confucian leaders from A.D. 351 to the present. Also contains numerous bibliographic references in notes, and an index.

WORKS OF MENCIUS

1580 Mencius; A New Translation Arranged and Annotated for the General Reader. Ed. and transl. by W. A. C. H. Dobson. Toronto, Univ. of Toronto Press, 1963 (UNESCO Collection of Representative Works: Chinese Series). 215 p.
Each selection is preceded by a brief introduction. Contains a finding list, and bibliographic references in footnotes.

1581 Mencius. The Book of Mencius. (Abridged.) Transl. by L. Giles. London, Murray, 1949 (1942) (Wisdom of the East Series). 128 p.
Contains the teaching of the great Confucian scholar divided into seven chapters.

1582 Mencius. Transl. by D. C. Lau from the Chinese with an Introd. Harmondsworth, Penguin, 1970. 280 p.
Presents a well-rendered translation of the teachings of the Confucian master.

CRITICAL STUDY OF MENCIUS

1583 Verwilghen, Albert F. Mencius; The Man and His Ideas. New York, St. John's Univ. Press, 1967 (Asian Philosophical Studies, no. 8). 122 p.
Presents a new study of the subject, with useful bibliographic references.

NEO-CONFUCIANISM

Anthology

1584 Chu, Hsi and Lü Tsu-ch'en, eds. Reflections on Things at Hand: The Neo-Confucian Anthology. Transl. with Notes by Wing-tsit Chan. New York, Columbia Univ. Press, 1967 (UNESCO Collection of Representative Works: Chinese Series). 441 p.
Contains a selection of readings from the most important Confucian writings. A select bibliography, a glossary of terms, and an index are provided.

Critical Studies

1585 Chang, Chia-sên. The Development of Neo-Confucian Thought, by Carsun, Chang. New York, Bookman Associates, 1957-62. 2 vols.
"Describes the main trends in Chinese thought covering the period ... of well over a thousand years"--Preface. Includes a select bibliography and an index.

1586 Levenson, Joseph R. Confucian China and Its Modern Fate. Berkeley, Univ. of Calif. Press, 1958-65. 3 vols.
Provides an analysis of intellectual conflict in the 20th century between Confucianism and its various counterparts. Selected bibliography and an index are provided at the end of each volume.

1587 Liang, Ch'i-ch'ao. Intellectual Trends in the Ch'ing Period. Transl. by I. C. Y. Hsu. Cambridge, Mass., Harvard Univ. Press, 1959 (Harvard East Asian Studies, v. 2). 147 p.
This excellent scholarly study concentrates on the developments of the more recent Neo-Confucian thought of the Ch'ing dynasty, 1644-1912. Contains an extensive bibliography of sources, a glossary of terms, and an index.

OTHER WORKS AND BELIEFS

MOHISTS AND LEGALISTS

1588 Basic Writings of Mo-Tsu, Hsün Tsu, and Han Fei Tsu. Transl. by Burton Watson. New York, Columbia Univ. Press, 1967 (Records of Civilization: Sources and Studies. UNESCO Collection of Representative Works: Chinese Series). 140, 177, 135 p.
Contains a selection of works by the three influential thinkers of classical China. Each selection is preceded by an informative introduction. Also contains some bibliographic references in footnotes, and an index.

1589 Kung-Sun, Yang. The Book of Lord Shang; A Classic of the Chinese School of Law. Transl. from the Chinese with Introd. and Notes by J. J. Duyvendak. Chicago, Univ. of Chicago Press, 1963 (1928) (UNESCO Collection of Representative Works: Chinese Series). 346 p.
This excellent book is comprised of a complete translation of the text with an informative introduction dealing with biographical details and the importance of the author as a social reformer and a "maker" of the school of law. It also discusses the authenticity and history of the text.

Includes some bibliographic references and an index of Chinese names and words.

FOLK RELIGIONS

1590 Ch'ü, Yüan, ed. and transl. The Nine Songs; A Study of Shamanism in Ancient China. London, Allen & Unwin, 1955. 64 p.

This interesting study is based on a collection of ancient poems. It discusses the place of the shaman (holy man) in ancient Chinese society. Also includes numerous bibliographic references in footnotes, and an index.

1591 Doré, Henri. Researches into Chinese Superstitions. Transl. by M. Kennelly and others. Taipei, Taiwan, Ch'eng-wen Pub. Co., 1966-(1926). 13 vols.

Translation of Manuel des superstitions chinoises (1926). Provides a catalog of Chinese superstitions and practices of Chinese popular religion in modern times, with numerous illustrations. Bibliographic references are included in footnotes.

1592 Morgan, Harry. Chinese Symbols and Superstitions. Detroit, Gale, 1972 (1942). 192 p.

A comprehensive survey which deals with the myth of creation, the legendary period, the conventionalized culture and hereditary rules, Buddhism and its symbols, amulets, charms, gems, and their mystique, as well as with folk gods and idols and their superstitions. A select bibliography and an index are supplied.

1593 Reichelt, Karl L. Religion in Chinese Garment. Transl. by J. Tetlie. New York, Philosophical Library, 1951 (Missionary Research Series, no. 16). 180 p.

A Norwegian missionary of long experience with the Chinese presents a survey of animistic folk beliefs in modern China, with descriptions of Confucian, Taoist, and Buddhist contributions to it. An index of sacred writings is added.

TAOISM

BIBLIOGRAPHY

1594 Soymié, Michael, and F. Litsch. "Bibliographie du taoisme; études dans les langues occidentales." Dokyo Kenkyu, v. 3 (1968), p. 1-72.

An extensive bibliography which lists monographs and periodical articles arranged alphabetically. A subject index is provided.

CLASSIC TEXTS

1595 The Sacred Books of China: The Texts of Taoism. Transl. by J. Legge. Delhi, Motilal Banarsidass, 1966 (Reprint of the Sacred Books of the East, v. 39-40). 2 vols.

An old, but still unchallenged scholarly translation of the Tao Te Ching by Lao Tsu, the writings of Chang Tzu, and the T'ai-shang tractate of actions and their retributions. Appendices, critical notes on sources, and a comprehensive index are added.

CHUANG-TZU

1596 Chuang-Tzu. Works. English 1968. The Complete Works of Chuang Tzu, transl. by B. Watson. New York, Columbia Univ. Press, 1968 (UNESCO Collection of Representative Works: Chinese Series). 397 p.

A more recent translation than Legge's (see no. 1595) with a concise but informative introduction. It has been also issued in an abridged version. Some bibliographic notes for further reading and an index are included.

LAO-TZU

1597 Lao-Tzu. The Way of Life; A New Translation of the Tao tê ching, by R. B. Blakney. New York, New American Library, 1955 (Mentor Book, M 129). 139 p.

Contains both a translation, and a paraphrase of each chapter, with an excellent introduction explaining many esoteric and complicated concepts.

1598 _______. The Way of Lao Tzu (Tao-tê ching). Transl. with Introd. Essays, Comments, and Notes by Wing-tsit Chan. Indianapolis, Bobbs-Merrill, 1963 (Library of Liberal Arts, 139). 285 p.

This modern translation is presented against the background of the entire history of Chinese philosophical thought. It brings a summary of the recent debates on Lao Tzu and his book. The bibliography includes a selection of books and periodical articles both in Western languages, as well as in Chinese and Japanese. An index is supplied.

1599 _______. Tao Te Ching; A New Translation, by Gia Fu Feng and J. English. New York, Vintage House, 1972. 1 vol.

A popularly presented rendition of the text, with numerous illustrations.

1600 _______. Tao te ching, transl. by D. S. Lau. Baltimore, Penguin, 1963 (Penguin Classics). 191 p.

This popular edition includes a well-presented translation and an informative introduction on the historical background of the work.

1601 ________. The Way and Its Power; A Study of the Tao Te Ching and Its Place in Chinese Thought. Ed. and transl. by A. Waley. London, Allen & Unwin, 1949. 262 p.
This translation is recognized as the best existing scholarly rendition of the text both for its accuracy and readability. It gives a translation of each chapter accompanied by an explanation of the more obscure phrases.

LIEH-TZU

1602 Lǐeh-Tzǔ. Taoist Teachings, Translated from the Book of Lieh-tzǔ, with Introd. and Notes by L. Giles. 2nd ed. London, Murray, 1947 (Wisdom of the East). 112 p.
A popularly presented translation with a brief informative introduction. Neither bibliography nor index is included.

1603 Lieh-Tzu. The Book of Lieh-tzu, transl. by A. C. Graham. London, Murray, 1961 (1960) (Wisdom of the East). 183 p.
Includes a complete collection of works by the great Taoist thinker. A short reading list is provided. Lacks an index.

T'AI I CHIN HUA TSUNG CHIH

1604 The Secret of the Golden Flower; A Chinese Book of Life with Part of a Chinese Meditation Text: The Book of Consciousness and Life. Transl. by R. Wilhelm. Rev. and enl. ed. New York, Harcourt, Brace, Jovanovich, 1962 (1931). 149 p.
Contains a Taoist mystical textbook on meditation preceded by a discussion of the texts. Some bibliographic references are given in the footnotes.

CRITICAL STUDIES

1605 Blofeld, John. The Secret and Sublime: Taoist Mysteries and Magic. London, Allen & Unwin, 1973. 216 p.
This popularly presented work brings together all aspects of Taoism: popular Taoism with its variety of colorful ceremonies, demon exorcism, oracles, ghosts; Yogic Taoism with its emphasis on rejuvenation achieved by means of sexual conservation or by "internal alchemy"; and the ancient philosophical Taoism. Neither bibliography nor index is included.

1606 Creel, Herrlee G. What Is Taoism? and Other Studies in Chinese Cultural History. Chicago, Univ. of Chicago Press, 1970. 192 p.

Contains a collection of papers dealing with various subjects in Chinese civilization. The title is taken from the very important study of Taoism. Bibliographic references in footnotes and an index are provided.

1607 Kaltenmark, Max. Lao Tzu and Taoism. Transl. from the French by R. Greaves. Stanford, Calif., Stanford Univ. Press, 1969 (1965). 158 p.

Translation of Lao tseu et le taoïsme (1965). Provides an interesting survey of Lao Tzu and his school, aimed at the beginner. Select bibliography includes sources and more important critical studies. An index is provided.

1608 Kenney, Edward Herbert. The Taoist Notebook, by Edward Herbert [pseud.]. London, Murray, 1966 (Wisdom of the East). 80 p.

Contains a brief survey of writings of special significance for Taoism and its schools. A brief bibliography and an index are included.

1609 Welch, Holmes. The Parting of the Way: Lao Tzu and the Movement. Boston, Beacon, 1957. 204 p.

An interpretation of the history and basic principles of Taoism. It is considered as the most satisfactory introduction to the Taoist movement as a whole from the ancient origins to contemporary American developments. A select bibliography and an index are provided.

JOURNALS

1610 The China Quarterly: An International Journal for the Study of China. Paris, 1960- .

Published by the Contemporary China Institute, School of Oriental and African Studies at the University of London. Indexed: P.A.I.S.

1611 Chinese Culture; A Quarterly Review, Taiwan, 1957- .

Published under the auspices of the Institute for Advanced Chinese Studies of the Chinese Academy. Carries articles on history, literature, religion, etc. Indexed: Bibliog. As. St.

1612 Chinese Studies in History; A Quarterly Journal of Translations. White Plains, N.Y., 1969- .

Continues Chinese Studies in History and Philosophy. Indexed: Bibliog. As. St.

1613 Chinese Studies in Philosophy; A Quarterly Journal of Translations. White Plains, N.Y., 1969- .
Continues Chinese Studies in History and Philosophy.

Part Four--Asian Religions (cont.)

VI JAPANESE RELIGIONS [for Japanese Buddhism, see nos 1496-1507]

REFERENCE WORKS

BIBLIOGRAPHIES AND GUIDES

1614 Blacker, C. "Religions of Japan." Bleeker, C. J. Historia religionum. Leiden Brill, 1969, p. 516-49.
See no. 38. An excellent bibliographic essay which deals with the essence of Japanese religions, their historical development, conception of deity, worship, and a brief history of the studies. Also includes a select bibliography.

1615 Borton, Hugh, et al. A Selected List of Books and Articles on Japan in English, French and German. Rev. and enl. ed. Cambridge, Mass., Harvard Univ. Press for the Harvard Yenching Institute, 1954. 272 p.
This is one of the best general bibliographies of materials on Japan. Especially interesting is Chapter XI, Mythology, Religion and Philosophy, p. 134-50.

1616 "Classics of Japanese Tradition." Columbia University. Columbia College. A Guide to Oriental Classics. Ed. by W. T. DeBary, and A. T. Embree. 2nd ed. New York, Columbia Univ. Press, 1975, p. 219-57.
Lists a number of the most famous classics: their editions, selections in Western translations, and also some critical works.

1617 "Japanese Religions." International Bibliography of the History of Religions. Leiden, Brill, 1954.
See no. 27. Provides an annual listing of selected monographs and periodical articles.

1618 Kitagawa, J. M. "The Religions of Japan." Adams, C. J. A. A Reader's Guide to the Religions. 2nd ed. New York, Free Press, 1977 (1965), p. 247-320.
See no. 22. An informative bibliographic essay which

contains an historical survey of research, with bibliographical appendices.

1619 Swyngedouw, Johannes. "A Brief Guide to English Language Materials on Japan's Religions." Contemporary Religions in Japan, v. 11:1-2 (March-June 1970), p. 80-97.
Provides a useful listing of readings on various issues of Japanese religious life.

DICTIONARY

1620 Goedertier, Joseph M. A Dictionary of Japanese History. New York, Walker-Weatherhill, 1968. 415 p.
"In the total of more than 1100 entries, this first volume offers concise explanations of such subjects as significant political events, major wars and battles, important feudal clans, features of government and social structure, styles of architecture and painting, outstanding works of literature, and major religious and social developments. The range is from prehistoric to modern times"--Preface. Lacks bibliographic information.

ANCIENT DOCUMENTS IN ENGLISH TRANSLATION

ANTHOLOGIES

1621 Tsunoda Ryusaku, et al., eds. Sources of the Japanese Tradition. New York, Columbia University Press, 1964 (1958). 2 vols.
Contains a well balanced and comprehensive selection of documents covering a broad area of subjects in Japanese culture and history. It includes a good presentation of the major Japanese religious and philosophical traditions, with excellent introductions to each chapter. A select bibliography of monographs and periodical articles, and an index are added.

1622 Wheeler, Post. The Sacred Scriptures of the Japanese.... London, Allen & Unwin, 1952.
Provides a new version of the Japanese scriptures: Fudoki, Kojiki, Nihongi, Kogo-Shui, Shojiroku, Engi-Shiki. Texts are accompanied by an excellent critical apparatus.

FUDOKI

1623 Izumo no Kuni fudoki. English. Izumo fudoki, transl. with an Introd. by Michiko Yamaguchi Aoiki. Tokyo, Sophia

Univ., 1971 (Monumenta Nipponica Monograph). 173 p.
Includes a translation of an ancient report from the Izumo Province with its historical background and a critical analysis. It belongs to the revered scriptures of Shinto containing early Japanese myths. A select bibliography of sources and critical studies is provided.

KOJIKI

1624 Kojiki. English. Kojiki, transl. with an Introd. and Notes by D. L. Philippi. Tokyo, Univ. of Tokyo Press, 1968. 655 p.
A controversial modern translation of a collection of ancient texts including the Japanese account of creation, Shinto mythology, and some early historical records. Also contains a glossary, a select bibliography, and an index.

1625 Yaku, Masao. The Kojiki in the Life of Japan. Transl. by G. W. Robinson. Tokyo, Centre for East Asian Cultural Studies, 1969 (East Asian Cultural Studies Series, no. 13). 208 p.
Provides a modern translation of Kojiki no inochi.

NIHONGI

1626 Nihongi, Chronicles of Japan, from the Earliest Times to A.D. 697. Transl. by W. G. Aston from the Original Chinese and Japanese. London, Allen & Unwin; New York, Macmillan, 1956. 443 p.
This repeats some of the Kojiki's accounts, but contains more historical records and descriptions of the ancient ritual practices.

NORITO

1627 Norito; A New Translation of the Ancient Japanese Ritual Prayers. Transl. by D. L. Philippi. Tokyo, Institute for Japanese Culture and Classics, Kokugakuin Univ., 1959. 59 p.
Includes information on the ancient Shinto liturgies, ritual prayers and ritualistic practices.

CRITICAL STUDIES

HISTORY OF JAPANESE CIVILIZATION

1628 Hane, Mikiso. Japan; A Historical Survey. New York,

Scribner's, 1973. 650 p.
A comprehensive one-volume history which deals with both traditional and modern periods. It attempts to present a balanced picture by scrutinizing all aspects of Japanese history: social, economic, political, cultural, and intellectual. Religious history is discussed within each period. A selected chapter bibliography and an index are provided.

1629 Japan. Nihon Yunesuko Kokunai Linkai. Japan, Its Land, People and Culture. Comp. by the Japanese National Commission for UNESCO. Tokyo, Bureau of Ministry of Finance, 1964 (1958). 885, 200 p.
Covers all aspects of Japanese life together with its geographical, historical, social, economic, and cultural background, while still keeping it concise in the treatment of subject. Of special interest is Pt. XIX dealing with development of Japanese thought and religious life of the people. Index is included, but lacks bibliographic references for further reading.

1630 Moore, Charles A., and A. V. Morris, ed. The Japanese Mind; Essentials of Japanese Philosophy and Culture. Honolulu, East-West Center Press, 1967. 357 p.
This interesting collection is comprised of 15 papers by outstanding authorities presented to the East-West Philosophers' Conferences at the University of Hawaii. The papers show the eclecticism of Japanese thought in welding together incompatible elements derived from India and China. Bibliographic references are included in notes, an index is added.

1631 Morton, William S. Japan; Its History and Culture. Newton Abbot, England, David and Charles, 1973. 243 p.
"This book is designed as an introduction ... both for the college student and for the general reader.... It attempts to approach history as a whole ... giving also the accompaniment of cultural, spiritual, artistic, and social life distinctive of Japan"--Preface. A glossary, a chronological table, a selected bibliography, and an index are provided.

1632 Nakamura, Hajime. A History of the Development of Japanese Thought from A.D. 592 to 1869, 2nd ed. Tokyo, Japan Publication, 1969 (1967) (Japanese Life and Culture). 2 vols.
Contains a collection of previously published articles. Vol. 1 covers the Nara, Heian, and Medieval eras; vol. 2, the Tokugawa era, 1600-1868. The selected bibliography includes monographs and periodical articles. There is no index.

1633 Varley, H. P. Japanese Culture: A Short History. New

York, Praeger, 1973. 227 p.

"This book is intended as a survey for the general reader of Japanese higher culture, including religion, the visual arts, literature; the theatre, thought, and those lesser arts, such as the tea ceremony, the landscape gardening, that have been uniquely cherished in Japan"--Preface. Also contains a selected list of English books and an index.

RELIGIOUS HISTORY

Atlas

1634 Christian Center for the Study of Japanese Religions. Religious Map of Japan. Kyoto, 1959. 51 p.

Presents to the reader the religious situation in today's Japan illustrated by maps. It provides the location of 167 Buddhist sects, 69 Shinto shrines, 168 new religions, and 60 Zen monasteries. For directory information consult also no. 1643.

Critical Studies

1635 Anesaki, Masaharu. History of Japanese Religion, with Special Reference to the Social and Moral Life of the Nation. Rutland, Vt., Tuttle, 1963 (1930). 423 p.

The most eminent Japanese scholar presents a survey of religious life in Japan on the historical background. Some bibliographic footnotes, and an index are included.

1636 ______. Religious Life of the Japanese People. Rev. by H. Kishimoto. Tokyo, Kokusai, 1970 (1936) (Series on Japanese Life and Culture, v. 4). 122 p.

A classic study presenting a review of Japanese religions. It has been criticized for its "evolutionary concept of the special moral qualities of the Japanese people." It discusses Shinto, Chinese influences: Confucianism and Taoism, Buddhism and its religious and social influence, etc. A brief bibliography and an index are supplied.

1637 Bellah, Robert N. Tokugawa Religion: The Values of Preindustrial Japan. Glencoe, Ill., Free Press, 1957. 249 p.

An excellent scholarly study presented by an outstanding sociologist. A selected bibliography contains references to works in Japanese and western languages. There is also a list of Japanese and Chinese terms, and an index.

1638 Earhart, H. B. Japanese Religion: Unity and Diversity.

Belmont, Calif., Dickenson, 1969 (Religious Life of Man). 270 p.

Gives an excellent survey of major religions, and their functions, practices, and life styles. Aimed at the beginner. Also contains an annotated list of books in Western languages, and an index. Should be used with the item below.

1639 ________. Religion in Japanese Experience; Sources and Interpretations. Belmont, Calif., Dickenson, 1974 (Religious Life of Man). 270 p.

This is a complementary source book to the author's earlier work, listed above, which contains a compilation of extracts from original texts. Aimed at the undergraduate student. Also includes a brief bibliography for each section and an index.

1640 Japan. Bunkacho. Japanese Religion; A Survey, by the Agency for Cultural Affairs, Tokyo-Palo Alto, Calif., Kodansha International, 1972. 272 p.

Pt. 1 describes and interprets the different religions in Japan; Pt. 2 is concerned with the present situation of specific religious organizations, and provides an account of the most important branches of Buddhism, Shinto, and Christianity, as well as of special phenomenons as Tenrikyo, Seicho no Ie, etc.; Pt. 3 is comprised of statistical data available at the end of 1970.

1641 Kishimoto, Hideo, ed. Japanese Religion in the Meiji Era. Transl. by J. F. Howes. Tokyo, Obunsha, 1956 (Japanese Culture in the Meiji Era, v. 2). 377 p.

Contains a collection of essays by prominent Japanese scholars. The introduction outlines the religious life during Tokugawa; Pt. 1 deals with Shinto and its development into a national religion; Pt. 2 describes the introduction and development of Buddhism; Pt. 3 presents Christianity and changes in cultural and social life; Pt. 4 discusses religion and social development.

1642 Kitagawa, Joseph M. Religion in Japanese History. New York, Columbia Univ. Press, 1966 (Lectures on the History of Religions, sponsored by the American Council of Learned Societies; new series no. 7). 475 p.

Presents the most up-to-date account of Japanese religions. Especially valuable is the study of Japanese folk religions. Also contains a chronological table, a glossary of terms, an extensive bibliography of monographs and periodical articles, and an index.

1643 Kokusai Shukyo Kenkyu Sho, Tokyo. Japan's Religions. Tokyo, International Institute for the Study of Religion, 1957-58. 6 vols.

"Attempts to meet the need for a directory with the

names, addresses, and other basic information required to get in touch with the denominational headquarters and some of their affiliated institutions"--Foreword. Contains information on Shinto, Christian Churches, Buddhist denominations, new religions, courses on religion in universities, etc.

1644 Smith, Robert J. Ancestor Worship in Contemporary Japan. Stanford, Calif., Stanford Univ. Press, 1974. 266 p.

The introductory chapter presents an historical explanation of ancestor worship. Following chapters discuss the nature of deities, the various kinds of spirits, the dividing line between human and divine, and the timing and character of memorialism and veneration. A glossary, a select bibliography and an index are appended.

1645 Supreme Commander for the Allied Powers. Civil Information and Education Section. Religions in Japan: Buddhism, Shinto, Christianity.... Rutland, Vt., Tuttle, 1955. 194 p.

Provides a solid introductory study of the three major religions, with brief information to major sub-sects. Also contains a classified selected bibliography and an index.

MYTHOLOGY

1646 Piggott, Julie. Japanese Mythology. London, Hamlyn, 1969. 141 p.

A brief popular presentation with numerous illustrations, and a brief list of books for further reading. An index is provided.

FOLK RELIGION

1647 Hori, Ichiro. Folk Religion of Japan: Continuity and Change. Ed. by J. M. Kitagawa and A. L. Miller. Tokyo, Univ. of Tokyo Press, 1968 (Haskell Lectures on History of Religions; new ser. no. 1). 263 p.

This scholarly study concentrates on characteristics shared by different religious traditions on the folk level throughout the history of Japan. Some bibliographic references are included.

See also no. 1642.

FESTIVALS

1648 Bauer, Helen, and S. Carlquist. Japanese Festivals. Garden City, N.Y., Doubleday, 1965. 224 p.

Provides a popular guide to Japanese festivals with a calendar. An index is added.

1649 Casal, U. A. The Five Sacred Festivals of Ancient Japan; Their Symbolism and Historical Development. Rutland, Vt., Tuttle, 1967. 114 p.

Traces the history and symbolism of the New Year's Festival, the Girls' Festival, the Boys' Festival, the Star Festival, and the Chrysanthemum Festival. An index is provided.

1650 Haga, Hideo. Japanese Folk Festivals, Illustrated. Transl. by F. H. Mayer. Tokyo, Japan's Publications, 1970. 127 p.

Translation of Nihon no matsuri. Presents an interesting description of major festivals, with a detailed list of festivals arranged by district including dates of celebrations.

AINU RELIGION

1651 Munro, Neil G. Ainu Creed and Cult. New York, Columbia Univ. Press, 1963. 182 p.

This excellent study is based on the author's personal observations of the Ainu of Hokkaido and their customs. It describes the fundamental religious concepts, the kanui, the inau, house building, and other rites, etc. A chapter on social organization by B. Z. Seligman is added. A bibliography of Japanese and Western language materials, a glossary, and an index are provided.

CONFUCIANISM IN JAPAN

1652 Smith, Warren W. Confucianism in Modern Japan; A Study of Conservatism in Japanese Intellectual History. Tokyo, Hokuseido, 1963. 285 p.

"The purpose of this study is to trace the varying fortunes of Confucianism in modern Japan and in this way shed light on the particular kind of situations in which the Japanese have attracted to Confucian thought rather than alternative philosophies"--Preface. The enclosed bibliography lists monographs and periodical articles in both Western and Oriental languages which were used in preparation of the study. An index is provided.

SHINTOISM

BIBLIOGRAPHIES

1653 Herbert, Jean. Bibliographie du shintô et des sectes shintôistes (Bibliography of Shinto and Shinto Sects). Leiden, Brill, 1968. 73 p.
Lists selected monographs, and periodical articles in English, French, German, and Japanese which deal with state Shinto, imperial Shinto, principal aspects of the popular Shinto, and the ancient and modern sects.

1654 Kato, Genchi, and others. A Bibliography of Shinto in Western Languages from the Oldest Times till 1952. Tokyo, Meiji Jingu Shamusho, 1953. 57 p.
Contains an alphabetical list of monographs and periodical articles. A general index is provided.

CRITICAL STUDIES

1655 Aston, William G. Shinto; The Way of Gods. London, Longmans Green, 1968 (1905). 390 p.
"The treatise has two objects. It is intended, primarily and chiefly, as a repertory of the more significant facts of Shinto.... It also comprises an outline theory of the origin and earlier stages of the development of religion..."--Preface. Also contains some bibliographic references in footnotes and an index.

1656 Creemers, Wilhelmus H. M. Shrine Shinto after World War II. Bibliographical Notes, Glossary, Appendixes, Bibliography, Japanese Texts. Leiden, Brill, 1968. 262 p.
Presents a scholarly study of various problems of shrine Shinto, its nature and historical development. A selected bibliography and an index are provided.

1657 Fujisawa, Chikao. Concrete Universality of the Japanese Way of Thinking; A New Interpretation of Shintoism. Tokyo, Hokuseido, 1958. 160 p.
"This book is a modest attempt to initiate Western people into ... the Japanese way of thinking..."--Preface. Neither bibliography nor index is provided.

1658 Herbert, Jean. Shinto at the Fountain-head of Japan, with a Preface by Y. Sasaki. London, Allen & Unwin, 1967. 622 p.
The only contemporary study in English which provides detailed information on the practices and mythology of Shinto. Also contains an extensive bibliography, and a useful glossary and index.

1659 Holton, Daniel C. Modern Japan and Shinto Nationalism; A Study of Present Day Trends in Japanese Religions, rev. ed. New York, Paragon Reprint, 1963 (1943). 226 p.

Presents state Shintoism as a formative power in the development of ultra-nationalism in Japan in the period before World War II. The study reflects a certain degree of wartime bias. Some bibliographic references are included.

1660 ______. National Faith of Japan: A Study in Modern Shinto. New York, Paragon Reprints, 1965 (1938). 329 p.

An older but still useful source of information on state Shinto, and Shinto sects. Also includes some bibliographic footnotes and an index.

1661 Kato, Genchi. A Study of Shinto, the Religion of the Japanese Nation. New York, Barnes & Noble, 1971 (1926). 250 p.

Presents a valuable scholarly study by an outstanding authority on Shintoism. The author supports the disputable "theory of evolution," and for this reason some caution must be advised. An extensive bibliography and an index are provided.

1662 Muraoka, Tsunetsugu. Studies in Shinto Thought. Transl. by D. M. Brown and J. T. Araoki. Chicago, Univ. of Chicago Press, 1964 (1947) (Philosophical Studies of Japan, v. 5). 264 p.

This collection is comprised of a series of eight papers, written between 1929-40, which are devoted to studies in Shinto ideas and practices. Some bibliographic references and an index are included.

1663 Ono, Motonari. Shinto, the Kami Way.... In collab. with W. P. Woodard. Rutland, Vt., Tuttle, 1964 (1960). 116 p.

Originally published under the title The Kami Way; An Introduction to Shrine Shinto. Presents a concise but reliable survey of the native religion of Japanese people.

1664 Ponsoby-Fane, Richard A. B. Studies in Shinto and Shrines; Papers Selected from the Works of R. A. B. Ponsoby-Fane, rev. ed. Kyoto, Ponsoby Memorial Society, 1956. (1942.)

1665 ______. The Vicissitudes of Shinto, with a Foreword by G. Kato. Kyoto, Ponsoby Memorial Society 1963 (1931). (Dr. R. Ponsoby Fane Series, v. 5).

Those two selections of papers, written by the eminent English "Japanophile," contain discussions of various aspects of Shinto beliefs and practices. Both volumes include indexes, but lack bibliographic references.

1666 Ross, Floyd H. Shinto; The Way of Japan. Boston, Beacon, 1965. 187 p.

This popular study for the beginner "presents the force of Shinto and the human mood, feelings, and the value-nuances which perpetuate it.... The reader visits a Shinto shrine; examines the basic myth of creation, and the Shinto conception of Kami (or deity); participates in festivals and rites ... and sees Shinto today..."--Publisher's note. Also includes an excellent brief list of books for further reading, a chronological table, and an index.

MODERN RELIGIOUS LIFE

NEW RELIGIONS

Bibliographies

1667 Christian Center for the Study of Japanese Religions. Bibliography on the New Religions. Comp. by H. Thomsen. Kyoto, 1960. 37 p.

"After the General Bibliography follows the main part of booklet: a bibliography of the most important new religions, one by one. Each paragraph is divided into two sections: sources in English, and sources in Japanese. In the case of English practically everything written in English (up to 1959) has been listed--in the case of Japanese only the works considered most important have been given"--Foreword.

1668 Earhart, H. B. The New Religions of Japan; A Bibliography of Western Language Materials. Tokyo, Sophia University, 1970 (Monumenta Niponnica Monograph). 96 p.

A comprehensive list of materials in English, French, and German. It covers both scholarly and popular studies, and voluminous literature issued by the "headquarters" of various sects.

Critical Studies

1669 McFarland, Horace N. The Rush Hour of the Gods; A Study of the New Religious Movements in Japan. New York, Macmillan, 1967. 267 p.

Contains a popularly presented survey of the new religions, with some bibliographic references in notes and an index.

1670 Offner, Clark B., and H. van Straelen. Modern Japanese Religions. New York, Twayne, 1963. 296 p.

Presents a popular survey of new religions, illustrated with photographs. Selected bibliography contains citations to monographs and periodical articles both in Western languages and in Japanese.

1671 Thomsen, Harry. The New Religions of Japan. Rutland, Vt., Tuttle, 1963. 269 p.
Provides a description of new religions and their sects. A brief classified bibliography lists both monographs and periodical articles.

RELIGIOUS LIFE

1672 Shukyo Mondai Kenkyujo. Religions of Japan at Present. Tokyo, 1958-64. 3 vols.
This extensive survey contains brief articles on various aspects of religious life in contemporary Japan.

See also nos. 1634-1640.

SOCIOLOGY OF JAPANESE RELIGION

1673 Morioka, Kiyomi and W. H. Newell, eds. The Sociology of Japanese Religion. Leiden, Brill, 1968 (International Studies in Sociology and Social Anthropology, 6). 145 p.
Contains a collection of papers presenting "the Japanese way of thinking." Includes also extensive bibliography, a general index, and an index of proper names.

JOURNALS

1674 Asiatic Society of Japan. Transactions. Yokohama, 1872- .
This publication, noted for its scholarship, often carries articles on various religious topics. Indexed: Bibliog. As. St.

1675 Japanese Journal of Religious Studies. Tokyo, 1974- (quarterly).
Formerly Contemporary Religions in Japan. Published for the International Institute for the Study of Religions. Gives a strong emphasis on scholarly presentation of religious perspectives, particularly Japanese Religion. Book reviews are included.

1676 Japanese Religions. Kyoto, 1959- (irregularly).
Published for the Center for the Study of Japanese Religions.

1677 <u>Monumenta Nipponica; Studies on Japanese Cultures, Past and Present</u>. Tokyo, 1938- (quarterly).
Contains outstanding scholarly articles and reliable signed book reviews. Indexed: Bibliog. As. St.

1678 <u>Tenri Journal of Religion</u>. Tenri, 1955- .
Published by the Oyasoto Research Institute at the Tenri University.

See also no. 1230-1251.

Part Four--Asian Religions (cont.)

VII EASTERN RELIGIONS IN THE WEST

1679 Bach, Marcus. Strangers at the Door. Nashville, Abingdon, 1971. 189 p.
A popular survey of new religious manifestations in North America. Contains an index, but lacks bibliographic references.

1680 Campbell, Anthony. The Mechanics of Enlightment; An Examination of the Teaching of Maharishi Mahesh Yogi. London, Gollancz, 1975. 223 p.
Attempts an explanation of various aspects of "a wave of interest in meditation." Bibliography and useful addresses are appended.

1681 Ellwood, Robert S. Religious and Spiritual Groups in Modern America. Englewood Cliffs, N.J., Prentice-Hall, 1973. 334 p.
Presents an informative survey of religious groups active at present in North America, from Abilitism to Zen. The descriptions of cults are illustrated by quotations from inspired sources. A brief select bibliography is provided.

1682 Evans, Christopher. Cults of Unreason. New York, Farrar, Straus, and Giroux, 1974. 258 p.
This interesting popular book deals with the upsurge of interest in Eastern mysticism, and other religious movements emerging from the counter-culture.

1683 Forem, Jack. Transcendental Meditation: Maharishi Mahesh Yogi and Science of Creative Intelligence. New York, Dutton, 1973. 274 p.
Presents a brief history of the movement with some selected references to further reading.

1684 French, Harold. The Swan's Wide Waters: Ramakrishna and Western Culture. New York, Kennikat Press, 1974.
This new critical study traces the origins and subsequent expansion in the West of the Ramakrishna movement,

based on the teachings of Vivekananda. It discusses the movement in relation to the total Indian religious tradition, and explores the complex patterns of cultural interaction created by its missionary activities in the West.

1685 Harper, Marvin H. Gurus, Swamis, and Avataras, Spiritual Masters and Their American Disciples. Philadelphia, Westminister, 1972. 271 p.
Provides a brief survey of Eastern cults, their historical background and teachings, in North America. Extensive bibliographic notes and an index are provided.

1686 Kory, Robert B. The Transcendental Meditation Program for Business People. New York, AMACOM, 1976.
The regional coordinator of the Transcendental Meditation program for New York discusses the values of TM for developing human potentials. Recommended additional readings supplied.

1687 Layman, E. M. Buddhism in America. Chicago, Nelson-Hall, 1976. 342 p.
Provides a psychological and sociological analysis of Buddhist groups in America. A glossary, selected bibliography, and an index are attached.

1688 Needleman, Jacob. The New Religions. Garden City, N.Y., Doubleday, 1970. 245 p.
In this treatise "new" means new to the North American continent. This interesting popular study gives information about Zen Buddhism, Meher Baba, Sufism, Krishnamurti, Transcendental Meditation, Tibetan Buddhism, Subud, Vedanta, and Humanistic Mysticism. Describes the teachings and practices, the nature of the organizations, and some accounts of the religious experience.

See also nos. 1460, 1463, 1468, 1469.

Part Five

NATIVE PEOPLES; MISCELLANEOUS

I GENERAL

DICTIONARIES

1689 Dictionary of Comparative Religion. Gen. ed.: S. G. F. Brandon. London, Weidenfeld & Nicolson, 1970. 704 p.
See no. 100. Provides brief informative articles with basic bibliographic references, e.g.: African, Aleutian, Altaic, Australian Aborigine, Bushman, Eskimo, Hawaiian, Melanesian, Polynesian, and Shamanism.

1690 Glasenapp, Helmuth von. Non-Christian Religions, A-Z. New York, Grosset & Dunlap, 1963 (1957). 278 p.
See no. 14. Consult the section, Primitive Tribal Religions, p. 192-206, and the Select Bibliography, p. 251-2. Also check brief articles on the Australian Aborigines, Oceanians, Indians of North America, Africans, and the primitive peoples of Asia.

1691 Larousse Encyclopedia of Mythology. London, Hamlyn, 1962 (1959). 500 p.
See no. 123. Presents informative articles on the myths of the two Americas, Oceania, and Africa. Consult the Select Bibliography, p. 494.

1692 Man, Myth, and Magic; An Illustrated Encyclopedia of the Supernatural. R. Cavendish, Ed. London, Purnell, 1970-71. 3152 p.
See no. 125.

1693 Parrinder, E. G. Dictionary of Non-Christian Religions. Amersham, England, Huton, 1971. 320 p.
See no. 18. Provides brief articles on a number of subjects pertaining to African, Australian, Polynesian and Melanesian religious beliefs. There is also a list of basic books for further reading.

1694 ________. Religions of the World, from Primitive Beliefs to Modern Faith. New York, Grosset & Dunlap, 1971. 440 p.

See no. 19. Contains informative and brief essays on the tribal religions in Asia, early Australasia, traditional Africa. Select elementary readings are at the end of articles.

1695 ________, et al. "Religions of Illiterate People." Bleeker, C. J. Historia religionum. Leiden, Brill, 1971. v. 2, p. 550-641.

See no. 38. An excellent survey comprised of articles by E. G. Parrinder on Africa; A. Class on North and Central Asia; J. R. Fox on North America; and T. G. H. Strehlow on Australia. Each article is supplied with a selective bibliography.

1696 "Religion of Primitive Peoples." McCasland, S. V., et al. Religions of the World. New York, Random House, 1969. p. 9-23, 26.

See no. 16. Presents a brief introductory essay, with a basic list for more extensive reading.

BIBLIOGRAPHIES, CATALOGS, ABSTRACTS

1697 Abstracts in Anthropology. Westport, Conn., 1970- (quarterly).

Abstracts are listed by geographical areas, e.g.: Mesoamerica, Africa, Oceania, etc. Subject index should be consulted under the name of a tribe, or religion.

1698 Harvard University. Peabody Museum of Archaeology and Ethnology. Library. Catalog: Authors, Subjects. Boston, G. K. Hall, 1963. 26 v.

This outstanding bibliography, covering some 50 years, includes periodical articles, papers from Festschriften, and proceedings of congresses, as well as monographs. The publication is up-dated by two supplements bringing the coverage up to 1971. One should consult the Index to Subject Headings under: Religion, and its subdivisions; names of tribes, or geographical areas.

1699 Human Relations Area Files. New Haven, Conn., HRAF, 1958- . A microfilm collection.

The files are comprised of collections of primary source materials, mainly published books and articles, as well as some unpublished manuscripts on selected cultures or societies representing all major areas of the world. Access to the files is through the two preliminary inventories: Outline of World Cultures, and Outline of Cultural Materials (1961), where one finds the codes for geographical areas, and information on various aspects of culture; topics dealing with religious life appear under the numbers 76-79.

1700 International Bibliography of Social and Cultural Anthropology.

London, Tavistock, 1956- (annually).
See no. 184. Religious topics are covered by Section F: Religion, Magic and Witchcraft. Of great help is the detailed subject index which should be checked for related topics, e.g.: Rites, Sacrifice; as well as the names of peoples, e.g. Dinka, Yoruba, etc.

1701 Long, C. H. "Primitive Religion." Adams, C. J. A Reader's Guide to Great Religions. 2nd ed. New York, Free Press, 1977 (1965), p. 1-38.
See no. 16. This informative introduction defines the subject and discusses fundamental terms such as animism, mana and taboo, animitism, totemism, etc. Also provides a list of basic bibliographic references.

1702 Ofori, Patrick E. Black African Traditional Religions and Philosophy: A Select Bibliographic Survey of the Sources from the Earliest Times to 1974. Nedein, Liechtenstein, Kraus-Tomson, 1975. 421 p.
An excellent list of some 2594 items which deal with beliefs and religious concepts, philosophy, psychology, cosmology, cult of ancestors, religious ceremonies and rites, divination, magic, sorcery, and medicine, myths, tabus, etc. An ethnical index and an author index are added. Lacks a subject index.

1703 "Prehistoric and Primitive Religion." International Bibliography of the History of Religions. Leiden, Brill, 1954- (annually).
See no. 27. Includes: Prehistoric Religion, Primitive Religion, Early European Religions. Lists monographs and journal articles.

1704 "Primitive Religions." Mitros, J. F. Religions: A Select Classified Bibliography. New York, Learned Publications, 1973. p. 97-106.
See no. 29. Provides a coverage of primitive religions in their geographical distribution.

CRITICAL STUDIES

1705 Eliade, Mircea. Shamanism: Archaic Techniques of Ecstasy, rev. and enl. ed. Transl. from the French by W. R. Trask. New York, Pantheon, 1964 (1951). 610 p.
"The book is the first to cover the entire phenomenon of shamanism, and at the same time to situate it in the general history of religion"--Foreword.

1706 La Barre, Weston. The Ghost Dance: Origins of Religion. New York, Doubleday, 1970. 677 p.
Presents a psychological and anthropological study of religion. It states that human religion is derived from

"the nature of human nature." Discusses first gods, ghost dances, cults, shamans, charisma and mana, sorcers, etc. Indexes of names and subjects are added. Also some bibliographic references are provided.

1707 Malinowski, Bronislaw. Magic, Science, and Religion, and Other Essays. New York, Doubleday, 1948 (Anchor Books, A23). 274 p.

Contains a selection of the renowned anthropologist's most famous essays on the primitive man and his religion, public and tribal character of primitive cults, magic and power of faith, myth in primitive psychology, etc. Neither an index nor bibliography is included.

1708 Mauss, Marcel. A General Theory of Magic. Transl. from the French by R. Brian. London, Routledge & Kegan Paul, 1972 (1950). 148 p.

Translation of Théorie de la magie. The famous French anthropologist presents an historical background of magic based on a careful analysis of all its elements, and then attempts to provide its definition. An index is included but the book lacks bibliographic citations.

1709 Wilson, Brayan R. Magic and the Millenium: A Sociological Study of Religious Movements of Protest Among Tribal and Third-World Peoples. New York, Harper & Row, 1973. 547 p.

This scholarly study analyzes new religious movements arising among less-developed peoples as a result of cultural contacts with the westerners. Some bibliographic references and an index are supplied.

JOURNALS

(Also consult lists of journals in Part One.)

1710 American Anthropologist. Menasha, Wisc., v. 1-11, 1889-1898; n.s. v. 1, 1899- (quarterly).

Supersedes: American Anthropological Society. Transactions. Publishes scholarly articles from all disciplines of anthropology. Also gives comprehensive review coverage to new publications of significance in the field. Indexed: Abstracts in Anthropology; Soc. Sci. Hum. Index; Anthropological Index to Current Periodicals.

1711 Anthropological Quarterly. Washington, D.C., 1953- .

Published by the Catholic University of America. Continues: Primitive Men, 1928-1952. Contains valuable research papers and book reviews.

1712 Anthropos; International Review of Ethnology and Linguistics. Salzburg, 1906- (3 issues a year).

Contains research papers in English, French, and German. Also provides an interesting survey of bibliographical news and includes reliable book reviews.

1713 Ethnos. Stockholm, 1936- (quarterly).
An official publication of the Ethnological Museum of Sweden. Carries scholarly articles, current research news, and book reviews.

1714 Man; The Journal of the Royal Anthropological Institute. London, 1901- (quarterly).
Brings highly valued research papers, current news in various disciplines of anthropology, and reliable book reviews.

Part Five--Native Peoples; Misc. (cont.)

II AFRICA

REFERENCE WORKS

ENCYCLOPEDIAS

1715 Balandier, G., and J. Maquet. Dictionary of Black African Civilization. Transl. by P. Neimark. New York, Amiel, 1974. 350 p.
Translation of Dictionaire des Civilisations africaines. Covers civilizations and black African societies in all their variety and individuality. Consult the entries: Religion, Ancestors, Divination, Divinities, Fetishes, Gods, Myths, Prayers, Sacrifice, etc.

1716 Standard Encyclopedia of Southern Africa. Capetown, NASOU, 1970. 10 v.
Main emphasis falls on South Africa. Included is also information on neighboring countries Congo, Kenya, Uganda, Tanzania, etc. Bibliographic references are supplied at end of articles.

BIBLIOGRAPHIES

1717 African Bibliographic Center. Special Bibliographic Series. New York, Negro Univ. Press, 1968- (annually).
Provides a current listing of materials on Africa. Of special interest is the section Religion.

1718 A Current Bibliography of African Affairs. Washington, D.C., African Bibliographic Center, v. 1-6, 1962-67; n.s. v. 1, 1968- (quarterly).
A comprehensive bibliography for African area studies arranged by subject, e.g., Culture, Religion, and also geographically by regions.

1719 Duignan, Peter, ed. Guide to Research and Reference Works on Sub-Saharan Africa. Stanford, Calif., Hoover Institution Press, 1971. 1102 p.

Aims to serve as a starting reference bibliography for the entire field of African studies covering Africa south of the Sahara. For religious subjects consult the index under Religion.

1720 International African Bibliography; Bibliographie Internationale Africaine. London, International African Institute, 1971- (monthly with annual cumulations).
Continues an annual bibliography previously appearing in Africa. Selects all useful materials which fall within the field of African studies. Of special interest is the section: Religion, Philosophy. See no. 1783.

1721 London. University. School of Oriental and African Studies. Library. Catalogue: Authors, Titles, Subjects. Boston, G. K. Hall, 1963. 28 v. and suppls.
Lists holdings of highly specialized collections of some half a million items dealing with languages, literatures, history, religious beliefs, law, anthropology and ethnology of the area. Coverage is up to 1972.

1722 Mitchell, Robert C., et al. A Comprehensive Bibliography of Modern African Religious Movements. Evanston, Ill., Northwestern Univ. Press, 1966. 132 p.
This valuable bibliography was brought up-to-date in: Journal of Religion in Africa, v. 1:3-3. Covers the literature on non-Islamic modern African religious movements in any language. Also includes journals and dissertations. Annotations indicate the main contents, special context, views on methodology.

1723 Schapera, Isaac, ed. Select Bibliography of South African Native Life and Problems. London, Oxford Univ. Press, 1941. 249 p. Suppl. 1950.
Provides a list of more important monographs, periodical articles, and reports, with brief annotations. Coverage is up to 1948. Also contains an author index.

1724 Zaretsky, Irving I. Bibliography on Spirit Possession and Spirit Mediumship. Berkeley, Univ. of California, Dept. of Anthropology, 1966, 106 p.
"This bibliography is a preliminary attempt to centralize the listings of ethnographic sources containing information about spirit possession or spirit mediumship on the African continent ... primarily sub-Saharan Africa..."--Introd. An ethnic group index, and an authors' list are included.

CRITICAL STUDIES

HISTORICAL BACKGROUND

1725 The Cambridge History of Africa. Cambridge, England,

Univ. Press, 1974- .
Attempts a presentation of an integrated history of the entire continent, from prehistoric to post-colonial times. Extensive bibliographic references, and a very detailed index are included.

1726 Davidson, Basil. The Africans; An Entry to Cultural History. London, Longmans, 1969. 367 p.
This informative book provides a summary of what is now known about the ideas and social systems, religious and moral values, magical beliefs, arts, and metaphysics of African peoples, mainly from tropical Africa. Of special interest in Pt. 3, Structures of Belief. Useful bibliographic notes, as well as a select bibliography add to the value of the book. An index is provided.

1727 Gibbs, James L., Jr. Peoples of Africa. New York, Holt, Rinehart and Winston, 1965. 594 p.
Describes 15 selected tribal groups from sub-Saharan Africa. Each section contains a chapter discussing religious beliefs and practices of the tribe. At the end of chapters very useful lists for further readings are supplied. For religious subjects consult also a well-designed index.

1728 A Horizon History of Africa, by A. Adu Boahen, et al. New York, American Heritage Pub., 1971. 528 p.
This popular book is comprised of very readable surveys by some of the best known scholars in the field. Each chapter is accompanied by a selection of original historical writings in English translation.

1729 July, Robert W. A History of the African People. New York, Scribner's, 1974 (1970). 731 p.
Presents a sound and comprehensive survey. "Each chapter has been provided with a list of readings particularly relevant to the materials in that chapter"--Biblio. Note. At the end, one also finds a listing of most relevant studies pertaining to Africa. An index is included.

1730 Murphy, E. J. History of African Civilization. Foreword by H. R. Lynch. New York, Crowell, 1972. 430 p.
Surveys major civilizations in various parts of Africa --their religious life, social customs, as well as economic and political institutions, from ancient Egypt to the Bantu States of southern Africa. Also contains a useful bibliography and an index.

1731 Oliver, Roland A., and J. D. Fage. A Short History of Africa, 3rd ed. Harmondsworth, England, Penguin, 1970 (1962) (Penguin African Library). 284 p.
This book has been acclaimed as the best introductory reading for both the student, and layman. It stresses

influence of the Islamic culture brought by the Arabs in northern and western Africa. A select bibliography and an index are provided.

STUDIES IN RELIGIOUS BELIEFS

1732 Ashton, Hugh. The Basuto: A Study of Traditional and Modern Lesotho, 2nd ed. London, Published for the International African Institute by Oxford Univ. Press, 1967 (1952). 359 p.
Describes the daily life of the Basuto people based on the author's field work. Deals with their historical and social background, social activities, as well as magic, medicine and sorcery. Also includes a select bibliography and an index.

1733 Barrett, David B. Schism and Renewal in Africa: An Analysis of Six Thousand Contemporary Religious Movements. Nairobi, Oxford Univ. Press, 1968. 363 p.
Provides an interesting examination of religious life in contemporary Africa. Also includes an author index, index of tribes and nations, index of movements, bodies and prophets, subject index, and a glossary of French terms. Some bibliographic citations are included.

1734 Bascom, William. Ifa Divination; Communications Between Gods and Men in West Africa. Bloomington, Indiana Univ. Press, 1969. 575 p.
This scholarly study describes one of the most respected systems of divination known among five million Yorubas in Nigeria, and many more in neighboring countries, as well as in the New World. A list of bibliographic references is cited. Lacks an index.

1735 Bitek, Okot p'. African Religions in Western Scholarship. Kampala, East African Literature Bureau, 1970. 139 p.
Presents a survey of the studies in African religious life by Western scholars, from the Classical times to the present day. A brief list of bibliographic references is added, but lacks an index.

1736 Burton, W. F. P. Luba Religion and Magic in Customs and Beliefs. Tervuren, Knk. Museum voor Midden-Afrika, 1961 (1939) (Annalen). 193 p.
Provides a scholarly study of the Luba culture which deals with the customs of death and the election of a new chief, worship of the dead "Bafu," spirits, use of charms, sorcery, secret societies, etc. A detailed index is added but there are no bibliographic references.

1737 Buxton, Jean. Religion and Healing in Mandari. Oxford, England, Clarendon Press, 1973. 443 p.

This scholarly study contains a discussion of cosmology and cults, personal identity, medico-religious practice, ritual and community, visual and sensory perception, etc. Also includes a bibliography and index.

1738 Colldén, Lisa. The Traditional Religion of the Sakota. Uppsala, Institutet för allmän och Jämnförande Etnografi, 1971. 173 p.
Provides a methodological survey of religious beliefs accompanied by proverbs, riddles, songs, legends and fables. Has an excellent bibliography but lacks an index.

1739 Daneel, M. L. The Gods of the Matopo Hills: An Essay on the Mwari Cult in Rhodesia. The Hague, Mouton, 1970. 95 p.
Describes the beliefs and ritual in the historical development and the existence of the Mwari Cult in the contemporary setting. Gives some bibliographic references, but lacks an index.

1740 Danquah, J. B. The Akan Doctrine of God: A Fragment of Gold Coast Religion, 2nd ed. with a New Introd. by K. A. Dickson. London, Cass, 1968. 206 p.
Contains a discussion of the doctrine, meaning of god, ethical canons. Some bibliographic references are given in footnotes. Also a glossary of Akan words is provided. Lacks an index.

1741 Downes, R. M. Tiv Religion, with a Foreword by J. W. Robertson. Ibadan, Univ. Press, 1971. 102 p.
Provides interesting observations of the religious beliefs and rituals among the Tiv people. Some bibliographic references and an index are provided.

1742 Evans-Pritchard, E. E. Nuer Religion. Oxford, Clarendon Press, 1956. 335 p.
An account of religious ideas and practices based on personal observations of the author. Bibliographic references are limited to a few citations. An index is included.

1743 Fabian, Johannes. Jamaa: A Charismatic Movement in Katanga. Evanston, Ill., Northwestern Univ. Press, 1971. 284 p.
Presents a summary of the author's observations of this new religious movement and its leaders. Also describes its basic doctrines and practices. Select bibliography and an index are supplied.

1744 Forde, Cyril D., ed. African World; Studies in the Cosmological Ideas and Social Values of African People. London, Pub. for the International African Institute, by the Oxford Univ. Press, 1968. 243 p.
Contains a collection of papers dealing with a variety

of religious ideas from Africa, presented from the sociological point of view. Some bibliographical references and an index are added.

1745 Gelfand, Michael. Shona Religion, with Special Reference to the Makorekore. Capetown, Juta, 1962. 184 p.
An interesting study by a physician who describes the religious beliefs and practices of the Shona people from Rhodesia. It takes into consideration tribal spirits, family guardian spirits, death, marriage, etc. Also includes bibliographic references in footnotes and an index.

1746 Goody, Jack. The Myth of the Bagre. Oxford, Clarendon, 1972. 381 p.
Pt. 1 provides an informative introduction dealing with the Lodagaa and their intellectual climate, religious actions, shrines, associations, etc. Pt. 2 is comprised of English translations of the myths. Some bibliographic notes are given within the text. An index to the introduction is supplied.

1747 Harris, W. T., and H. Sawyerr. The Springs of Mende Belief and Conduct: A Discussion of the Influence of the Belief in the Supernatural Among the Mende. Freetown, Sierra Leone Univ. Press, 1968. 152 p.
Deals with the beliefs of the Mende People from West Africa, their supreme god, ancestral spirits, nature divinities, medicine man, and other supernatural agencies. Bibliographic information is included in the notes. Also contains an index.

1748 Herskovits, M. J., and F. S. Herskovits. An Outline of Dahomean Religious Beliefs. New York, Kraus Reprint, 1964 (1933) (American Anthropological Association. Memoires, no. 41). 77 p.
Deals with general concepts underlying Dahomean religious beliefs: great gods, ancestral cults, cult practices, personal spirits and powers, as well as magic. Some bibliographic references, and a glossary are included.

1749 Historical Study of African Religion. Ed. by T. O. Ranger and I. N. Kimambo. Berkeley, Calif., African Studies Center, 1972. 307 p.
This collection is comprised of papers dealing with methods used in the reconstruction of early religious history. Subjects range from a discussion of kinship, to the interaction between African religion and Christianity in the 20th century. Contains bibliographical references at the end of each paper, a general index, and an index of themes.

1750 Horton, Robin. The Gods as Guests: An Aspect of Kalabari

Religious Life. Lagos, Federal Gov. Printer, 1960 (Nigeria Magazine Special Publications). 71 p.
A popular presentation of Kalabari beliefs and practices with numerous illustrations. Lacks bibliographic references and an index.

1751 Idowu, E. B. African Traditional Religion: A Definition. New York, Orbis Books, 1973. 228 p.
Consists of informative discussions on the study of religion in general and especially of African traditional religion, its nature, structure and prospects. Also contains a useful select bibliography and an index.

1752 ________. Olódùmarè: God in Yoruba Beliefs. London, Longmans, 1962. 221 p.
Contains a study "of the beliefs of the Yoruba with the specific aim of emphasizing their concept of the deity"--Preface. Indexes of subjects and names, as well as some bibliographic footnotes are included.

1753 International African Seminar, 3rd, Salisbury, 1960. African Systems of Thought. London, Oxford Univ. Press, 1960.
Consists of a collection of 21 papers on indigenous religious systems, ritual and symbolism, ancestor worship, witchcraft and sorcery, Islam, Christianity, and "Systèmes de connaissance." Bibliographic notes and an index are provided.

1754 Jahn, J. Muntu: An Outline of Neo-African Culture. Transl. by M. Grene. London, Faber and Faber, 1961. 267 p.
"The book is ... the first attempt to sketch neo-African culture as an independent culture of equal value with other cultures..."--Chapter 1. Also includes a bibliography of monographs, journal and newspaper articles, and indexes of names and subjects.

1755 Junod, H. A. The Life of a South African Tribe. New Hyde Park, N.Y., University Books, 1962 (1927). 2 v.
Pt. 1: Social Life; Pt. 2: Mental Life. Presents a detailed study based on personal observations. Consult detailed table of contents. Index and a glossary are added.

1756 King, Noel Q. Religions of Africa: A Pilgrimage into Traditional Religions. New York, Harper & Row, 1970. 116 p.
Provides an excellent brief account of traditional African religions, myths and legends, observation of rituals, kings and prophets, medicine men and earth priests. Also includes an excellent classified bibliography of the most important studies in the field, a brief list of

periodicals, a glossary, and an index.

1757 Knappert, Jan. Myths and Legends of the Swahili. Nairobi, Heinemann Educational Books, 1970 (African Writers Series, no. 75). 212 p.

Contains a collection of stories on the creation, prophets, miracles of Muhammad, mysterious destinies, spirits and sorcerers, etc.

1758 Lienhardt, Godfrey. Divinity and Experience: The Religion of Dinka. Oxford, Clarendon Press, 1961. 328 p.

This interesting survey based upon two years' work among the Dinka people. Some bibliographic references are included in footnotes. An index.

1759 Lukas, J. O. The Religion of the Yorubas; Being an Account of the Religious Beliefs and Practices of Yoruba Peoples of Southern Nigeria, Especially in Relation to the Religion of Ancient Egypt. Lagos, C. M. S. Bookshop, 1948. 420 p.

Presents a scholarly survey dealing with the supreme deity, deified spirits of the ancestors and other spirits, priesthood and worship, magic, etc. A select bibliography and a list of periodicals is included.

1760 Mbiti, John S. African Religions and Philosophy. London, Heinemann, 1969. 290 p.

This scholarly study, written by an African, brings new insight into the understanding of African beliefs. Contains a discussion of god and nature, worship, ethnic groups, kingships, and the individual, etc. Also includes a select bibliography, and separate indexes for authors and subjects.

1761 ________. Introduction to African Religion. London, Heinemann, 1975. 211 p.

This excellent textbook, by the outstanding African scholar, aims at the readers "who do not know anything or much about African Religion"--Preface. It discusses the African heritage, views of the universe, belief in god, spirits, birth, marriage, death, rituals and festivals, religious objects and places, leaders, morals, etc. A list for advanced reading and an index are included. Of great interest also is the author's selection of 300 prayers: The Prayers of African Religion (London, S. P. C. K., 1975, 193 p.).

1762 Meyerowitz, Eva L. R. The Akan of Ghana: Their Ancient Beliefs. London, Faber & Faber, 1958. 164 p.

Presents a brief but informative survey of religious beliefs and practices among the Akan people. Provides some select bibliographic references in footnotes and an index. Also consult the author's: The Sacred State of the Akan and Akan Traditions of Origin (1952).

1763 Middleton, John. Lugbara Religion; Ritual and Authority Among an East African People. London, Pub. for the International African Institute by Oxford Univ. Press, 1960. 276 p.
Presents a sociological analysis of religious beliefs and practices in the daily life of the Lugbara. Some bibliographic references are given in footnotes; an index is added.

1764 Millroth, Berta. Lyuba: Traditional Religion of the Sukuma. Uppsala, Almquist, 1965 (Studia Etnographica Upsaliensia, 22). 217 p.
This scholarly survey of religious ideas and practices deals with the names of god, the cults, sacrifices and offering, secret societies, as well as myths and traditions. Includes a select bibliography of more important studies on the Lyuba. Lacks a subject index.

1765 Nadel, Siegfried. Nupe Religion. London, Routledge & Paul, 1954. 288 p.
An interesting study of the religious life among the Nupe people in East Africa which discusses the creeds, divination, rituals, medicine, witchcraft, etc. Some bibliographic references in footnotes and an index are supplied.

1766 Parrinder, Edward G. African Mythology. London, Hamlyn, 1967. 139 p.
A brief popular presentation with some bibliographic references for further reading and an index, abundantly illustrated.

1767 ________. African Traditional Religions, 3rd ed. London, S.P.C.K., 1962 (1954). 156 p.
A standard work for study of the religious life of the Africans, presented in its third thoroughly revised version. Subjects discussed range from a description of traditional beliefs and practices to modern religious movements. Also includes a brief bibliography and an index.

1768 ________. Religion in Africa. London, Pall Mall; New York, Praeger, 1969. 253 p.
Contains a discussion of traditional religions, Christianity, and Islam. Some bibliographic references and an index are provided.

1769 ________. West African Religion: A Study of the Beliefs and Practices of Akan, Ewe, Yoruba, Ibo, and Kindred, 2nd ed. London, Epworth Press, 1961 (1949). 203 p.
Provides an informative study of various aspects of

religious life in West Africa. It deals with the supreme god, temple and worship, priests and devotees, personal religious rites, charms and magic, totems and taboos, etc. A select bibliography and an index are provided.

1770 Ray, Benjamin. African Religions: Symbol, Ritual, and Community. Englewood Cliffs, N.J., Prentice-Hall, 1976 (Prentice-Hall Studies in Religion Series). 238 p.
Provides a survey of different approaches to the study of African Religion. It deals with the myth and history, divinity and man, ritual expression and control, religious authorities, etc. A select bibliography and an index are added.

1771 Reynolds, Barrie. Magic, Divination and Witchcraft Among the Barotse of Northern Rhodesia. Berkeley, Univ. of Calif. Press, 1963. 181 p.
"This report is based on ... information and material collected during witchcraft investigations.... The object of this study is the description of the witchcraft and allied practices and beliefs..."--Preface. A select bibliography comprising monographs and periodical articles and an index are included.

1772 Schapera, Isaac. The Bantu Speaking Tribes of South Africa: An Ethnographical Survey. Ed. for the South African Inter-University Committee for African Studies. London, Routledge & Kegan Paul, 1959. 453 p.
A standard work on the tribes of South Africa which contains some scholarly accounts of religious life and practices. Bibliographic references are given in footnotes and in a select bibliography. An index is lacking.

1773 Smith, Edwin W., ed. African Ideas of God; A Symposium, 2nd rev. ed. by E. G. Parrinder. London, Edinburgh House Press, 1961. 308 p.
Provides an exposition of the religious ideas and practices among the Africans. A selective bibliography and a general index are added.

1774 Swantz, M. L. Ritual and Symbol in Transitional Zaramo Society, with Special Reference to Women. Uppsala, Gleerup, 1970 (Studia Missionalia Upsaliensia). 430 p.
A scholarly sociological study which deals with the social organization, religious and cultural identification, ritual in transition, spirit concepts and practices, myth and symbol, etc. Also contains a glossary of terms, select bibliography of monographs and periodical articles, and an index.

1775 Talbot, P. A. Some Nigerian Fertility Cults. London, Cass, 1967 (1927). 140 p.
A study devoted to some aspects of Ibo and Ijaw

religious beliefs and practices. There is an index but the book lacks a bibliographic guide.

1776 Turnbull, Colin. The Forest People: A Study of the Pygmies of the Congo. New York, Simon & Schuster, 1962 (1961). 295 p.

This is an account of the daily life of the Pygmies based on the personal observation of the author. A glossary and an index are provided. Lacks bibliographic information.

1777 ________. The Mountain People. New York, Simon & Schuster, 1972. 309 p.

Presented in popular style, this picture of the daily life of the Ik people describes also their religious beliefs, ceremonies and rituals. A glossary and an index are added. Lacks any leads for further reading.

1778 Turner, V. W. The Drums of Affliction: A Study of Religious Processes Among the Ndembu of Zambia. Oxford, Clarendon Press, 1968. 326 p.

This is a sociological study of divination and its symbolism, and the morphology of rituals and affliction. A select bibliography and an index are provided.

1779 Wilson, Monica. Religion and the Transformation of the Society; A Social Change in Africa. Cambridge, Univ. Press, 1971 (Scott Holland Memorial Lectures, 15). 165 p.

An outstanding study, with very useful bibliographic references.

AFRICAN CULTS IN THE AMERICAS

1780 Bastide, Roger. African Civilizations in the New World. Transl. from the French by P. Green, with a Foreword by E. G. Parrinder. New York, Harper & Row, 1971 (1967) (Torchbook). 232 p.

Translation of Les Amériques noires. Provides an expert's survey of all African cults which survive in the Americas under a variety of disguises. Bibliographic references and an index are provided.

1781 Williams, E. L., and C. F. Brown, eds. Afro-American Religious Studies: A Comprehensive Bibliography with Locations in American Libraries. Metuchen, N.J., Scarecrow Press, 1972. 454 p.

Entries are arranged topically under five general headings: I. African Heritage; II. Christianity and slavery in the new world; III. The American negro and the American religious life; IV. The civil rights movement; V. The contemporary religious scene. Index.

JOURNALS

PERIODICAL LIST/INDEX

1782 Liste mondiale des périodiques specialisés: Etudes africaines; World List of Specialized Periodicals: African Studies. Established with the Collab. of the CARDAN (Centre d'Analyze et de Recherche Documentaire pour l'Afrique Noire). Paris, Mouton, 1969. 214 p.
This extensive listing is arranged by country of publication, e.g.: France, Italy etc. Also contains an index of subjects, geographical names, institutions and titles.

THE JOURNALS

1783 Africa: Journal of the International African Institute; Journal de l'Institut Internationale africain. London, 1928- .
Includes informative research papers, notes, and current news, as well as reliable book reviews. From 1929-70, it carried an annual bibliography now issued separately as International African Bibliography (see no. 1720).

1784 African Affairs; Journal of the Royal African Society. Oxford, England, 1901- .
One of the best journals in the field. Carries excellent research articles, and short notes on new developments. Also is known for reliable book reviews. Periodically issues subject bibliographies.

1785 African Religious History. Los Angeles, 1971- .
Published by the African Studies Center, Univ. of Calif., Los Angeles. Covers east, central and south Africa; excludes studies on West Africa.

1786 African Studies. Johannesburg, 1942- .
Published at the Witwatersrand Univ., South Africa. Continues: Bantu Studies, 15 vo., 1921-41.

1787 African Studies Review. 1970- (3 issues a year).
Issued by the Institute of International Studies, Univ. of Calif., Berkeley; and the Hoover Institution, Stanford Univ. Continues: African Studies Bulletin, 1958-69.

1788 Africana Library Journal; A Quarterly Bibliography and Resources Guide. New York, 1970- .
Carries bibliographic articles, reports on research and teaching resources, book reviews, and a comprehensive current bibliography. Covers all areas related to African studies.

1789 Canadian Journal of African Studies; Le Journal canadien des études africaines. Montréal, 1967- .

Published for the Committee on African Studies in Canada. Materials are in English or French.

1790 Génève-Afrique; Geneva-Africa; Acta africana. Geneva, 1971- .

Published for the Institut Africain de Genève. Articles are in English or French.

1791 International Journal of African Historical Studies. Brookline, Mass., 1972- (quarterly).

Continues: African Historical Studies, 1968-71.

1792 Journal of African History. London, 1960- (semiannually).

Contains scholarly articles, reliable book reviews and short bibliographic notices of new materials.

1793 Journal of Religion in Africa; Religion en Afrique. Leiden, Brill, 1968- (3 issues a year).

Text of publications is either English or French. Contains excellent research papers, survey bibliographies of selected subjects, and dependable book reviews.

III THE AMERICAS

NORTH AMERICA

REFERENCE WORKS

ENCYCLOPEDIAS

1794 Encyclopedia of Indians of the Americas. St. Claire Shores, Mich., 1974- .

Vol. 1 contains the conspectus articles. Of special interest is the chapter, Religion and Philosophy, p. 165. Comprehensive coverage of the field is to be found within the main alphabetical part of the reference work.

1795 Reference Encyclopedia of the American Indian. B. T. Klein, ed., with an Introd. by R. C. B. Morton. New York, Todd, 1973- (1967-).

Provides "the most thorough compilation of related source materials on the North American Indian. These information sources are arranged either alphabetically or geographically..."--Preface. Also contains two bibliographic listings: alphabetical and by subject.

BIBLIOGRAPHIES AND INDEXES

1796 Arctic Bibliography, Prepared for and with Cooperation with the Department of Defense under the Direction of the Arctic Institute of America. Washington, D.C., Dept. of Defense, 1953- (annually).

Provides a fundamental reference tool to the existing knowledge of the Arctic. It consists of two parts: 1. an alphabetical listing by author, with full bibliographic descriptions and annotations, or abstracts; 2. a comprehensive subject-geographical index. For religious materials, consult the index under: Religion, or other related subjects.

1797 Index to the Literature of the American Indian. San Francisco, Indian Historical Press, 1970- (annually).
Provides a comprehensive coverage of materials pertinent to American Indian studies. Includes an index by author and subject. Of special interest are the topics, Ceremony, Dance, Folklore, Religion, as well as the names of tribes, or broader terms, e.g., Plains Indians.

1798 Marken, Jack W. The Indians and Eskimos of North America; A Bibliography of Books Printed Through 1972. Vermillion, S.D., Dakota Press, 1973. 200 p.
Consists of references to books and some non-printed materials. One should consult the select subject index.

1799 Murdock, George P., and T. J. O'Leary. Ethnographic Bibliography of North America, 4th ed. New Haven, Conn., Human Relations Area Files, 1975 (Behavior Science Bibliographies). 5 vols.
One of the best reference tools for North American Indian studies. Contains a selective classified bibliography, arranged by areas and then within by tribal groups.

1800 Smith, Dwight L. Indians of the United States and Canada; A Bibliography. Santa Barbara, Calif., CLIO, 1974 (Clio Bibliography Series). 453 p.
International in coverage, this bibliography lists 1687 periodical articles published between 1954 and 1972. Consult the index under Religion and Ceremony.

CRITICAL STUDIES

INDIAN BELIEFS

1801 Alexander, H. B. The World's Rim: Great Mysteries of the North American Indians. Lincoln, Univ. of Nebraska Press, 1953. 259 p.
"...Provides an accurate and sympathetic insight into the life and mind of the North American Indians as expressed through the symbolism of their art and ritual..." --Cover. A detailed subject index is included. Bibliographic references are in Notes.

1802 Boas, Franz. The Religion of the Kwakiutl Indians. New York, Columbia Univ. Press, 1930 (Columbia University Contributions to Anthropology, v. 10). 2 v.
See also the author's: Kwakiutl Culture as Reflected in Mythology (1935); and Kwakiutl Culture (1935).

1803 Goldman, Irving. The Mouth of Heaven. New York, Wiley, 1975. 265 p.
Provides an interpretation of religious myths and

ritual. The first several chapters seek out the religious foundations of lineage, rank, and marriage. The following two chapters deal specifically with the winter ceremonial and its ritual exchange of wealth. A select bibliography and an index are provided.

1804 Hultkrantz, Åke. Conceptions of the Soul Among North American Indians. Stockholm, Statens Etnografiska Museum, 1953 (Monograph Series, no. 1). 544 p.

A scholarly study which investigates the Indians' eschatological conceptions and their associated beliefs. It discusses the basic soul dualism, secondary soul systems, phenomenology, life-cycle of the soul, etc. Numerous bibliographic references are given in footnotes. A very useful index is supplied.

1805 _______. The North American Indian Orpheus Tradition: A Contribution to Comparative Religion. Stockholm, Statens Etnografiska Museum, 1957. 339 p.

Presents a scholarly discussion on the North American Indians' conceptions of the realm of the dead. Also it deals with the Orpheus motif's distribution, its elements, and its origin and history. Includes a select bibliography of books and periodical articles, and an index.

1806 _______. "North American Indian Religion in the History of Research." History of Religions, v. 6:2, p. 91-107; v. 6:3, p. 183-207; v. 7:1, p. 13-34, p. 112-48.

Concentrates mainly on European and American research. Bibliographic references are included in the text and footnotes.

1807 Hurdy, John M. American Indian Religion. Los Angeles, Sherbourne Press, 1970. 192 p.

Contains an excellent introductory text with a strong emphasis on mysticism, and the development of supernatural talents. Of special interest are accounts on the ghost dance, Peyote cults, and the snake dance. A list of sources and a select bibliography are included, but lacks an index.

1808 LaBarre, Weston. The Peyote Cult; with a New Preface. Enl. ed. New York, Schocken Books, 1969 (1938). 260 p.

Consists of excellent scholarly studies on Peyote religious ideas and practices, as well as their mythology. Some bibliographic references are included.

1809 Lowie, Robert H. "The Religion of the Crow Indians." American Museum of Natural History. Anthropological Papers, v. 25:2 (1922), p. 313-451.

Provides a summary of research on religious beliefs and practices of the Crow Indians' culture. It deals with supernatural beings, visions and dreams, shamans, medicine men, magic, offerings, and prayers. A detailed index is added. Also recommended is the author's: "Myth Traditions of the Crow Indians" in the same issue, p. 1-308.

1810 Park, Willard Z. Shamanism in Western North America. Evanston, Northwestern Univ. Press, 1938 (Northwestern University Study in the Social Sciences, no. 2). 166 p.
An older but still useful survey, with some bibliographic references.

1811 Radin, Paul. The Trickster: A Study in American Indian Mythology. With commentaries by K. Kerényi and C. G. Jung. New York, Philosophical Library, 1956. 211 p.
Presents a thorough study of the Trickster myth found among the Winnebago Indians. Also analyzes the Hare myth in full, and fragmentarily with the Assiniboine and Tlingit versions. Includes some bibliographic references in footnotes. An index is lacking.

1812 Reichard, Gladys. Navaho Religion: A Study of Symbolism, 2nd ed. New York, Bollingen Foundation, 1970 (Bollingen series, 18). 804 p.
An excellent anthropological study which discusses dogma, symbolism, and ritual. Also includes three special concordances: a. Supernatural Beings; b. Ritualistic Ideas; c. Rites. A select bibliography and an index are provided.

1813 Slotkin, James S. The Peyote Religion: A Study in Indian-White Relations. Glencoe, Ill., Free Press, 1956. 195 p.
The most comprehensive account of the cult ever attempted, written by a professional anthropologist who joined the cult and was elected an official to the cult. Highly recommended.

1814 Spence, Lewis. The Myths of the North American Indians. London, Harrap, 1914. 392 p.
A collection of myths which is accompanied by still useful historical and ethnological information. Contains myths of the Algonquins, Iroquois, Sioux, Pawnees, and northern and northwestern Indians. There is a bibliography and a combined glossary and index.

1815 Starkloff, Carl F. The People of the Center: American Indian Religion and Christianity. New York, Seabury, 1974 (Crossroad Books). 144 p.
"The data of this book are both documentary and personal." Deals with doctrines and myths, rituals, ethical and social aspects, etc. Some bibliographic sources are listed in bibliography. Lacks an index.

1816 Thompson, Stith. Tales of the North American Indians. Bloomington, Indiana, Univ. Press, 1966 (1929). 386 p.

Explores folklore and legends of North American Indians.

1817 Underhill, Ruth M. Red Men's Religion; Beliefs and Practices of Indians North of Mexico. Chicago, Univ. of Chicago Press, 1965. 302 p.

A comprehensive study which includes discussions of the supernatural, attitudes towards the dead, the role of shaman, ceremonies, hunting and gathering rituals, as well as some modern religious developments. Each chapter contains special bibliographic references. Also includes an extensive general bibliography, and an index with numerous cross-references.

1818 Wissler, Clark. "Ceremonial Bundles of the Blackfoot Indians." American Museum of Natural History. Anthropological Papers, v. 7:2 (1912), p. 65-289.

Contains a detailed study of ceremonials which are called medicine bundles. Describes medicinemen's experiences, origin of the ritual, and ceremonial features. Some bibliographic references are added.

1819 ______. "The Sun Dance of the Plain Indians; Its Development and Diffusion." American Museum of Natural History. Anthropological Papers, v. 16:7 (1921). 548 p.

Presents an extensive report of investigations of the many existing rites of the Sun Dance. A select bibliography and an index are provided.

ESKIMO-ALEUT (INUIT) BELIEFS

1820 Jochelson, Vladimir I. History, Ethnology, and Anthropology of the Aleut. Oosterhout N. B., Anthropological Pubs., 1968 (1933) (Carnegie Institution of Washington. Pub. no. 432). 91 p.

Of special interest is Chapter VI.: Mythology of the Aleut. Some bibliographic references are supplied. Become acquainted also with the author's: Archaeological Investigations in the Aleutian Islands (1925).

1821 Marsh, Gordon H. "A Comparative Survey of Eskimo-Aleut Religion." Alaska. University. Anthropological Papers, v. 3 (1954), p. 21-36.

Provides an informative survey of the field, with extensive bibliographic documentation.

SOUTH AMERICA

[For material on the ancient religions of South and Central America see nos. 377-388.]

HANDBOOK

1822 Steward, Julius H. Handbook of South American Indians. Washington, D. C., U.S. Govt. Print. Office, 1946-50 (U.S. Bureau of American Ethnology. Bulletin, 143). 7 vols.

Presents a comprehensive survey with extensive bibliographical data. The beginner should consult first vol. 7, Index, under Religion and other related topics; e. g.: God, Deities, Shaman, Shamanism, etc.

BIBLIOGRAPHY

1823 O'Leary, Timothy J. Ethnographic Bibliography of South America. New Haven, Conn., Human Relations Area Files, 1963 (Behavior Sciences Bibliographies). 387 p.

Includes monographs, periodical articles, governmental reports, etc. Arranged by geographical area, and then by tribes.

CRITICAL STUDY

1824 Lyon, Patricia J., ed. Native South Americans: Ethnology of the Least Known Continent. Boston, Little, Brown, 1974. 433 p.

Presents a collection of informative studies, by a group of specialists, concentrating on those areas of South America which still encompass functioning native Indian cultures. Especially interesting in Chapter IV, Relationship with the Supernatural, p. 235-321. Also includes A Guide to the Bibliography of South American Ethnology, dealing with old and new literature. Lacks an index, but the detailed table of contents may be of great help in locating information in the text.

CARIBBEANS

1825 Deren, Maya. Divine Horsemen: The Living Gods of Haiti. London, Thames and Hudson, 1953. 350 p.

The author, one of the pioneers of American avant-garde cinema, attempts a comprehensive survey based on firsthand observation. Deals with the trinity, "Les serviteurs," divine horsemen, rites, drums, and dance, etc. Also includes a glossary, selected bibliographic references and an index.

1826 Métraux, Alfred. Voodoo in Haiti. Transl. by H. Charteris. New York, Oxford Univ. Press, 1959. 400 p.
This excellent scholarly survey deals with the history of voodoo, the supernatural world, ritual, magic and sorcery, as well as voodoo and Christianity. Also contains the voodoo glossary, select bibliography, and a detailed index.

1827 Simpson, George E. Religious Cults of the Caribbean: Trinidad, Jamaica, and Haiti, rev. ed. Rio Piedras, Puerto Rico, Institute of Carribbean Studies, Univ. of Puerto Rico, 1970 (Caribbean Monograph Series, 7). 308 p.
An outstanding Afro-Americanist provides an excellent scholarly description and analysis of Afro-American religious cult practices and behaviors. Also contains a well-selected bibliography for broader study, and an index.

Part Five: Native Peoples; Misc. (cont.)

IV AUSTRALIA AND NEW ZEALAND

AUSTRALIA

REFERENCE WORKS

ENCYCLOPEDIA

1828 The Australian Encyclopedia. E. Lansing, Mich., Michigan State Univ. Press, 1958. 10 vols.
Provides a comprehensive source of information on the history on Australia. Especially important is the article Aborigines, v. 1, p. 3-99, with an extensive bibliography.

BIBLIOGRAPHIES

1829 Australian Institute of Aboriginal Studies, Canberra. Current Bibliography. Canberra, 1967- (semiannually).
Provides a comprehensive list of monographs and periodical articles.

1830 Eliade, Mircea. "Australian Religions." History of Religions, v. 6, p. 108-34, p. 208-35, v. 7, p. 61-90, p. 149-83, p. 244-68.
Evaluates contributions made to the studies of the native religious beliefs and practices. Useful bibliographic citations are given in footnotes.

1831 Greenway, John. Bibliography of the Australian Aborigines and the Native Peoples of the Torres Strait to 1959. Sydney, Angus and Robertson, 1963. 420 p.
Contains some 10,000 references to monographs and periodical articles. Consult the subject index under the entries Religion, p. 396, Mythology and Legend, p. 394, etc.

1832 Pilling, Arnold R. Aborigine Culture History; A Survey of Publications, 1954-57. Detroit, Wayne State Univ. Press,

1962. 217 p.
"Draws together threads of information provided by ... archaeologists, ethnographers, ethnologists, social and physical anthropologists, paleontologists, linguists, folklorists and historians"--Preface. For topics dealing with religious life check the index.

CRITICAL STUDIES

HISTORICAL BACKGROUND

1833 Clark, C. M. H. A History of Australia. Melbourne, Univ. Press, 1962- (3 vols. already pub.).
Presents a comprehensive survey, with an excellent bibliographic section. Indexes are supplied in each volume. Use also its abridged version, A Short History of Australia (1969).

1834 McLeod, Allan L., ed. The Pattern of Australian Culture. Ithaca, N.Y., Cornell Univ. Press, 1963. 486 p.
This collective work attempts a comprehensive survey of the Australian "intellectural history." Each section concludes with a selection of the most important bibliographic references including periodical articles. Of special interest is the last section, The Culture of Aborigines.

STUDIES IN BELIEFS

1835 Berndt, Ronald M., ed. Aboriginal Man in Australia; Essays in Honour of A. P. Elkin. Sydney, Angus and Robertson, 1965. 491 p.
Contains an interesting collection of papers on a variety of selected subjects. Of great importance is the study by W. E. H. Stanner, "Religion, Totemism, and Symbolism," p. 207-37.

1836 ________. Australian Aboriginal Religion. Leiden, Brill, 1974 (Iconography of Religions, Sec. 5). 4 fascs. in 1 v.
Provides a detailed survey of religious ideas and practices of the tribes living in the southeastern, northeastern, northern and central regions of the Australian continent. Also contains a discussion of the most important myths. Some bibliographic references are included.

1837 ________. Kunapipi; A Study of an Australian Aboriginal Cult. Melbourne, Cheshire, 1951. 223 p.
"The main purpose of this work is to indicate some fundamental features of an Australian Aboriginal religious cult from Arnhem Land..."--Preface. Includes some bibliographic footnotes and an index.

1838 ________. The World of the First Australians; An Introduction to the Traditional Life of the Australian Aborigines. Sydney, Smith, 1964 (1952). 509 p.

An introductory textbook which deals with the social organization and structure, the life cycle, religious beliefs and practices, magic and sorcery, etc. An extensive bibliography and an index are included.

1839 Conference on Aboriginal Studies. Australian National University, 1961. Australian Aboriginal Studies; A Symposium of Papers Presented at the 1961 Research Conference. Ed. by H. Sheils. Melbourne, Oxford Univ. Press for the Australian Institute of Aboriginal Studies, 1963. 505 p.

The most useful part of this selection is the section Religious and Artistic Life, including a paper by E. A. Worms, "Religion," with excellent bibliographical leads. An index is supplied.

1840 Eliade, Mircea. Australian Religions; An Introduction. Ithaca, N. Y., Cornell Univ. Press, 1973 (Symbol, Myth, and Ritual). 205 p.

Attempts a reconstruction of cultural history of the Aborigines into certain patterns, with a special regard to their ritual and belief. Also examines some gods and heroes, mythical geography and theogony initiation rites and secret cults, death and eschatology, etc. An evaluation of existing literature is provided. Contains a detailed index.

1841 Elkin, Adolphus P. The Australian Aborigines; How to Understand Them, 4th ed. Sydney, Angus and Robertson, 1964 (1958). 393 p.

This study "seeks to understand aboriginal tribal and social organization, law, beliefs, ritual, and philosophy..." --Preface. Some bibliographical footnotes and an index are provided.

1842 Róheim, Geza. Animism, Magic and the Divine King. New York, International Universities Press, 1972 (1930). 390 p.

This is an older but still useful study with excellent bibliographic documentation.

1843 ________. Australian Totemism; A Psycho-analytic Study in Anthropology. New York, Humanities Press, 1971 (1925). 487 p.

Presents a scholarly study of problems encountered in research on Australian totemism. Deals with the prototemic complex, sex totems, negative totemism, Alcheringa myth, conceptional totemism, Intichiuma ceremonies, etc. Numerous bibliographical footnotes, a list of authorities, and an index are included.

1844 _______. The Children of the Desert: The Western Tribes of Central Australia. Ed. with an Introd. by W. Muensterberger. New York, Basic Books, 1974.

A thorough scholarly study based on personal observations made by the author while living among the Aborigines. A glossary of terms, and some bibliographic references are supplied.

1845 _______. The Eternal Ones of the Dream; A Psychoanalytic Interpretation of Australian Myth and Ritual. New York, International Univ. Press, 1945. 270 p.

A scholarly work which deals with religious and magical symbolism, beliefs concerning conception, circumcision rites, fertility ceremonies, and ancestral cults. Includes some bibliographic references in the text and footnotes, as well as a useful index.

1846 Smith, W. R. Myths and Legends of the Australian Aboriginals. New York, 1970 (1932). 355 p.

"It is a collection of narratives as told by pure-blooded Aboriginals of various tribes..."--Preface. An index is added.

1847 Strehlow, T. G. H. Aranda Traditions. New York, Johnson Reprint, 1968 (1947) (Landmarks in Anthropology). 181 p.

Contains three papers describing the sacred traditions of the Aranda people as they have been handed down by ancestors. Very few bibliographic references, but an index is included.

NEW ZEALAND

ENCYCLOPEDIA

1848 An Encyclopedia of New Zealand. Ed. by A. H. McLintock. Wellington, N. Z., Owen, 1966. 3 v.

A comprehensive source of information on various aspects of life in New Zealand. Of special interest are articles on Maoris, p. 408-87, with selected bibliographies at the end of each article. The last volume contains an index with numerous cross-references.

BIBLIOGRAPHY

1849 Taylor, Clyde R. H. A Bibliography of Publications on the New Zealand Maori and the Moriori of the Chatham Islands. Oxford, England, Clarendon Press, 1972. 161 p.

This is "a revision and updating of the New Zealand

and the Maori section of "the author's Pacific Bibliography (see no. 1862). Especially interesting are the two sections Religion, and Magic and Sorcery.

CRITICAL STUDIES

Historical Background

1850 McLeod, Alan L., ed. The Patterns of New Zealand Culture. Ithaca, N.Y., Cornell Univ. Press, 1968. 301 p.
This collective work attempts a comprehensive survey of the "intellectual history" of New Zealand. Especially recommended are the chapters Religion; Maori Culture. Each section contains a selection of bibliographical references. An index is appended.

1851 Oliver, W. H. The Story of New Zealand. London, Faber & Faber, 1960. 301 p.
Presents "an overall picture of origins and development"--Preface. Also contains an annotated bibliography, and an index.

1852 Sinclair, Keith. A History of New Zealand, rev. ed. Harmondsworth, England, Penguin, 1970 (1961) (Pelican Book). 335 p.
Presents a brief account of the country's historical events from 1642 to the 1970's. A list of suggestions for further reading, and an index are provided.

Studies in Beliefs

1853 Best, Elsdon. Maori Religion and Mythology, Being an Account of the Cosmogony, Anthropogeny. Religious Beliefs and Rites, Magic and Folk Lore of New Zealand. Wellington, N.Z., Skinner, 1924 (Dominion Museum. Bulletin, 10). 2 v. in 1.
"Embraces many forms of Maori beliefs from the highest to the lowest phases..."--Preface. Some bibliographic references, and an index are provided. Also consult the author's The Maori as He Was (1952).

1854 Buck, Peter. The Coming of the Maori; by Te Rangi Hiroa Sir P. Buck. Wellington, N.Z., Maori Purposes Fund Board, 1950. 552 p.
Presents opinions and conclusions of the greatest authority on the Maori people, their history, traditions, customs, culture, and social life. Of special interest is Book IV: Religion, dealing with the myths of creation, gods, priesthood, and varieties of religious experience. Numerous bibliographical citations to monographs and periodical articles are given in the notes at the end.

There is also an index.

1855 Grey, George. Polynesian Mythology and Ancient Traditional History of the Maori as Told by Their Priests and Chiefs. Ed. by W. W. Bird. Illus. R. Clark. Christchurch, Whitcombe & Rombes, 1956 (1854). 250 p.
Presents a collection of the most prominent myths. An index of proper names is appended.

1856 Henderson, J. M. Ratana: The Origins and the Story of the Movement. Wellington, N. Z., Polynesian Society, 1963. (Polynesian Society. Memoir, v. 36). 128 p.
Presents a history of a political movement which grew from a religious alliance among the Maori. A glossary combined with an index, and an extensive bibliography of primary and secondary sources are provided.

1857 Izett, James, ed. Maori Lore: The Traditions of the Maori People.... Wellington, N. Z., Mackay, 1904. 451 p.
Presents a critical edition of Maori legends showing a variety of versions accepted by different tribes.

1858 Schwimmer, Erik G., ed. The Maori People in the Nineteen-Sixties: A Symposium. London, Hurst, 1968. 396 p.
Brings together a collection of papers by specialists on various aspects of Maori life. An extensive bibliography, and an index are provided. It is also recommended that one consult the author's The World of Maori (1966).

1859 Taylor, R. Te Ika a Maui, or New Zealand and Its Inhabitants, 2nd ed. London, Macintosh, 1870 (1855). 713 p.
An older but still valuable survey which describes the origin, manners, customs, mythology, religion, rites, songs, proverbs, fables, and the language of the native people of New Zealand.

V OCEANIA; SIBERIA

PACIFIC ISLANDS

REFERENCE WORKS

Encyclopedia

1860 Encyclopedia of Papua and New Guinea. Melbourne, Univ. Press, 1972. 3 vols.
A comprehensive record of information on various aspects of history of daily life, with numerous bibliographic references.

Bibliographies

1861 O'Reily, P., and E. Reitman. Bibliographie de Tahiti et de la Polynésie française. Paris, Musée de l'Homme, 1967. 1047 p.
This extensive bibliography covers general reference works, history of discoveries, geographical descriptions, ethnology, history, economics, literature. There is also a list of journals. For religious topics one should consult the subject index (Index analytique).

1862 Taylor, Clyde R. H. A Pacific Bibliography: Printed Matter Relating to Native Peoples of Polynesia, Melanesia, and Micronesia, 2nd ed. Oxford, England, Clarendon Press, 1965 (1951). 692 p.
Provides a selective list of monographs and periodical articles. Of special interest are sections on religion, magic and sorcery under each island and archipelago. One should consult first the Guide to Subjects, and the Guide to Arrangement. See also no. 1849.

CRITICAL STUDIES

1863 Alpers, Anthony. Legends of the South Seas; The World of

the Polynesians Seen Through Their Myths and Legends, Poetry and Art. New York, Crowell, 1970. 476 p.
This collection in English translation "tries to produce for English speaking readers some impression of what the Polynesian oral literature must have been, what the life was like from which it arose, and what view of life they took..."--Preface. Includes useful bibliographic references, and an index. A glossary of terms is appended.

1864 Andersen, Johannes C. Myths and Legends of the Polynesians. Rutland, Vt., Tuttle, 1969. 513 p.
Presents a selection of the most important myths and legends as preserved by the Kahunas. Also contains a brief selected bibliography and an index.

1865 Beckwith, Martha W. Hawaiian Mythology, with a New Introd. by K. Luomala. Honolulu, Univ. of Hawaii Press, 1970 (1940). 575 p.
This is a scholarly critical edition of the Hawaiian myths and legends, with extensive bibliographical documentation.

1866 Burridge, Kenelm. Tangu Traditions; A Study of the Way of Life, Mythology, and Developing Experience of a New Guinea People. Oxford, England, Clarendon Press, 1969. 513 p.
Of special interest is the section Moral and Divine, p. 124, and Pt. 2: Mythology. Contains a very useful index.

1867 Codrington, Robert H. The Melanesians: Studies in Their Anthropology and Folklore. New Haven, Conn., HRAF, 1957 (1891) (Behavior Science Reprints). 419 p.
An older but still unexcelled monumental study which provides a summary of many years' research among the peoples of Melanesia.

1868 Elkin, A. P. Social Anthropology in Melanesia: A Review of Research. Pub. under auspices of the South Pacific Commission. London, Oxford Univ. Press, 1953. 166 p.
"This survey is concerned mainly with our knowledge of the social structure and culture of the peoples in the region ... [and] the total complex of institutions, beliefs, and customary ways of life"--Introd. Includes some bibliographic references in footnotes, and an index.

1869 Fortune, R. F. Manus Religion; An Ethnological Study of the Manus Natives of the Admiralty Islands. Lincoln, Univ. of Nebraska Press, 1935. 391 p.
Provides a description of the spiritualistic cult of the Manus, their system of morals, oracles, magic, sorcery, etc. A glossary and an index are appended, but there

are no bibliographical references.

1870 Goldman, Irving. Ancient Polynesian Society. Chicago, Univ. of Chicago Press, 1970. 625 p.
Presents a comprehensive survey of the subject, with an extensive bibliography of monographs and periodical articles. Also contains an elaborate index in which religious topics are easily found.

1871 Handy, Edward S. C. Polynesian Religion. Honolulu, Bishop Museum, 1927 (Ernice P. Bishop Museum. Bulletin, 34). 342 p.
An older but still useful survey of the ancient religious beliefs and practices, with some bibliographic references.

1872 Kamma, Freerk C. Koreri; Messianic Movements in the Biak-Numfor Culture Area. The Hague, Nijhoff, 1972 (Knk. Instituut voor Taal-, Land-, en Volkenkunde. Translation Ser. 15). 328 p.
A scholarly study based on observations of daily life among the Biak people of West New Guinea. It attempts to compare this movement to seemingly similar ones elsewhere in the world. An extensive bibliography of monographs and periodical articles, as well as an index are provided.

1873 The Kumulipo; A Hawaiian Creation Chant. Transl. and ed. with commentary by M. W. Beckwith. Chicago, Univ. of Chicago Press, 1951. 257 p.
This excellent work is comprised of a critical translation of the text, and an informative exposition of its mythological and historical background. Extensive bibliography lists printed and manuscript sources, including periodical articles, monographs, and reports of various institutions involved in the research of the area.

1874 Luomala, Kathrine. Maui-of-thousand-tricks, His Oceanic and European Biographers. Honolulu, Bishop Museum, 1949. 300 p.
Presents a summary of research on the Maui, a Polynesian god, myth. A useful bibliography and an index are appended.

1875 ________. Voices on the Wind; Polynesian Myths and Chants. Honolulu, Bishop Museum Press, 1955. 191 p.
Contains a critically edited collection of Polynesian texts.

1876 Mackenzie, Donald A. Myths and Legends of the South Sea Islands. London, Gresham, n.d.
"This is a study of the civilization and the religious ideas and practices of the Polynesian peoples, with

comparative evidence from Melanesia, Micronesia, Indonesia, and beyond..."--Preface. Some bibliographic footnotes and an index are supplied.

1877 Oceanic Mythology; The Myths of Polynesia, Micronesia, Melanesia, and Australia. London, Hamlyn, 1967. 141 p.

A brief popular presentation with numerous illustrations. A short select list for further reading is provided.

1878 Williamson, R. W. Religion and Social Organization in Central Polynesia. Ed. by R. Piddington, with a Preface by R. Firth. Cambridge, Eng., Univ. Press, 1937. 340 p.

Pt. 1 deals with gods and worship; Pt. 2 presents the place of religion in the cultures of central Polynesia. An extensive bibliography covers monographs, periodical articles, reports and memoires. An index is included. Also consult the author's Essays in Polynesian Ethnology (1939), which provides an extensive bibliography.

1879 ________. Religious and Cosmic Beliefs of Central Polynesia. Cambridge, England, Univ. Press, 1933. 3 vols.

Covers a "number of myths of creation, the religions of the people, including their beliefs as to the soul and the after life ... and their great army of gods and spirits.... Also includes some bibliographic references in footnotes and an index.

1880 Worsley, Peter. The Trumpet Shall Sound; A Study of "Cargo" Cults of Melanesia, 2nd ed. New York, Schocken Books, 1968 (1951). 300 p.

Attempts to find an origin and explanation of the Melanesians' belief that ancestral spirits will come back and bring untold quantities of "trade goods." Also contains a select bibliography and an index.

JOURNALS

1881 The Journal of Pacific History. Canberra, 1966- .

Published by the Australian National University. Articles and features deal with political, economic, religious and cultural history, archaeology, prehistory, and ethnohistory. Also carries a list of current publications, and reliable book reviews.

1882 Oceania; A Journal Devoted to the Study of the Native Peoples of Australia, New Guinea, and the Islands of the Pacific Ocean. Sydney, 1930- (quarterly).

Published by the University of Sydney.

1883 Papua and New Guinea Society. Journal. Port Moresby, Papua, 1966- .
The journal concerns itself with the past, and the study of traditional cultures of the indigenous peoples.

1884 Polynesian Society. Journal; A Quarterly Study of the Peoples of the Pacific Area. Wellington, N. Z., 1892- .
Includes research papers, shorter communications on recent research, reliable book reviews, and a list of currently published materials.

1885 Société des Océanists. Journal. Paris, 1945- (irregularly).
Published by the Musée de l'Homme. Articles are either in French or English.

JAVA

1886 Geertz, Clifford. The Religion of Java. Glencoe, Ill., Free Press, 1960. 392 p.
Presents the only substantial study of Java's religion available in English. It describes various aspects of contemporary religious life in an actual, in many respects, typical place in east central Java. Part of the material included in this study was published previously under the title, Modjokuto, Religion in Java. An index is included.

OKINAWA

1887 Lebra, William P. Okinawan Religion: Belief, Ritual, and Social Structure. Honolulu, Univ. of Hawaii Press, 1966. 241 p.
"The primary intent of the book ... is to provide a systematic, descriptive account of the indigenous religion of Okinawa..."--Preface. It describes the beliefs, ritual, and structure of the autochthonous religious system. A glossary, some bibliographic references and an index are included.

SIBERIAN (ALTAIC) PEOPLES

1888 Czaplicka, M. A. Aboriginal Siberia; A Study in Social Anthropology... with Pref. by R. R. Marett. Oxford, England, Clarendon Press, 1914. 374 p.
This is a classic which still holds its value as the

most comprehensive and compact handbook for the study of anthropology of the area. Presents systematically the results of firsthand research done by outstanding authorities. Of special interest is Pt. II, Religion, p. 166-306. Bibliographical references are given in footnotes as well as in an extensive bibliography of the older literature at the end. A glossary, and an index are also appended.

1889 Diószegi, Vilmos. Tracing Shamans in Siberia; The Story of an Ethnological Research Expedition. Transl. from the Hungarian by A. Rajkay Babo. Oosterhout, Anthropological Pubs., 1960. 328 p.

Surveys some of the existing forms of shamanism among the peoples living on the vast areas of Siberia. Neither a bibliography nor an index are provided.

1890 Jochelson, Wladimir I. The Peoples of Asiatic Russia. New York, American Museum of Natural History, 1928. 277 p.

Presents an excellent handbook which deals with the peoples of Siberia of Ural-Altaic, Palaeo-Asiatic, Arian, and Semitic descent. It describes their somatological, linguistic and cultural characters. Sections discussing religious topics are easily accessible through the index. An extensive bibliography of older materials covers monographs, periodical articles, and reports of expeditions.

1891 Michael, H. N., ed. Studies in Siberian Ethnogenesis. Toronto, Pub. for the Arctic Institute of North America by the Univ. of Toronto Press, 1962 (Anthropology of the North: Translations from Russian Sources, no. 2). 313 p.

1892 ________. Studies in Siberian Shamanism. Toronto, Pub. for the Arctic Institute of North America by the Univ. of Toronto Press, 1963 (Anthropology of the North: Translations from Russian Sources, no. 4). 229 p.

Both of the works listed above contain translations of papers by outstanding Russian authorities in anthropological studies of Siberia. Some bibliographic references and indexes of subjects are appended.

Part Five--Native Peoples; Misc. (cont.)

VI CHURCH AND STATE

GENERAL

ENCYCLOPEDIAS

1893 "Church and State." Corpus Dictionary of Western Churches. Washington, D.C., Corpus, 1970, p. 177-83.
See also Pt. III, no. 587. Presents a brief informative historical survey, with a few selected bibliographical recommendations.

1894 "Church and State." Encyclopaedia Britannica. Chicago, 1974. Macropaedia, v. 4, p. 590-5.
An excellent brief historical account of the varying relations of church and state, with some well-selected bibliographical references.

1895 "Church and State." Maclintock, J. Cyclopedia of Biblical, Theological, and Ecclesiastical Literature. Grand Rapids, Mich., 1969, v. 2, p. 329-33.
A brief historical survey, with some bibliographic references. See also: Pt. I, no. 14, of The New Schaff-Herzog Encyclopedia of Religious Knowledge, v. 3, p. 105-12. Both works present the Protestant viewpoint.

BIBLIOGRAPHY

1896 Menendez, Albert J. Church-State Relations. New York, Garland, 1976. 126 p.
This annotated bibliography is comprised of English language monographs which discuss the subject in some depth and completeness.

1897 International Bibliography of Political Sciences. London, Tavistock, 1952- (annually).
Prepared by the International Committee for Social Science Information and Documentation, provides current international coverage of periodical articles and monographs.

Entries relevant to the topic are listed in the subject index under: Religion and State.

CRITICAL STUDIES

1898 Barth, Karl. Community, State, and Church; Three Essays, with an Introd. by W. Herberg. Garden City, N.Y., Doubleday, 1960 (Anchor Book, 221). 193 p.
The Swiss master of theologians expresses his views on the state-church relationship.

1899 Ehler, S., and J. Morrall, eds. and transls. Church and State Through the Centuries: A Collection of Historic Documents with Commentaries. Westminster, Newman, 1954. 625 p.
"[A]im of this book is to provide reliable English translations of the most significant official documents in ... the story of the Church's relationship with the secular political power through the various metamorphoses of that power over twenty centuries of that history"--Introd. A useful index is appended.

1900 Gavin, Frank. Seven Centuries of the Problems of Church and State. New York, Fertig, 1971 (1938). 132 p.
Contains a collection of lectures which attempt a scholarly evaluation of the church-state relationship. Bibliographical references are given in the notes at the end of each chapter. Lacks an index.

1901 Lewy, G. Religion and Revolution. New York, Oxford Univ. Press, 1974. 694 p.
"Examines the general relationship of religion and revolution on a larger cross-cultural scale from a comparative perspective"--Preface. The case material is divided into six parts: a brief historical introduction; millenarian revolts; religion and anticolonial strife; church and revolution; religion and the legitimation of revolutionary change; religion and revolution-theoretical perspective.

1902 Murray, Albert V. The State and the Church in a Free Society. Cambridge, Eng., Univ. Press, 1958 (Hibbert Lectures, 1957). 190 p.
Presents a liberal Protestant point of view on goals and possibilities for the relationship of church and state in a free democratic society. An index is appended.

1903 Pfeffer, L. Church, State, and Freedom, rev. ed. Boston, Beacon, 1967. 832 p.
Presents a survey of events leading to the establishment of the principles of religious liberty and separation of government and religion. Excellent bibliographic

sources and an index are provided. Also check the author's God, Caesar, and the Constitution (1975).

1904 Religion and Political Modernization. Ed. by D. E. Smith. New Haven, Conn., Yale Univ. Press, 1974. 340 p.
This volume is comprised of papers which attempt to analyze the interaction of religion and politics in the transitional societies of the Third World. Includes some bibliographic footnotes and an index. Also consult the author's earlier selection, Religion, Politics, and Social Change in the Third World (1971).

1905 Stroup, Herbert H. Church and State in Confrontation. New York, Seabury, 1967. 246 p.
Presents an historical examination of church-state relations from ancient to contemporary times. Describes church-state problems in the setting of modern secular, totalitarian and welfare states. Also deals with state-church relationship in "Non-Christian" countries. Contains some bibliographical references and an index of names and subjects.

1906 Sturzo, Luigi. Church and State. With an Introd. by A. R. Caponigri. Transl. by B. B. Carter. Notre Dame, Ind., Notre Dame Univ. Press, 1962 (1939) (Notre Dame Paperback 132-6). 2 vols.
Translation of Chiesa e stato. An older but still unsurpassed classic, with an excellent bibliographical documentation.

EASTERN EUROPE AND THE SOVIET UNION

1907 Beeson, Trevor, ed. Discretion and Valour: Religious Conditions in Russia and Eastern Europe. Huntington, N.Y., Fontana, 1975. 348 p.
Contains a collection of papers furnished by a panel of specialists on Eastern Europe. Covers Russia, Poland, East Germany, Czechoslovakia, Hungary, Yugoslavia, Albania, Bulgaria and Romania.

1908 Bourdeaux, Michael. Opium of the People; The Christian Religion in the U.S.S.R. Indianapolis, Bobbs-Merrill, 1966. 244 p.
Presents a picture of relationships between the church and the state. Notes for further reading are provided.

1909 Conquest, Robert. Religion in the U.S.S.R. London, Bodley Head, 1968 (Soviet Studies Series). 135 p.
Provides an historical survey of religious developments in Russia after the revolution. Also includes materials

on non-Christian religions: Judaism, Buddhism, Islam. A select bibliography is provided, but there is no index.

1910 Curtiss, John S. The Russian Church and the Soviet State, 1917-1950. Boston, Little, Brown, 1953. 387 p.
Limited to discussion of the Russian Orthodox Church; no attempt is made to include other denominations. A selected bibliography and an index are appended.

1911 Kolarz, Walter. Religion in the Soviet Union. New York, St. Martin's Press, 1961. 518 p.
"It is an attempt to provide a fuller understanding of Russian reality...." Describes the survival of religion in the Soviet Union, the Russian Orthodox Church, the Old Believers, Western Protestantism, etc. Also contains an appendix: The Peoples of the Soviet Union and Their Religious Beliefs. Some bibliographic information and an index are included.

1912 Marshall, Richard H., Jr., ed. Aspects of Religion in the Soviet Union, 1917-1967. Chicago, Univ. of Chicago Press, 1971. 489 p.
Contains a selection of papers which discuss various aspects of the relationship between the state and the Orthodox Church, Jews, Catholics, Protestants, and Muslims. Also includes bibliographical information in footnotes and an index.

1913 Mid-European Law Project. Church and State Behind the Iron Curtain: Czechoslovakia, Hungary, Poland, Romania, with an Introduction on the Soviet Union. Prepared under the general editorship of V. Gsovski. New York, Pub. for the Mid-European Studies Center of the Free Europe Committee by Praeger, 1955 (Praeger Publications in Russian History and World Communism, no. 17). 311 p.
"This valuable collection is comprised of studies written by a group of lawyers, now refugees of cruel governmental effort to transform churches into supporters of governmental policies and ultimately into bureaus of a socialist state..."--Catholic World review. A select list of readings and an index are appended.

1914 Religion and the Search for New Ideals in the U.S.S.R. Ed. by W. C. Fletcher and A. J. Strover. New York, Praeger, 1967 (Praeger Publications in Russian History and World Communism, no. 187). 135 p.
Includes a collection of papers which deal with various problems of spiritual life in Russia, e.g.: life without spiritual or religious ideals, pseudo-religious rites introduced by Party authorities, etc. Some bibliographic footnotes are given, but lacks an index.

1915 Struve, Nikita. Christians in Contemporary Russia. Transl.

by L. Sheppard and A. Manson. New York, Scribner's, 1967. 464 p.

Translation of Les Chrétiens en U. R. S. S. Focuses mainly on the Russian Orthodox Church. An extensive appendix contains a significant store of valuable data of an historical and legislative nature. Some bibliographic information is provided in notes.

VII CONTEMPORARY TRENDS IN NORTH AMERICA

[For additional materials on Christianity consult nos. 519-783; and on the eastern religions, 1199-1688. For a dictionary of modern cults and minority religious groups in America, see no. 1921.]

GUIDES

1916 Biteaux, A. The New Consciousness. Willits, Calif., Oliver Press, 1975 (Finder's Guide, 5). 164 p.

1916a A Pilgrims Guide to Planet Earth: Traveler's Handbook and Spiritual Directory. San Rafael, Calif., Spiritual Community Publications, 1974. 1 v.

These two works are the best sources of information available of names, addresses, and phone numbers of "New Age" religions. Includes descriptions of one hundred different spiritual groups in North America.

INDEX

1917 Alternative Press Index: An Index to the Publications Which Amplify the Cry for Social Change and Social Justice. Ipswitch, Mass., Radical Research Center, 1969- (quarterly).

Entries are arranged by subject; e.g., Alternative Life Styles for Counterculture, International Society for Krishna Consciousness, Meditation, etc.

CRITICAL STUDIES

1918 Altizer, Thomas J. J., and W. Hamilton. Radical Theology and the Death of God. Indianapolis, Bobbs-Merrill, 1966. 202 p.

Presents a brief explanation of its philosophical ideas, and present development within Protestantism, with some Jewish, Roman-Catholic, and non-religious response. A reading list of selected works is appended.

1919 Berger, Peter L. A Rumor of the Angels; Modern Society and the Rediscovery of Supernatural. Garden City, N.Y., Doubleday, 1969. 129 p.
A renowned sociologist presents a popular analysis of the present religious situation. Some bibliographic references are included in notes. An index is lacking.

1920 Boyd, Malcolm, ed. The Underground Church. New York, Sheed and Ward, 1968. 246 p.
This interesting selection of papers includes discussions on "the role of church in solving painful problems of the present reality which bear a character of grievance against traditional Christianity"--Preface. Of great interest is the Source Material appendix comprised of litanies, new sacramental rites, a Report on Community Centre Activities, and a 'Diary from the Underground" by D. Berrigan. Some bibliographic footnotes are provided.

1921 Braden, Charles S. These Also Believe. New York, Macmillan, 1960 (1949). 481 p.
Consists of outstanding studies on American minority religions and cults. It is restricted to indigenous movements. It discusses the Peace Mission, Psychiana, New Thought, Unity School of Christianity, Christian Science, Theosophy, the I Am Movement, etc. Also includes a "Brief Dictionary of Modern Cults and Minority Religious Groups in America." A select bibliography is provided.

1922 Braden, William. The Private Sea: LSD and the Search for God. Chicago, Quadrangle Books, 1967. 255 p.
This interesting study connects the LSD experience to some of the main currents of the new theology, especially "The Death of God Theology." Also deals with the growing influx of Eastern cults, as well as the renewed interest in metaphysics. An index is included.

1923 Clark, Walter H. Chemical Ecstasy: Psychedelic Drugs and Religion. New York, Sheed and Ward, 1969. 179 p.
Contains interesting observations of the psychedelic culture, with some bibliographical references and an index.

1924 Cohen, Daniel. The New Believers: Young Religion in America. Philadelphia, Lippincott, 1975. 192 p.
This chatty informal book gives an informative account of 11 new religious movements: Children of God, Unification Church, Transcendental Meditation, Hare Krishna, Satanism, the Process, etc. A short directory is included. Lacks an index. Consult also the author's: Not of the World: A History of the Commune in America (1973).

1925 Coleman, John E. The Quiet Mind. London, Rider, 1971.

239 p.
Contains a popularly presented discussion of meditation, peace of mind, Buddhism, and psychical research. Also includes an index.

1926 Cooper, John C. Religion in the Age of Aquarius. Philadelphia, Westminster, 1971. 175 p.
Contains a discussion of present developments in contemporary spiritual life. Of special interest are the parts dealing with the occult in America today, its new meaning and symbols, etc. Some bibliographic references are given in notes; lacks an index.

1927 Enroth, Ronald M., and E. E. Ericson. The Jesus People: Old-time Religion in the Age of Aquarius. Grand Rapids, Mich., Eerdmans, 1972. 249 p.
Examines "the origin and growth of each of the brands of the new religious revival and their fundamental beliefs as seen from the sociological, theological and psychological angle"--Preface. Also contains a bibliographical essay and an index.

1928 ________, and G. E. Jamison. The Gay Church. Grand Rapids, Mich., Eerdmans, 1974. 144 p.
Two sociologists examine and report on many aspects of the phenomena of homosexual churches and religious parishes.

1929 Furst, Peter T., ed. Flesh of the Gods: The Ritual Use of Hallucinogens. New York, Praeger, 1972. 304 p.
This collection is comprised of papers which provide information about the use of "mind-alternating botanicals" by primitive subcultures and present interesting theories about the historical importance of hallucinogens in our own culture. A select bibliography and an index are appended.

1930 Glock, C. Y., and R. N. Bellah. The New Religious Consciousness. Berkeley, Univ. of California Press, 1976. 408 p.
Provides a selection of studies on new religious and quasi-religious groups from Hare Krishna sect to "est," Synanon, and the Church of Satan.

1931 Götz, Ignacio L. The Psychedelic Teacher: Drug Mysticism and Schools. Philadelphia, Westminster, 1972. 154 p.
Includes a discussion on the drug phenomenon as symptom; drugs and ultimate concerns; and the role of schools. A selected bibliography and an index are provided.

1932 Harrell, David E. All Things Are Possible: The Healing and Charismatic Revivals in Modern America. Bloomington,

Indiana Univ. Press, 1976. 304 p.
This impartial and thorough historical survey reviews the post-World War II revival movement in the U.S., drawing from writings from and about evangelists, their sermons, and personal contacts. Also analyzes the origins, personalities, techniques and problems of the healing revivals, and the large scale charismatic revivals which had a stronger spiritual impact than healing alone. Also contains a bibliographical essay.

1933 Holzer, Hans W. The Aquarian Age; Is There Intelligent Life on Earth? Indianapolis, Bobbs-Merrill. 1971. 131 p.
Presents a popular discussion of new spiritual values in human life. Neither bibliography nor an index is appended.

1934 Judah, J. S. Hare Krishna and the Counterculture. New York, Wiley, 1974 (Contemporary Religious Movements). 301 p.
One of the most comprehensive scholarly studies on the modern cult movements in America. It is based on extensive observations, interviewing, and questionnaire analysis.

1935 Leary, Timothy L. High Priest. New York, World Pub. Co., 1968. 353 p.
One of the leading personalities of American counterculture presents a selection of documents which illustrate the spiritual background of the psychedelic culture. Some selected readings are given. No index is provided.

1936 Ling, Trevor O. "Counterculture: Towards a New Perspective." Religion, v. 5 (1975), p. 168-74.
An informative review article, with useful bibliographic information.

1937 Needleman, J.; A. K. Bierman; and J. A. Gould. Religion for a New Generation. New York, Macmillan, 1973. 592 p.
"The aim of this text is to present teachable material that illuminates ... major directions of the new religious mind..."--Preface. Additional readings and an index are added.

1938 Perry, Whitall N. "Gurdjieff in the Light of Tradition." Studies in Comparative Religion, Pt. I (autumn 1974), p. 211-39; Pt. II (winter 1975), p. 20-35; Pt. III (spring 1975), p. 97-126.
This "condensed study," reflecting renewed interests in the works of the Armenian-born mystic philosopher, attempts a new evaluation of his enigmatic ideas. Bibliographic documentation is provided in Pt. I, p. 213.

1939 Pope, Harrison. The Road to East, America's New Discovery of Eastern Wisdom. Boston, Beacon, 1974. 158 p.
Contains a study of religious aspects of the American youth counterculture. It deals with Transcendental Meditation, Gurdjieff, Guru Maharaj Ji, Krishna, and Tai Chi. Also includes a list of bibliographic references mainly in the area of scientific research on Eastern techniques and altered states of consciousness.

1940 Reich, Charles A. The Greening of America: How the Youth Revolution Is Trying to Make America Living. New York, Random House, 1970. 399 p.
This controversial book gives a description of the author's schematic arrangement of American consciousness into three categories: 1. Behind the Original American Dream; 2. That of Corporate State Traditionally Liberal; 3. What Has Begun to Emerge from All This in the Young. Some bibliographic citations are included. Also recommended is the sternly critical selection in: Nobile, P., ed., The Con III Controversy (New York, 1971, 274 p.).

1941 Romm, Ethel G., et al. The Open Conspiracy: What America's Angry Generation Is Saying; by E. G. Romm and Many Named and Unnamed Writers of these Uncensored Excerpts from the Underground and the Movement Press. Harrisburg, Pa., Stackpole Books, 1970. 256 p.
Contains an interesting collection of primary materials, with annotated bibliographic documentation, and an index.

1942 Roszak, Theodor. The Making of Counter-Culture: Reflections on the Technocratic Society and Its Youthful Opposition. New York, Doubleday, 1969. 303 p.
Examines "some of the leading influences on the youthful culture: H. Marouse, N. Brown, A. Ginsberg, A. Watts, T. Leary, P. Goodman--and shows how each has helped to call into question the conventional scientific world view, and in so doing has set about undermining the foundations of the technocracy... "--Publisher's Note. Also contains some bibliographic references, but lacks an index.

1943 Rowley, Peter. New Gods of America: An Informal Investigation into the New Religions of American Youth Today. New York, McKay, 1971. 208 p.
"This book is a factual account... " based on facts. Deals with the Baha'i, Gurdjieff, Subud, Spiritual Science, Witchcraft, religious communes, etc. Includes a selection of bibliographical notes.

1944 Wuthnow, Robert. The Consciousness Reformation. Berkeley, Univ. of California Press, 1976. 320 p.

Attempts a survey of recent changes in American social patterns with a special reference to new religious movements, based on evidence and finds.

1945 Zaehner, Robert C. Zen, Drugs, and Mysticism. New York, Pantheon, 1973. 223 p.

An outstanding authority in the field of religious studies presents a popular discussion on the vitalist heresy, mysticism and LSD, LSD and Zen, etc. Contains numerous bibliographic references in footnotes, and an index.

1946 Zaretsky, I. I., and M. P. Leone, eds. Religious Movements in Contemporary America. Princeton, N.J., Princeton Univ. Press, 1974. 837 p.

"The papers in this volume present the most current empirical and theoretical research on a contemporary marginal religious movements in the United States"--Preface. An extensive bibliography of monographs and periodical articles and an index are provided.

Part Six

THE OCCULT, MAGIC, PARAPSYCHOLOGY

REFERENCE WORKS

ENCYCLOPEDIAS

1947 Cavendish, Richard, ed. Encyclopedia of the Unexplained: Magic, Occultism, and Parapsychology. Special Consultant on Parapsychology: J. B. Rhine. London, Routledge & Kegan Paul, 1974. 304 p.

This highly praised reference work explains terms, organizations and persons associated with parapsychology, magic, spiritualism, and the occult. Articles, varying in length, express modern Western views. Bibliographic references are appended at the end. Also contains an index of persons.

1948 Daniels, C., and C. M. Stevans, eds. Encyclopedia of Superstitions, Folklore, and the Occult Sciences of the World; A Comprehensive Library of Human Belief and Practice in the Mysteries of Life Through More than Six Thousand Years of Experience and Progress. Detroit, Gale, 1971 (1903). 3 vols.

This older but still useful work contains information on intuition and instincts, mythology, demonology, magic, witchcraft, esoteric philosophy, signs, omens, oracles, sorceries, divinations, methods and means employed in revealing fortune and fate, systems and formulas for the use of psychical forces. Each volume is provided with a detailed table of contents. Vol. 3 includes an index.

1949 Fodor, Nandor. Encyclopedia of Psychic Science. New York, Univ. Books, 1966. 416 p.

This comprehensive survey "covers the entire field of psychic phenomena and spiritualism, including mediumship, extrasensory perception, and parapsychology. Every kind of psychical phenomenon ... is listed, all the important and lesser known items, with precise information and detailed biographical and bibliographical materials..." --Preface.

1950 Man, Myth, and Magic; An Illustrated Encyclopedia of Supernatural. Richard Cavendish, ed. London, Purnell, 1970-71. 3152 p.

See also no. 125. Provides a comprehensive survey of magic, mythology and religion. Pt. 1 contains introductory articles explaining more clearly the alphabetically arranged dictionary section. Most of the entries are followed by selective bibliographies. A complete index with cross references to related subjects appears at the end.

1951 Newall, Valentia. The Encyclopedia of Witchcraft and Magic. Introd. by R. M. Dorson. New York, Dial Press, 1974. 192 p.

Presents an alphabetically-arranged popular guide to the complex and intriguing issues of magic and witchcraft. Also includes a selected bibliography and an index.

1952 Robbins, R. H. The Encyclopedia of Witchcraft and Demonology. New York, Crown Publishers, 1959. 571 p.

An excellent source of information on the subject. A select bibliography and a subject index are included.

1953 Spence, Lewis. Encyclopedia of Occultism; A Compendium of Information on the Occult Sciences, Occult Personalities, Psychic Science, Magic, Demonology, Spiritism and Mysticism. New Hyde Park, N.Y., University Books, 1960 (1920). 440 p.

Articles are arranged alphabetically. Also contains a select bibliography and an index.

BIBLIOGRAPHIES

1954 Abbot, A. E. A Guide to Occult Books and Sacred Writings of the Ages. London, Emerson, 1963. 64 p.

Addressed primarily to the layman; this list includes basic books on occult movements and communities.

1955 Galbreath, Robert. "The History of Modern Occultism; A Bibliographic Survey." Journal of Popular Culture, v. 5 (1971), p. 726-54.

Also published in the author's: The Occult: Studies and Evaluations (1972).

1956 White, Rhea A., and L. A. Dale. Parapsychology: Sources of Information. Comp. under Auspices of the American Society for Psychical Research. Metuchen, N.J., Scarecrow Press, 1973. 302 p.

The entries are arranged in numerical order by item and alphabetically by author under 24 broad subjects, e.g.: Anthropology and PSI Phenomena, Hauntings and Poltergeists, Religion and PSI Phenomena, etc.... Includes doctoral dissertations, master's theses, opportunities for graduate work. Also contains a glossary of terms, and a name-subject index.

CRITICAL STUDIES

GENERAL

1957 Angoff, Allan, ed. The Psychic Force. Ed. with an Introd. and Notes. New York, Putnam, 1970. 345 p.
This collection of papers is comprised of studies of the struggle for recognition, mesmerism and hypnosis, sleep and dreams, vision and hallucinations, religion and parapsychology, reincarnation, survival and communication with the dead. Also contains some bibliographical leads in notes, a glossary, and an index.

1958 Barrett, Francis. The Magus or Celestial Intelligence, Being a Complete System of Occult Philosophy. With a New Introd. by d'Arch Smith. New Hyde Park, N.Y., University Books, 1967 (1801). 198 p.
A classical work which still holds its extraordinary importance for studies in magic.

1959 Carroll, David. The Magic Makers: Magic and Sorcery Through the Ages. New York, Arbor House, 1974. 286 p.
Presents a popular historical survey. Neither bibliography nor an index is appended.

1960 Castiglioni, Arturo. Adventures of the Mind. Transl. from the Italian by V. Gianfurco. New York, Knopf, 1946. 428 p.
Part of the book was previously published under the title Incantesimo e magia. It is "an attempt to present some historical facts that appear to have common character in their origin, development and consequences..." --Preface. It describes the magic world and gives its historical survey from antiquity to modern times. A select bibliography and an index are added.

1961 Cavendish, Richard. The Black Art. London, Routledge and Paul, 1967. 373 p.
An excellent, popularly presented survey which describes the theory and practice of magic in Europe and England from ancient times to the present. It deals with numerology, satanism, astrology, alchemy, and ritual magic and also discusses the Kabbalah and the Tarot. Includes a select bibliography and an index.

1962 ________. The Powers of Evil in Western Religion, Magic and Folk Belief. New York, Putnam, 1976. 299 p.

This popular study leads the reader through well-researched sections on vampires, "devouring dog," the Antichrist, furies and titans, witchcraft, hell and devil. Also provides a well-selected list of books for further reading, and an index.

1963 Christopher, Milbourne. ESP: Seers and Psychics. New York, Crowell, 1970. 268 p.

Includes a popular explanation of the occult, extrasensory perception, thought reading, fortune telling, astrology, poltergeists, fire walking, etc. A select bibliography and an index are appended.

1964 Cohen, Daniel. Voodoo, Devils, and the New Invisible World. New York, Dodd, Mead, 1972. 204 p.

Presented in popular style, this book explores the many facets of modern occultism, from Adventism to Zoroastrianism. Contains informative discussions on witchcraft, satanism and voodoo, along with a well-researched section on secret societies which examines the present status of organizations such as the Masons and Rosicrucians. The author considers the persistence of occult practices to be a sign of "widespread disenchantment with the modern view of the world." A selected list of bibliographic references and an index are included.

1965 Freedland, Nat. The Occult Explosion. New York, Putnam, 1972. 270 p.

Attempts a survey of old achievements and new developments in the occult sciences. An index is included.

1966 Galbreath, Robert, ed. The Occult: Studies and Evaluations. Bowling Green, Ohio, Bowling Green Univ. Popular Books, 1972. 126 p.

This collection is comprised of excellent brief surveys on various aspects of the occult sciences. A very useful bibliography is given in notes, and in a bibliographic essay.

1967 Grillot de Givry, Emile A. Picture Museum of Sorcery, Magic, and Alchemy. Transl. by J. Courtenay Locke. New Hyde Park, N.Y., University Books, 1963 (1929). 394 p.

Translation of Le Musée des sorciers, mages et alchemists. Presents a "collection of the iconography containing everything with which it is essential to be conversant..."--Preface. Book I: Sorcers; deals with the diabolic manifestations in the religious life, the sabbath, spells, etc.; Book II: Magicians; provides information on cabbalists, astrology and microcosm, metoscopy, physiognomy, cheiromancy, cartomancy, the Tarot, talismans, etc.; Book III: Alchemists; explains the doctrine, alchemic materials, etc. Contains abundant illustration. Also includes some bibliographical references in the text and an index.

1968 Jacobson, Nils O. Life without Death? On Parapsychology, Mysticism and the Question of Survival. Transl. from the Swedish by S. La Farge. New York, Delacorte, 1974. 339 p.
Translation of Liv efter döden? Provides a survey of current developments and findings. A select bibliography, a glossary, and an index are provided.

1969 LeShan, Lawrence. The Medium, the Mystic and the Physicist: Towards a General Theory of the Paranormal. New York, Viking, 1974 (Esalen Book). 299 p.
Presents a popular account of research on the paranormal experience with extensive bibliographic references at the end of each chapter. An index is lacking.

1970 Logan, Daniel. America Bewitched: The Rise of Black Magic and Spiritism. New York, Morrow, 1974. 187 p.
The aim "in this book is to help to discover the difference between good and evil in spiritual or occult endeavors"--Preface. Contains a brief bibliography and an index.

1971 McConnell, R. A. ESP Curriculum Guide. New York, Simon and Schuster, 1971. 128 p.
Gives useful instructions explaining how to teach extra-sensory perception and related subjects. Of special importance is Pt. III, "Books and Articles Recommended."

1972 Moss, Thelma. The Probability of the Impossible: Scientific Discoveries and Explorations in the Psychic World. Los Angeles, Tarcher, 1974. 410 p.
A scholarly study by a medical psychologist which surveys phenomena associated with inspiration, multiple personality, and meditative states. Her observations are based on research in parapsychology, religion, and yoga. Also includes a select bibliography and an index.

1973 Oesterreich, T. K. Possession: Demoniacal and Other, Among Primitive Races, in Antiquity, the Middle Ages, and Modern Times. New Hyde Park, N.Y., University Books, 1966 (1921). 400 p.
Presents a scholarly account gathered from widely scattered literary sources. It examines the nature of the state of possession, and the distribution of possession and its importance from the standpoint of religious psychology. An appendix on parapsychology is added. Includes numerous bibliographic citations in the text, and an index.

1974 Ostander, S., and L. Schroeder. Psychic Discoveries Behind the Iron Curtain. Introd. by I. T. Sanderson. Englewood Cliffs, N.J., Prentice-Hall, 1970. 443 p.
Provides a survey of developments in psychic sciences in Russia, Bulgaria, and Czechoslovakia. A select bibliography and an index are appended.

1975 Panati, Charles. Supersenses: Our Potential for Parasensory Experience. New York, Quadrangle, 1974. 274 p.
A comprehensive survey for the layman which discusses recent research in the telepathy, clairvoyance, precognition, psychokinesis, and psychic healing. Also contains a selective bibliography and subject and author indexes.

1976 Pitois, Christian. The History and Practice of Magic, by Paul Christian. Transl. by J. Kirkup and J. Shaw. Supplementary articles by M. Bashir, M. Lawrence, and J. Shaw. Ed. and rev. by R. Nichols. New York, Citadel Press, 1963 (1870). 2 vols.
Translation of Histoire de la magie, du mond surnaturel. This is an older classic which is still considered as a standard historical work.

1977 Psychic Exploration: A Challenge for Science. E. D. Mitchell and others. Ed. by J. White. New York, Putnam, 1974. 708 p.
Contains a selection of papers on various aspects of parapsychology, with a selected list of readings and an index.

1978 Richard, John. But Deliver Us from Evil: An Interpretation of the Demonic Dimension in Pastoral Care. London, Darton, Longman and Todd, 1974. 244 p.
Contains a popular explanation of exorcism, demonic possession, and occult sciences. Also includes a select bibliography and an index.

1979 Rogo, D. S., ed. Parapsychology: A Century of Inquiry. New York, Taplinger, 1975. 319 p.
This interesting collection of papers presents an up-to-date survey of research into various aspects of psychic sciences. Some bibliographic references and an index are appended.

1980 Rush, John A. Witchcraft and Sorcery: An Anthropological Perspective of the Occult. Springfield, Ill., Thomas, 1974. 166 p.
Provides a popular explanation of occult beliefs and practices around the world as viewed by an anthropologist. Also contains a select list for additional reading, and an index.

1981 Seligmann, Kurt. Magic, Supernaturalism, and Religion, 2nd ed. New York, Pantheon Books, 1971. 342 p.

The 1st edition (1948) was issued under the title, The History of Magic. "The aim of this book is to present to the general reader a condensed account of magical ideas and operations in the civilized western world..." --Introd. References for further reading are given in the bibliographic résumé. An index is added.

1982 Sladek, John T. The New Apocrypha; A Guide to Strange Science and Occult Beliefs. New York, Stein & Day, 1973. 375 p.

"The chapters ... are meant to show a representative sample of the New Apocrypha: Thou shalt and must...." A selected bibliography and an index are included.

1983 Swann, Ingo. To Kiss Earth Good-bye. New York, Hawthorn, 1975. 217 p.

Presents a popular explanation of psychic phenomena with some bibliographic references and an index.

1984 Thorndike, L. A History of Magic and Experimental Science. New York, Macmillan, 1923-58. 8 vols.

Presents a thorough historical survey of the study of magic from ancient times to the present. Numerous bibliographical citations are appended in footnotes. Each volume contains a bibliographical and a general index.

1985 Tiryakian, Edward A., ed. On the Margin of the Invisible: Sociology, the Esoteric, and the Occult. New York, Wiley, 1974 (Contemporary Religious Movements; Wiley Interscience Series). 364 p.

Contains a selection of papers by outstanding authorities in the field, divided into two sections: I. Representative Esoteric Doctrines and Their Social Forms of Expansion; II. The Social Setting of the Occult: Witchcraft. Also includes a bibliography and an index.

1986 Truzzi, Marcello. "Definition and Dimension of the Occult: Towards a Sociological Perspective." Journal of Popular Culture, v. 5 (1971), p. 635-46.

A brief survey of the subject, with an excellent selection of readings. Also published in: Galbreath, R., ed. The Occult: Studies and Evaluations (1972). See no. 1966.

1987 Varaolachari, Vankeenpuram. Psychic Research, Occultism and Yoga. Madras, Higginbotham, 1970. 257 p.

Includes a comparative study of clairvoyance, telepathy, psychometry, psychokinetics, precognition, and autoscopy as investigated in the West, with the results of the yoga techniques developed in the East. Some bibliographic leads are provided. Lacks an index.

1988 Waite, Arthur E. The Book of Black Magic and the Facts Including the Rites and Mysteries of Goetic Theurgy, Sorcery, and Infernal Necromancy. Chicago, Occult Publishing House, 1910. 326 p.
An old but still useful work.

1989 Watson, Lyall. Supernature. Garden City, N.Y., Doubleday, (Anchor Press), 1973. 344 p.
Provides a popular introduction to the history of the supernatural, with a well-selected list of books for further reading. There is no index.

1990 Webb, James. The Occult Underground. La Salle, Ill., Library Press Book, 1974. 387 p.
This popularly written book introduces the layman to the history and current developments in occult sciences. Also contains a bibliography in notes, and an index.

1991 Wheatley, Dennis. The Devil and His Works. New York, American Heritage Press, 1971. 302 p.
This well selected anthology examines how the forces of good and evil have been utilized throughout history.

1992 Wilson, Colin. The Occult. London, Hodder & Stoughton, 1971. 601 p.
A useful general introduction to the subject, with well selected additional readings, and an index.

1993 Yalman, Nur. "Magic." International Encyclopedia of the Social Sciences. New York, Macmillan, 1968; v. 5, p. 521-8.
Presents a brief informative discussion of witchcraft, sorcery, and magic. A select bibliography is appended at the end of the article.

ALCHEMY

1994 Burckhardt, Titus. Alchemy: Science of Cosmos, Science of the Soul. Transl. from the German by W. Stoddart. Baltimore, Penguin, 1972 (1971). 206 p.
Translation of Alchemie, Sinn und Weltbild. An excellent introduction to the history and basic problems of alchemy. A select bibliography and an index are supplied.

1995 Holmyard, Eric J. Alchemy. Harmondsworth, England, Penguin, 1957. 281 p.
Contains a popular account of history and elementary doctrines for the beginner. A useful list for further readings, and an index are provided.

1996 Redgrove, Herbert S. Alchemy: Ancient and Modern, Being a Brief Account of the Alchemistic Doctrines, and Their Relations to Mysticism on the One Hand and the Recent Discoveries in Physical Sciences on the Other Hand Together with some Particulars Regarding the Lives and Teachings of the Most Noted Alchemists, 2nd rev. ed., with an Introd. by H. J. Sheppard. Wakefield, E. P. Publishing, 1973 (1922). 141 p.

An older but still valuable study with excellent information regarding the locating of documents. Lacks an index.

APPARITIONS AND GHOSTS

1997 MacKenzie, Andrew. Apparitions and Ghosts; A Modern Study, with a Foreword by G. W. Lambert. London, Barker, 1971. 180 p.

This is one of the few recent books that is scholarly as well as interesting and geared to the non-specialist reader.

1998 Rogo, D. S. An Experience of Phantoms. New York, Taplinger, 1974. 214 p.

This popular book attempts to "illustrate the many different kinds of encounters people had with phantoms, hauntings, and other psychical events..."--Preface. Also contains an annotated bibliography of selected monographs, and a very useful index.

ASTROLOGY

1999 Lindsay, Jack. Origins of Astrology. London, Muller, 1971. 480 p.

An historical survey which covers the ancient Middle East and the Greco-Roman civilization. Also contains a select bibliography and an index.

2000 McIntosh, Christopher. The Astrologers and Their Creed: An Historical Outline, with a Foreword by Agehanada Bharati. London, Hutchinson, 1969.

This popular introduction outlines the origins and history from the ancient to the present times. Also contains an interesting section explaining certain aspects of modern astrology e.g.: the horoscope techniques. Includes some bibliographic references in footnotes and an index.

2001 Naylor, Phyllis I. H. Astrology: An Historical Examination. London, Maxwell, 1967. 242 p.

Presents an historical summary of the 3000 years of development in the field. A selected bibliography and an index are appended.

2002 Parker, Derek. Astrology in the Modern World. New York, Taplinger, 1970. 254 p.
A popular investigation for the lay reader which explains how the ancient science uses its 3000 years' experience for warning or advice, in medicine, weather forecasting, and business. Also includes some bibliographic references in footnotes, a glossary of terms, and an index.

CRYSTALLOMANCY

2003 Besterman, Theodore. Crystal Gazing: A Study in the History, Distribution Theory and Practice of Scrying. Introd. by E. Juster. New Hyde Park, N.Y., University Books, 1965. 183 p.
Contains an informative introduction to history, methods and rationale of crystallomancy. A select bibliography and an index are appended.

EXORCISM

2004 Baker, Roger. Binding the Devil: Exorcism; Past and Present. London, Sheldon Press, 1974. 187 p.
This is a wide ranging study of the ways in which man has dealt with the physical manifestations of evil through the ages. It traces the history of devilry and possession from Biblical times, through witchcraft, to the age of reason and the advent of psychiatry. Also deals with modern existence of black magic and the occult. Includes a list of selected readings, a glossary, and an index.

2005 Ebon, Martin. The Devil's Bride; Exorcism, Past and Present. New York, Harper, 1974. 245 p.
Contains a popular presentation, from a parapsychologist's point of view, of case histories which examine the myths of demons. Emphasizes recent psychological research, and also explains how various cultures have accounted for the phenomenon. A select bibliography is provided but it lacks an index.

2006 Nauman, St. Elmo, ed. Exorcism Through the Ages. New York, Philosophical Library, 1974. 311 p.
Provides an historical survey for the beginner, with some bibliographic references.

NUMEROLOGY

2007 Butler, Christopher. Number Symbolism. New York, Barnes & Noble, 1970. 186 p.

Introduces a brief explanation in a popular style of complex systems of numbers which were invented in the past. Also describes some modern developments in the art of number reading. A select bibliography is very useful in pursuing the study. An index is appended.

PROPHECY AND FORTUNE-TELLING

2008 Ellis, Keith. Prediction and Prophecy. London, Weyland, 1973. 192 p.

This popular book investigates human attempts to delve into the secrets of the future. A list of books for further reading and an index are included.

2009 Gibson, W. B., and L. R. Gibson. The Complete Illustrated Book of Divination and Prophecy. Garden City, N.Y., Doubleday, 1973. 336 p.

Provides a popular explanation of the ways whereby the future is foretold to an appreciable degree. It deals with the arithmancy, tasseomancy, the Tarot, cartomancy, cheiromancy, etc. A glossary of methods of divination and an index are added.

SECRET SOCIETIES; MASONRY

Dictionaries

2010 Preuss, Arthur, ed. A Dictionary of Secret Societies, Comprising Masonic Rites, Lodges and Clubs ... Mystical and Occult Societies. London, Herder, 1924. 543 p.

An older but still well-used compendium of knowledge on the subject. Entries are arranged alphabetically with some bibliographical references appended.

2011 Waite, Arthur E. A New Encyclopedia of Free-masonry (Ars magna latomorum) and of Cognate Instituted Mysteries: Their Rites, Literature, and History, new and rev. ed. London, Rider, 1928. 2 vols.

Articles are arranged alphabetically.

Guide

2012 Jones, Bernard E. Freemason's Guide and Compendium, new and rev. ed. London, Harrap, 1956. 604 p.

This is a handbook prepared for members of Masonic societies. A selected list of bibliographic references is appended.

Critical Studies

2013 Hankins, F. H. "Masonry." Encyclopedia of the Social Sciences. New York, Macmillan, 1963; v. 10, p. 177-84.
See no. 181. A brief introductory survey of the subject, with a useful bibliography.

2014 Lewis, H. S. Rosicrucian: Questions and Answers with Complete History of the Rosicrucian Order. San José, Calif., AMORC, 1947. 340 p.
An official manual for Rosicrucian students. A select bibliography is appended.

2015 MacKenzie, Norman I., ed. Secret Societies. New York, Rinehart and Winston, 1968. 350 p.
This collection of papers, by outstanding authorities, includes studies on primitive secret societies, Rosicrucians, Freemasonry, etc. Also contains some bibliographic references and an index.

2016 Pick, R. L., and G. N. Knight. The Pocket History of Freemasonry, 4th ed. London, Muller, 1963 (1953). 303 p.
It is "in no sense a mere epitome of any of the larger histories, although in its compilation the standard authorities and records have been consulted.... [E]specially useful to the young Master mason..."--Preface. Contains a select bibliography and an index.

2017 Roberts, John M. The Mythology of the Secret Societies. New York, Scribner's, 1972. 370 p.
This scholarly study describes the actual relationships among the Freemasons, Illuminati, Carbonari, and the Jacobins on the historical background. It helps to understand their attitudes and beliefs. Unfortunately neither bibliography nor index are adequate.

WITCHCRAFT AND DEMONOLOGY

2018 Caro Baroja, Julio. The World of Witches. Transl. from the Spanish by N. Glendinning. London, Weidenfeld & Nicolson, 1964 (Nature of Human Society). 313 p.
Translation of Las brujas y su mundo. Provides a survey of European witchcraft, in popular style, with some bibliographic references in notes.

2019 Cohn, Norman R. C. Europe's Inner Demons; An Enquiry Inspired by the Great Witch-Hunt. New York, Basic Books, 1975 (Columbus Series). 320 p.
Contains a scholarly study of European witchcraft and demonology presented in the historical context. Also includes a select bibliography and an index.

2020 Franklyn, Julian. Death by Enchantment; An Examination of Ancient and Modern Witchcraft. New York, Putnam, 1971. 244 p.

Presents a popular historical survey with some bibliographic references in footnotes and an index.

2021 Holzer, Hans W. The Truth about Witchcraft. Garden City, N.Y., Doubleday, 1969. 254 p.

A specialist in ESP and parapsychology presents the "how to" and "who's who" in contemporary witchcraft. He provides firsthand information of the practices of the cult in today's society.

2022 Hughes, Pennethorne. Witchcraft. Harmondsworth, England, Penguin, 1952. 220 p.

An historian attempts an analysis of the entire substance of witchcraft. It deals with prehistoric beliefs and customs, relationships to ancient religions of the Middle East, events of the Middle Ages, as well as with the existing evidence of the present practice of witchcraft. Includes a selective bibliography and an index.

2023 Kors, A. C., and E. Peters, eds. Witchcraft in Europe, 1100-1700; Documentary History. London, Dent, 1974. 382 p.

Contains a collection of documents, selected from original sources, which illustrates the rise and fall of the wave of witchcraft in Europe between the 11th and 18th centuries. Also provides some bibliographical references and an index.

2024 Lyons, Arthur. The Second Coming: Satanism in America. New York, Dodd, Mead, 1970. 211 p.

"Gives an insight into certain aspects of human nature..."--Preface. A select bibliography and an index are added.

2025 Mair, Lucy. Witchcraft. London, Weidenfeld & Nicolson, 1973 (1969) (World University Library).

An authoritive introduction for the general reader, with well-selected bibliographical citations of journal articles and monographs in notes.

2026 Martello, Leo L. Witchcraft, the Old Religion. Secausus, N.J., University Books, 1973. 287 p.

Informs the reader of the true nature of the witch cult, maintaining that it is based on reverence and happiness and lacks the sense of evil, avenging god or hell-bent theology of most modern religions. Some bibliographic references are provided.

2027 Monter, E. W. "The Historiography of European Witchcraft: Progress and Prospects." Journal of Interdisciplinary

History, v. 2 (1972), p. 435-51.
Presents a brief historical survey of European witchcraft viewed, by the author, as a social development. Numerous bibliographic references are given in footnotes.

2028 Nugent, Donald. "Witchcraft Studies, 1959-1971; a Bibliographical Survey." Journal of Popular Culture, v. 5 (1971), p. 711-25.
Also published in: Galbreath, R., ed., The Occult: Studies and Evaluations (1972) (see no. 1966). Includes a brief bibliographic survey of selected monographs, papers published in collections, and periodical articles.

2029 Parrinder, Edward G. Witchcraft European and African, rev. and enl. ed. London, Faber, 1963 (1958). 215 p.
First examines the historical content of European witchcraft, and then attempts to find parallels among certain beliefs and craft practices. The book is an excellent introduction for the beginner.

2030 Scth, Ronald. Witches and Their Craft. New York, Taplinger, 1968. 255 p.
Beginning with a brief historical account, the author describes both the demonic and the gentler aspects of the craft of The Coven, The Sabbot, Familiars, White Witchcraft, The Black Mass, and other witchcraft groups. Provides a select bibliography and an index.

2031 Summers, Montague. The History of Witchcraft and Demonology. London, Routledge & Kegan Paul, 1973 (1926). 353 p.
Presents an informative survey of the witchcraft, sorcery, black magic, necromancy, secret divination, satanism, and other kinds of occult practices. Also provides an extensive bibliography and an index.

2032 Wedeck, Harry E. Treasury of Witchcraft. New York, Philosophical Library, 1961. 271 p.
A well-selected anthology of materials pertaining to the magic arts which includes discussion of the divination and astrology, lycanthropy and necromancy, and all the varieties of thaumaturgical practices from the earliest times to the present day. Each section is preceded by an informative introduction to the subject. Some bibliographic notes are provided.

GENERAL INDEX

(Authors, Titles, Subjects)

ABBOT, A. E. 1954
'Abd al-Malik Ibn Hisham 1041
ABERNETHY, G. L. 157
Aboriginal Man in Australia 1835
Aboriginal Siberia 1888
Aborigine Culture History 1832
Abstracta Islamica 1016
Abstracts in Anthropology 1697
Academy of Religion and Mental Health 206
ACKROYD, P. A. 818
ADAMS, C. J. 22, 259, 425, 541, 1002, 1287, 1396, 1520, 1618, 1701
ADEN, L. 210
Adi-Granth 1376
ADKINS, A. W. H. 336
Admiralty Islands 1869
African Bibliographic Center 1717
African Civilizations in the New World 1780
African Ideas of God 1773
African Mythology 1766
African Religions 1770
African Religions and Philosophy 1760
African Religions in Western Scholarship 1735
African Systems of Thought 1753
African Traditional Religion 1751
African Traditional Religions 1767
African World 1744
The Africans 1726
Afro-American Religious Studies 1173, 1781
After Auschwitz 483
Aftermath 46
AGEHANANDA, B. S. 1474
AHLSTRÖM, S. E. 738
Ahmadiyyah 1166
Ainu Creed and Cult 1651
Akan 1769
The Akan Doctrine of God 1740
The Akan of Ghana 1762
The Akan Traditions of Origin 1762
AKEN, A. R. A. 319
ALBRIGHT, W. F. 546, 862, 863
Alchemy 1994-6
Aleut 1820-1
ALEXANDER, H. B. 1801
Algonquins 1814
ALI, M. M. 1029, 1047, 1060
All Things Are Possible 1932
Allah's Commonwealth 1095
ALLEN, C. J. 832
ALLEN, G. 1408
ALLEN, J. B. 717
ALLPORT, G. W. 207
ALPERS, A. 1863
An Alphabetical Subject Index and Index Encyclopedia to Periodical Articles on Religion 35
Alternative Press Index 1917
ALTIZER, T. J. J. 1918
America Bewitched 1970
American Baptist Historical Society 692
The American Churches in the Ecumenical Movement 752
American Doctoral Dissertations 61
American Indian Religion 1807
American Judaism 471

The American Religious Experience 757
American Religious History 734
AMIR-ALI, HASHIN 1024
The Analects 1574
Analytical Concordance to the Bible 846
Analytical Guide to the Bibliographies on the Arabian Peninsula 1008
Anatomy of the New Testament 950
Ancestor Worship in Contemporary Japan 1644
The Ancestry of Our English Bible 790
Anchor Bible 791, 830
Ancient Buddhism in Japan 1502
The Ancient Civilization of Peru 386
Ancient Civilizations of the Andes 387
Ancient Egyptian Religion 295, 297
The Ancient Gods 285
Ancient Greek Religion 335
Ancient Iran and Zoroastrianism 316
Ancient Israel 880
Ancient Judaism 490
An Ancient Library of Qumran 978
Ancient Maya 382
Ancient Mesopotamia 303
The Ancient Near East 288
The Ancient Near East in Pictures 289
Ancient Near East Texts 289, 875
Ancient Near Eastern Literature 280
Ancient Pagan Symbols 120
Ancient Polynesian Society 1870
Ancient Roman Religion 335, 348
The Ancient Supplementary Texts 289
ANDERSEN, J. C. 1864
ANDERSON, B. W. 905
ANDERSON, C. C. 954
ANDERSON, C. P. 247
ANDERSON, G. H. 639
ANDERSON, G. W. 906
ANDERSON, H. 955
ANDERSON, J. N. D. 1131
ANDERSON, N. 716
ANDERSON, R. T. 547
ANDRAE, T. 1042
ANDREWS, E. D. 726
ANESAKI, MASAHARU 1635, 1636
Anglicanism 690
Anglicanism in History and Today 691
ANGOFF, A. 1957
Animism, Magic and the Divine King 1842
Annotated Bibliography in Religion and Psychology 206
Annual Bibliography of Indian Archaeology 1252
Annual Egyptological Bibliography 291
Anthology of Islamic Literature 1056
Anthology of Zen 1451
Anthropological Approaches to the Study of Religion 186
ANURUDDHA, R. P. 1475
The Apocryphal Literature 971
Apollinarian Heresy 625
Apparitions and Ghosts 1997
Approaches to Asian Civilization 1260
Approaches to the Philosophy of Religion 161
The Aquarian Age 1933
Arab Civilization to A.D. 1500 1087
Arab Islamic Bibliography 1014
Arab Painting 1114
Arabia Before Muhammad 1098
Arabic Literature 1137
Arabic Thought in the Liberal Age 1106
The Arabs 1088
The Arabs in History 1092
Aranda Traditions 1847
ARBERRY, A. J. 548, 1025, 1053, 1061, 1143, 1155
Archaeological Bibliography 273
Archaeology and Old Testament

878
Archaeology in Biblical Research 882
Archaeology in the Holy Land 868
Archaic Roman Religion 346
Archäologische Bibliographie 273
Archeology and Religion of Israel 861
The Archeology of the New Testament 934
The Archeology of World Religions 45
ARCHER, J. C. 1378
Arctic Bibliography 1796
ARGYLE, M. 208
Arian Heresy 625
Arithmacy 2009
Armenian Church 665, 668
ARMSTRONG, M. M. 693
ARMSTRONG, O. K. 693
ARMSTRONG, R. C. 1503
ARNDT, I. 144
ARNETT, W. E. 158, 159
ARNOLD, T. W. 1062, 1085, 1125
ARNOLD, W. 202
ARONSON, E. 205
Art of Islam 1113
ASHBY, P. 1352
ASHTON, H. 1732
Asia: A Guide to Paperbacks 1199
Asian Religions 1221
The Asians 1229
ASLIB 62
ASMUSSEN, J. P. 356
Aspects of Islam in Post-colonial Indonesia 1185
Aspects of Islamic Civilization 1053
Aspects of Rabbinic Theology 484
Aspects of Religion in the Soviet Union 1912
Assiniboine 1811
Association for the History of Religions 27
Association of Social Anthropologists. Monographs 186
Associations, Buddhist 1406
ASTON, W. G. 1626, 1655
The Astrologers and Their Creed 2000
Astrology 2001
Astrology in the Modern World 2002
ATIYEH, G. N. 1003
Atlas of Biblical World 852
Atlas of Islamic History 1018
Atlas to the Bible 853
ATTIYA, A. S. 587, 665
ATTWATER, D. 654, 656, 666, 673
Australian Aboriginal Religion 1836
Australian Aboriginal Studies 1839
The Australian Aborigines 1841
The Australian Encyclopedia 1828
Australian Religions 1840
Australian Totemism 1843
Autoscopy 1987
AUZOU, G. 885
AVERY, C. B. 323
AVI-YONAH, M. 863
AYER, J. C. 573
AZIZ, A. 1182, 1183
The Aztecs 381
AZZAM, A. R. 1063

Baal in the Ras Shamra Texts 306
Babylonian and Assyrian Religion 300
BACH, M. 1679
BACHARACH, J. L. 1004
BACON, M. H. 722
Badarayana 1329
BAEK, L. 458, 459
Bafu 1736
Bagre 1746
The Baha'i Faith 1186
BAINTON, R. H. 549, 574, 582, 591, 594
BAIRD, R. 1217
BAKER, R. 2004
BALANDIER, G. 1715
BALDWIN, M. W. 583
BALFOUR, E. 1254
BALY, D. 852, 856, 857

BANCROFT, A. 1218
BANDO, S. 1496
BANERJEA, J. 1277
BANERJEE, A. C. 1417
BANERJEE, P. 1266
The Bantu Speaking Tribes of South Africa 1772
BAPAT, P. V. 1418
A Baptist Bibliography 692
BARKER, W. P. 519
BARON, S. W. 446, 449
Barotse 1771
BARRETT, D. B. 1733
BARRETT, F. 1958
BARRIER, N. G. 1372
BARROW, J. G. 23
BARTH, K. 550, 1898
BARTHELL, E. E. 337
BASCOM, W. 1734
BASHAM, A. L. 1258, 1412
BASHIR, M. 1976
A Basic Bibliographic Guide for New Testament Exegesis 922
Basic Judaism 488
Basic Modern Philosophy of Religion 164
Basic Writings of Mo-Tsu, Hsun Tsu, and Han Fei Tsu 1588
BASKIN, W. 257, 1548
BASTIDE, R. 1780
The Basuto 1732
BATEY, R. A. 928
BAUER, H. 1648
BAUER, J. 801
BAVIER, R. 430
BECKFORD, J. A. 699
BECKWITH, M. W. 1865, 1873
BEEBE, H. K. 907
BEESON, T. 1907
A Believing Jew 488
BELL, C. A. 1476
BELL, R. 1026, 1034
BELLAH, R. N. 221, 1637, 1930
BENNINGSEN, A. 1178
BENZ, E. 667
BERGENDORFF, C. 704
BERGER, P. 225, 1919
BERKEY, R. F. 871
BERKOWITZ, M. I. 24
BERLIN, C. 423
BERLIN, M. 416
BERNDT, R. M. 1835-8
BERRIGAN, D. 1920
BERRY, T. M. 1267
BERTOCCI, P. A. 160
BEST, E. 1853
BESTERMAN, T. 2003
BETTENSON, H. S. 575
Between God and Men 474
BEWER, J. A. 908
Bhagavadgita 1314-6
BHARATI, A. 180
BHARDWAJ, S. M. 1275
BHATTACHARJI, S. 1281
BHATTACHARYA, S. 1255
BHUDDASA, B. 1419
Biak-Numfor 1872
BIANCHI, U. 4
The Bible and the Ancient Near East 881
Bible, Archaeology, and Faith 865
The Bible as Literature 893
Bible Bibliography 818
The Bible Companion 841
The Bible in the Making 898
The Biblical Archaeologist Reader 866
Biblical Archaeology 883
Biblical Archaeology and History 870
Biblical Bibliography 824
Biblical Criticism 849
Biblical Structuralism 901
The Biblical World 812
A Bibliographical Guide to the History of Christianity 537
A Bibliographical Guide to the New Testament Research 918
Bibliographie Biblique 824
Bibliographie Bouddhique 1393
Bibliographie de la Réform 593
Bibliographie de Tahiti 1861
Bibliographie du Shintô 1653
Bibliographie Védique 1289
Bibliographie zur alteuropäischen Religionsgeschichte, 1954-64 258
Bibliographie zur Symbolik, Ikonographie und Mythologie

113
Bibliographie zur Symbolkunde 115
A Bibliography of Anabaptism 707
Bibliography of Asian Studies 1200
A Bibliography of Bible Study for Theological Students 825
A Bibliography of Bibliographies in Religion 23
Bibliography of Indian Philosophies 1322
A Bibliography of Japanese Buddhism 1496
Bibliography of Jewish Bibliographies 428
A Bibliography of Middle East Folklore 1013
A Bibliography of New Testament Bibliographies 919
Bibliography of Philosophy 155
A Bibliography of Pre-Islamic Persia 313
A Bibliography of Publications on the New Zealand Maori 1849
A Bibliography of Sex Rites and Customs 114
A Bibliography of Shinto in Western Languages 1654
Bibliography of Symbolism 113, 114
Bibliography of the Architecture, Arts, and Crafts of Islam 1112
Bibliography of the Australian Aborigines 1831
Bibliography of the Continental Reformation 591
Bibliography of the Dead Sea Scrolls 975-977
A Bibliography of the Peoples and Cultures of Mainland Southeast Asia 1203
Bibliography of Tibetan Studies 1387
Bibliography on Buddhism 1395
A Bibliography on Judaism and Jewish-Christian Relations 424
Bibliography on Spirit Possession 1724
Bibliotheca Orientalis 274
BIERMAN, A. K. 1937
BIFOLCK, W. S. 1208
BIJLEFELD, W. A. 1005
Binding the Devil 2004
A Biographical Dictionary of the Saints 657
Biographies, Christian 522, 526, 528, 533-5
Biography, Early Islamic 999
BIRGE, J. K. 1180
BIRNBAUM, E. 1111, 1201
BIRNBAUM, N. 226
The Birth of the Gods 272
BITEAUX, A. 1916
BITEK, O. 1735
BLACK, D. M. 63
BLACK, M. 831
Black African Traditional Religions and Philosophy 1702
The Black Art 1961
The Black Mass 2030
Blackfoots 1818
BLAU, J. 446, 460, 492
BLEEKER, C. J. 38, 292, 299, 309, 312, 315, 336, 353, 355, 356, 359, 376, 383, 385, 431, 1397, 1614, 1695
BLOCK-HOEL, N. 719
BLOFELD, J. E. C. 1477, 1605
BLOOM, A. 1217
BLOOMFIELD, M. 1299, 1336
BLYTH, R. H. 1455, 1468
BOAHEN, A. A. 1728
BOAS, F. 1802
BODENSIECK, J. 702
BOER, T. J. 1152
BOLAND, B. J. 1185
BOND, M. F. 527
BONNERJEA, B. 116
The Book of Black Magic 1988
Book of Changes 1562-5
The Book of Documents 1558
The Book of Lord Shang 1589
The Book of Mormon 718
Book of Odes 1559-61
Book of Rites 1566

The Book of Rituals 1566
The Book of Saints 655
The Book of Songs 1561
Books in English on Islam 1009
The Books of Splendor 506
Books on Asia 1111, 1201
Books on Buddhism 1398
BORNKAMM, G. 956, 968
BORTON, H. 1615
BOSWORTH, C. E. 1023, 1062
BOTTERWECK, G. J. 816
BOUQUET, A. C. 101, 1337
BOURDEAUX, M. 1908
BOUYER, L. 520
BOYCE, M. 1284
BOYD, M. 1920
BRADEN, C. S. 39, 1921
BRADEN, W. 1922
The Brahma Sutra 1329
BRANDON, S. G. F. 100, 275, 1399, 1689
BRANNEN, N. S. 1504
BRASCH, R. 462
BRATTON, F. G. 281, 886
BRAUER, J. B. 536
BRAVMANN, M. M. 1097
BREASTED, J. H. 293
BRENNER, L. 1144
BRENT, P. L. 1338
BREWERS, E. C. 633
BRIDGER, D. 418
A Brief Dictionary of Modern Cults and Minority Religious Groups in America 1921
A Brief History of the Liturgy 629
BRIGGS, R. C. 929
BRIGGS, W. 1451
BRINTON, H. 723
British Humanities Index 31
Broadman Bible Commentary 832
BROCK, S. P. 819
BROCKELMANN, C. 1086, 1137
BROCKINGTON, L. H. 970
BRONSTEIN, D. J. 161
Our Brothers in Christ 561
BROWN, C. F. 1173, 1781
BROWN, R. E. 833
BROWNE, E. G. 1140
BROWNRIGG, R. 923
BRUCE, F. F. 788, 930
BUBER, M. 463
BUCHHOLZ, P. 258
BUCK, L. P. 602
BUCK, P. 1854
The Buddha 1493
The Buddha's Philosophy 1408
The Buddha's Way 1434
Buddhica 1393, 1501
Buddhism 14, 18, 22, 38, 45, 48, 51, 55, 1393-1517
Buddhism; A Historical Introduction to Buddhist Values 1432
Buddhism; A Non Theistic Religion 1426
Buddhism; A Religion of Infinite Compassion 1414
Buddhism; A Subject Index 1406
Buddhism and Society 1511
Buddhism for the West 1423
Buddhism in America 1687
Buddhism in China 1481
Buddhism in Chinese History 1488
Buddhism in India and Abroad 1417
Buddhism in Japan 1500
Buddhism in Transition 1435
Buddhism in Translations 1471
Buddhism, Its Essence and Development 1420
Buddhism, Its Origins and Spread in Words 1440
Buddhism under Mao 1485
Buddhist Background of the Burmese Revolution 1509
The Buddhist Bible 1413
The Buddhist Conquest of China 1489
Buddhist Dictionary 1404
The Buddhist Library 1421
Buddhist Mahayana Texts 1443
Buddhist Meditation 1409
The Buddhist Nirvana and Its Western Interpreters 1439
Buddhist Philosophy in India and Ceylon 1492
The Buddhist Religion 1433
The Buddhist Revival in China 1486

Buddhist Sacred Books 1471
The Buddhist Sects of Japan 1506
A Buddhist Student's Manual 1428
Buddhist Texts Through the Ages 1411
Buddhist Thought in India 1490
The Buddhist Tradition in India, China, and Japan 1412
BUDGE, E. A. T. W. 294
BUITENEN, J. A. B. VAN 1311, 1330
BULFINCH, T. 117
Bulgaria 1974
BULLOUGH, S. 677
BULTMANN, R. K. 576
BURCKHARDT, T. 1113, 1994
BURKHARDT, V. R. 1542
BURLAND, A. 377, 380
Burma 1509, 1511
Burmese Supernaturalism 1511
BURNABY, S. B. 507
BURR, N. R. 731-2
BURRIDGE, K. 1866
BURTON, W. F. P. 1736
BURTT, E. A. 102, 1409-10
BUSH, R. C. 1539
But Deliver Us From Evil 1978
BUTLER, A. 656
BUTLER, C. 2007
BUXTON, J. 1737

CAIN, S. 425
CAINS, G. E. 16
Calendar, Perpetual Jewish: 1920-2020 414
The Caliphate 1125
The Call of Minaret 1067
CALVERLEY, E. E. 1064
The Cambridge Ancient History 276
Cambridge Bible Commentary 834
The Cambridge History of Africa 1725
The Cambridge History of India 1259
Cambridge History of Iran 1174
Cambridge History of the Bible 820
CAMPBELL, A. 1680
CAMPBELL, J. 128-9
CAMPENHAUSEN, H. von 887
Canaanite Myths and Legend 304
The Canaanites 305
Canadian Catholic Church 743
Canadian Experience of Church Union 746
Canadian Graduate Theses in the Humanities and Social Sciences 66
Canadian Society for the Study of Religion 247
Canadian Theses 64
CANNEY, M. A. 9
ÇANU, J. 641
CAPPS, D. 204
CAPPS, W. H. 40
Cargo Cults 1880
CARLEN, M. C. 649
CARLQUIST, S. 1648
CARO BAROJA, J. 2018
CARROLL, D. 1959
Carthage, Churches of 665
Cartomancy 1967, 2009
CASA, C. della 1365
CASAL, U. A. 1649
CASE, S. J. 537
CASO, A. 381
CASPER, B. M. 433
CASTIGLIONI, A. 1960
Cathedral and Crusade 554
Catholic Apostolic Congregation 661
Catholic Biblical Association of America 797
The Catholic Church in America 737
The Catholic Church in the Modern World 679
A Catholic Dictionary 673
A Catholic Dictionary of Theology 521
Catholic Encyclopedia 522
Catholic Periodical Index 542
The Catholic Reformation 556
CAVENDISH, R. 125, 1692, 1947, 1950, 1961-2
CAVERT, S. M. 739, 752
CAYRE, F. 577
CELNIK, I. 424

Celtic Heritage 372
Celtic Mysteries 373
Celtic Mythology 370
ČERNY, J. 295
CHADWICK, H. 578
CHADWICK, N. 368
CHADWICK, O. 538, 597
CHAI, C. 1568
CHAI, W. 1568
Chaldean Rite 668
CHAN, W. T. 1213, 1436, 1540, 1547, 1549, 1598
Ch'an and Zen Teaching 1453
Chan Buddhism 1454
CHANG, C. 1456
Change and Continuity in Indian Religion 1269
Changing Perspectives in the Scientific Study of Religion 44
CHATTERJEE, S. 1339
CHATTOPADHYAYA, S. 1354
CHEETHAM, S. 533
Cheiromancy 1967, 2009
Chemical Ecstasy 1923
CH'EN, K. K. S. 1481-2
The Children of the Desert 1844
China; A Critical Bibliography 1521
China; A Short Cultural History 1525
Chinese Civilization 1524
The Chinese Classics 1557
Chinese Creeds and Customs 1542
Chinese Festivals 1543
The Chinese Mind 1555
Chinese Mystics 1536
Chinese Religion 1534
Chinese Religions 1518, 1532
Chinese Symbols and Superstitions 1592
Chinese Thought and Institutions 1570
Chinese Thought from Confucius to Mao Tse-Tung 1552
The Chinese Transformation of Buddhism 1482
Chinese Way in Religion 1535
CHITRITA, D. 1304
Christendom 661
Christendom Divided 600
CHRISTIAN, P. 1976
Christian Center for the Study of Japanese Religions 1634, 1667
The Christian Centuries 678
The Christian Church in Canada 749
The Christian Churches of the East 666
Christian Missions 637
Christian Myth and Ritual 646
Christian Science 695, 1921
Christianity; A Psychologist's Translation 571
Christianity Among the Religions of the World 569
Christianity and the Development of Canadian Culture 745
Christianity in a Revolutionary Age 607
Christianity in the Twentieth Century 606
Christians in Contemporary Russia 1915
The Christology of the Faith and Order Movement 622
CHRISTOPHER, J. B. 1066
CHRISTOPHER, M. 1963
CHU, H. 1584
CH'U, Y. 1590
Chuang-tzu 1596
CHUDHURI, S. 1387
Chung Yung 1568
Church and Sects in Canada 744
Church and State 1906
Church and State Behind the Iron Curtain 1913
Church and State in Confrontation 1905
Church and State Through the Centuries 1899
The Church and the Age of Reason 605
Church Cooperation and Unity in America 739
Church Dogmatics 550
The Church in an Age of Revolution 559, 610
The Church in Crisis 617
The Church in the Dark Ages 553

The Church in the Eighteenth Century 558
The Church in the Seventeenth Century 557
Church of New Jerusalem 661
Church of South India 666
The Church of the Apostles and Martyrs 552
The Church of the Lutheran Reformation 704
Church, State and Freedom 1903
Church-State Relations 1896
Church Symbolism 648
CIRLOT, J. E. 118
The Civilization of the American Indians Series 381
Clairvoyance 1975
CLARK, C. M. H. 1833
CLARK, E. T. 753
CLARK, S. D. 744
CLARK, W. H. 209, 1923
CLASS, A. 1694
Classical and Contemporary Reading in the Philosophy of Religion 167
Classical Approaches to the Study of Religion 8
A Classical Dictionary of Hindu Mythology and Religion 1280
A Classical Dictionary of India 1256
Classical Islam 1100
Classical Mythology 330
Classics in Chinese Philosophy 1548
A Classified Bibliography of Literature on the Acts of the Apostles 920
A Classified Bibliography of the Finds in the Desert of Judah 976
A Classified Bibliography of the Septuagint 819
CLEBSCH, W. A. 246
CLEMEN, C. C. 41
The Code of Maimonides 442
CODRINGTON, R. H. 1867
COHEN, A. A. 685
COHEN, D. 1924, 1964
COHN, H. 957
COHN, N. R. C. 2019
COHON, S. S. 465-6
COLEMAN, J. E. 1925
COLLDEN, L. 1738
Colonialism and Christian Missions 638
COLWELL, E. C. 888, 931
COMAY, J. 802
The Coming of the Maori 1854
Community, State and Church 1898
The Companion to the Bible 840
Companion to the Qur'an 1033
Comparative Religion 101, 104, 106
The Comparative Study of Religion 110
The Complete Illustrated Book of Divination and Prophecy 2009
A Comprehensive Bibliography of Modern African Religious Movements 1722
COMSTOCK, W. R. 42, 43
The Con III Controversy 1940
The Concept of Deity 105
Conceptions of Soul Among North American Indians 1804
Concise Dictionary of the Christian World Missions 639
Concise Encyclopedia of Islam 1000
The Concise Encyclopedia of Living Faith 21, 1210, 1364
Concise Encyclopedia of the Middle East 997
Concise Theological Dictionary 530
A Concordance to the Principal Upanishads and Bhagavadgita 1308, 1317
Concrete Universality of the Japanese Way of Thinking 1657
Condition of Jewish Belief 467
Conference on Oriental Civilization in General Education 1260
Conference on Religion in South Asia 1268

The Conflict Between El and Baal in Canaanite Religion 308
Confucian China and Its Modern Fate 1586
A Confucian Notebook 1569
Confucian Personalities 1579
The Confucian Persuasion 1578
Confucianism 38, 45, 48, 55, 1568-87
Confucianism in Action 1572
Confucianism in Modern Japan 1652
CONFUCIUS 1574
Confucius and Chinese Humanism 1576
Confucius and the Chinese Way 1575
Confucius, the Man of the Myth 1575
The Congregational Way 698
CONNICK, C. M. 958
CONQUEST, R. 1909
The Consciousness Reformation 1944
Conservative Jews 471, 492
A Constructive Survey of Upanishadic Philosophy 1310
Contact and Conflict 1541
The Contemporary Middle East 1003
Contemporary Protestant Thought 683
CONTENAU, G. 282
CONZE, E. 1411, 1420, 1421-2, 1490
COOPER, J. C. 1926
Coptic Church 665, 668
CORNFELD, G. 803
Corpus Dictionary of the Western Churches 659, 721, 1893
CORSWANT, W. 804
Cosmological Doctrines in Islam 1157
COULING, S. 1523
COULSON, N. J. 1132
The Councils of the Church 620
Counsels in Contemporary Islam 1104
The Coven 2030
CRAGG, G. R. 605
CRAGG, K. 1035, 1067-8, 1104
Creeds of Christendom 614
Creeds of the Churches 613
CREEL, H. G. 1552, 1575, 1606
CREEMERS, W. H. M. 1656
CRESSWELL, K. A. C. 1112
A Critical Bibliography of Religion in America 731
Critical Guide to Catholic Reference 676
A Critical Introduction to the Apocrypha 970
The Critical Introduction to the Old Testament 906
Critical Quest of Jesus 954
Critical Study of Bhagavadgita 1318
A Critical Survey of Indian Philosophy 1326
CROON, J. H. 320
CROOSE, G. 527
CROSS, F. L. 528
CROSS, F. M. 983, 978
CROW, P. A. 615
Crow Indians 1809
Crowell's Handbook of Classical Mythology 325
CRUDEN, A. 842
The Crusade 587
CRYSDALE, S. 742
Crystal Gazing 2003
Cults of Unreason 1682
The Cultural Heritage of India 1261
CUMONT, F. V. M. 314
Cuneiform Bibliography 279
A Current Bibliography of African Affairs 1718
CURTIS, C. J. 683
CURTISS, J. C. 1910
Cyclopedia of Biblical, Theological and Ecclesiastical Literature 1895
The Cyclopedia of India 1254
CZAPLICKA, M. A. 1888

Dahomey 1748
DALE, L. A. 1956
DANDEKAR, R. N. 1286, 1340

DANEEL, M. L. 1739
DANIEL, N. 1163-4
DANIEL-ROPS, H. 551-61, 959
DANIELOU, A. 1341
DANIELOU, J. 678
DANIELS, C. 1948
DANKER, F. W. 821
DANQUAH, J. B. 1740
Darbyites 661
DASGUPTA, S. 1478
DASGUPTA, S. N. 1324
DAVIDSON, B. 1726
DAVIDSON, H. R. E. 359-61
DAVIDSON, R. 849
DAVIES, J. G. 627-8
DAVIES, R. E. 712
DAVIES, W. D. 932
DAVIS, H. F. 521
DAWLEY, P. M. 689
The Dawn and Twilight of Zoroastrianism 318
DAWOOD, N. J. 1027
The Dead Sea Scrolls 972-7
DEANESLEY, M. 584
Death by Enchantment 2020
The Death of God Theology 1922
DE BARY, W. T. 1213, 1260, 1412, 1519, 1616
A Decade of Bible Bibliography 828
DECARREUX, J. 642
DEIGHTON, L. C. 245
DEISSMANN, A. 969
DEMARTINO, R. 1458
DEMERATH, N. J. 227
DEMETRAKOPOULOS, G. H. 664
DEMIEVILLE, P. 1401
DEREN, M. 1825
Desert Saints 716
DEUSSEN, P. 1309
DEUTSCH, E. 1330
The Development of Hindu Iconography 1277
Development of Muslim Theology, Jurisprudence, and Constitutional Theory 1156
The Development of Neo-Confucian Thought 1585
Development of Religion and Thought in Ancient Egypt 293
The Devil and His Works 1991
The Devil's Bride 2005
Devouring Dog 1962
A Dialog between Theology and Psychology 210
Diary from the Underground 1920
Dictionary of Anthropology 183
Dictionary of Bible Place Names 813
Dictionary of Black African Civilization 1715
A Dictionary of Buddhism 1399
A Dictionary of Chinese Buddhist Terms 1405
A Dictionary of Chinese Mythology 1544
A Dictionary of Christian Antiquities 533
A Dictionary of Christian Biography and Literature 535
Dictionary of Christian Biography, Literature, Sects, Doctrines 534
A Dictionary of Christian Theology 531
Dictionary of Classical Mythology 285, 326
A Dictionary of Comparative Religion 100, 1399, 1689
Dictionary of Ecclesiastical Terms 529
A Dictionary of English Church History 527
A Dictionary of Indian History 1255
A Dictionary of Islam 998
A Dictionary of Life in the Bible Times 804
A Dictionary of Liturgy and Worship 627
Dictionary of Mysticism 145
Dictionary of Mythology 321
Dictionary of Mythology, Folklore and Symbols 122
Dictionary of Non-Christian Religions 18, 1209, 1663
Dictionary of Orthodox Theology 664
Dictionary of Pagan Religions 257

Dictionary of Papal Pronouncements 649
Dictionary of Religion and Ethics 17
A Dictionary of Secret Societies 2010
A Dictionary of Superstitions and Mythology 116
A Dictionary of Symbols 118
Dictionary of the History of Ideas 10
Dictionary of the Miracles 633
DIEHL, K. S. 25
DIETRICH, B. C. 338
DILLINBERGER, J. 684
DILLISTONE, F. W. 130
DIMAND, M. S. 1119
DIMONT, M. I. 450-1
Dinka 1758
DIOSZEGI, V. 1889
Discoveries in Judean Desert 984
Discretion and Valour 1907
Dissertation Abstracts 65
DITTIES, J. E. 201
Divine Horsemen 1825
Divinity and Experience 1758
Dix Années de Bibliographie Classique, 1914-24 329
DOBSON, W. A. C. H. 1520
Doctrine and Argument in Indian Philosophy 1327
Documents from Old Testament Times 879
DO-DINGH, P. 1576
DOI, A. R. I. 1048
DOLAN, J. P. 563, 598
DOLLEN, C. 616
DONALDSON, D. M. 1124, 1175
DONATH, D. C. 1423
DORE, H. 1591
DOTSON, L. O. 1203
DOUGHERTY, J. J. 889
DOUGLAS, J. D. 523
DOUGLAS, M. 131
DOWNES, R. M. 1741
DOWSON, J. 1280
DRAAK, M. 369
DRIOTON, E. 282
DRIVER, G. R. 304, 979
The Druids 371
The Drums of Affliction 1778
DUBNOV, S. M. 452
DUCASSE, C. J. 162
DUIGNAN, P. 1719
DUMEZIL, G. 346, 362
DUMOULIN, H. 1457
DUNLOP, D. M. 1087
DUPONT-SOMMER, A. 980
DURKHEIM, E. 228
DUSCHESNE-GUILLEMIN, J. 282, 315
DUTT, N. 1444
DUYVENDAK, J. J. 1589
DYCK, C. 708
The Dynamics of Emancipation 447

ESP Curriculum Guide 1971
ESP; Seers and Psychics 1963
EARHART, H. B. 1638-9, 1668
Early Buddhism and Its Origins 1438
Early Buddhist Japan 1498
Early Chinese Literature 1527
Early Christendom 672
Early Christian Fathers 575
Early Christianity 574
Early Church 578
Early Highland People of Anatolia 311
Early Indian Religions 1266
Early Madhyamika in India and China 1446
East-West Philosopher's Conference 1262
Eastern Christendom 672
Eastern Civilization 1224
The Eastern Orthodox Church 667
Eastern Orthodoxy 664-72
EBERHARD, W. 1543
EBON, M. 2005
Ecumenical Councils of the Catholic Church 619
Education Index 249
EDWARDES, M. 1263
EDWARDS, P. 154
Egyptian Mythology 296
Egyptian Religion 298
EHLER, S. 1899
EHRMAN, A. 444

EICHHORN, W. 1524
EISSFELDT, O. 890
EISTER, A. W. 44
EKVALL, R. B. 1390
Elementary Forms of the Religious Life 228
Elements of Hindu Iconography 1278
Elements of the Jewish and Muhammedan Calendars 507
Elenchus Bibliographicus Biblicus 822
Eleven Years of Bible Bibliography 827
ELIADE, M. 1, 47, 103, 132-3, 1705, 1830, 1840
ELIOT, C. N. E. 1219, 1424, 1497
ELKIN, A. P. 1835, 1841, 1868
ELLIS, J. T. 733
ELLIS, K. 2008
ELLISON, J. W. 843
ELLWOOD, R. S. 1681
EMBREE, A. T. 1199, 1203, 1260, 1294, 1519, 1616
EMENEAU, M. B. 1292
Encyclopedia Judaica 414, 505
Encyclopedia of Archaeological Excavations in the Holy Land 863
Encyclopedia of Bible Life 810
Encyclopedia of Biblical Prophesy 811
Encyclopedia of Biblical Theology 801
Encyclopedia of Buddhism 1400
The Encyclopedia of Classical Mythology 319
Encyclopedia of East Asia 1208
The Encyclopedia of Education 245
The Encyclopedia of Indian Philosophies 1322
Encyclopedia of Indians of the Americas 1794
Encyclopedia of Islam 995
The Encyclopedia of Jewish Religion 422
The Encyclopedia of Lutheran Church 702
An Encyclopedia of New Zealand 1848
Encyclopedia of Occultism 1953
Encyclopedia of Papua and New Guinea 1860
Encyclopedia of Philosophy 146, 154
Encyclopedia of Psychic Science 1949
Encyclopedia of Psychology 202
Encyclopedia of Religion 12
Encyclopedia of Religion and Ethics 11
An Encyclopedia of Religions 9
Encyclopedia of Superstitions, Folklore and the Occult Sciences 1948
The Encyclopedia of the Classical World 320
Encyclopedia of the Middle East 996
Encyclopedia of the Papacy 652
Encyclopedia of the Social Sciences 181
Encyclopedia of the Unexplained 1947
Encyclopedia of Theology 524
The Encyclopedia of Witchcraft and Demonology 1952
Encyclopedia of World Methodism 713
Encyclopedia of Yoga 1332
Encyclopedia of Zionism and Israel 415
The Encyclopedia Sinica 1523
Encyclopedia Talmudica 416
Encyclopedic Dictionary of the Bible 805
Encyclopedic History of the Church of Jesus Christ of Latter Saints 718
The English Bible 788
English Church 527
The Enjoyment of Scripture 437
ENROTH, R. M. 1927-28
Enuma Elish 301
Episcopal Church and Its Work 689

EPSTEIN, I. 443, 453, 468
ERICSON, E. E. 1927
Essays in Polynesian Ethnology 1878
Essays in Zen Buddhism 1463
The Essence of Chinese Civilization 1550
The Essence of Judaism 458
The Essene Writing from Qumran 980
Essentials of Bible History 871
The Essentials of Buddhist Philosophy 1436
Eternal Faith, Eternal People 489
The Eternal Flame 462
The Eternal Message of Muhammed 1063
The Eternal Ones of the Dream 1845
Ethico-religious Concepts of the Qur'an 1037
Ethiopic Church 668
Ethnographic Bibliography of North America 1799
Ethnographic Bibliography of South America 1823
ETTINGHAUSEN, R. 1006, 1114
Europe, Ancient Religions 258
Europe's Inner Demons 2019
EUSTACE, H. W. 695
Eutychian heresy 625
EVANS, A. P. 624
EVANS, B. 321
EVANS, C. 1682
EVANS-PRITCHARD, E. E. 262, 1742
The Event of the Qur'an 1035
EVERS, H. D. 1491
Everyday Life in Old Testament Times 867
Everyman's Dictionary of Non-Classical Mythology 126
Evolution of Hindu Sects 1354
Ewe 1769
The Exhaustive Concordance of the Bible 845
Exorcism Through the Ages 2006
An Experience of Phantoms 1998
Exploring Mysticism 151
EYSENCK, H. J. 202

FABIAN, J. 1743
FAGE, J. D. 1731
FAIRBANKS, J. K. 1570
Faith and Knowledge 447
The Faith of Christendom 612
Faith of Man 13
Faith, Reason, and Existence 168
The Faiths Men Live By 52
FAKHRY, M. 1152
Falashas 494
FALLDING, H. 229
Familiars 2030
Far Eastern Bibliography 1200
FARAH, C. E. 1069
FARQUHAR, J. N. 1291, 1353
al-FARUQI, I. R. 98
Fathers of the Church 579
A Feast of Liturgy 500
FEAVER, J. C. 163
FÊNG, YÜ-LAN 1553-4
FERGUSON, C. W. 714
FERGUSSON, J. 347
FERM, V. T. A. 12, 277
FERRE, F. 164
Festivals and Holidays of India 1276
Festivals and Songs of Ancient China 1559
Festivals of the Jewish Year 508
FIEGENBAUM, J. W. 1007
The Fight for God 560
FILSON, F. V. 855, 933
Finding the Historical Jesus 965
FINEGAN, J. 45, 851, 934
FINKELSTEIN, L. 454, 493
Fire Walking 1963
FIRTH, R. 134
FISCHER, P. B. 547
FISHER, H. J. 1166
FISHER, W. B. 1174
FITZGERALD, C. P. 1525
FITZMYER, J. A. 823, 974
The Five Ancient Festivals of Ancient Japan 1649
Flesh of the Gods 1929

FODOR, N. 1949
Folk Buddhist Religion 1483
Folk Religion of Japan 1647
FORDE, C. D. 1744
The Foreign Vocabulary of the Qur'an 1038
FOREM, J. 1683
The Forest People 1776
Forgotten Religions 277
FORLONG, J. G. R. 13
The Formation of Islamic Art 1115
The Formation of the Babylonian Talmud 436
The Formation of the Bible 885
The Formation of the Christian Bible 887
The Formation of the New Testament 936
FORTUNE, R. F. 1869
FOUCHER, A. C. A. 1441
Foundations of Tibetan Mysticism 1479
The Four Books 1567
The Four Great Heresies 625
The Four Major Cults 696
Four Religions of Asia 1228
FOX, J. R. 1694
FOZDAR, J. 1425
France. Centre National de la Recherche Scientifique 26
FRANCE, R. T. 918
FRANK, H. T. 865
FRANKFORT, H. 297
FRANKLYN, J. 2020
FRAZER, J. G. 46, 263
FRAZIER, A. M. 1214
FREEDLAND, N. 1965
FREEDMAN, D. N. 866, 872
FREEDMAN, H. 441
FREEMAN, D. H. 165
FREEMAN-GRENVILLE, G. S. P. 1123
FREITAG, A. 544
FRENCH, G. S. 745
FRENCH, H. 1684
FREUD, S. 211, 264
FRITSCH, C. T. 819
FROELICH, K. 941
From Fetish to God in Ancient Egypt 294
From Stone Age to Christianity 546
FROMM, E. 212, 909
FUJISAWA, C. 1657
FULLER, R. 835
The Fundamentals of Hinduism 1339
Funk and Wagnals Standard Dictionary of Folklore, Mythology, and Legend 119
Furies and Titans 1962
FURST, P. T. 1929
The Future of an Illusion 211
Fyzee, A. A. A. 1133

GABRIELI, F. 1043, 1088
GALBREATH, R. 1955, 1966
GANT, W. J. 844
GARDET, L. 1070
GARLAND, G. F. 847
GARRET, J. 1256
GASTER, T. 283, 508, 973
Gateway to Judaism 420
GÄTJE, H. 1036
GAUDEFROY-DOMOMBINE, M. 1126
GAUSTAD, E. S. 729, 734
GAVIN, F. 1900
GAYNOR, F. 145
GEDDES, C. L. 1008-9
GEERTZ, C. 182
GEHMAN, H. S. 806
GELFAND, M. 1745
A General Theory of Magic 1708
Geographical and Topographical Texts of the Old Testament 859
Geographical Companion to the Bible 856
Geography of Religions 99
Geography of the Bible 857
GERRISH, B. A. 612
GERSH, H. 434
Ghana 1762
The Ghost Dance 1706
GIBB, H. A. R. 1071, 1105, 1137
GIBBS, J. L. 1727
GIBSON, L. R. 2009
GIBSON, W. B. 2009
GILES, L. 1602
Gilgamesh 301

GILLOW, J. 674
GIMBUTAS, M. 374
GINZBERG, L. 448
The Gita in the Light of Modern Science 1319
GLANZMAN, G. S. 823
GLASENAPP, H. 14, 1426, 1690
GLATZER, N. N. 447
GLOCK, C. Y. 1930
GLUBB, J. B. 1044, 1089
God and Man in the Qur'an 1037
God, Caesar, and the Constitution 1903
God in Hindu Thought 1340
The God of Buddha 1425
God of Justice 1039
GODDARD, D. 1413
Godmen of India 1338
Gods and Goddesses of Ancient Greece 337
The Gods as Guests 1750
The Gods of Mexico 380
Gods of the Ancient Northmen 362
Gods with Bronze Swords 333
GOEDERTIER, J. M. 1620
Goetic theurgy 1988
GOITEIN, S. D. F. 1127
Golden Bough 46
GOLDIN, H. E. 509
GOLDIN, J. 425
GOLDINGAY, J. 910
GOLDMAN, I. 1803, 1870
GOLDSMITH, E. 120
GOLDZIHER, I. 1049
GONDA, J. 1269, 1355
GONTARD, F. 650
GOODE, W. J. 265
GOODLAND, R. 114
GOODSPEED, E. J. 891
GOODWIN, J. 639
GOODY, J. 1746
GOPALAN, S. 1368
GOPINATHA, R. T. A. 1278
GORDIS, R. 469
The Gospel of the Churches 662
The Gospels, Their Origins and Their Growth 935
GOTTWALD, N. K. 911
GÖTZ, I. L. 1931
GOULD, J. A. 1937
GOVINDA, A. B. 1479
GRABAR, O. 1115
GRAEF, H. 645
GRAHAM, A. C. 1603
GRANET, M. 1559
GRANT, F. C. 348, 354, 935
GRANT, J. W. 745-7
GRANT, M. 322, 331, 349
GRANT, R. M. 936-7
GRAVES, R. 339
GRAY, J. 284, 305
GRAY, L. H. 11
Great Asian Religions 1215
The Great Religions of the Modern World 48
Great Religious Festivals Series 1543
The Greater Judaism in Making 476
Greek Mythology 343
The Greek Myths 339
The Greeks and Their Gods 340
Greening of America 1940
GREENWAY, J. 1831
GREY, G. 1855
GRILLOT de GIVRY, E. A. 1967
GRIMM, H. J. 592, 599
GRIMM, J. L. K. 363
GRIMWOOD-JONES, D. 1010
GROLLENBERG, L. H. 853
GROOT, J. J. M. 1528
GROS LOUIS, K. R. R. 892
The Growth of the Bible Tradition 897
GRUBE, E. 1116
A Guide to American Catholic History 733
A Guide to Eastern Literatures 1135
Guide to Indexed Periodicals in Religion 33
Guide to Lists of Master's Theses 63
A Guide to Occult Books and Sacred Writings of the Ages 1954
A Guide to Oriental Classics 1285, 1518, 1616
Guide to Religious Studies in Canada 247

Guide to Research and Reference Works on Sub-Saharan Africa 1719
Guide to the Encyclicals of the Roman Pontiffs 649
A Guide to the Study of Holiness Movement 735
Guide to Theses and Dissertations 69
Guide to Turkish Area Studies 1180
Guides to Biblical Scholarship 943, 946
GUILLAUME, A. 1050, 1062, 1072
GUPTA, H. R. 1379
GUPTA, R. S. 1279
Gurdjieff, G. I. 1938
GURNEY, O. R. 310
Gurus, Swamis, and Avataras 1685
GUTHRIE, W. K. C. 340-1
GUTTMANN, J. 470
GUY, H. A. 924
gZi-brjid 1388-9

HAGA, H. 1650
Hagadah 497
HAGLUND, A. 1541
HAIM, S. G. 1125
Haiti 1825-7
HAKEDA, V. 1412
al-HAKIM al-NISABURI, M. 1051
HALES, E. E. Y. 679
HALVERSON, M. 685
HAMILTON, C. H. 1414
HAMILTON, R. W. 854
HAMILTON, W. 1918
HAMMOND, P. E. 227
HAMPSON, R. M. 1167
HAN FEI TSU 1588
HANAYAMA, S. 1395
Handbook of Biblical Chronology 851
A Handbook of Christian Theology 685
Handbook of Church History 563
Handbook of Denominations in the United States 755
A Handbook of Greek Mythology 344
Handbook of Muhammedan Art 1119
Handbook of Social Psychology 205
Handbook of South American Indians 1822
A Handbook of Theological Terms 525
HANDY, E. S. C. 1871
HANE, M. 1628
HANGEN, E. C. 121
HANKINS, F. H. 2013
HAPPOLD, F. C. 147
HARDON, J. A. 471, 606
Hare Krishna and the Counter-culture 1934
Hare Myth 1811
HARMON, N. B. 713
HARPER, E. B. 1268
HARPER, M. H. 1685
Harper's Bible Commentary 839
Harper's Topical Concordance 848
HARRELL, D. E. 1932
HARRIS, W. T. 1747
HARRISON, E. F. 938
HARRISON, I. 750
Harvard Oriental Series 1211, 1299, 1300
Harvard University. Peabody Museum. Catalog 1698
HARVEY, A. E. 926
HARVEY, V. A. 525
HASAN, H. I. 1073
HASTINGS, J. 11, 807, 952
Hawaii 1873
Hawaiian Mythology 1865
HAWRYLUK, M. 996
HAYES, J. H. 960
HAZARD, H. W. 1018
HAZEL, J. 322
Healing, psychic 1975
The Heart of Jainism 1370
The Heathens 266
HEATON, E. W. 867
The Hebrew Religion 873
HEIN, N. J. 1287
HELFER, J. S. 5
Hellenistic Religions 354
HENDERSON, G. D. 721
HENDERSON, J. M. 1856

HENN, T. 893
HENSHAW, T. 939
HERAVI, M. 997
HERBERG, W. 472
HERBERMANN, C. G. 522
HERBERT, E. [pseud.] 1569, 1608
HERBERT, J. 1653, 1658
HERCLOTS, H. G. G. 894
Heresies of the Middle Ages 624
The Heretics 623
HERSKOVITS, F. S. 1748
HERSKOVITS, M. J. 1748
HERTZBERG, A. 473
HESCHEL, A. J. 474
HEWETT, A. P. 727
HICKS, J. 166-7
High Priest 1935
HILL, D. 1117
HILL, M. S. 717
Hillel the Elder 447
HILLERBRAND, H. J. 600, 707
Hindu Cults in America 732
Hindu Places of Pilgrimage 1275
Hindu Polytheism 1341
Hindu Quest for the Perfection of Man 1347
The Hindu Religious Tradition 1343
Hindu Scriptures 1295-6
The Hindu Tradition 1294
Hindu World 1290
Hinduism 14, 18, 22, 38, 45, 48, 55, 1252-1363
Hinduism and Buddhism 1219, 1424
Hinduism at a Glance 1346
Hinduism Through the Ages 1348
HINES, T. C. 33
Historia Religionum 38, 299, 309, 312, 315, 336, 353, 355-6, 359, 369, 376, 383, 385, 431, 1397, 1614, 1695
An Historian's Approach to Religion 58
Historical Atlas of Religion in America 729
Historical Atlas of the Muslim Peoples 1022
Historical Atlas of the Religions of the World 98
The Historical Geography of the Holy Land 860
Historical Selections in the Philosophy of Religion 173
Historical Study of African Religion 1749
History and Culture of the Indian People 1264
The History and Practice of Magic 1976
History, Ethnology and Anthropology of the Aleut 1820
A History of Australia 1833
History of Buddhism in Ceylon 1494
The History of Buddhist Thought 1437
A History of Chinese Philosophy 1553
A History of Christianity 565
A History of Crusades 590
A History of Eastern Christianity 665
A History of Greek Religion 342
A History of India 1263
The History of Islam Law 1132
History of Islamic Literature 1141
A History of Islamic Philosophy 1152
History of Islamic Spain 1179
History of Israelite Religion 864
History of Japanese Religion 1635
A History of Magic and Experimental Science 1984
A History of Medieval Christianity 585
A History of Medieval Church 584
A History of New Zealand 1852
History of North Africa 1168
The History of Philosophy of Islam 1151
The History of Philosophy of the Metaphysical Movement in America 697

A History of Protestantism 686
History of Religion in the United States 756
The History of Religions 4, 47, 50, 1830
The History of Salvation Army 725
A History of the African People 1729
History of the Arabs 1090
A History of the Baptist 694
A History of the Bible 886
History of the Catholic Church 682
A History of the Christian Church 567, 570
History of the Christian Church in Canada 747
History of the Church 538
The History of the Church of Christ 551-61
A History of the Development of Japanese Thought 1632
A History of the Early Church to A.D. 500 581
A History of the Ecumenical Movement 621
A History of the Expansion of Christianity 635
The History of the Incas 388
History of the Jewish People 455
History of the Jews 452
A History of the Modern Church 611
History of the New Testament Times 947
History of the Popes 653
History of the Reformation 598
History of the Sikh Gurus 1379
The History of the Sikhs 1384
The History of Witchcraft and Demonology 2031
A History of Zen Buddhism 1457
HITTI, P. 1074, 1090, 1165
The Hittites 310
Hôbôgrin 1401
HODGSON, M. G. S. 1091
HOEKEMA, A. A. 696
HOFFMAN, Y. 1452
HOFFMANN, H. 1480
HOFMAN, H. F. 1142
HOLBROOK, C. A. 250
HOLLENWEGER, W. J. 720
HOLT, P. M. 1065
HOLTOM, D. C. 1659-60
HOLWECK, F. G. 657
The Holy Qur'an 1032
HOLZER, H. W. 1933, 2021
HOMANS, P. 210
Homo Religiosus 3
Homosexual Churches 1928
HOOK, D. F. 1562
HOOKE, S. H. 300
HOPKINS, T. J. 1343
HOPWOOD, D. 1010
HORDER, D. 251
HORI, I. 1647
A Horizon History of Africa 1728
The Horizon History of Christianity 549
HORNSBY, S. 895
Horoscope Technique 2000
HOROSH, W. 163
HORSCH, J. 709
HORTON, R. 1750
HOURANI, A. H. 1106
The House of Islam 1068
How the Bible Came to Us 894
HOWELL, W. 266
HOWES, J. F. 1641
Hsiao Ching 1568
HSUN TSU 1568, 1588
HUCKER, C. O. 1521
HUDSON, W. S. 740
HUGHES, E. 1530
HUGHES, K. 1530
HUGHES, P. 562, 601, 617, 680
HUGHES, PENNETHORNE 2022
HULTKRANTZ, A. 1804-6
Human Relations Area Files 1699
HUMPHREYS, C. 1402, 1415, 1427-8, 1447, 1459-60
HUNT, G. N. S. 854
HURD, J. C. 919
HURDY, J. M. 1807
HURVITZ, L. 1412
HUTCHINSON, J. A. 168

Hymns of Guru Nanak 1377

The I Am Movement 1921
I and Thou 463
I Ching 1562-5
The I Ching and You 1562
IBN KHALLIKAN 999
Ibo 1769, 1775
Iconography of the Hindus, Buddhist, and Jains 1279
Ideals and Realities of Islam 1077
IDELSOHN, A. Z. 496
IDOWU, E. B. 1751
Ifa Divination 1734
Ijaw 1775
Illuminati 2017
Images and Symbols 132
In Search of Historical Jesus 963
In Time and Eternity 447
INDEN, R. B. 1202
The Indestructible Jews 450
Index Islamicus 1017
Index to Jewish Periodicals 432
Index to Periodical Literature on Christ and the Gospels 953
Index to Religious Periodical Literature 30
Index to the Literature on the American Indian 1797
India; A Critical Bibliography 1253
Indian and Far Eastern Religious Tradition 1217
Indian Buddhism 1495
The Indian Mind 1262
Indian Mythology 1282
Indian Philosophy 1325
The Indian Religious Tradition 1273
The Indian Theogony 1281
The Indians and Eskimos of North America 1798
Indians of thc United States and Canada 1800
India's Past 1265
The Individual and His Religion 207
The Indus Civilization 1259, 1286
The Influence of Islam upon Africa 1171
Instituut Kern, Leiden 1252
An Intellectual History of Islam in India 1182
Intellectual Trends in the Ching Period 1587
International African Bibliography 1720
International African Seminar, 3rd 1753
International Association of Egyptologists 291
International Bibliography of Periodical Literature 32
International Bibliography of Political Science 1897
International Bibliography of Social and Cultural Anthropology 184, 1700
International Bibliography of Sociology 222
International Bibliography of the History of Religions 27, 260, 426, 539, 1288, 1394, 1518, 1703
International Critical Commentary on the Holy Scriptures 836
International Encyclopedia of Religion and Philosophy 15
International Encyclopedia of the Social Sciences 182, 201, 221
International Folklore and Folklife Bibliography 185
Internationale ökumenische Bibliographie 618
The Interpretation of the New Testament 945
Interpretations of American History 717
The Interpreter's Bible 837
The Interpreter's Dictionary of the Bible 808
Interpreting Religion 60
Interpreting the Gospels 929
Interpreting the New Testament 948
Introduction to a Science of Mythology 137
Introduction to African Religion

1761
An Introduction to Asian Religions 1223
An Introduction to Chinese Civilization 1526
An Introduction to Christianity 547
Introduction to Civilization of India, South Asia 1202
Introduction to Classical Scholarship 328
Introduction to Indian Religious Thought 1274
An Introduction to Islamic Cosmological Doctrines 1157
An Introduction to Islamic Law 1134
An Introduction to Japanese Buddhist Sects 1503
An Introduction to Lamaism 1475
The Introduction to Mennonite History 708
Introduction to Religious Philosophy 172
Introduction to Tantric Buddhism 1478
An Introduction to the Books of the Old Testament 914
Introduction to the Hadith 1048
Introduction to the Old Testament 915
Introduction to the Philosophy of Religion 160
Introduction to the Qur'an 1048
Introduction to the Science of Tradition 1051
Introduction to the Talmud and Midrash 439
An Introductory Bibliography for the Study of Scripture 823
IONS, V. 1282
Iroquois 1814
Isa 1307
Islam 14, 18, 22, 38, 45, 48, 548, 995-1198
Islam; A Religious, Political, Social and Economic Study 1073
Islam; A Way of Life 1074
Islam and the Integration of Society 1129
Islam and the Muslim World 1160
Islam and the West 1163, 1165
Islam; Beliefs and Observances 1069
Islam; Beliefs and Institutions 1160
Islam, Europe and Empire 1164
Islam in Africa 1169
Islam in America 732
Islam in East Africa 1171
Islam in Ethiopia and Islam in the Sudan 1171
Islam in History 1093
Islam in Modern History 1108
Islam in South Africa 1167
Islam in the Modern National State 1107
Islam in the Soviet Union 1178
Islam: Muhammad and His Religion 1054
Islam the Straight Path 1076
Islamic Architecture and Its Decoration 1117
Islamic Art 1120
Islamic Art and Architecture 1118
Islamic Calligraphy 1122
Islamic History 1099
The Islamic Jesus 1052
Islamic Law in Modern World 1131
Islamic Literature 1136
Islamic Modernism in India and Pakistan 1183
Islamic Painting 1121
Islamic Philosophy and Theology 1154
Islamic Revelation in the Modern World 1110
Islamic Surveys 1023, 1034, 1104, 1132, 1154, 1179, 1182
The Islamic Tradition 1066
Israelite Religion 877
ITZKOWITZ, N. 1181
Iwingites 661
IZETT, J. 1857
Izumo no Kuni fudoki 1623

IZUTSU, T. 1037

JACKSON, S. M. 20
JACOB, G. A. 1308, 1317
JACOBI, H. G. 1367
Jacobins 2017
Jacobite Church 665
JACOBS, L. 475
JACOBSEN, T. 301
JACOBSON, N. O. 1968
JAHN, J. 1754
Jaina Sutras 1367
Jaina View of Life 1369
Jainism 38, 45, 1364-71
Jamaa 1743
Jamaica 1827
JAMES, E. O. 104-5, 135, 267, 285-6, 646
JAMES, W. 213
JAMISON, G. E. 1928
JANSSEN, J. 291
Japan and Korea 1205
Japan; Its History and Culture 1631
Japan, Its Land, People, and Culture 1629
Japanese Buddhism 1496-1507
Japanese Culture 1633
Japanese Culture in the Meiji Era 1641
Japanese-English Buddhist Dictionary 1403
Japanese Festivals 1648
Japanese Folk Festivals 1650
Japanese Life and Culture 1632, 1636
The Japanese Mind 1630
Japanese Mythology 1646
Japanese Religion; A Survey 1640
Japanese Religion in the Meiji Era 1641
Japanese Religion: Unity and Diversity 1638
Japanese Religions 18, 22, 38, 48-9, 51, 55, 1614-78
Japan's New Buddhism 1505, 1643
Japan's Religions 1643
JEDIN, H. 545, 563, 619
JEFFERY, A. 1038, 1054-5
The Jehovah's Witnesses 701
JELLICOE, S. 819, 912
JENSEN, A. E. 268
JEREMIAS, J. 940
The Jerome Biblical Commentary 833
Jerusalem Bible 795
Jesus 952-66
Jesus and Christian Origins 955
Jesus and His Times 959
Jesus in History 862
Jesus of Nazareth 956
The Jesus People 1927
Jesus, the Man, the Mission and the Message 958
Jewish Antiquites 445
The Jewish Encyclopedia 417
Jewish Liturgy and Its Development 496
Jewish Mind 456
Jewish Sects in the Times of Jesus 495
Jewish War 445
Jewish Worship 499
The Jews, Their History 454
Jews, Gods, and History 451
JOBES, G. 122
JOCHELSON, V. I. 1820, 1890
JOHN, E. 651
JOHNSON, D. C. 1207
JOHNSON, J. E. 24
JONES, B. E. 2012
JONES, C. E. 735
JONGELING, B. 976
JORDAN, L. H. 106
JOSEPHUS FLAVIUS 445
JOY, C. R. 848
JUDAH, J. S. 697
Judaism 22, 38, 48, 51, 55, 414-518
Judaism; A Historical Presentation 453
Judaism; A Portrait 482
Judaism: A Sociology 485
Judaism and Modern Man 472
Judaism as a Civilization 477
Judaism in a Christian World 469
Judaism in America 732
Judaism: Postbiblical and Talmudic Period 446
Judaism; The Way of Life 466

The Judean Scrolls 979
JULIEN, C. A. 1168
JULY, R. W. 1729
JUNG, C. G. 214, 1811
JUNOD, H. A. 1755
JURJI, E. J. 48

Kabalah 504
Kabbalah 503, 505
KÄHLER, M. 961
Kalabari 1750
KALGHATGI, T. G. 1369
Kalpa Sutra 1367
KALTENMARK, M. 1607
The Kami Way 1663
KAMMA, F. C. 1872
KAPERLUND, A. S. 306
KAPLAN, M. M. 476
KAPLEAU, P. 1461
Karaites 494
Karika 1307
KARLGREN, B. 1558, 1560
KARMAY, S. G. 1389
Katanga 1743
Katha 1307
KATO, G. 1654, 1661
KAUFMANN, J. 478
KEE, H. 941, 962
Keilschriftbibliographie 279
KEITH, A. B. 1300, 1492
KELM, A. 385
Kena 1307
KENNEDY, J. R. 28
KENNEY, E. H. 1569, 1608
KENYON, F. C. 896
KENYON, K. M. 868-9
KERENYI, K. 332, 1811
Kern Institute 1252
KERR, H. T. 564
KHAIR, G. S. 1318
KIDDER, J. E. 1498
KING, A. A. 668
KING, N. Q. 1756
KISHIMOTO, H. 2, 1641
al-Kitab al-Agdas 1186
KITAGAWA, J. M. 47, 1220, 1618, 1642
KITTEL, G. 925
KLAUSER, T. 629-30
KLEIN, B. T. 1795
KLEIN, F. A. 1075
KNAPPERT, J. 1757
KNIGHT, G. N. 2016
KOCH, K. 897
Kojiki 1624-5
KOLARZ, W. 1911
KOLATCH, A. J. 435
KONOW, S. 1270
The Koran Interpreted 1025
Koreri 1872
KORS, A. C. 2023
KORY, R. B. 1686
KRAMER, S. N. 278, 302
KRICKENBERG, W. 378
Krishna Consciousness 1684, 1688
KRISTENSEN, W. B. 169
KRITZECK, J. 1056-7, 1169
KÜHNEL, E. 1118
KÜHNER, H. 652
KÜMMEL, W. G. 942
Kumulipo 1873
Kunapipi 1837
KUNG-SUN, YANG 1589
Kwakiutl 1802

LA BARRE, W. 1706, 1808
LAL, P. 1312
LAL, R. B. 1319
LAMMENS, H. 1160
LANDIS, B. Y. 49
LANDMAN, I. 421
The Lands of the Eastern Caliphate 1020
LANE-POOLE, S. 1023
LANFORD, T. K. 157
LANG, D. M. 1135
LANGEVIN, P. E. 824
LANMAN, C. R. 1211
Lao-Tzu 1597-1601
Lao Tzu and Taoism 1607
LAPP, P. W. 870
Larousse Encyclopedia of Mythology 123, 375, 1691
LARSEN, E. 660
LARSON, G. J. 364
LASOR, W. S. 977, 981
LASTRANGE, G. 1019-20
The Later Christian Fathers 575
LATOURETTE, K. S. 545, 565, 607, 635
LAU, D. 1582, 1600
LAWRENCE, M. 1976

LAYMAN, E. M. 1687
LAYMON, C. M. 838
LEACH, M. 119
LEANEY, A. R. C. 849
LEARY, T. 1935
LEBRA, W. P. 1887
LEBRAS, G. 223
LEEMING, D. A. 136
LEEUW, G. van der 170
The Legacy of Islam 1062
Legends of the Jews 448
LEGGE, J. 1531, 1557, 1595
Legs-bshad-mdzod 1389
LEHRBURGER, E. 660
LEIMAN, S. Z. 427
LEITH, J. M. 613
LENZER, G. 226
LEONARD, E. G. 686
LEONE, M. P. 1946
LESHAN, L. 1969
Lesotho 1732
LESSA, W. A. 107
LESTER, R. 1472
LEVENSON, J. R. 1586
LEVI, S. 1401
LEVI-STRAUSS, C. 137-8
LEVY, I. 498
LEVY, R. 1128
LEWIS, B. 1092-1094
LEWIS, C. S. 634
LEWIS, H. D. 171
LEWIS, H. S. 2014
LEWIS, W. H. 1169
LEWY, G. 1901
LI, DUN J. 1550
Li Chi 1566
LIANG, C. C. 1587
Library Research Guide to Religion and Theology 28
Lieh-tzu 1602-3
LIENHARDT, G. 1758
The Life and Times of Muhammad 1044
The Life of a South African Tribe 1755
The Life of Buddha 1441-2
The Life of Muhammad 1041
Life of Muhammad from Original Sources 1045
Life Without Death 1968
The Light of the Nations 911
Like a Great River 1350
LIN, Y. 1216
LINDSAY, J. 1999
LINDZEY, G. 205
LING, T. O. 1493, 1936
A Literary Approach to the New Testament 949
A Literary History of Persia 1140
A Literary History of the Arabs 1138
Literary Interpretations of Biblical Narratives 892
Literature and Zen 1468
The Literature of the Old Testament 913
LITSCH, F. 1594
LITTLE, L. C. 67
Liturgies of the Western Church 632
LIU, W. C. 1571
Living Religions of the World 57
Living Thought of the Prophet Muhammad 1060
LLOYD, S. 311
Lodagaa 1746
LOEWENICH, W. von 681
LOGAN, D. 1970
LONG, C. H. 47, 259, 1701
LOVELL, E. K. 1172
LOVERDO, C. de 333
LOWIE, R. H. 269, 1809
LU K'UAN YÜ 1453
Luba Religions and Magic in Customs and Beliefs 1736
LUEKER, E. L. 703
Lugbara Religions 1763
LUK, C. 1453
LUKAS, J. O. 1759
LUOMALA, K. 1874-5
LURKER, M. 115
Lutheran Cyclopedia 703
Lutheranism in North America 705
LYON, P. J. 1824
LYONS, A. 2024
Lyuba 1764

MCARTHUR, H. K. 963
MACAULIFFE, M. A. 1380
MCCABE, J. P. 676
MACCANA, P. 370
MACCASLAND, S. V. 16,

261, 1011, 1204, 1366, 1374, 1696
MCCONNELL, R. A. 1971
MACCULLOCH, J. A. 124
MACDONALD, D. B. 1156
MACDONELL, A. A. 1265, 1298, 1301
MCFARLAND, H. N. 1669
MACGREGOR, G. 898-9
MCGUIRE, M. R. P. 328
MACHOVEC, M. 964
MCINTOSH, C. 2000
MCKELWAY, A. J. 570
MACKENZIE, A. 1997
MACKENZIE, D. A. 1876
MCKENZIE, J. L. 809
MACKENZIE, N. I. 2015
MCKINNEY, G. D. 700
MCKNIGHT, E. V. 900, 943
MCLEAN, G. F. 540
MCLEOD, A. L. 1834, 1850
MCLEOD, W. H. 1381
MCLINTOCK, A. H. 1848
MACLINTOCK, J. 1895
MCNEIL, W. K. 1013
MACNICOL, N. 1295
Magic and the Millenium 1709
Magic, Divination, and Witchcraft Among the Barotse 1771
The Magic Makers 1959
Magic, Science, and Other Essays 1707
Magic, Supernaturalism, and Religion 1981
The Magus or Celestial Intelligencer 1958
Mahabharata 1311-16
MAHADEVAN, T. M. D. 1344
MAHAR, J. M. 1253
Mahayana Buddhism 1443-8
Maimonides 442
MAIR, L. 2025
Major Trends in Jewish Mysticism 502
Majumdar, R. C. 1264
The Making of Counter-Culture 1942
Makorekore 1745
MALINOWSKI, B. 1707
Man and His Religion 218
Man, Myth, and Magic 125, 1692, 1950
The Man of Many Qualities 1565
Man Seeks the Divine 102
Man; The New Hamanism 609
Mandari 1737
Mandrikya 1307
Mani 357
MANI, V. 1257
Mani and Manicheism 358
Manichean Literature 356
Manicheism 277
Man's Religions 51
MANSON, T. W. 840
MANSOOR, M. 982
Manual of Patrology and History of Theology 577
Manual of Zen Buddhism 1464
Manus Religion 1869
Maori Lore 1857
The Maori People 1858
Maori Religion and Mythology 1853
MAQUET, J. 1715
MARANDA, P. 139
MARGOLIS, M. 455
MARGULL, M. J. 620
MARKEN, J. W. 1798
Maronite Church 665, 668
MAROUZEAU, J. 329
MARROU, H. 678
MARSH, G. H. 1821
MARSHALL, R. H. 1912
MARTELLO, L. L. 2026
MARTIN, S. 545
MARTY, M. E. 687
MARX, A. 455
Marxist Looks at Jesus 964
The Mary Knoll Catholic Dictionary 675
The Masks of God 128
MASON, J. A. 386
Masons 1964, 2010-17
Masters Abstracts 68
Materials for the History of the Text of the Quran 1038
MATHEWS, S. 17
MATHIOT, M. 112
MATSUO, K. 1506
MATTIL, A. J. 920
MATTIL, M. B. 920
Maui-of-Thousand-Tricks 1874
MAUSS, M. 1708
MAY, H. G. 789, 799, 854

Maya History and Religion 384
MAYER, F. E. 754
MAYER, H. E. 588
MAZAR, B. 457
Mazdakism 277
MBITI, J. S. 1760-1
MEAD, F. S. 755
A Meaning and End of Religions 56
The Meaning of Religion 169
The Meaning of the Glorious Koran 1031
MEANS, P. A. 387
The Mediaeval Church 582-6
Medieval Islam 1103
The Medium, the Mystic, and the Physicist 1969
MEISSNER, W. W. 206
Melanesia 1862, 1867-8
The Melanesians 1867
MELTRAUX, A. 388
Mencius 1580-3
Mende 1747
MENDELSOHN, I. 287
MENDELSOHN, J. 728
MENENDEZ, A. J. 1896
The Mennonite Church in America 711
The Mennonite ·Encyclopedia 706
Mennonite History 709, 711
Mennonites and Their Heritage 710
Mennonites in Europe 709
MESKILL, J. 1526
The Message of Holy Qur'an 1024
The Message of the Scrolls 985
METHA, J. M. 1321
Methodism 712
Methodists 715
Metoscopy 1967
METRAUX, A. 1826
METZGER, B. M. 799, 944, 953, 967
Mexican and Central American Mythology 377
MEYENDORFF, J. 669
MEYEROWITZ, E. L. R. 1762
MICHAEL, H. N. 1891-2
Micronesia 1862
Middle East and Islam 1010
MIDDLETON, J. 1763
Midrash rabbah 441
Millennial Church 726
MILLER, A. L. 1647
MILLER, J. 1302
MILLER, J. L. 810
MILLER, M. 810
MILLER, W. M. 1186
MILLGRAM, A. E. 499
MILLROTH, B. 1764
The Mind of the Qur'an 1035
Miracles 634
Mission Handbook 636
MITCHELL, E. D. 1977
MITCHELL, R. C. 1722
Mithraism 277, 314, 317
Mithras, the Secret God 317
MITROS, J. F. 29, 1704
MIZUNO, K. 1429
MO TSU 1588
MODE, P. G. 736
Modern Catholicism 681
Modern Islam 1109
Modern Islam in India 1184
Modern Islamic Literature 1057
Modern Japan and Shinto Nationalism 1659
Modern Japanese Religions 1670
A Modern Philosophy of Religion 174
A Modern Reader in the Philosophy of Religion 158
The Modern Reader's Guide to the Bible 850
Modern Religious Movements in India 1353
Modern Trends in Hinduism 1352
Modern Trends in Islam 1105
Modern Varieties of Judaism 492
The Modernist Muslim Movement in Indonesia 1185
MOFFATT, J. 796
The Moffatt Bible Concordance 844
Mohammed, the Man and His Faith 1042
Mohammedanism 1071
MOIR, J. S. 748
MOLLAND, E. 661

Monks and Civilization 642
The Monks of the West 643
Monks, Priests, and Peasants 1491
MONTALAMBERT, C. F. 643
MONTER, E. W. 2027
MOORE, C. A. 1323, 1436, 1555, 1630
MOORE, G. F. 50, 913
Moravians 661
MORENZ, S. 298
MORGAN, H. 1592
MORGAN, K. 1076, 1221, 1345, 1430
MORLEY, S. G. 382
Mormonism in American Culture 717
MORRALL, J. 1899
MORRIS, A. V. 1630
MORTON, W. S. 1631
MOSES BEN MAIMON 442
MOSS, T. 1972
MOULD, E. W. K. 871
The Mountain People 1777
The Mouth of Heaven 1803
Muhammad and the Conquest of Islam 1043
Muhammad at Mecca 1046
Muhammad at Medina 1046
Muhammad: Prophet and Statesman 1046
The Muhammedan Dynasties 1023
Muhammedan Festivals 1162
MUIR, W. 1045
MÜLLER, F. 1212
Multipurpose Tools for Bible Study 821
MUNCH, P. A. 365
MUNRO, N. G. 1651
Muntu 1754
MURAOKA, T. 1662
MURATA, K. 1505
Murdaka 1307
MURDOCK, G. P. 1799
MURPHY, E. J. 1730
MURPHY, H. S. 921
MURPHY, R. E. 833
MURRAY, A. V. 1902
MURTI, T. R. U. 1445
The Muslim and Christian Calenders 1123
The Muslim Creed 1158
Muslim Devotions 1161
Muslim Institutions 1126
The Muslim World 1096
The Mysteries of Mithra 314
Mystical Dimensions of Islam 1147
Mystical Experience 149
Mysticism 144
Mysticism; A Study and Anthology 147
Mysticism; A Study in the Nature 153
Mysticism in World Religion 150
The Mystics of Islam 1145
Myth and Cult among Primitives 268
Myth and Reality 133
Myth and Religion of the North 367
Myth and Ritual in Christianity 647
Myth and Ritual in the Ancient Near East 286
Myth in Indo-European Antiquity 364
The Myth of Asia 1227
The Myth of the Bagre 1746
The Mythic Image 129
Mythologies of the Ancient World 278
Mythology 139
The Mythology of All Races 124
Mythology of Americas 377
The Mythology of Secret Societies 2017
Mythology: The Age of Fable 117
Myths and Legends of China 1546
Myths and Legends of the Ancient Near East 281
Myths and Legends of the Australian Aboriginals 1846
Myths and Legends of the Polynesians 1864
Myths and Legends of the South Sea Islands 1876
Myths and Legends of the Swahili 1757
Myths and Symbols in Indian Arts and Civilization 1283

Myths of Greeks and Romans 331
The Myths of Mexico and Peru 379
The Myths of the North American Indians 1814

NADEL, S. 1765
NAJIB ULLAH 1136
NAKAMURA, H. 1222, 1632
Nanak 1377
NASR, H. 1077-8, 1157
National Faith of Japan 1660
Native South Americans 1824
Natural Symbols 131
NAUMAN, S. E. 2006
Navaho Religion 1812
NAVALANI, K. 1373
NAYLOR, P. I. H. 2001
The Near East 1015
A Near East Studies Handbook 1004
Near Eastern Mythology 284
NEBESKY-WOJKOWITZ, R. de 1391
Necromancy 1988
NEEDLEMAN, J. 1688, 1937
NEIL, W. 839, 841
NEILL, S. C. 608, 621, 637-9, 690, 945
NEILL, T. P. 682
NELSON, E. C. 705
Nelson's Complete Concordance to the Bible 843
NENNEY, M. C. 817
Nestorian Heresy 625
NEUSNER, J. 436, 479
NEVINS, A. 675
The New Apocrypha 1982
The New Believers 1924
New Catholic Encyclopedia 526
The New Century Handbook of Greek Mythology and Legend 323
The New Consciousness 1916
New Dictionary of the Liturgy 631
New Directions in Biblical Archaeology 872
A New Encyclopedia of Freemasonry 2011
New English Bible 798
The New English Bible Companion 926
The New Face of Buddha 1510
New Gods of America 1943
The New International Dictionary of the Christian Church 523
The New Jewish Encyclopedia 418
New Movements in Religious Education 251
The New Oxford Annotated Bible 799
The New Religions 1688
The New Religions of Japan 1667-71
The New Religious Consciousness 1930
The New Schaff-Herzog Encyclopedia of Religious Knowledge 20, 1895
The New Standard Jewish Encyclopedia 419
New Testament Abstracts 927
New Testament History 930
New Testament Introduction 951
New Testament Issues 928
New Testament Literature in the Light of Modern Scholarship 939
New Testament Theology 940
New Testament Tools and Studies 953, 967
New Thought 1921
The New Westminster Dictionary of the Bible 806
NEWALL, V. 1951
NEWELL, W. H. 1673
NHAT-HANH, T. 1508
NICHOLLS, W. 566
NICHOLS, R. 1976
NICHOLSON, I. 377
NICHOLSON, R. A. 1138, 1145-6
NIESEL, W. 662
NIEUWENHUIJZE, C. A. O. van 1185
Nigeria 1775
NIGG, W. 623, 644
Nihongi 1626
NILSSON, M. P. 342
NIMTZ, A. H. 1170

The Nine Songs 1590
The Nine Ways of Bon 1388
NIRVEDANANDA, S. 1346
NIVISON, D. S. 1572
NOBILE, P. 1940
NOER, D. 1185
Non-Christian Religions 14, 1690
NORBECK, E. 270
NORRIS, H. 658
Norse Mythology 365
NOSS, J. B. 51
North American Indian Mythology 377
The North American Indian Orpheus Tradition 1805
Not of the World 1924
NOTTINGHAM, E. K. 230
Nubia, Church of 665
Nuer Religion 1742
NUGENT, D. 2028
Number Symbolism 2007
Numerology 1961, 2007
Nupe Religion 1765
NYANATILOKA, B. 1404, 1470

OBERMANN, J. 307
O'BRIEN, E. 148
O'BRIEN, T. C. 659
The Occult 1966, 1992
The Occult Explosion 1965
The Occult Underground 1990
Oceanic Mythology 1877
O'DEA, T. F. 231, 718
OESTERLEY, W. O. E. 873, 914
OESTERREICH, T. K. 1973
OFFNER, C. B. 1670
OFORI, P. E. 1702
OGILVIE, R. M. 350
Okinawan Religion 1887
Old Catholics 661
Old Testament Commentary Survey 910
The Old Testament, Including the Apocrypha 890
The Old Testament, Its Formation and Development 917
OLDENBURG, U. 308
The Oldest Stories in the World 283
O'LEARY, de Lacy E. 1098
O'LEARY, T. J. 1799, 1823
OLIVER, R. A. 1731
OLIVER, W. H. 1851
OLLARD, S. L. 527
OLMSTEAD, C. E. 756
Olódúmaré 1752
On Indian Mahayana 1448
On Judaism 464
On Method in the History of Religion 5
On the Margin of the Invisible 1985
ONO, M. 1663
The Open Conspiracy 1941
Opium of the People 1908
OPPENHEIM, L. 303
Oracles and Demons of Tibet 1391
O'REILY, P. 1861
ORGAN, T. W. 1347
Organizing to Beat the Devil 714
Orientalism and History 1226
The Origin and Development of the State Cult of Confucius 1573
Original Teachings of the Chan Buddhism 1454
Origins of Astrology 1999
The Origins of Greek Religion 338
Origins of Sacrifice 135
ORLIN, L. L. 280
ORLINSKY, H. M. 874
ORT, L. J. R. 357
The Orthodox Church 671
The Orthodox Church, Its Past and Its Role in the World 669
Orthodox Jews 471, 492
OSBORNE, H. 377
OSTANDER, S. 1974
OTTEN, H. 312
Ottoman Empire and Islamic Tradition 1181
Our Bible and the Ancient Manuscripts 896
Our English Bible in Making 789
An Outline and Annotated Bibliography of Chinese Philosophy 1547
Outline of Cultural Materials

1699
An Outline of Dahomean Religious Beliefs 1748
Outline of World Cultures 1699
Outlines of Hinduism 1344
Outlines of Jainism 1368
Outlines of Muhammedan Law 1133
OVERMYER, D. 1483
The Oxford Classical Dictionary 324
The Oxford Dictionary of the Christian Church 528
OXTOBY, W. G. 316

A Pacific Bibliography 1862
PADWICK, C. E. 1161
Palestine under the Moslems 1019
Pali Text Society 1407
PALMER, E. H. 1030
PALMER, R. E. A. 351
PANATI, C. 1975
PANDE, G. C. 1431
PANNIKAR, R. 1303
Parapsychology: A Century of Inquiry 1979
Parapsychology: Sources of Information 1956
PARK, W. Z. 1810
PARKER, D. 2002
PARRINDER, E. G. 18-19, 108, 140, 1209, 1223, 1693-5, 1766-9, 1773, 2029
Parting of the Way 1609
Past and Present 334
Pastor, L. 653
PATAI, R. 415, 456
PATANJALI 1335
The Path of Buddha 1430
Patrology 580
Patron Saints of Occupations and Professions 675
Patrons and Their Feasts 675
The Pattern of Australian Culture 1834
Patterns in Comparative Relition 103
PATTERSON, M. L. P. 1202
Paul 968
Pawnees 1814
PAYNE, J. B. 811
Peace Mission 1921
PEARSON, J. D. 313, 1014, 1017
PELICAN, J. 670
Pelican Guide to Modern Theology 566
The Pelican History of the Church 578, 586, 597, 605, 610, 638
The Penguin Dictionary of Saints 654
PENNER, H. H. 6
Pentapolis, Church of 665
The Pentecostal Movement 719
The Pentecostals 720
The People Called Quakers 724
The People Called Shakers 726
The People of the Center 1815
People of the Old Testament Times 867
Peoples of Africa 1727
The Peoples of Asiatic Russia 1890
PERADOTTO, J. 330
PERDUE, P. A. 1432
PEROWNE, S. 352
PERRIN, N. 946
PERRY, W. N. 1938
Persia in Islamic Times 1177
Persian Literature 1139
PETER, J. 965
PETERS, F. E. 1095
PETERSON, K. G. 825
The Peyote Cult 1808
The Peyote Religion 1813
PFEFFER, L. 1903
PFEIFFER, C. F. 812, 858, 915
PFEIFFER, F. H. 915, 947
The Pharisees 493
PHILIPPI, D. L. 1624, 1627
Philological Annual 327
A Philosophical Scrutiny of Religion 162
A Philosophical Study of Relition 165
Philosophies of Judaism 470
Philosophy of Religion. Abernethy, G. L. 157
Philosophy of Religion. Hick,

J. 166
Philosophy of Religion. Trueblood, D. E. 175
The Philosophy of the Kalam 1159
Philosophy of the 20th Century: Catholic and Christian 540
The Philosophy of the Upanishads 1309
Physiognomy 1967
PICK, F. L. 2016
PICKTHALL, M. 1031
Pictorial Biblical Encyclopedia 803
Picture Museum of Sorcery, Magic and Alchemy 1967
PIDDINGTON, R. 1878
PIGGOTT, J. 1646
PIGGOTT, S. 371
A Pilgrim's Guide to Planet Earth 1916a
PILLING, A. R. 1832
PINSENT, J. 343
PITOIS, C. 1976
PLANHOL, X. de 1021
PLAUT, W. G. 480
Plymouth Brethren 661
The Pocket History of Freemasonry 2016
PODHRADSKY, G. 631
POLITELLA, J. 248
Poltergeists 1963
Polynesia 1862-4, 1870
Polynesian Mythology and Ancient Traditional History of the Maori 1855
Polynesian Religion 1871
POLZIN, R. M. 901
PONCE, C. 503
PONSOBY-FANE, R. A. B. 1664-5
Pontificio Instituto Biblico 822
POPE, H. 1939
The Popes 650
The Popes; A Concise Biographical History 651
A Popular Dictionary of Buddhism 1402
A Popular History of the Catholic Church 680
Possession, Demonical and Other 1973
POTTER, C. F. 52
POTTER, K. H. 1322
The Powers of Evil in Western Religion 1962
Practice of Chinese Buddhism 1487
The Practice of Zen 1456
Prasna 1307
The Prayers of African Religion 1761
The Preaching of Islam 1085
Precognition 1975, 1987
Pre-Columbian American Religions 378
Prediction and Prophecy 2008
Prehistoric Religions 267
Presbyterianism 721
PREUSS, A. 2010
PRICE, I. M. 790
PRICE, J. L. 948
Primitive Buddhism 1429
Primitive Christianity in Its Primitive Setting 576
Primitive Religion 42, 45, 46, 51, 257-72
Primitive Religion. Lowie, R. H. 269
Primitive Religion; Its Nature and Origin 271
Principles and Problems of Biblical Translation 903
Principles of the Jewish Faith 475
PRITCHARD, J. B. 288-9, 875
The Private Sea 1922
Protestant Christianity Interpreted Through Its Development 684
The Protestant Ethic and Spirit of Protestantism 688
The Protestant Reformation 555
Protestantism 48
Protestantism. Marty, M. E. 687
The Psychedelic Teacher 1931
Psychiana 1921
Psychic Discoveries Behind the Iron Curtain 1974
Psychic Exploration 1977
The Psychic Force 1957
Psychic healing 1975
Psychoanalysis and Religion

212
Psychokinesis 1975, 1987
Psychological Abstracts 203
Psychology of Religion. Capps, D. 204
The Psychology of Religion. Jung, C. G. 214
Psychology of Religion. Scobie, G. E. W. 216
Psychology of Religion. Spinks, G. S. 217
Psychotherapy and Religion 215
PUMMER, R. 7
Puranic Encyclopedia 1257
PURVIS, J. S. 529
PUSALKAR, A. D. 1264
Pygmies 1776

QUALE, G. R. 1224
QUASTEN, J. 580
Quest for the Original Gita 1318
The Quiet Mind 1925
The Quiet Rebels 722
Qumran and the History of the Biblical Text 983
The Qur'an as Scripture 1038

RADHAKRISHNAN, S. S. 1306, 1315, 1323, 1325, 1329
A Radical Reformation 604
Radical Theology and the Death of God 1918
RADIN, P. 271, 1811
RAHBAR, DAUD 1039
RAHMAN, F. 1079
RAHNER, K. 530, 532
RAHULA, W. 1473, 1494
RAI, R. K. 1332
Ramakrishna Movement 1684, 1688
The Ramayana 1320-1
RAMBO, L. 204
RAMSEY, P. 253
RANADE, R. D. 1310, 1331
Te Rangi Hiroa 1854
RANSOHOFF, P. 204
RAPHAEL, C. 500
RAST, W. 902
Ratana 1856
The Raw and the Cooked 137
RAY, B. 1770
RAY, N. 1382
Reader in Comparative Religion 107
A Reader on Islam 1055
A Reader's Guide to Great Religion 22, 259, 425, 541, 1002, 1287, 1396, 1520, 1618, 1701
Readings from the Mystics of Islam 1148
Readings in Christian Thought 564
Readings in Eastern Religious Thought 1214
Reasons for Jewish Customs and Traditions 501
Red Men's Religion 1817
Rediscovering Judaism 491
REES, A. 372
REES, B. 372
Reference Encyclopedia of the American Indian 1795
Reflections on Things at Hand 1584
Reform Jews 471, 480, 492
The Reformation. Chadwick, O. 597
Reformation. Todd, J. M. 603
The Reformation Era 599
The Reformation in England 601
The Reformation in Recent Historical Thought 592
The Reformation of the Sixteenth Century 596
REGAZZI, J. J. 33
REICH, C. A. 1940
REICHARD, G. 1812
REICHELT, K. L. 1484, 1593
REINHOLD, M. 334
REISCHAUER, A. K. 1499
REITMAN, E. 1861
Religion: A Humanistic Field 250
Religion; A Sociological View 230
Religion Among the Primitives 265
Religion; An Anthropological View 187

Religion and Change in Contemporary Asia 1225
Religion and Healing in Mandari 1737
Religion and Judgement 159
The Religion and Mythology of the Greeks 341
Religion and Political Modernization 1904
Religion and Revolution 1901
Religion and Social Organization in Central Polynesia 1878
The Religion and the Philosophy of the Vedas 1300
Religion and the Search for New Ideals in the USSR 1914
Religion and the Transformation of the Society 1779
La Religion au Canada 742
Religion, Culture, and Society 233
Religion for a New Generation 1937
Religion in Africa 1768
Religion in American Life 731-2
Religion in Ancient History 275
Religion in Canada 742
Religion in Canadian Society 742
Religion in China 1530
Religion in Chinese Garment 1593
Religion in Chinese Society 1538
Religion in Communist China 1539
Religion in Education 248
Religion in Essence and Manifestation 170
Religion in Greece and Rome 335
Religion in Japanese Experience 1639
Religion in Philosophical and Cultural Perspective 163
Religion in Primitive Society 270
Religion in Social Context 227
Religion in South Asia 1268
Religion in the Age of Aquarius 1926
Religion in the Soviet Union 1911
Religion in the U.S.S.R. 1909
The Religion of Ancient Greece 345
The Religion of China 1537
The Religion of Greeks and Romans 332
The Religion of India 1272
The Religion of Islam 1050
Religion of Israel 876
The Religion of the Chinese 1528
The Religion of the Hindus 1345
The Religion of the Sikhs 1383
The Religion of the Veda 1336
The Religion of the Yorubas 1759
The Religion of Tibet 1476
Religion, Politics, and Social Change in the Third World 1904
Religion, Society, and the Individual 238
Religions; A Select Classified Bibliography 29, 1704
Religions and Man 42
Religions in a Changing World 59
Religions in Japan 1645
Religions in the Middle East 548
Religions, Mythologies, Folklores 25
Religions of Africa 1756
Religions of Ancient India 1271
Religions of India. Berry, T. M. 1267
Religions of India. Konow & Tuxen 1270
Religions of Japan at Present 1672
The Religions of Man 55
The Religions of Mankind 54
Religions of Mankind Today and Yesterday 53
Religions of the Ancient East 282
Religions of the Ancient Near East. Mendelsohn, I. 287
Religions of the Ancient Near East. Ringgren, H. 290

Religions of the East. Bancroft, A. 1218
Religions of the East. Kitagawa, J. M. 1220
The Religions of the Roman Empire 347
Religions of the World. Clemen, C. C. 41
Religions of the World. McCasland, S. V. 16, 261, 1011, 1204, 1366, 1374, 1696
Religions of the World from Primitive Beliefs to Modern Faith 19, 1694
Religions of the World, Their Nature and Their History 41
The Religions of Tibet 1480
Religious and Cosmic Beliefs of Central Polynesia 1879
Religious and Spiritual Groups in Modern America 1681
Religious and Theological Abstracts 34
Religious Behaviour 208
The Religious Bodies of America 754
Religious Cults of the Caribbean 1827
Religious Education 254
The Religious Experience of Mankind 109
Religious Issues in American Life 734
A Religious History of America 734
A Religious History of American People 738
Religious Life of Japanese People 1636
The Religious Life of Man 1343, 1433, 1535, 1638-9
Religious Map of Japan 1634
Religious Movements in Contemporary America 1946
Religious Observances in Tibet 1390
Religious Orders of Men 641
Religious Sects 663
Religious Sects of the Hindus 1356
The Religious Systems of China 1529
Religious Trends in Modern China 1540
Renaissance of Hinduism 1348
RENCKENS, H. 876
RENOU, L. 1271, 1289
Repertoire Bibliographique de la Philosophie 156
Research in Personality, Character, and Religious Education 67
Research on Religious Development 252
Researches into Chinese Superstitions 1591
Revelation and Reason in Islam 1155
Revolution and Religion 1901
REYNOLDS, B. 1771
REYNOLDS, F. E. 1396
REYNOLDS, M. M. 69
Rhodesia 1745
RICE, D. T. 1120-1
RICHARD, J. 1978
RICHARDSON, A. 531
RICHARDSON, E. C. 35
RICHARDSON, H. N. 871
RINGGREN, H. 53, 290, 309, 816, 877
The Rise and Fall of Maya Civilization 384
The Rise of Reform Judaism 480
Rites of Eastern Christendom 668
Ritual and Symbol in Transitional Zaramo 1774
The Road to East 1939
ROBBINS, R. H. 1952
ROBERTS, J. M. 2017
ROBERTSON, R. 232
ROBINSON, R. H. 1433, 1446
ROBINSON, T. H. 873, 914
ROBSON, J. 1051
ROGO, D. S. 1979, 1998
ROHEIM, G. 1842-5
Roman Catholicism 677
Roman Mythology 352
Roman Myths 349
Roman Religion and Roman Empire 351
The Romans and Their Gods in the Age of Augustus 350
RÖMER, W. H. P. 299
ROMM, E. G. 1941

RONART, S. 1000
ROSE, H. J. 335, 344
ROSENTHAL, E. I. S. 1107
ROSENZWEIG, F. 481
ROSHWALD, M. 494
Rosicrucians 1964, 2014-15
ROSS, F. H. 1666
ROSS, N. W. 1462
ROSZAK, T. 1942
ROTH, C. 414, 419, 497
ROTH, J. K. 757
ROTH, L. 482
ROUSE, R. 621
ROWLEY, H. H. 813-4
ROWLEY, P. 1943
Royal Cities of the Old Testament 869
RUBENSTEIN, R. L. 483
RUDIN, J. 215
The Rumor of the Angels 1919
RUNCIMAN, S. 589
RUSH, J. A. 1980
The Rush Hour of the Gods 1669
The Russian Church and the Soviet State 1910
RUSSELL, J. B. 585
RYDBERG, V. 366
RYPKA, J. 1141

The Sabbot 2030
Sacramentum mundi 532
The Sacred and the Profane 1
The Sacred Books of China 1557, 1595
The Sacred Books of Confucius and Other Confucian Classics 1568
Sacred Books of the Buddhist 1407
Sacred Books of the East 1212, 1595
The Sacred Books of the Jews 434
Sacred Canopy 225
The Sacred Scriptures of the Japanese 1622
The Sacred State of the Akan 1762
SADDHATISSA, H. 1434
SADDIQUI, H. 1032
St. Thomas Christians 665
Sakota 1738
Saliba, J. A. 3
Samaritans 494
SANDALL, R. 725
SANDERS, S. A. 972
SANDMEL, S. 437
SARKISYANZ, E. 1509
SARMA, D. S. 1348
SAUNDERS, E. D. 1500
The Savage Mind 138
SAVORY, R. M. 1080, 1177
SAWYERR, H. 1747
Scandinavian Mythology 361
SCHACHT, J. 1062, 1134
SCHAFF, F. 567, 614
SCHAPERA, I. 1723, 1772
SCHARFSTEIN, B. A. 149
SCHECTER, J. 1510
SCHECHTER, S. 484
SCHILLING, R. 353
SCHIMMEL, A. 1122, 1147
Schism and Renewal in Africa 1733
SCHMANDT, R. H. 682
SCHNEIDER, L. 233-4
SCHOEPS, H. J. 54
SCHOLEM, G. 502, 504-5
SCHOLER, D. M. 922
SCHROEDER, L. 1974
SCHUBERT, P. 921
SCHULMAN, A. 420
SCHULWEIS, H. M. 161
SCHWARTZ, W. 903
SCHWEIZER, E. 966
SCHWIMMER, E. 1858
Science and Civilization of Islam 1078
Sciences Religieuses 26
The Scientific Study of Religion 239
SCOBIE, G. E. W. 216
SCOTT, R. B. Y. 916
Scrying 2003
Searching the Scriptures 889
The Second Coming 2024
The Secret of the Golden Flower 1604
The Secret of the Sublime 1605
SEJOURNE, L. 383
SELBIE, J. 11
Select Bibliography of Sikhs and Sikhism 1375

Select Bibliography on Arab Islamic Civilization 1012
A Select Liturgical Lexicon 628
A Selected and Annotated Bibliography ... Dealing with the Near and Middle East 1006
A Selected Annotated Bibliography of "Store-front" Churches 750
SELIGMAN, B. Z. 1651
SELIGMANN, K. 1981
SEN, K. M. 1349
The Septuagint and Modern Study 912
SETH, R. 2030
SETTON, K. M. 590
Seven Centuries of the Problems of Church and State 1900
SHABAN, M. A. 1099
Shamanism 1705
Shamanism in Western North America 1810
SHARIF, M. M. 1153
SHARKEY, J. 373
SHARMA, C. D. 1326
SHARMA, U. 144
SHAROT, S. 485
SHASTRI, H. P. 1320
SHEILS, H. 1839
Shih Ching 1559-61
Shi'ite Islam 1176
The Shi'ite Religion 1175
Shin Buddhism 1507
SHINN, R. L. 609
Shinto at the Fountain-head of Japan 1658
Shinto, the Kami Way 1663
Shinto, the Way of Gods 1655
Shinto, the Way of Japan 1666
SHOKO, W. 1501
Shona Religion 1745
Short Dictionary of Bible Personal Names 814
A Short History of Africa 1731
A Short History of Australia 1833
Short History of Buddhism 1421
A Short History of Chinese Philosophy 1553
A Short History of Confucian Philosophy 1571
A Short History of the Arab People 1089
A Short History of the Western Liturgy 630
Shorter Encyclopedia of Islam 1001
Shrine Shinto after World War II 1656
SHRYOCK, J. K. 1573
Shu ching 1558
SHUNAMI, S. 428
Siberia 1888-92
Siddhanta 1367
The Sikh Gurus and the Sikh Society 1382
The Sikh Religion 1380
Sikhism 1385
The Sikhs and Their Literature 1372
The Sikhs in Relation to Hindus 1378
SILBERMAN, B. S. 1205
SILVER, ABBA H. 486
SIMAN, M. 441
SIMON, J. J. 859
SIMON, M. 495, 506
SIMONSEN, C. 622
SIMPSON, G. E. 1827
SINCLAIR, K. 1852
SINGER, I. 417
SINGH, G. 1375, 1383
SINGH, K. 1384
SINGH, T. 1376, 1385
Sioux 1814
SIU, R. G. H. 1565
6000 Years of the Bible 904
SLADEK, J. T. 1982
The Slave 374
SLOTKIN, J. S. 1813
The Small Sects in America 753
SMART, N. 109, 146, 173, 251, 1327
SMITH, D. E. 1904
SMITH, D. H. 1532
SMITH, D. L. 1800
SMITH, D. M. 950
SMITH, E. W. 1773
SMITH, G. A. 860
SMITH, G. B. 17
SMITH, H. 55
SMITH, M. 1148-9

SMITH, R. J. 1644
SMITH, W. 533-4, 815
SMITH, W. C. 56, 1108, 1184
SMITH, W. M. 950
SMITH, W. R. 1846
SMITH, W. W. 1652
SNELLGROVE, D. L. 1388
The So-Called Historical Jesus 961
Social Anthropology of Melanesia 1868
The Social History of the Reformation 602
Social Sciences and Humanities Index 36
Social Sciences Citation Index 37
Social Sciences Index 36
Social Scientific Studies of Religion 24
The Social Structure of Islam 1128
Sociological Abstracts 224
Sociological Approach to Religion 234
The Sociological Interpretation of Religion 232
Sociology and Religion 226
Sociology and the Study of Religion 231
The Sociology of Japanese Religion 1673
Sociology of Religion. Fallding, H. 229
The Sociology of Religion. Stark, W. 235
Sociology of Religion. Wach, J. 236
The Sociology of Religion. Weber, M. 237
Sōka Gakkai 1504
Some Aspects of the History of Hinduism 1340
Some Nigerian Fertility Cults 1775
Son of God to Superstar 960
SONTAG, F. 757
SOOTHILL, W. E. 1405, 1533
SOPHER, D. E. 98-9
The Sound of the One Hand 1452
Source Book and Bibliographical Guide for American Church History 736
A Source Book in Indian Philosophy 1323
A Source Book of Advaita Vendanta 1330
A Source Book of Chinese Philosophy 1549
Sources of Chinese Tradition 1213
Sources of Indian Tradition 1293
Sources of the Japanese Tradition 1621
SOURDEL, D. 1081
South American Mythology 377
Southeast Asia 1207
SOUTHERN, R. W. 586
SOYMIE, M. 1594
SPEISER, E. A. 457
SPENCE, L. 1814, 1953
SPENCER, R. F. 1225
SPENCER, S. 150
SPERLING, A. I. 501
SPERLING, H. 506
SPIEGELBERG, F. 57
SPINKS, G. S. 217
The Spirit of Chinese Philosophy 1554
The Spirit of Eastern Christendom 670
The Spirit of Zen 1466
The Spiritual Background of Early Islam 1097
Spiritual Community 1916
SPIRO, M. E. 1511
SPIVEY, R. A. 950
The Springs of Mende 1747
SPULER, B. 1096
Ssŭ Shu 1567
STAAL, F. 151
STACE, W. T. 152
Standard Encyclopedia of Southern Africa 1716
STANNER, W. E. H. 1835
STANTON, H. U. W. 1040
The Star of David 462
STARK, W. W. 235
STARKEY, M. L. 698
STARKLOFF, C. F. 1815
STARR, E. C. 692
The State and the Church in a Free Society 1902
STEADMAN, J. M. 1227

STEIN, R. A. 1392
STEINBERG, M. 488
STEINILBER-OBERLIN, E. 1506
STERN, M. H. 429
STERN, W. B. 1130
STEVANS, C. M. 1948
STEVENSON, M. 1370
STEWARD, J. H. 1822
The Stones and the Scriptures 884
STOREY, C. A. 1139
The Story of Mysticism 645
The Story of New Zealand 1851
The Story of the Bible 891
STRACK, H. L. 439
STRAELEN, H. van 1670
Strange Sects and Cults 660
Strangers at the Door 1679
STREHLOW, T. G. H. 1847
STRØM, Å. U. 53
STROMMEN, M. P. 252
STRONG, J. 845
STROUP, H. H. 701, 1228, 1350, 1905
The Structure of the Ethical Terms in the Qur'an 1037
The Struggle of Islam in Modern Indonesia 1185
STRUVE, N. 1915
STRYK, L. 1416
Studies in Chinese Religion 1522
Studies in Chinese Thought 1556
Studies in Islamic Mysticism 1146
Studies in Jaina Philosophy 1371
Studies in Japanese Buddhism 1499
Studies in Muslim Ethics 1124
Studies in Shinto Thought 1662
Studies in Siberian Ethnogenesis 1891
Studies in Siberian Shamanism 1892
Studies in the Origins of Buddhism 1431
Study in Islamic History and Institutions 1127
The Study of Judaism 430
The Study of Religion and Primitive Religions 43
The Study of Religion in Colleges and Universities 253
A Study of Shinto 1661
The Study of the Bible 888
STURZO, L. 1906
Subject Guide to the Bible Stories 847
The Sufi Orders in Islam 1150
The Sufi Path of Love 1149
Sufism 1143
Sumerian Mythology 302
SUMMERS, M. 2031
Sun Dance 1819
SUNDARARAJAN, K. R. 1342
Supernature 1989
Supersenses 1975
Sutrakritanga 1367
SUZUKI, B. L. 1447
SUZUKI, D. T. 1447-8, 1458, 1463-5, 1507
Svetaśvatara 1307
Swahili 1757
SWANN, I. 1983
The Swan's Wide Waters 1684
SWANSON, G. E. 272
SWANTZ, M. L. 1774
SWEARER, D. K. 1435
Swedenborgians 661
SWEET, W. W. 715
SWYNGEDOUW, J. 1619
SYKES, E. 126
Symbols and Legends in Western Art 142
Symbols--Our Universal Language 121
Symbols, Signs, and Their Meaning 141
The Synagogue 498
Syrian Church 668
Syro-Malabar Rite 668
Systematic and Philosophical Theology 566
Systematic Theology 568
The Systematic Theology of Paul Tillich 570

Ta Hsüeh 1568
TABATABA'I, A. S. M. H. 1176
Tahiti 1861
T'ai I Chin Hua Tsung Chih 1604

TAKAKUSU, J. 1401, 1413
TALBOT, P. A. 1775
Tales of the North American Indians 1816
TALMON, S. 983
Talmud 435-6, 439, 443-4
Tangu Traditions 1866
Tantric Buddhism 1474-80
The Tantric Mysticism of Tibet 1477
A Tantric Tradition 1474
Tao tê Ching 1599-601
Taoism 38, 45, 48, 55, 1594-609
Taoist Teachings 1602
TAO-YÜAN, S. 1454
The Tarot 1967, 2009
Tasseomancy 2009
TATIA, N. 1371
TAYLOR, C. R. H. 1849, 1862
TAYLOR, M. S. 254
TAYLOR, R. 1859
Te Ika a Maui 1859
The Teaching of the Qur'an 1040
The Teachings of the Compassionate Buddha 1410
The Teachings of the Mystics 152
Telepathy 1975
Tents of Jacob 456
Teutonic Mythology 363, 366
The Text of the New Testament 944
Thai Buddhism 1512
Themes in Islamic Civilization 1059
Theological Abstracting and Bibliographical Services 543
Theological and Religious Index 543
Theological Dictionary of the New Testament 925
Theological Dictionary of the Old Testament 816
The Theology of Jehovah's Witnesses 700
Theories of Primitive Religion 262
Theosophy 1921
Theravada Buddhism in Southeast Asia 1472
These Also Believe 1921
Theurgy, Goetic 1988
THICH, Thien-An 1469
Thirty Years of Buddhist Studies 1422
This People Israel 459
THOMAS, D. W. 878-9
THOMAS, E. J. 1437, 1442
THOMAS, P. 1276
THOMPSON, B. 632
THOMPSON, J. E. S. 384
THOMPSON, L. 1534
THOMPSON, L. G. 1522
THOMPSON, S. 1816
THOMPSON, S. M. 174
THOMSEN, H. 1671
THORNDIKE, L. 1984
The Three Pillars of Zen 1461
The Three Religions of China 1533
Three Ways of Thought in Ancient China 1551
THURSON, H. 656
Tibetan Civilization 1392
TILLICH, P. 570
TIRYAKIAN, E. A. 1985
Titans 1962
Tiv Religion 1741
Tlingit 1811
To Kiss Earth Goodbye 1983
TODD, J. M. 603
Tokugawa Religion 1637
The Torah 440
TORBET, R. G. 694
TORREY, C. C. 971
Totem and Taboo 264
Totemism and Exogamy 263
TOYNBEE, A. 58, 569
Tracing Shamans in Siberia 1889
Trade Gods 1880
Tradition, History, and the Old Testament 902
The Traditional Religion of the Sakota 1738
Traditional Symbols of the Contemporary World 130
The Traditions of Islam 1050
The Transcendental Meditation 1686
Transmission of the Lamp

1454
The Treasure of Darkness 301
A Treasury of Good Sayings 1389
The Treasury of Jewish Holidays 509
Treasury of Witchcraft 2032
TREPP, L. 489
The Trial and Death of Jesus 957
The Trickster 1811
TRIMMINGHAM, J. S. 1150, 1171
Trinidad 1827
TRIPP, E. 325
TRITTON, A. S. 1082
TRUEBLOOD, D. E. 175, 724
The Trumpet of Prophecy 699
The Trumpet Shall Sound 1880
The Truth about Witchcraft 2021
Truth and Tradition in Chinese Buddhism 1484
TRUZZI, M. 1986
TSUNODA, R. 1412
Tung Chung-Shu 1568
Turkish Literature 1142
TURNBULL, C. 1776-7
TURNER, V. W. 1778
TURVILLE-PETRE, G. 367
TUSHINGHAM, A. D. 852
TUXEN, P. 1270
2500 Years of Buddhism 1418
TWITCHETT, D. 1579

Ugaritic Mythology 307
The Underground Church 1920
UNDERHILL, E. 153
UNDERHILL, R. M. 1817
Understanding the Bible Through History and Archaeology 874
Understanding the New Testament 941
Understanding the Old Testament 905
An Unfettered Faith 727
A Union List of Printed Indic Texts 1292
United Society of Believers in Christ's Second Coming 726
Unity School of Christianity 1921
The Universal Jewish Encyclopedia 421
Universe Atlas of the Christian World 544
The Unknown Sanctuary 462
Upaniṣads for All 1304
Upanishads 1304-7
Uttaradhyayna 1367

VALK, A. de 743
Valmiki 1320-1
Vampires 1962
VAN OVER, R. 1536
VARAOLACHARI, V. 1987
Varieties of Mystic Experience 148
The Varieties of Religious Experience 213
VARLEY, H. P. 1633
VARMA, V. P. 1438
VAUX, R. de 880-1
Vedanta Dictionary 1328
Vedanta, the Culmination of Indian Thought 1331
The Vedas 1211-2, 1297-8, 1302
Vedic Bibliography 1286
A Vedic Concordance 1299
The Vedic Experience 1303
The Vedic Mythology 1301
A Vedic Reader for Students 1298
The Venture of Islam 1091
VERMASEREN, M. J. 317, 355
VERMES, G. 984
VERWILGHEN, A. F. 1583
VESSIE, P. A. 1449
The Vicissitudes of Shinto 1665
VIDLER, A. R. 610
Vietnam 1508
Viśnavaism and Sivaism 1355
VISSER, M. W. de 1502
VOGT, E. Z. 107
Voices on the Wind 1875
VOLLMAR, E. R. 737
Von Grunebaum 1083, 1100, 1103
Voodoo, Devils and the New Invisible World 1964
Voodoo in Haiti 1826
VORGLIMLER, H. 530

VOS, H. F. 59, 858
VYNCKE, F. 376

WAARDENBURG, J. J. 8
WACE, H. 534-5
WACH, J. 47, 110, 236
WAITE, A. E. 1988, 2011
WAKEFIELD, W. 624
Waldesian Church 661
WALEY, A. 1551, 1561, 1601
WALHOUT, D. 60
WALKER, B. 1290
WALKER, W. 570
WALLACE, A. F. C. 187
WALSH, H. H. 541, 749
WAND, J. W. C. 581, 611, 625, 691
WARDER, A. K. 1495
WARE, K. 671
WARREN, H. C. 1471
Warriors of God 644
WATSON, B. 1213, 1527, 1588
WATSON, L. 1989
WATSON, W. J. 1177
WATT, W. M. 1033, 1046, 1084, 1110, 1129, 1154, 1179
WATTS, A. W. 647, 1466-7
WATTS, H. H. 850
The Way and Its Power 1601
The Way of Lao Tzu 1598
The Way of Wisdom in the Old Testament 916
The Way of Zen 1467
WAYMAN, A. 1397
Ways of Thinking of Eastern People 1222
Ways of Understanding Religion 40
WEBB, J. 1990
WEBBER, F. R. 648
WEBER, M. 237, 490, 688, 1272, 1537
WEDECK, H. E. 257, 2032
WEGENER, G. S. 904
WEISER, A. 917
WELBON, G. R. 1439
WELCH, C. 684
WELCH, H. 1485-7, 1609
WELFORD, A. T. 571
WELLS, K. E. 1512
WELTY, P. T. 1229
WENGER, J. C. 711
WENSINCK, A. J. 1158
WERBLOWSKY, R. J. Z. 422, 431
WERNER, E. T. C. 1544, 1546
West African Religion 1769
Western Society and the Church in the Middle Ages 586
The Westminster Dictionary of the Church History 536
Westminster Historical Atlas to the Bible 855
What Is Form Criticism? 900, 943
What Is Taoism? 1606
What the Buddha Taught 1473
WHEATLEY, P. 1991
WHEELER, M. 1259
WHEELER, P. 1622
WHITE, J. 1977
WHITE, R. A. 1956
White Witchcraft 2030
WHITTICK, A. 141
WHITTLESEY, E. S. 142
Who's Who in Church History 519
Who's Who in the Gospels 924
Who's Who in the New Testament 923
Who's Who in the Old Testament 802
Who's Who in the Talmud 435
Why I Am a Unitarian Universalist 728
WICKENS, G. M. 1177
WIDENGREN, G. 38, 358
WIENER, P. P. 10
WIGODER, G. 419, 422
WIKENHAUSER, A. 951
WILHELM, R. 1604
WILLIAMS, E. L. 1781
WILLIAMS, G. H. 604
WILLIAMS, J. A. 1058-9
WILLIAMS, W. G. 882
WILLIAMSON, R. W. 1878-9
WILSON, B. R. 663, 1709
WILSON, C. 1992
WILSON, H. H. 1356
WILSON, M. 1779
WINICK, C. 183

Winnebago Indians 1811
A Wisdom of Buddhism 1415
The Wisdom of China and India 1216
WISEMAN, D. J. 867
WISMER, D. 1052
WISSLER, C. 1818-9
Witchcraft. Hughes, P. 2022
Witchcraft. Mair, L. 2025
Witchcraft and Sorcery 1980
Witchcraft in Europe 2023
Witchcraft, the Old Religion 2026
Witches and Their Craft 2030
WOLF, A. J. 491
WOLFSON, H. A. 1159
The Wonder That Was India 1258
WOOD, E. 1328, 1333, 1335, 1450
The Word of the Buddha 1470
Working Bibliography for the Old Testament 921
World Christian Handbook 572
The World History of the Jewish People 457
World Methodism Council 713
World of Buddha 1416
World of Islam. Grube, E. 1116
The World of Islam. Lewis, B. 1094
The World of Islam. Planhol, X. 1021
The World of the First Australians 1838
The World of Witches 2018
The World of Zen 1462
World Religions 49
The World's Religions 39
The World's Rim 1801
Worship in the World's Religion 140
WORSLEY, P. 1880
WRIGHT, A. F. 1488, 1556, 1572, 1578-9
WRIGHT, G. E. 855, 866, 883
WUTHNOW, R. 1944
The Wycliff Historical Geography of Bible Lands 858
YADIN, Y. 985
Yahweh and the Gods of Caanan 862
Yaku, M. 1625
YALMAN, N. 1993
YAMAMOTO, K. 1429
YAMAUCHI, E. M. 884
YAMPOLSKY, P. 1412
YANG, C. K. 1526, 1538
Yearbook of American Churches 730
YINGER, J. M. 238-9
Yoga 1335
Yoga Dictionary 1333
Yoga: Immortality and Freedom 1334
Yoga Sutra 1335
YOO, Y. 1398, 1406
Yorubas 1734, 1752, 1759, 1769
You Shall Be as Gods 909
YOUNG, R. 846
YOUNGER, P. 1273-4
YU, D. C. 16

ZAEHNER, R. C. 21, 318, 1210, 1296, 1351, 1945
Zaramo 1774
ZARETSKY, I. I. 1724, 1945
Zen; A Way of Life 1459
Zen and Zen Classics 1455
Zen Buddhism. Humphreys, C. 1460
Zen Buddhism. Vessie, P. A. 1449
Zen Buddhism and Psychoanalysis 1485
Zen Dictionary 1450
Zen, Drugs and Mysticism 1945
Zen in English Literature and Oriental Classics 1468
Zen Philosophy 1469
ZERNOV, N. 672
ZIELINSKI, T. 345
ZIMMER, H. R. 1283
ZIMMERMAN, J. E. 326
Zohar 506
The Zondervan Pictorial Encyclopedia of the Bible 817
ZOPHY, J. W. 602
Zoroastrianism 45, 318

ZUNINI, G. 218
ZÜRCHER, E. 1440, 1489
ZUWIYYA, J. 1015

PERIODICALS INDEX

Acta Asiatica 1230
Acta Orientalia (Budapest) 1231
Acta Orientalia (Copenhagen) 1232
Africa 1783
African Affairs 1784
African Historical Studies 1791
African Religious History 1785
African Studies 1786
African Studies Review 1787
Africana Library Journal 1788
American Academy in Rome. Memoirs 389
American Academy of Religion 70
American Anthropologist 390, 1710
American Antiquity 391
The American Benedictine Review 758
The American Jewish Historical Quarterly 510
American Journal of Archaeology 392
American Journal of Philology 393
American Journal of Sociology 240
American Museum of Natural History. Anthropological Papers 394
American Oriental Society. Journal 1233
American Schools of Oriental Research. Bulletin 71
Anatolian Studies 395
Annual Review of Anthropology 193
Anthropologica 188
Anthropological Journal of Canada 189
Anthropological Quarterly 190, 1711
Anthropological Society of Oxford. Journal 191
Anthropos 192, 1712
Antiquity 396
Archaeology 397
Archiv für Reformationsgeschichte 759
Archiv Orientalní 72, 1234
Ars Islamica 1187
Ars Orientalis 1187
Asia Major 1235
Asian Affairs 1236
Asian Perspectives 1237
Asiatic Society of Japan. Transactions 1674

Berytus 398
Biblica 987
Biblical Archaeologist 988
Biblical Research 989
British School in Rome. Papers 400
British School of Athens. Annual 399

Canadian Church Historical Society. Journal 760
Canadian Church Historical Society. Occasional Publications 761
Canadian Journal of African Studies 1789
Canadian Journal of Theology 762
Catholic Historical Review 763
Central Asiatic Journal 1238
The China Quarterly 1610

Chinese Culture 1611
Chinese Studies in History 1612
Chinese Studies in History and Philosophy 1613
Chinese Studies in Philosophy 1613
The Christian Century 764
Church History 765
Cithara 73
Classical Philology 401
Classical Quarterly 402
Classical Review 403
Classical World 404
Current Anthropology 194

Daedalus 74
Diogenes 75

East and West 76, 1239
Ecumenical Review 766
Eranos 77
Ethnology 195
Ethnos 196, 1713
The Expository Times 78

Folk Lore 143

Geneva-Africa 1790
Génève-Afrique 1790
Greece and Rome 405

Harvard Journal of Asiatic Studies 1240
Harvard Theological Review 767
Hebrew Union College Annual 511
Hesperia 406
History of Religions 79
Huguenot Society of London. Proceedings 768
Huguenot Society of London. Publications 769

Indian Horizon 1357
Indian Studies 1358
Indiana. University. Folklore Institute. Journal 197
Indo-Iranian Journal 1359
International Journal for Philosophy of Religion 176
International Journal of African Historical Studies 1791
International Journal of Middle Eastern Studies 1188
International Review of Missions 770
International Yearbook for the Sociology of Religion 241
Internationales Jahrbuch für Religionssoziologie 241
Iraq 407
Der Islam 1189
Islam and the Modern Age 1190
Islamic Culture 1191
Islamic Quarterly 1192
Islamic Studies 1193
Israel Exploration Journal 512

Japanese Journal of Religious Studies 1675
Japanese Religions 1676
The Jewish Journal of Sociology 513
Jewish Quarterly Review 514
Jewish Social Studies 515
Journal for the Scientific Study of Religion 80
Journal for the Studies of Judaism in the Persian, Hellenistic and Roman Period 516
Journal of African History 1792
Journal of Anthropological Research 198
Journal of Asian and African Studies 81
Journal of Asian History 1241
Journal of Asian Studies 1242
Journal of Biblical Literature 990
Journal of Christian Education 255
Journal of Cuneiform Studies 409
The Journal of Ecclesiastical History 771

Journal of Hellenic Studies 408
Journal of Indian History 1360
Journal of Indian Philosophy 1361
Journal of Near Eastern Studies 411
Journal of Oriental Research 1243
Journal of Oriental Studies 82, 1244
The Journal of Pacific History 1881
Journal of Religion 83
Journal of Religion and Health 219
Journal of Religion in Africa 84, 1793
The Journal of Religious History 85
Journal of Roman Studies 410
Journal of Semitic Studies 517
Journal of Social Psychology 220
Journal of Southeast Asian Studies 1245
The Journal of Theological Studies 772

Laval Théologique et Philosophique 773
Liste Mondiale des Périodiques Specialisés: Etudes Africaines 1782
London. University. School of Oriental and African Studies. Bulletin 86, 1246

Man 199, 1714
Mankind 200
Middle Eastern Affairs 1194
Middle Eastern Studies 1195
The Month 774
Monumenta Nipponica 1677
Monumenta Serica 87, 1247
Mother India 1362
Muslim World 1196

New Testament Studies 991
Novum Testamentum 992
Numen 88

Oceania 1882
Oriens Extremus 1248
Orientalia 89

Palestine Exploration Quarterly 518
Papua and New Guinea Society. Journal 1883
Philosophy and Phenomenological Research 177
Philosophy East and West 1249
Polynesian Society. Journal 1884

Recherches de Théologie Ancienne et Médiévale 775
Recusant History 776
Religion and Society 242
Religion in Communist Dominated Areas 90
Religion in Life 777
Religious Education 256
Religious Humanism 91
Religious Studies 92
Religious Studies Review 93
Research in Phenomenology 178
Review of Religious Research 94
Revue de Qumran 986
Revue d'Historie Ecclesiastique 778
Royal Asiatic Society of Great Britain and Ireland. Journal 1250

Scottish Journal of Theology 779
Sikh Review 1386
Social Compass 243
Société Canadienne d'Histoire de l'Eglise Catholique 780
Société de Océanist. Journal 1885
Sociological Analysis 244
Sophia 179
Studia Islamica 1197
Studia Liturgica 781

Studies in Religion 95

Tenri Journal of Religion 1678
Textus 993
Theological Studies 782
Theology Today 783
Thought 96

Visvabharati Quarterly 1363

Die Welt der Islams 1198
World Archaeology 412

Yale Classical Studies 413

Zeitschrift für die Alttestamentliche Wissenschaft 994
Zygon 97